Uncontained:
Urban Fiction in
Postwar America

Uncontained

Urban Fiction in Postwar America

ELIZABETH A. WHEELER

RUTGERS UNIVERSITY PRESS
New Brunswick, New Jersey, and London

Library of Congress Cataloging-in-Publication Data

Wheeler, Elizabeth A., 1959–
  Uncontained : urban fiction in postwar America / Elizabeth A. Wheeler.
    p. cm.
  Includes bibliographical references and index.
  ISBN 0-8135-2972-7 (cloth : alk. paper)—ISBN 0-8135-2973-5 (pbk. : alk.
  paper)
    1. American fiction—20th century—History and criticism.   2. City and
town life in literature.   3. Literature and society—United States—History—
20th century.   4. World War, 1939–1945—Influence.   5. Cities and towns
in literature.   6. Social problems in literature.   I. Title.

  PS374.C5 W48 2001
  813′.5409321732—cd21

                                                            00-045894

British Cataloging-in-Publication information is available from the British
Library.

Some material in chapter 2 appeared in a different form in *Southern
California Quarterly* 10:1 (Winter 1996–97). Copyright Historical Society of
Southern California. Reprinted by permission.

Manufactured in the United States of America

For Mama, John, and Kevin
"Love has kissed me in a
beautiful way."

Contents

Acknowledgments

In writing a book about literary communities, I have benefited immeasurably from my own literary community. At the University of Oregon, research funds from the Center for the Study of Women in Society, the College of Arts and Sciences, and the English Department enabled the book's completion. My wonderful colleagues read portions of the manuscript and offered other invaluable help. I particularly thank John Gage, Richard Stevenson, Shari Huhndorf, Elizabeth Bohls, Henry Wonham, Suzanne Clark, Ian Duncan, Karen Ford, Kathleen Rowe Karlyn, Sandy Morgen, and Arlene Stein. I also thank my research assistants, Hilary Hart and Jordana Dolowich, and my students in the American Novel classes. I thank my mentors at the University of California at Berkeley, Julio Ramos and the late, great Barbara Christian. I thank my friends Jane Boatner, Margaret Holub, Wendy Simon, Laurie Ozone, Dora Wang, Maxine Craig, Francesca Royster, Elizabeth Busbee, Faizal Deen, and Marcy Jane for our conversations over the years about cities and literature. I thank my insightful and adept editor, Leslie Mitchner, for seeing this project through many stages. I thank Maureen Reddy for her useful comments and Hisaye Yamamoto for her inspiration. I thank my grandmother, Edith Milnes Wheeler, and my nephew, Adam Nathan Wheeler. I remember my late father, brothers, and grandparents with much love.

I dedicate this book to my immediate family circle. My mother, Phyllis Huntley Wheeler, has always inspired and encouraged my writing and has celebrated each step along the way. Mama, you may not agree with my conclusions about your generation, but at least you'll know I was listening to your stories. To John Shin, my husband, I offer boundless gratitude and devotion. You helped in every possible way. You mapped out ideas on endless yellow pads, listened to each new revelation, cooked, repaired, carried, babysat, and even typed. Above all, you kept the faith, week in and week out. This book is yours and so am I. Finally, I thank my infant son, Kevin Annik Shin-Wheeler, who gestated in me along with this book. Thank you for your excellent company during the solitary hours of writing. I wish you a wide open world.

Uncontained:
Urban Fiction in
Postwar America

Introduction

In the era between World War II and the mid-1960s, imagery of containment dominated urban American fiction. Containment logic neutralizes the shocks of history. It encapsulates memory and geography to control pain and conflict. Containment was also the official political ideology of the Cold War era. In this book, however, I approach containment not as an abstract ideology but as material history and lived experience. Analyzing the many genres of postwar fiction, I reveal how sense of place changed drastically in U.S. cities after World War II. I draw analogies between two forms of containment, one geographic, the other emotional. These two forms are urban segregation and repressed trauma. Segregation and trauma merge to reshape the postwar fictional city. Postwar fiction transfers difficult memories from the individual to the urban landscape.

This book not only analyzes urban containment but moves beyond it as well. Postwar fiction writers did not stop at mapping the city's containment zones. They also contested containment logic itself, overcoming the rigid divisions between different states of mind and parts of town. Subcultural fiction of the late 1950s and early 1960s presents an escape from containment. An exhilarating, open vision of city life transcends barriers and old griefs. I call this freeing vision "the Open City," with all its wartime connotations of liberation after constraint. Although often unheard and unremarked, alternatives to containment discourse exist within postwar fiction itself.

Uncontained critiques a pervasive containment story linking the postwar city to the lone, alienated, often violent man. I place this narrative in the broader context of other postwar stories that do not rely on masculine alienation. The book also draws analogies between the segregation of city space and the repression of traumatic memory. Finally, it moves beyond geographic and emotional containment into new postwar visions of urban community life.

Analyzing the time period from 1944 through 1964, the book covers film, short stories, novels, and novellas from a cross section of American cities. Part I focuses mainly on Los Angeles, a city profoundly affected by World War II. Almost overnight, Pearl Harbor transformed Los Angeles into an industrial powerhouse and a major deployment zone for the Pacific theater. Confronted with a new diversity of population, Los Angeles had a wartime racial climate prefiguring the containment logic of postwar segregation. After the war, Los Angeles epitomized the national trends toward suburbanization, mobility, and a fresh start. Part II, "The Segregated Imagination," shows the widespread effects of segregation by analyzing three cities far apart in region, size, and character: Chicago, Seattle, and New Orleans. Finally, Part III, "The Open City," focuses on New York City, the postwar "Capital of the Free World." With its beatniks, avant-garde artists, and new gay communities, New York also became the subcultural capital of the world and the source of the cult novel.

The Lone Violent Man and the Postwar Literary Canon

I challenge a containment story common in postwar fiction: the association of city life with the figure of the lone, violent man. This figure still walks through today's urban stories, from rap music to action films. In postwar fiction he metamorphoses from film noir detective to returning war veteran to urban hipster. In postwar cult novels like *Naked Lunch* and *Last Exit to Brooklyn,* male violence and loneliness represent everything real and compelling about city life. In the noir fictions discussed in chapter 1, the hero can see the city only after an act of symbolic violence. This focus on the solitary hero makes it impossible to imagine a safe, healthy urban community. The city becomes a fundamentally dangerous place only a lone expert can occupy. The idea of community itself comes to look effeminate and naive. Postwar fiction by men often displays a philosophy of rootlessness, an abstract American sense of place bound to no particular locality. Alienation becomes an existential stance rather than a psychological problem to be aired and resolved.

The lone, alienated man often seems the sole narrator of postwar fiction, drowning out all competing voices. "The voice of Male Experience" begins in the wisecracking descriptions of noir and resounds in postwar classics like *The Catcher in the Rye* and *Invisible Man*.[1] Although his own reputation may be tarnished, the lone man has a privileged standpoint on urban reality unavailable to those who surround him. This book places his voice in dialogue with the other, lesser-known voices of postwar fiction. Sociologist Wini Breines sees in postwar containment culture "a defense of masculinity and whiteness; the changes that accompanied the formation of an advanced capitalist society were perceived and experienced as threats from those outside American borders and from those who had been excluded within those borders, women and blacks and homosexuals."[2] I place the discourse of straight white men in the context of gay, African American, Asian American, and women's discourses. I also oppose urban solitude to visions of urban community.

The lone man's voice still drowns out women's voices in recent studies of postwar American literature. In *American Fiction in the Cold War* Thomas Schaub writes, "Perhaps inevitably, the discourses of strong, democratic individualism and sexual freedom that were essentially gender-neutral often produced a male-dominated rhetoric, in which society (totalitarianism, conformity) was associated with an emasculating femininity, and the rebel was always a man."[3] In *October Cities* Carlo Rotella writes, "It bears mentioning that the literature examined in this study is dominated by men, and at times it can be buffoonishly male. . . . More often than not, violent young men and family patriarchs in various stages of ascent and decline are those who do the work of moving through the cityscape, standing for urban peoples and orders, and dramatizing the situations of urban intellectuals."[4]

Certainly, postwar discourse often associated conformity with effeminacy and cities with violent men. However, the postwar rebel wasn't always a man, and the city produced many female and nonviolent voices. My book places works by postwar male writers such as Ralph Ellison, J. D. Salinger, Jack Kerouac, John Cheever, Walker Percy, Philip Roth, Hubert Selby Jr., William Burroughs, and Truman Capote in the context of postwar fiction by women such as Tillie Olsen, Grace Paley, Paule Marshall, Hisaye Yamamoto, Jo Sinclair, Ann Bannon, Sylvia Plath, and Gwendolyn Brooks.

This book also challenges the containment of racial difference and sexuality as well as gender. It broadens the canon of postwar fiction by comparing works from opposite sides of the literary tracks. For instance, I analyze the Caribbean American womanist author Paule Marshall in tandem with the Jewish American, resolutely phallocentric Philip Roth. Such combinations allow us to see what's going on in adjacent neighborhoods and compare their doings with one another. Postwar urban fiction takes place in segregated enclaves such as Chicago's Black Belt, Seattle's

Japantown, the gay bars of Greenwich Village, and the all-white Connecticut suburb of Shady Hill. It is difficult to see the wider, shared cultural context from within these enclaves. The relationships become clearer through comparison.

For example, the writings of John Okada and Hisaye Yamamoto demonstrate the "articulate silences" of Asian American literature.[5] However, their strategic silences also interact with a repressed wartime trauma widely shared beyond the Japanese American community. Both Sylvia Plath's German American college girl and Charles S. Wright's African American hustler regard with unease postwar New York's corporate gloss, even though one hangs out on Madison Avenue and the other in Hell's Kitchen. Walker Percy, John Cheever, and film noir director Billy Wilder satirize the blandness and clichés of affluent white culture. I interpret their satire in the larger context of racial segregation, a context invisible from within the confines of separate texts. Their fictions vague malaise responds to a larger problem sensed rather than seen.

This book, then, moves back and forth among different neighborhoods in the same time frame. Writers of many backgrounds and experiences respond to the same postwar containment logic. By contrast, Carlo Rotella's *October Cities* views postwar urban writing diachronically while I see it synchronically. Rotella traces a movement across time from a white industrial community to an African American postindustrial community in one particular kind of urban area, the inner-city neighborhood. On the other hand, I see postwar fiction occupying a liminal zone far different from the traditional neighborhood. The postwar urban novel takes place not in one area but in the interstices between areas. It responds to a newly mobile, abstract, and generic sense of place—often, a diaspora sense of place, where "home" names multiple sites. People camp out on the landscape rather than rooting in it.

My synchronic focus requires a new approach to the postwar literary canon. To convey the broad diversity of the postwar city, I compare works considered definitive of the era with works forgotten after their own time. In this endeavor I build on the accomplishments of such literary activists and scholars as Barbara Christian, the *Aiieeee!* editors, King-Kok Cheung, Mike Davis, Lawrence Hogue, and Robert Corber, who have brought belated attention to works that remained out of print for decades.[6] These rediscovered works include Chester Himes's novel *If He Hollers Let Him Go* (1945), Gore Vidal's *The City and the Pillar* (1948), Hisaye Yamamoto's short stories, Gwendolyn Brooks's *Maud Martha* (1953), Jo Sinclair's *The Changelings* (1955), John Okada's *No-No Boy* (1957), Paule Marshall's *Brown Girl, Brownstones* (1959), Ann Bannon's lesbian pulp novels (1957–1962), and Charles S. Wright's *The Messenger* (1963).

Critics have only just begun to consider these works as definitive of the postwar canon. They seem atypical in many ways. For instance, *Maud Martha, No-No Boy,* and *Brown Girl, Brownstones* may escape critical notice because they do not employ the first-person narration considered a defining characteristic of postwar fiction. The fifties novels of Sylvia Plath, Paule Marshall, and John Okada are often regarded as forebears to subsequent white feminist, African American, and Asian American writers rather than in their original fifties context. Nonetheless, their writing addresses that context as forcefully as the work of John Cheever or Jack Kerouac, whose names are synonymous with the postwar era. As Gavin Jones observes of Paule Marshall's first novel, *Brown Girl, Brownstones,* "rather than a peripheral womanist text, *Brown Girl* should be placed at the heart of a developing political philosophy of the 1950s, a philosophy that emphasized how far blackness and whiteness were intertwined in America, and how far the oppression of black identity was culturally destructive, both to oppressor and oppressed."[7] Similarly, the "womanist" fiction of Gwendolyn Brooks, Hisaye Yamamoto, and Ann Bannon is central rather than peripheral to understanding the postwar city.

Unlikely Pairs

In keeping with a synchronic approach, each section of the book reveals similarities between two or more authors who wrote in the same time and place but who rarely appear together in literary criticism. Such comparisons show generational and local affinities, without erasing sexual and racial difference. Part I, "Hipster versus Housewife," treats two important subgenres of postwar fiction, the noir narrative and the suspiciously impeccable fifties short story. Unlikely pairs of works share characteristics across huge discrepancies of race, gender, and experience. Chapter 1 analyzes the racial politics of film noir by comparing Billy Wilder's Hollywood version with Chester Himes's African American rewriting of the genre. In Chapter 2, the beautifully crafted short stories of Hisaye Yamamoto and John Cheever share the same post-traumatic subtext. Stories set in Little Tokyo or Connecticut bedroom towns betray the same repression of wartime memory and the same vexed marital relations.

Part II, "The Segregated Imagination," treats three novels, each set in an isolated single-race enclave: *Maud Martha,* by Gwendolyn Brooks; *No-No Boy,* by John Okada; and *The Moviegoer,* by Walker Percy. I compare the segregation of the black Chicago ghetto with the segregation of Seattle's Japantown and New Orleans's white suburbs. Despite the vast differences among these three communities, the novels display similar narrative contours. Ironically, their very segregation from one another links the novels most closely.

Finally, Part III, "The Open City," opens out the pairing of twos and threes into a crowd scene. Authors start to overcome segregation, facing one another directly across lines of race, sex, and sexuality. The shared sensibility of the postwar generation expresses itself in the freedom and exhilaration of the Open City. Across two rivers, Philip Roth's Jewish suburbanites and Paule Marshall's Barbadian immigrants walk parallel paths of upward mobility. Charles S. Wright's squatter and Sylvia Plath's college girl mirror each other's disillusionment across Central Park. The "literary" cult novels of Charles S. Wright, Truman Capote, Jack Kerouac, and Gore Vidal show up at the same Village shindigs with the pulp fiction of Ann Bannon and the shock fiction of William Burroughs and Hubert Selby Jr. Female hipsters appear as the often invisible doubles of male hipsters, while gay subcultures appear as the often invisible doubles of straight subcultures.

Housewife Discourse

One of this books most important revisions lies in its reassessment of the housewife's voice. I stress the importance of fifties housewife discourse to postwar fiction, even though the era is often regarded as one of the most masculine phases of American literature. The housewife's voice may seem a contradiction in terms, because she is often ridiculed as unable to think or speak for herself. The housewife serves as the male hipster's constant foil and butt of jokes. She stands for everything he rebels against: conformity, unreality, boredom, suburbia. She represents all the blandness and consumerism of the stereotypical 1950s: what *Fortune* editor William Whyte once called "the pink lampshade in the picture window."[8]

Nonetheless, fifties housewives still managed to write and speak for themselves. A mother of school-age children, Grace Paley started writing short stories "in 1954 or 55" despite the overwhelming masculinity of the literary climate. She discovered her best material in the disparaged housewifely world around her. "I had been reading the current fiction, fifties fiction, a masculine fiction, whether traditional, avant-garde, or—later—Beat. As a former boy myself (in the sense that many little girls reading *Tom Sawyer* know they've found their true boy selves) I had been sold pretty early on the idea that I might not be writing the important serious stuff. As a grown-up woman, I had no choice. Everyday life, kitchen life, children life, had been handed to me, my portion, the beginning of big luck, though I didn't know it."[9]

In American literature, a housewife's experience seems an unlikely source of "big luck." American culture is still in rebellion against the fifties housewife. Although few of us come from conventional fifties families, picket-fence conformity still serves as whipping girl in contemporary popular culture. In *Commodify Your Dissent* Thomas Frank observes, "The evils of conformity are most conveniently summarized with images of 1950s suburban correctness. You know, that land of sedate music, sexual repression, deference to authority, Red Scares, and smiling white people standing politely in line to go to church. Constantly appearing as a symbol of archbackwardness in advertising and movies, it is an image we find easy to evoke."[10] From hip consumerism to feminist scholarship to girl zines, all kinds of contemporary discourses keep insisting they're "not June Cleaver."[11] In neo-fifties films like *American Beauty* (1999) and *Pleasantville* (1998), the housewife's naïveté and determined cheerfulness look absurd to a male viewer who claims superior insight. America still hates a sissy.

Nonetheless, the great fifties women writers discussed in this book practice an acute social criticism from within hat shops and housewife discourse. Claiming space for family and community, they refute the postwar city's image as the sole preserve of lone, violent men. Gwendolyn Brooks, Tillie Olsen, Grace Paley, and Hisaye Yamamoto demonstrate the power of housewife discourse for social critique. They also refute the stereotype that all fifties housewives were white, affluent, and suburban. Yamamoto's tidy, modest tone of voice calls readers to witness postwar racism and collective amnesia. She finds the potential for a new multiracial city after the war. In portraying Japanese Americans returning home from wartime internment in concentration camps, her tales also show how women and families were war veterans along with men.

These postwar writers did not reject the image of "the pink lampshade." Rather, they worked it hard. As Daniel Boyarin writes, "Feminism needs to liberate not only women but also femininity."[12] Postwar housewife discourse has strong affinities with the camp discourse of gay male culture newly prominent in the late fifties and early sixties. Like the drag queens closely associated with camp, these women writers use conventional femininity as an oppositional gesture. They reveal the strength within a seeming weakness. For example, Gwendolyn Brooks seems to exaggerate feminine stereotypes in order to refute them. Her novel *Maud Martha* fiercely defends the deep roots of the black community despite the threats of urban renewal and intensified segregation. Maud Martha's resistance to racism seems to grow from her love of flowers and her experiments in sewing. Heroism appears not as one grand fatal gesture but in small acts of dignity asserted in everyday neighborhood life.

The novels of Ann Bannon and Paule Marshall undo the binary opposition between hipster and housewife. Marshall depicts the female hipster and her conventional mother as two halves of a whole, two chapters in a multigenerational history. Indeed, the housewife shocks bohemia with doses of repressed truth. Even Ann Bannon's lesbian pulp fiction emerges from housewife discourse. Bannon was herself a housewife while writing these books; she visited Greenwich Village occasionally when her husband was away on business. Bannon uses a classic housewifely form, the soap opera, to clear safe space for lesbian community in a sexist and homophobic city. Her melodrama challenges what I call "the discourse of sadomasochistic violence": the idea that homosexuality, like the city itself, invites its own destruction.

Yamamoto, Brooks, Marshall, Bannon, and housewife-activists Janice Smith and Mary Sharmat use family and community as the excluded terms that explode male hyperseriousness. They make urban dread look ridiculous. They lampoon the containment logic of the lone, violent man. While men are saying, "The city is dangerous and you don't belong here," urban housewives go calmly about their business.

A Concrete Island: The Material History of Containment

As recent scholars have shown, containment culture influenced Cold War thought far beyond foreign policy. Alan Nadel writes, "Containment was the name of a privileged American narrative during the cold war. Although technically referring to U.S. foreign policy from 1948 until at least the mid-1960s, it also describes American life in numerous venues and under sundry rubrics during that period. . . . In attempts to keep the narrative straight, containment equated containment of communism with containment of atomic secrets, of sexual license, of gender roles, of nuclear energy, and of artistic expression."[13] This list omits two important aspects of containment culture that form the main emphasis of my book: racial segregation and traumatic memory. I interpret containment culture as a sensual force reshaping the American landscape. While several critics have defined various films, novels, and other narratives as part of containment culture, their readings have been primarily ideological. For instance, Thomas Schaub sees the ahistoricism and alienation of Cold War fiction as a response to "postwar liberalism's contempt for the naive politics of the thirties."[14]

By contrast, I focus on the material history of containment. I compare the cities of postwar fiction with their literal counterparts, right down to events on individual street corners. This materialist approach regrounds postwar fiction's dislocated sense of place. The dialectic between the literal city and the figurative city has particular importance in a world of segregated enclaves. As this book reveals, discourses that seem conceptually and culturally disconnected are indeed materially and geographically akin.

Postwar sense of place was highly contradictory, marked by new freedom of movement and new restrictions on movement. Paradoxically, containment culture emerged in an era of unprecedented mobility. The World War II armed forces served as a "giant centrifuge," shaking up and rearranging all of American culture.[15] Troop deployments, the defense industry, and the removal of all West Coast Japanese Americans caused massive flows of population in and out of American cities. This mobilization broke down regional differences and sparked a new postwar interest in relocation (and, of course, relocation was not a matter of choice for Japanese Americans). GI benefits for mortgages and higher education, new suburbs, and new freeways made massive relocation possible. The postwar era saw a simultaneous opening-up and closing-down of public space and civil liberties. With the 1950s came a greatly intensified racial segregation and the worst repression of gays and lesbians in U.S. history but also the birth of the civil rights movement and the modern gay community. I map the contradictions of urban movement and containment in three kinds of city space: the City of Dread, with its new mixing of peoples and fears of violence; the split between new suburbs and tighter ghettos; and the rise of the subcultural city.

This book draws close analogies between material and intellectual history. I compare the literal construction of the city with its imaginative construction in literature. I show how the mental structure of containment logic reshaped the physical landscape, while the physical containment of segregation reshaped the structure of fiction. My approach is structural on many levels, finding structural similarities among culturally disparate authors and emphasizing structural inequality over personal failings. Throughout this book one piece of city infrastructure keeps reappearing to symbolize mental and physical containment: the image of the concrete island in the midst of traffic. The concrete island represents postwar fictional style and the postwar city itself.

Postwar fiction is concrete because of its vivid directness, newly accessible to a wide public in mass-market paperback. However, postwar fiction is also concrete because its emotions are paved over. The postwar fictional city is a concrete island, holding itself above and apart from the flow of unfortunate memory. The repressed, the hidden, and the unsaid determine the shape of the city and the shape of narrative. For instance, the fifties short story portrays wartime trauma and postwar readjustment within the tight confines of marriage satire and suspiciously impeccable prose. The paving-over of memory typified the literal postwar city along with the literary one. During the Age of Concrete from the 1930s through the 1960s, enthusiastic builders believed they could tame history by altering the landscape. Concrete and bulldozers became ways to forget past conflicts and start fresh.

After the war, urban renewal drastically altered the face of American cities. The phrase "urban renewal" has a spiritual tone, in line with an old and continuing American idea that cities need to be razed and restarted periodically for their redemption. This idea travels from the Pilgrim Fathers through Nathaniel Hawthorne's *Marble Faun* and into current explosions in action films.[16] However, starting over means the erasure of urban history. In the postwar context of segregation, it also means erasing the knowledge of racial contact. The chancellor of the University of Chicago scribbled to himself in notes for a 1954 meeting on urban renewal: "Tear it down and begin over again. Negroes."[17]

As racial division acquired a new absoluteness, concrete reinforced the logic of segregation. In home building, the heated concrete slab replaced the basement and permitted the boom in whites-only suburban subdivisions. Meanwhile, back in the inner city, urban renewal bulldozed old neighborhoods and replaced them with enormous concrete block housing projects. By 1960, the segregated black community on Chicago's South Side "was solidly institutionalized and frozen in concrete."[18] Occasionally, a concrete wall divided neighborhoods along racial lines to satisfy federal mortgage insurance rules.[19]

With these divisions frozen in concrete, containment logic realized itself on the landscape. The metaphor of quarantine often determined the style of containment. Andrew Ross notes the widespread use of public health metaphors in postwar discourse; he quotes many intellectuals describing mass culture as a contagion in need of quarantine.[20] In the postwar city, quarantine strategies served to hush up racial conflicts all along the color line. The new racial diversity of the wartime city caused white anxiety and even paranoia. In 1943, racist riots toward nonwhites erupted in New York City, Detroit, Los Angeles, and other cities. Fearing the spread of violence, the Chicago Commission on Human Rights bragged about its own quarantine strategy: "[We] seek to quarantine the most explosive Human Relations elements and situations so that they will not and cannot infect the rest of the city."[21]

Postwar urban fiction's emotional indirectness and unnameable malaise grow from this era of hidden violence. A domestic Cold War affected not only the African American community but also gays and lesbians and other purported subversives. Fiction responds to this climate by containing violence through the prose style itself. For example, film noir sets the stage for postwar quarantine logic. Its urban dread divides the city into safe and dangerous zones, making it easy to identify scapegoats and eliminate them. Even though noir concerns murder, the genre's heavy stylization allows the sublimation of grief. Noir creates emotional distance so we can consume a violent city with pleasure.

The containment of violence through style runs through the many varieties of postwar fiction. In the segregation novels discussed in Part II, writers erect a neutral zone to contain rage and injustice so that the truce between neighborhoods stands. The cult novels discussed in Part III transform shock from a personal trauma to a mass-market commodity. Like film noir, the urban cult novel allows the pleasurable consumption of a violent city. The cult novel presents gay, delinquent, and beatnik subcultures paperback-marketed as "shocking" to a readership of combined hips and squares.

The quarantine of memory goes together with the fictional containment of violence and the quarantine of neighborhoods. In postwar fiction, traumatic memory becomes another form of concrete island—vivid yet separate from the rest of experience. The two main components of post-traumatic stress disorder, flashback and psychic numbing, are both containment narratives. Although vivid and overwhelming, flashback is also a form of emotional containment. Past trauma lives in the psyche as an encapsulated island, quarantined away from the rest of memory. Psychic numbing is by nature a form of emotional containment, whether through avoidance of feeling, amnesia, or the inability to feel. We can detect psychic numbing in the inappropriate neutrality common to postwar discourse. In his 1967 study of Hiroshima survivors Robert Jay Lifton wrote, "It is no exaggeration to say that psychic numbing is one of the great problems of our age."[22]

Although post-traumatic stress disorder (PTSD) is most commonly associated with Vietnam War veterans, it was a huge, if submerged, problem in World War II. As my book shows, trauma touched not only returning veterans but a wide variety of civilians as well. The American Psychiatric Association did not officially acknowledge PTSD until 1980. However, the original research leading to the new diagnostic category was conducted with Nazi concentration camp survivors, not Vietnam War veterans.[23] In *Trauma and Recovery* Judith Herman describes the widespread yet forgotten problem of World War II psychiatric casualties.

> According to one report, 80 percent of the American fighting men who succumbed to acute stress in the Second World War were

returned to some kind of duty, usually within a week. Thirty percent were returned to combat units. Little attention was paid to the fate of these men once they returned to active duty, let alone after they returned home from the war. As long as they could function on a minimal level, they were thought to have recovered. With the end of the war, the familiar process of amnesia set in once again. There was little medical or public interest in the psychological condition of returning soldiers. The lasting effects of war trauma were once again forgotten.[24]

One can never erase the memory of violence; one can only encapsulate it, and the capsule always leaks. Postwar fiction recapitulates the process of amnesia Herman describes. The shape of postwar prose is the shape of overlooking: a smooth and polished capsule of almost forgetting, bobbing on the sea of time. Trauma is what Lawrence Langer calls a "deep memory," almost unspeakable, held apart from a shared and articulated "common memory."[25] For Cheever, Yamamoto, Okada, Percy, and Kerouac, war is an island adrift and separate from postwar experience. In *The Moviegoer* Walker Percy describes war memory as "the sudden confrontation of a time past, a time so terrible and splendid in its archreality; and so lost—cut adrift like a great ship in the flood of years."[26] In 1976 Hisaye Yamamoto referred to her wartime concentration camp experience as "a lump in my subconscious": "I didn't know myself what a lump it was in my subconscious until a few years ago when I watched one of the earlier television documentaries on the subject, narrated by the mellow voice of Walter Cronkite."[27] In her 1950 short story "Wilshire Bus," Yamamoto uses submerged metaphors of a beach ball and a tumor to describe the capsule of traumatic memory.

The internment of all West Coast Japanese Americans is an infamous example of World War II containment logic. The internment contradicted the war's unprecedented chance to bring people together in a shared cause and expand the definitions of democracy. The dislocation of entire communities made it nearly impossible for Nisei (second-generation Japanese American) writers to relate urban past to urban present. In *No-No Boy,* John Okada's main character, Ichiro Yamada, relentlessly questions his own sense of place and belonging. Since Ichiro represses the memory of white racism, he simply cannot remember why he and Seattle have changed so much. His amnesia causes him to transfer shame and rage from his history onto the landscape. Seattle itself seems sick, soiled, and in desperate need of urban renewal.

The encapsulation of wartime memory bears a close relationship to the segregated enclaves of the postwar city. The novels, novellas, short stories, and films analyzed here take place in a series of concrete islands: Japantown, South Central Los Angeles, downtown Newark, a haunted brownstone on the Upper East Side, a kitchenette building in Bronzeville, the gay and lesbian bars of Greenwich Village, and the suburbs of Los Feliz, Gentilly, Short Hills, and Shady Hill. Containment logic dictates that different groups must hold themselves apart from one another for fear of emotional meltdown.

Asian American and African American writers convey the tremendous pressure on segregated ghettos from within and without. In the Jim Crow world of South Central Los Angeles, Chester Himes's main character physically and ethically "pushes it" as a form of racial protest. He leans out against the neighborhood's barriers. Contemplating assimilation into mainstream America, John Okada's main character speculates, "Maybe the whole damned country is pushing and shoving and screaming to get into someplace that doesn't exist, because they don't know that the outside could be the inside if only they would stop all this pushing and shoving and realize that."[28]

The tension of containment keeps racial conflict hidden. A great stillness lies at the heart of Gwendolyn Brooks's *Maud Martha,* but this is the stillness of tremendous pressure from both sides. The Black Belt's wildly overcrowded buildings must soon burst outward into the surrounding white neighborhoods, despite the threat of violence. The white neighborhood is "always hunched and ready to close in on you but never doing so."[29] Maud Martha maintains her peace by keeping her perceptions inward. The novel's vignettes segregate her experiences from one another so they won't add up to an explosion. The reader learns to understand containment from the inside. Black anger rushes forward, then dams itself up vertically, as if it had hit an invisible wall.

For Brooks, Okada, and Himes, segregation makes the world ugly, harsh, and violent. The main spiritual problems are rage and despair. For white middle-class observers like Billy Wilder, John Cheever, and Walker Percy, segregation makes the world too pretty, soft, and banal. The main spiritual problems are malaise and triviality. One cannot see the direct effects of racial segregation from inside the walls of white privilege. Rather, segregation appears as a vague not-rightness or excessive tidiness. Wilder, Cheever, and Percy satirize white bourgeois culture for its constrictions, yet they do not fully reveal how a bigger worldview might look.

Instead, they let us know how it feels to live within a segregated imagination. In *Double Indemnity,* director/screenwriter Billy Wilder casts an ironic lens on the banality of white domestic enclaves. Like the endlessly repeated baby food boxes in the film's grocery store scene, the boxes of consciousness are too small for full humanity. Whether contemplating a cliché, a movie screen, or a new suburban building, Walker Percy's protagonist dwells on the tidy order of the frame in order to raise suspicions about the frame's limits. Nonetheless, *The Moviegoer* falls utterly silent about a civil rights movement happening in the same locales of New Orleans at the same time period. There is an unsettling contrast between the charged, contested urban spaces of the civil rights movement and Percy's bemused, pleasantly detached observations of those exact same spaces.

The encapsulation of landscape allows one to stand back and notice its strangeness. Postwar fiction has a dislocated sense of place that never takes belonging for granted. Wilder, Cheever, and Percy inspire a sense of wonder at the most ordinary things. Percy's moviegoer feels "as if I had come to myself on a strange island. And what does a castaway do? Why, he pokes around the neighborhood and he doesn't miss a trick."[30] John Cheever's suburban satire documents what he calls "an atmosphere of intense and misplaced domesticity."[31] Home is completely homelike yet somehow out of place. Postwar fiction keeps wondering at the strange commute from wartime shock to postwar calm. Characters ask in various tones of voice, What have I done? What am I doing back here? Many in the postwar generation require what Sylvia Plath calls "a ritual for being born twice."[32]

American culture usually did not speak about itself as divided into separate small islands. In fact, a discourse of shared Americanness characterizes wartime and postwar writing to a degree unmatched before or since. The rallying of the citizenry during World War II gave rise to a new multiracial discourse analogous to the multiculturalism of the 1980s. People of all races and backgrounds came together to fight fascism. People of color expected their wartime sacrifices to reap domestic justice and inclusion after the war. However, inclusion also relied on exclusion. An optimistic postwar discourse promoted a vision of progress whereby everyone would have a new suburban home, everyone would share in the new prosperity, and everyone would be happy. Segregated, traumatized, and impoverished people were just exceptions to the rule. Despite its blind spots, this vision of progress helped the civil rights movement and other liberation movements stake their claims to full equality.

Throughout this book I explore the problem of one's own inclusion and happiness in the face of others' exclusion and pain. The freedom to move, express, and reinvent oneself is one of U.S. culture's greatest gifts. American mobility and self-reinvention speeded up dramatically after World War II, and postwar writers often present America through their rearview mirrors. However, I have used the phrase "dislocated sense of place" because mobility is painful as well as freeing. The uprooting of the wartime era brought fun to some people and trauma to others. For instance, relocation means something very different to the joyous white bohemians of *On the Road* than it does to the Nisei writers who spent time in concentration camps. If we label the postwar generation "post-traumatic," we run the risk of erasing individual experiences. As Kali Tal cautions, we must acknowledge the power differences and agendas involved in any literary reworking of trauma.[33] It is important to ask: Does the text call on the reader to join a community of witnesses, or does the text reinforce silence and alienation? As we shall see, it is much easier to remain stylishly detached from violence if you aren't on the receiving end.

Beyond Containment

Two overlapping kinds of postwar fiction witness the freedom of moving out beyond containment logic: the coming-of-age novel and the cult novel. In these genres, the postwar generation declares itself ready to abandon old griefs and find new communities. The concrete island transforms itself into an asylum or cocoon, sheltering the rebirth from which the postwar city emerges. It is no accident that most of these novels take place in subcultures, communities based on affinities rather than family ties. The postwar generation could create a new city vision only by going outside the lines of traditional gender roles, segregation, and conventional behavior.

This new vision draws on a philosophy of witness inherent in previous works of postwar fiction. From noir to the fifties short story to the Beats, the protagonist of postwar fiction is a social watcher, calling readers to witness what others cannot see. Even the segregation novel allows readers to observe conflict as it surfaces and then disappears. The reader holds on to the deep memory as it vanishes beneath common memory. Although protagonists may lack social interaction in their own worlds, they cultivate a great intimacy with the reader. In the cult novel, this intimacy between narrator and reader turns into a full-fledged imagined community.[34] Lesbians and gay men read cult novels to affirm group identity in repressive times. Ann Bannon, Gore Vidal, Hubert Selby Jr., and Truman Capote employ melodrama, camp, and the Open City vision to clear safe gay space within a violent atmosphere.

In the cult novel, "underground" subcultures come above ground to occupy the entire city. The Subterranean City becomes the Open City, pulsing with life. The most telltale image from the Open City is a group of young people laughing and running freely down a city street. This image is the precise opposite of the lone, alienated man, tensed for inevitable violence. The Open City impels us to speak "as if": as if we were already freed from fear and violence; as if we had room to play. Ann Bannon's lesbian pulp novels burst forth from the closet into full enjoyment of the Village's sexual liberation. The release from intense confinement shapes her fiction's intense erotics.

Two geographies characterize the uncontained city of postwar fiction: a diaspora sense of place and a philosophy of camping out. Both geographies resist amnesia and containment. In coming-of-age novels by Louis Chu, Paule Marshall, and Philip Roth, a diaspora sense of place responds to the mobile climate by imagining "home" in multiple sites. As Khachig Tölölyan notes, a crucial distinction between a diaspora and other dispersed transnational ethnic groups is that "diasporan communities actively maintain a *collective* memory that is a foundational element of their distinct identity."[35] Diaspora becomes a way to accept displacement while resisting amnesia. Thus the postwar generation reclaims history and reads the past onto the present landscape. "Camping out" also responds to the climate of uprooting. Like urban renewal its sense of place is transient, but it resists containment logic and rests more lightly on the city. The openness and freedom of camping out provide ways to have fun with one's own dislocation.

The subcultural novel still takes place in a segregated enclave of its own. Nonetheless, it makes limited yet important strides toward a more inclusive vision of community. Cult novels emerge from a cross-cultural urban world. Gay and straight writers both hung out at the San Remo bar in Greenwich Village, and their writing speaks back and forth to each other. There was some contact and awareness across different races, sexes, and sexualities. As poet Audre Lorde remembered, "Lesbians were probably the only Black and white women in New York City in the fifties who were making any real attempt to communicate with each other; we learned lessons from each other, the values of which were not lessened by what we did not learn."[36] The postwar generation of writers emerged from a subtext of dread and division to occupy a new city.

PART
I
Hipster versus Housewife

1 | The Lone Violent Man

Los Angeles epitomizes the changes World War II brought to American cities. After the war, Los Angeles headed the national trends toward suburbanization, mobility, and a fresh start. Fictional styles responded to a new landscape where men and women interacted differently and racial politics changed drastically. Many novelists and screenwriters tied the American city to the figure of the lone, alienated, sometimes violent man. This linkage was not entirely new; earlier periods of American literature also drew a connection between cities and male violence. During and after World War II, however, the idea of city life as fundamentally male, dangerous, and decadent acquired a new centrality and importance. Chapter 1 looks at film noir as an important fictional force in this redefinition of the American city.

Straddling the line between the literary elite and the mass market, noir is a highly ritualized type of novel and film emerging from the traditional murder mystery. Originating in 1930s novels, noir reached its classic form in stylish films of the forties and early fifties. In many ways, it serves as the template for postwar urban fiction. I argue that the detached, wisecracking noir hero becomes the model for postwar fiction's key figures: the hipster, the existentialist, and alienated narrators like Holden Caulfield and the Invisible Man. Critic James Naremore calls noir narration "the voice of Male Experience."[1] This voice predominates throughout the various styles of postwar fiction, and its influence continues. The knowing voice of male experience still resounds wherever American men confront cities, in rap music, police stories, and action films.

At the heart of this chapter lies a comparison between director Billy Wilder's 1944 noir film *Double Indemnity* and Chester Himes's 1945 noir novel *If He Hollers Let Him Go*. These texts illustrate particularly well the new wartime relationship between the city and the lone, violent man. The city of Los Angeles becomes a main character in both stories. The audience sees the city through the eyes of sympathetic heroes who also have homicidal tendencies. The heroes' lack of moral compass steers the stories' decadent sense of place. I also examine the racial politics of film noir. While many critics have discussed gender in noir, fewer have explored its significant racial dynamic.[2] Denied screenwriting work in Hollywood because of his race, Chester Himes used his novel to rewrite film noir from an African American viewpoint and to expose the whiteness of cinematic perspectives. Himes's contribution to noir remained ignored until 1991, when Mike Davis drew attention to Himes's Los Angeles novels.[3] On the other hand, *Double Indemnity* has always been considered canonical. James Naremore calls it "a definitive film noir and one of the most influential movies in Hollywood history."[4]

A comparison of these two noir fictions reveals both racial difference and a shared masculine creed. When white and African American men write noir fiction, they share a common ideal of male expertise, free movement, and alienation. Regardless of race, noir heroes aim to roam all parts of town and question all kinds of people. A certain cultural detachment accompanies this ideal. In Dean MacCannell's formulation, the noir "hero demands a paradoxical combination of rights: to be completely detached from society *and* at the same time to be allowed total access to every part of it. . . . He holds himself external to and above specific class, domestic and institutional relations in order not to be marked by any specificity. He is thus free to enter into everything."[5] Everything includes violence.

This freedom dovetails with the new mobility and social reinvention of the wartime era. In a segregated city, however, the African American noir hero cannot have total access or avoid racial specificity. He is marked by race, and this marking confines him to certain parts of town. However, this bitter limitation creates a paradoxical advantage, if not for him, then for postwar fiction. The black noir hero cannot walk away from community life as easily as the white noir hero can. His struggle against physical containment requires him to be less emotionally contained than his white counterpart. Thus, Chester Himes's rewriting of noir suggests an alternative city model beyond lone masculinity, even within the alienated phallocentrism of noir discourse. All the chapters of this book engage in the dual project of analyzing lone male discourse while also looking beyond it for alternative community models.

The Wartime Context

Film noir reacts to an American city greatly changed by World War II. These changes included a new mobility of the population thanks to defense industries and troop deployments; new race and gender mixing on the job; and a great fear of violence before the twin threats of racial conflict and enemy bombing. The huge movement of population into and out of wartime Los Angeles serves as a model of postwar cities to come. Urban sense of place would never regain its old fixity. Wartime changes evident all over the United States revealed themselves with particular clarity in Los Angeles, because of its rapid industrialization and intense paranoia. World War II transformed Los Angeles economically, racially, and emotionally. Almost overnight, Pearl Harbor converted Los Angeles into an industrial powerhouse. Tapping into the power of the new Hoover Dam, Los Angeles became a center of the defense industry.[6]

New workers of many races poured into the city, often blacks and whites from the rural South. Although many African Americans spent their time in defense plants pushing brooms[7] the war brought an unprecedented level of prosperity to black workers. Under threat of a mass march on Washington, President Roosevelt signed Executive Order 8802 in June 1941, ordering the end of racial discrimination in the defense industries. Over the next four years, almost one million African Americans entered the industrial workforce.[8] "Los Angeles was particularly alluring to many of these westward migrants because of its booming military-industrial complex. No industrial area of the United States was more important to the war effort; total war contracts for Los Angeles amounted to more than $11 billion, and upwards of 550,000 were employed in shipbuilding, aircraft production, and other war-related industries."[9] The black population of Los Angeles doubled between 1940 and 1944.[10]

At that time, Los Angeles was the whitest city in America.[11] Many white newcomers were fleeing the racial diversity they disliked back home. African American newcomers met considerable hostility. Deputy Mayor Orville Caldwell proposed banning black migrants. "The Negro who was born and reared here fits into our picture, but these Southern Negroes are a serious problem. They don't get along with the Negroes who were born and reared here, nor with the white residents. . . . If this immigration is not stopped, until such a time as these people can be properly absorbed into the community, dire results will ensue."[12] In *If He Hollers Let Him Go,* Chester Himes's narrator Bob Jones, an African American shipyard worker, describes the racial intensity of Los Angeles right after Pearl Harbor: "After that it was everything. It was the look in the white people's faces when I walked down the streets. It was that crazy, wild–eyed, unleashed hatred that the first Jap bomb on Pearl Harbor let loose in a flood. All that tight, crazy feeling of race as thick in the street as gas fumes."[13]

Racist paranoia took hold among many white citizens who feared both Japanese bombing and their new nonwhite neighbors. A take-turns variety of scapegoating emerged, with one racial group replacing another as the target. The removal of all West Coast Japanese Americans into concentration camps eliminated thriving and well-established communities. After the expulsion of the Japanese Americans, white servicemen attacked young Chicanos and African Americans in the Zoot Suit Riots of 1943.[14] The Los Angeles racist riots were not an anomaly; other such incidents occurred the same year in New York and Detroit.

The racial conflict of the war years led to permanent changes on the urban landscape. Efforts to contain racial fear led to the literal containment of nonwhites in tighter ghettos. This domestic containment parallels the efforts of U.S. Cold War foreign policy to "contain" Communism. Wartime film noir already reveals this containment strategy at work. Film noir views society as fundamentally violent yet also provides ways to contain and channel that violence. Violence serves as a way not to express feeling but to replace feeling. Noir locates the violence in the character of one single man or woman who can represent the scapegoat and be eliminated. Film noir empties out the city streets, offering loneliness as the best alternative to continuous violence. It cannot imagine a peaceful community. The threatening nature of city life shapes the character of the urban hero. He must remain perpetually vigilant. Like city dwellers who fear enemy bombing, he scans the empty skies for signs of danger.

Noir as the Template for Postwar Fiction

As I have suggested, the noir hero provides a model for the alienated male narrator of postwar fiction. Noir serves as a template for postwar narrative in other ways as well. In its preoccupation with containment, urban decadence, and post-traumatic numbness, noir anticipates the fiction of the subsequent twenty years. Noir contains genre, personality, and city space. The mass-mediated, baroque conventions of noir style work together with the hero's emotional detachment and an encapsulated portrayal of the American city. All noirs zero in on a vision of contained violence. As Vivian Sobchack points out, the degenerate men and women of noir must be confined in "hermetically sealed— quarantined—social space" away from respectable citizens. Sobchack is quite right that noir segregates the clean-cut spaces of hard work away from the seedy and decadent world of "lounge time."[15] However, we can also read this division as a greater harbinger of the new postwar city, with its lack of intermingled public space. Noir's division between safe and seedy areas prefigures the coming split between gated community and urban dread.

Although noir presents a violent and dangerous city, the viewer maintains a sense of distance and visual pleasure. The high style of the noir genre creates this pleasurable distance. Noir narration is a subset of the murder mystery genre, and in some ways the mystery is about the sublimation of grief. Its reading would not be pleasurable if readers felt the tragedy of the murder too deeply. The detective sublimates this grief through what Raymond Chandler calls "a cool spirit of detachment." In Chandler's famous image, the detective belongs to the noir city, yet the elements that characterize it do not characterize him. "But down these mean streets a man must go who is not himself mean, who is neither tarnished nor afraid. . . . He has a range of awareness that startles you, but it belongs to him by right, because it belongs to the world he lives in."[16] The voice of Male Experience describes the city exhaustively, yet the hero remains aloof.

Film noir invents a new city vision that will dominate urban literature for the next twenty years. It sets the stage for postwar sense of place. Of course, noir began long before World War II, in the depression-era fiction of Dashiell Hammett, James M. Cain, Raymond Chandler, and others. Noir emerges from the 1930s social context, not the wartime American city.[17] Furthermore, the decadent noir city has many antecedents, from thirties gangster movies to the poetry of T. S. Eliot and Charles Baudelaire.[18] However, noir offers an important legacy to postwar fiction: the hero's special bond with his city. While noir novels of the 1930s rendered their settings in brilliant detail, it was the film noir of the 1940s and 1950s that sealed the pact between city and hero. Urban representation in the novels is more literal, whereas in the films the city becomes figurative and atmospheric, representing some universal truth of dread.

The ritualized, premeditated, and ceremonial nature of noir violence saturates its surroundings. The city is the church where noir enacts the ritual of violence. Even though wholesome, law-abiding, family-loving people live in big cities, noir brushes them aside. The hero and the city share their violence. As Richard Schickel writes, *Double Indemnity* "deliciously proved the adage that landscape is character. You could charge L.A. as co-conspirator in the crimes this movie relates."[19] Noir projects the hero's loneliness onto the landscape, as in the film noir title *In a Lonely Place*. If noir exists in a liminal space between the world of criminality and the world of respectable work, then this liminal space encompasses the entire city. The city's peaceful zones come to look naive and immature from the viewpoint of male experience.

Before the 1940s, noir already had an unhomelike sense of place, but this unhominess took on a strong cultural charge during and after the war's displacements. In the postwar era, noir speaks to a larger cultural feeling of estrangement and displacement, a sense of place repeated frequently in postwar fiction.[20] Lack of hominess may provide noir's greatest form of social critique. The decadent city of noir casts a shadow over a determinedly cheerful postwar optimism. It mocks an ideal of community based on hypocrisy, false prettiness, and false consensus. At a time when the picket-fence family home seemed the greatest reward for wartime sacrifice and Cold War conformity, noir turns that sentimental image into its nightmare opposite. Mike Davis's idea of noir as "transformational grammar" works as well for the postwar era as it does for the 1930s: "Noir was like a transformational grammar turning each charming ingredient of the boosters' arcadia into a sinister equivalent."[21]

Nonetheless, noir offers no alternative vision of community. Instead it offers lone manhood. No shared public space mediates between the hero's keen solitude and the peaceful citizens' deluded enclaves. This lack of public space echoes the postwar split between inner city and commuter suburb. Two urban spaces predominate in noir, the enclave and the trajectory. These spaces resemble the suburb and the freeway, key features of the postwar landscape. Noir associates the trajectory with the hero. Intent, expert, and larger than life, the hero is always on the move, and his movement is linear—as they say in *Double Indemnity,* his trajectory goes "straight down the line." The trajectory appears in dangerous shapes: the careening car chase, the homicidal obsession, the trail of blood. The hero's lack of moral compass takes geographic form in film noir's horizontal vertigo.[22]

The enclave is an enclosed bubble, the opposite of the trajectory. The enclave can represent either the decadent world of "lounge time" or the respectable world of the feminine and the domestic. In *If He Hollers Let Him Go* and *Double Indemnity*, the enclave primarily takes feminine and domestic forms. The main character in *If He Hollers Let Him Go* uses women as straight men for his jokes, playing hip to their squareness. Similarly, *Double Indemnity* uses domestic space as straight man in contrast to the murder plot. From inside the smug and snug enclave, witnesses can't see danger lurking. Only the lone, violent man understands the homicidal truth of city life. The enclave provides necessary contrast to his superior and far-reaching knowledge. Thus, both texts reinforce as well as mock the logic of segregation.

Wartime Trauma and the City of Dread

Relying on forms invented in the 1930s, film noir provided a way to deal with the war's anxieties stylishly and indirectly. The war colored the noir presentations of the city and the hero. The 1930s noir hero takes on a special resonance in the 1940s context of returning veterans. In her work on trauma Judith Herman describes the returning war veteran in terms that would also suit the noir hero: "The veteran is isolated not only by the images of the horror that he has witnessed and perpetrated but also by his special status as an initiate in the cult of war. . . . He views himself . . . as at once superior and defiled."[23] The noir hero's lonely isolation has to do with his knowledge of violence on the urban landscape, a violence others cannot see. This knowledge grants him superior vision, but it also makes him one with the city's most decadent aspects.

In his 1936 novel *Double Indemnity,* James M. Cain describes homicide as a kind of post-traumatic numbness. "If that seems funny to you, that I would kill a man just to pick up a stack of chips, it might not seem so funny if you were back of that wheel, instead of out front. I had seen so many houses burned down, so many cars wrecked, so many corpses with blue holes in their temples, so many awful things that people had pulled to crook the wheel, that that stuff didn't seem real to me any more."[24] Walter, the insurance agent protagonist, has seen so many fatal accidents on the job that death no longer affects him. Although Cain writes before the war, his noir hero already seems to suffer from battle fatigue. By the time Billy Wilder filmed *Double Indemnity* during the war in 1944, Walter's post-traumatic numbness took on extra cultural significance. The noir hero is like a parody version of a trauma victim. Noir exaggerates and stylizes the post-traumatic subject's emotional constriction, explosive rage, estrangement, heightened startle response, and vague feelings of foreboding.[25] Himes's hero Bob Jones lives in constant tension, ready to kill or to die: "Every day I had to make one decision a thousand times: Is it now? Is now the time?" (4). The hero's post-traumatic numbness leads him to speak as if he were already dead. The protagonists of *Double Indemnity* and *If He Hollers Let Him Go* tell their stories while they are dying or while they imagine themselves dying or dead. (Billy Wilder reuses the dead narrator to maximum effect in the 1952 film noir *Sunset Boulevard*). After he commits murder, *Double Indemnity*'s Walter Neff reports: "It sounds crazy, Keyes, but it's true, so help me. I couldn't hear my own footsteps. It was the walk of a dead man."[26] This sense of being already dead will haunt postwar fiction writers, from John Okada to Walker Percy and Sylvia Plath.

Accompanying the already dead narrator is a sense of the city as already dead, abandoned, evacuated. As Reid and Walker point out, the noir city foreshadows the postwar abandonment of cities during urban renewal and suburbanization.[27] However, and perhaps more important, film noir of the forties and fifties reflects a crucial way World War II altered the perception of city life. For the first time, the city became a place to be bombed. The massive, continuous bombing of cities was a brand-new nightmare. The Germans and then the British initiated the "bombing of cities aimed at the breaking of civilian morale."[28] The gruesome list includes Warsaw (1939–40); London, Liverpool, and other British cities (1940–41); Berlin, Cologne, Hamburg, Dresden, and other German cities (1942–45); and Tokyo (first in 1942 and then, along with sixty-four other Japanese cities, 1944–45), culminating in the atomic bombing of Hiroshima and Nagasaki in August 1945.[29] Nicholas Christopher argues that movie theater newsreels of global bombing inspired film noir's vision of urban horror, even though mainland American cities remained untouched. "It is from images of these foreign cities (ironically, transmitted through the medium of film) and their entrances into the dream-life of Americans, that the film noir springs."[30]

The noir hero's superhuman detachment and skill allow us to view the threatening city from a comfortable distance. Film noir contains and distances urban horror not only through the male expertise of its heroes but also through the professionalism of its writers, directors, actors, and technical staff.[31] Film noir's wit and beauty remind us that the noir city is not a real threat but an atmosphere skillfully created for our entertainment. In an interview Cameron Crowe asked director Billy Wilder, "I just wondered if there was a key event in your life that continued to inspire you." Wilder responded elliptically, "To do something better than I did last time. But my life was kind of . . . Except for the fact that three-quarters of my family was extinguished in Auschwitz, I don't really think that . . ."[32] Wilder's perfectionism of craft seems related to his subdued expression of loss. Grief and horror can be sublimated into craft. While Wilder waited to learn what had happened to his family, he turned the Los Angeles of *Double Indemnity* into a spectacularly beautiful city of dread.

Black in Another Language

Noir means "black" in another language, the French of the postwar cinema critics who gave film noir its name. This translation of an American form into another language reflects the acts of translation involved in film noir itself. Film noir translates violence into a mass-market commodity, a witty play with evil. Urban decay appears not as lived experience but as stylized visual and narrative pleasure. The racial politics of film noir also involve multiple acts of translation. Noir translates white experience into the vocabulary of darkness: the dark side of town, the dark side of human nature. White masculinity, as Richard Dyer observes, often involves giving way to darkness but ultimately containing it. "Thus it is that the whiteness of white men resides in the tragic quality of their giving way to darkness and the heroism of their channelling or resisting it."[33] An African American noir writer like Chester Himes translates black experience into the vocabulary of a white-dominated fictional style. To this day, noir remains a useful form for black novelists and screenwriters because it draws attention to urban safety and danger zones, police brutality, all the city's dirty little secrets. It maps out social codes and prohibitions and makes them visible. African American noir can take the nameless, atmospheric dread of forties film noir and name it as racial injustice.

However, something always gets lost, or changed, in translation. For example, violence is only beautiful and distant if you're not on the receiving end. In the city's racially charged atmosphere, the African American man often finds himself and his community on the receiving end of racist violence. Therefore, the violence of *Double Indemnity* looks and feels different from the violence of *If He Hollers Let Him Go.* Chester Himes embraces violence. In classic noir fashion, Himes intertwines the violence of the city with the violence of the hero. Indeed, his narrator can only see the landscape after he has committed an act of literal or symbolic violence.

Nonetheless, the violence of Himes's work comes across differently than the violence of forties film noir. Himes's novel is painful, not pleasurable, to read. The city seems too real for casual consumption. The African American noir hero cannot detach himself so easily from his community's losses, even though he shares the noir ideal of masculine detachment. Himes uses the classic noir structure of a strong man giving way to wrongful desires, even employing the stock figure of the femme fatale. In the end, however, he does not channel or resist masculine rage. Bob Jones's anger remains uncontrolled and threatens the future. Jones uses "pushing it" as a form of political resistance. Himes takes the intent linearity of the noir hero, plotting his trajectory "straight down the line," and translates it into a protest march.

Double Indemnity:
The Hero's Superior Gaze

Double Indemnity simultaneously mocks and reinforces the logic of containment. The lead characters' homicidal intentions color the landscape; however, murder produces not chaos but excessive neatness, planning, and boundaries. In his visual choices director Billy Wilder mocks excessive order. He renders absurd both the hero's self-absorption and the desire to contain urban threat and dread. Nonetheless, the mocking of excessive order also reinforces the superior gaze of the lone hero. Only the hero, and the audience through him, can discern the banality and naïveté of safe urban space.

The movie's first scene drives home the contrast between the city's peaceful enclaves and the hero's intent trajectory. In the opening scene of *Double Indemnity,* the headlights of a rapidly speeding car come over a rise and head straight for the audience. The shot startles and compels the viewers, as if they were wearing 3-D glasses and the car were about to crash into them. The street has become an accident waiting to happen. The geography slips and careens out of control, just as the hero lacks moral control. We will soon learn that the car's driver is Walter Neff, on his way to his office in the Pacific Building to confess to a double homicide. However, Wilder immediately undercuts this startling image by presenting the first of the movie's many peaceful work enclaves. The opening sequence showcases not only Walter Neff's speeding car but also the city's beautiful electric lights (courtesy of Hoover Dam) against the nighttime darkness. The fast car swerves to avoid a flagman and crew repairing the electric railway line.

The workers stand below street level, as if they formed part of the street itself. In a brilliant flash, the welder's torch lights up a sign that reads, "Los Angeles Railway Corp. Maintenance Dept." The scene restores our sense of moral and geographic order, with its diligent workers, helpfully explicit sign, and routine sense of place. While some men plot, other men maintain. To a certain extent this peaceful work enclave mocks the hero's urgent self-absorption. Noir sometimes dwells on urban danger to a campy extreme, and Wilder undercuts this tendency with his characteristic wit. The shot reminds the audience that *Double Indemnity* is only a movie, and an expertly crafted movie at that. The intensity of the nighttime lighting, the beautifully timed contrast between trajectory and enclave, draw attention to their own cinematic perfection. Relax and enjoy, the scene tells us, you're in the hands of professionals. After all, film crews also work odd hours under intense lights.

Thus, the film allows us to stay a comfortable distance from urban danger. However, the opening scene glorifies the dangerous man along with undercutting him. The noir hero needs the lesser mortal, the everyday worker, to witness his extraordinary actions. Furthermore, there is something odd about this peaceful work enclave. It sits in the middle of a lonely and dangerous street. A car almost runs the men over, but they work on as if they didn't notice. As I have suggested, home and community seem displaced in the postwar era. Similarly, this homey work site seems misplaced in the middle of the dangerous street. The men are repairing electric railroad tracks; eventually the railroad track becomes the film's main metaphor for homicide. Danger is omnipresent, even on a quiet job. This is a maintenance crew. The film points out how much work it takes to maintain one's sense of peace in a fundamentally dangerous city. Only noir heroes see danger, while the residents of peaceful enclaves work hard to ignore its existence. Violence appears as the essence of city life, despite these denials.

"It Just Can't Be the Way It Looks"

Like its female protagonist, *Double Indemnity* declares itself "Californian. Born right here in Los Angeles." In overstated fashion, the movie labels its city three times in the opening five and a half minutes—twice in signs, once in the heading on an ironic "office memorandum."[34] As in his other noir masterpiece, *Sunset Boulevard,* Billy Wilder renders Los Angeles with remarkable knowledge and intimacy. He chooses the places that set Los Angeles apart: the hillside tile-roofed home, the drive-in restaurant, the Hollywood Bowl. The city seems vivid and knowable on one hand yet strangely remote on the other. How does *Double Indemnity* contain the film's uncontrollable violence and passion? One form of emotional containment lies in its dialogue. As Alan Spiegel observes, Chandler and Wilder's witty script "becomes a 'crack wise' way of holding virtually any serious subject at arm's length."[35]

The film's visual style also offers the viewer emotional distance from its troubling subject matter. It creates this distance through a contradiction between what is shown and what is said. As one character describes the death of another: "It just can't be the way it looks." Like the murder's solution, Los Angeles becomes "something you couldn't see because it was smack up against your nose." Although the voiceover and dialogue tell of murder plots, fatal accidents and "monoxide jobs," the film shows a series of protected, sunny enclaves: children playing safely in the street outside a lovely hillside home; a clean and stylish Pacific Building with beautiful indoor balconies; a market that displays its oranges and grapefruits in ample bins on the sidewalk. Everything seems to be out in the open.

Within their safe enclaves, however, characters chatter on about fatal accidents past, future, and hypothetical. Sitting on comfy cushions or pacing in their offices, the film's insurance agents produce an endless stream of fatal possibilities.

Suicide by leaps, subdivided by leaps from high places, under the wheels of trains, under the wheels of trucks, under the feet of horses, from steamboats—but Mr. Norton, of all the cases on record there is not one single case of suicide by leap from the rear end of a moving train. And do you know how fast that train was going at the point where the body was found? Fifteen miles an hour! Now how can anybody jump off a slow-moving train like that with any expectation that he would kill himself? [Barton Keyes, elucidating the actuarial tables to the company president]

Then if some dark night that crown block *did* fall on him . . . only sometimes it can't quite make it on its own, it has to have a little help. . . . Of course, it doesn't have to be a crown block, it can be a car backing over him, or he could fall out of the upstairs window— any little thing, so long as it's a morgue job. [Walter Neff, letting Phyllis Dietrichson know he grasps her homicidal intentions in taking out accident insurance]

This contradiction between sight and sound reproduces the texture of life in a segregated city. Segregation designates safety zones and quarantines them away from the designated danger zones. People who live inside the safety zone sense that danger lurks on the periphery, but they have no visual proof. They hear about violence, but they don't see it. In Walter's Dictaphone confession of murder, he describes himself in police-blotter terms: "I killed Dietrichson. Me, Walter Neff, insurance salesman, thirty–five years old, no visible scars—'til a while ago, that is." Until Walter leaves the safety zone, he has no visible connection to violence.

Double Indemnity contrasts bright, sunny, definitively labeled spaces with the unnamed dark side street where the couple commits the murder. Once again, "it just can't be the way it looks." The viewer cannot understand the murder visually. Although the camera shows every detail of Walter's alibi, down to the card placed on the doorbell, it fails to show the setting or actual moment of the murder. The murder victim asks, "What are you doing that for? What are you honking the horn for?" but he receives no answer. We hear a bit of offscreen struggle, but we see the luminous face of Barbara Stanwyck. Like Walter Neff's mocking self-description, the scene bears "no visible scars."

For narrative purposes, the bodies of the noir man and woman signify passion and danger; for visual purposes, their bodies signify containment. The wounding of Walter Neff marks him as the ritual scapegoat whose elimination will halt urban violence. Like the white hero, the film gives way to darkness and then contains it. Collapsed in the doorway of the Pacific Building, Fred MacMurray as Walter Neff crumples over and sweats profusely as he tries to contain his bleeding within his torso. Aside from his actual wounding, Walter Neff also spends part of the film on crutches, faking an injury in order to impersonate his murder victim. The film begins with this image, drawing special attention to it. The opening credits roll over the shadowed silhouette of the man on crutches coming straight toward us, until the shadow fills the screen. This man is ritually wounded yet threatening, a scapegoat who requires elimination for our own self-defense.

The visuals also encapsulate and contain the body of Barbara Stanwyck, who plays Phyllis Dietrichson, Walter's paramour and co-conspirator. The camera keeps delineating her edges, highlighting the artificiality of her blond wig, her clothes, her skin. Her artifice is so conspicuous, she even discusses it. Turning to the hall mirror and filling in her lipstick, she says, "Hope I've got my face on straight," and Walter replies, "Perfect, for my money." The camera looks at Walter and Phyllis in the hallway mirror. The mirroring contains them in a double frame: the frame of the mirror inside the frame of the camera. This excessive mirroring distances the viewer with a double stylization.

Sitting behind the wheel while Walter commits the murder from the passenger seat, Stanwyck becomes a one-woman white suburb. Wilder shoots her face so that it looks luminous, supremely transcendent—a peaceful enclave surrounded by evil darkness. Discussing how cinematic lighting constructs race, Richard Dyer writes, "Idealised white women are bathed in and permeated by light. It streams through them and falls on to them from above. In short, they glow."[36] We know evil resides in Phyllis, but the camera doesn't show it here. Basking in her excessive blondness and whiteness all radiating and contained, the viewer ignores the unseen violence happening on the other side of the car (or the other side of town). Or, rather, Wilder mocks the viewer who could ignore violence because of a pretty face. He flatters the viewer who recognizes the contradiction between sight and sound.

Ironic Banality

Although the noir hero may be weak, criminal, and unheroic, his intensity makes the city's safety zones look naive and stupid. Thus his perspective emerges as superior despite his inadequacies. The night porter's "Hello, there, Mr. Neff. Working pretty late, aren't cha, Mr. Neff?" are the prosaic opening lines of *Double Indemnity*. This everyday banality provides sharp contrast to a hero intent on going upstairs, confessing to murder, and bleeding to death.

Obsessively repeated images of movement convey an intent city. Intent motion appears even in the spaces of refuge Walter seeks out when first shaken by Phyllis Dietrichson's homicidal suggestion. Walter goes to a drive-in for a beer, drinking it in his car while carhops and customers dash back and forth in front of the hood. In the bowling alley, Walter sends the ball purposefully down his lane while a lady in the next row, oblivious to him, repeats the motion. Postwar public space becomes a series of encapsulated enclaves, and the hero moves intently through them.

Double Indemnity loves to dwell on the visual banality of everyday city life. One by one, the film displays comfortable domestic enclaves and then floods them with irony. Mocking excessive tidiness and order, the film argues for violence as the fundamental truth of city life. It becomes impossible to think of the city as safe for everyday living, for even trivial objects signify violence at an emotional remove. For instance, Phyllis and Walter meet secretly at Jerry's Market for intense, hushed conversations about the murder. In one brilliant shot, the camera views Walter and Phyllis from the back, talking intently, while the same baby face grins at us dozens of times from identical stacked boxes of farina. The shot reminds us of the boring family unit Phyllis and Walter plan to destroy.

The uncanny, excessive repetition of the stacked boxes is like the mirror shot of Walter and Phyllis: it repeats the ordinary to the point of absurd strangeness. The market's excessive commodities would have been especially obvious to the film's original audience. *Double Indemnity* is a historical film, shot in 1944 but set in 1938. The film's first viewers would have noticed the look of a city untouched by war: young, able-bodied men in civilian clothes, careening cars unchecked by gas rationing. In the Jerry's Market scene, the store's ample display of goods would have jumped out at an audience enduring food rationing and shortages. During the filming, the Los Angeles Police Department had to guard the market's shelves, well stocked to reproduce prewar conditions.[37] Throughout the film, the excessive stocking and stacking of goods mock the desire for urban order.

Walter's apartment is another cozy domestic space rendered unlivable. At first glance, the bachelor pad seems to argue that the film is comfortably settled in the city and reflects no sense of estrangement. Friends visit Walter there. He can walk to work or to the corner for a bite. Cars sit row by shining row in the basement garage underneath the apartment building, waiting their turn to be washed by Charlie, the genial garage attendant. (Of course, the excessively repeated rows of cars should makes us immediately suspicious.) Walter's apartment is pleasantly impersonal, like a hotel room, but also like a hotel room it can set the stage for independence, chance encounters, and desirable isolation. Phyllis Dietrichson can visit him there.

Phyllis: It's nice here, Walter. Who takes care of it for you?
Walter: Colored woman comes in a coupla times a week.
Phyllis: Cook your own breakfast?
Walter: Squeeze a grapefruit once in a while. Get the rest down at the corner drugstore.
Phyllis: Sounds wonderful. Just strangers beside you. You don't know them and you don't hate them.

However, this praise of anonymity comes from a murderess, sick of sharing a suburban dinner table with her husband. The femme fatale praises Walter's independence while persuading him to help her commit a domestic murder. Phyllis's visit converts Walter's rooms into the site of adulterous and homicidal plans. Paradoxically, this moral chaos produces excessive order. Walter's apartment becomes a place where he can only plot and plan, where he can no longer relax. From Phyllis's visit onward, *Double Indemnity* takes on a dead-ahead, timetable quality, as if the whole film and not just one aspect of the murder took place on a train.

Walter: Call me tomorrow, but not from your house, from a booth, and watch your step every single minute. This has got to be perfect, you understand? Straight down the line.
Phyllis: Straight down the line.

Immediately after this exchange, Walter goes to his living-room window to watch Phyllis depart in her car. Not, however, before he has made a telling gesture. Walter walks almost to the window and then turns back to smooth with his foot a folded-under corner of the rug. Walter Neff has become a creature of pure, driving intention, moving straight ahead, perfectionist, no longer at ease in his own home. Domestic images come to signify violence at an emotional remove. Walter's apartment is decorated with nineteenth-century boxing prints, the perfect decor for a bachelor pad. Walter stands calmly in his apartment finishing a drink while Barton Keyes tells him he suspects Phyllis of murder. Between the two men, however, a tiny boxer aims a perfect punch at Keyes's nose. The boxing picture expresses violence in framed and mediated form, just as *Double Indemnity* does. Like the boxer, the film itself is just a picture.

The visual distancing of violence echoes the emotional distance of the noir hero. The city is built for the intent and expert man. As Walter says, tightly gripping Phyllis's shoulder: "We're gonna do it and we're gonna do it right. And I'm the guy that knows how." Neff knows the city intimately and describes it exhaustively in the film's voiceover, yet he remains emotionally aloof. This combination of corruption and superhuman detachment renders the world of *Double Indemnity* fascinating but unlivable. Noir suggests that you have to be very special or very desperate to live in the city.

When Walter Neff impersonates the murder victim, he boards a train on crutches and passes through what John Cheever calls "an atmosphere of intense and misplaced domesticity."[38] In the observation car's comfortably boring atmosphere of soft lamplight and comfy armchairs, a middle-aged lady knits on one side of the aisle and a middle-aged man naps on the other. They seem to sit in their own living room. Their coziness reflects the displacement of home in the wartime era. The couple looks as if they sit in a living room, but it's a living room on wheels. Domestic space has become public space—public space in transit. Meanwhile, a murderer cuts between husband and wife on his own violent trajectory. The dullness of the scene reinforces the hero's extraordinary character and throws the intent city into sharper relief. In *Double Indemnity,* office banter, overtime, and a dull evening in an armchair all serve as alibis for murder. The hero makes routine mortals witness him. Their boredom is his adventure.

White Hero, Black Workers

Interestingly, *Double Indemnity* does not place its dark-skinned characters on the dark, unsafe side of town. Rather, African American minor characters maintain the white world's peaceful enclaves and support its illusion of safety. The film associates a series of black workers with an exaggerated and therefore suspect sense of order. The screenplay's use of black actors seems in deliberate contrast to prevalent Hollywood stereotypes of obsequious Stepin Fetchits and to local resentment of the city's new black working population. Instead, Chandler and Wilder's screenplay presents black men as decent, dignified, competent workers. African American men create a world of neat and humming order for white people. In every locale *Double Indemnity* answers Phyllis's question, "Who takes care of it for you?" The workers' tidy diligence draws attention to the constructedness and unnaturalness of peaceful white enclaves. Black workers maintain an atmosphere of normality and order viewers know to be false.

An airtight order suggests its opposite, a fundamental disorder. Under the surface, violence is the order of the day. All the film's African American workers form part of the murder alibi or part of the murder's discovery. The Pullman porters on the train reinforce the world of conventional courtesies in the midst of the murder sequence. A porter nods graciously at Walter's rejection of his help and then places a polite hand under Phyllis's arm. Meanwhile, Charlie remains downstairs in the gleaming rows of automobiles under Walter's apartment building, carefully polishing Walter's car and unknowingly furnishing Walter's alibi. Walter needs Charlie as a witness: "I had to go down to the garage. I wanted Charlie to see me again." Charlie's genial smiles and pleasant speech bracket the murder scene with ironic normality. In the first scene at the Pacific Building, suspenseful music swells as the camera tilts down. We expect a shock, but instead we see a janitor smoking a pipe and straightening endless neat rows of insurance company desks. Later, he will report Walter's bloody intrusion.

> *Neff:*   I was wondering what time you got down to the office. Or did that little man of yours pull you out of bed?
>
> *Keyes:*   The janitor did. It seems you leaked a little blood on the way in here.

The hero's violent trajectory intrudes into the peaceful order of the Pacific Building. Cleverly, the script has the janitor discover Walter's trail of blood. Even a really good janitor can't tidy a mess of this magnitude.

Wanda Coleman, a distinguished African American poet from Los Angeles, has commented on racial stereotyping in film noir and its effect on black viewers. She describes her own pleasure in watching noir films and then her response when black characters appear on screen, always in the narrow stereotypical roles of servants or entertainers. "My husband groans and my son laughs. Someone black has suddenly appeared onscreen. My stomach tightens and I feel the rage start to rise. . . . To enjoy that sentimental journey back to yesteryear, I have to pretend I live in a perfect world." Coleman remarks, "Like murder, the cultural subtext will out."[39] However, *Double Indemnity* may use the conjunction of murder and cultural subtext on purpose. Wilder asks viewers to pretend they live in a perfect world and then watch that effort fail. We can't squeeze ourselves into those rows of desks or those boxes of baby food. Murder provokes the larger cultural revelation that those perfect white enclaves weren't perfect after all.

This filmmaking strategy is problematic for black viewers, however. The African American workers of 1940s Los Angeles probably did not need a film noir to tell them the white world wasn't perfect. It is easy to understand Coleman's rage in watching the black servants of film noir, even the dignified portrayals in *Double Indemnity.* Ultimately, the film relies on black workers' staying in their place. If their movements were free and unpredictable, the white hero would have no alibi. He needs routine workers to witness his extraordinary feats. Black men function for others, whereas Walter Neff and his co-conspirator function only for themselves. There's no percentage in community. To be a white man is to be uniquely special. Even though the African American workers are hard-working, decent, and likeable, they are interchangeable. Even though Walter is a murderer and often a fool, he's the hero—both superior and defiled.

If He Hollers Let Him Go:
The African American Noir Hero

Like Billy Wilder or James M. Cain, Chester Himes intended to become a mass-media success. It just didn't work out that way. He was trying to write a noir adventure thriller, not a vanguard cry against racial protest that would stay out of print for twenty-three years. The novel confronts the pain of city life too directly to allow for its comfortable consumption as genre fiction. Nonetheless, the novel works within the noir narrative conventions. It belongs to the same noir subgenre as *Double Indemnity*. In this subgenre, the hero takes on a criminal frame of mind and meets his downfall through his obsession with a treacherous woman (a femme fatale, in the parlance of film noir critics).

However, Himes also reworks noir conventions to introduce a black man's gaze. Locked out of the studio system because of his race,[40] Chester Himes uses Hollywood styles to critique Hollywood. He rewrites forties film noir, converting the African American worker from supporting player into hero. Although a work of fiction, *If He Hollers Let Him Go* provides an exceptionally vivid social history of African American defense workers. Its protagonist, Bob Jones, takes pride in his supervisory job as a leaderman at the fictional Atlas Shipyard in Los Angeles. "I felt a swagger in my stance when I stepped over to the dresser to get my keys and wallet, identifications, badge, handkerchief, cigarettes" (9). In his first-person narration Bob Jones explicitly critiques African American actors' subservient roles in Hollywood movies: "I never found out the name of the picture or what it was about. After about five minutes a big fat black Hollywood mammy came on the screen saying 'Yassum' and 'Noam,' and grinning at her young white missy; and I got up and walked out" (79).

Himes rewrites white Hollywood film noir from the viewpoint of the black male spectator. The novel's perspective on women grows from this revision of film. Bob Jones views women with sexism and even with sexual violence in mind, but also with a racial difference. As bell hooks observes, the movies offered a rare place in segregated America where black men could commit the rebellious act of looking directly at white women. Bob Jones's narrative gaze constitutes such a rebellious act. Hooks explains, "Before racial integration, black viewers of movies and television experienced visual pleasure in a context where looking was also about contestation and confrontation. . . . Given the real life public circumstances wherein black men were murdered/lynched for looking at white womanhood, where the black male gaze was always subject to control and/or punishment by the powerful white Other, the private realm of television screens or dark theaters could unleash the repressed gaze."[41]

When Bob Jones criticizes segregation, he speaks as if he were starring in a film noir. He embraces the noir hero's creed of universal access and emotional detachment. In his mental picture of freedom, Jones swings down Hollywood Boulevard like a movie star. He defines freedom in terms of the contrast between enclave and trajectory. *If He Hollers Let Him Go* documents the black community in a moment of relative affluence. Rather than staying in a limited black, middle-class enclave, Bob flaunts the ideal of going anywhere in the city and still being safe. As Bob argues for free movement through every part of town, he imagines himself making a pass at the movie star Lana Turner. This is the rebellious male gaze bell hooks describes among African American spectators in segregated movie theaters.

> If you couldn't swing down Hollywood Boulevard and know that you belonged; if you couldn't make a polite pass at Lana Turner at Ciro's without having the gendarmes beat the black off you for getting out of your place; if you couldn't eat a thirty-dollar dinner at a hotel without choking on the insults, being a great big "Mister" nigger didn't mean a thing. Anyone who wanted to could be nigger-rich, nigger-important, have their Jim Crow religion, and go to nigger heaven. I'd settle for a leaderman job at Atlas Shipyard—if I could be a man, defined by Webster as a male human being. That's all I'd ever wanted—just to be accepted as a man—without ambition, without distinction, either of race, creed, or color; just a simple Joe walking down an American street, going my simple way, without any other identifying characteristics but weight, height, and gender. (153)

Bob Jones's vision of a better Los Angeles echoes Raymond Chandler's vision of the noir detective: "But down these mean streets a man must go who is not himself mean, who is neither tarnished nor afraid. . . . He has a range of awareness that startles you, but it belongs to him by right, because it belongs to the world he lives in."[42] Bob Jones claims the right to be not just any man but to be a noir hero, identified in police-blotter terms by weight, height and gender. He may be an anonymous working man, but he always stays a man. However, one great difference between Himes's main character and the protagonist of forties film noir lies in the changed relationship between individual and community. As his name indicates, Bob Jones is an Everyman, who shares the situation of many black men. Note that Jones declares his right to free movement in second person: "if *you* couldn't make a polite pass at Lana Turner." Any number of men reading this book could walk in Jones's shoes. The special, unique gaze of the Hollywood noir hero doesn't work for Himes's rewrite. Jones tries to embrace the noir creed of lone manhood, but he keeps falling back into a collective vision of the black community.

Chester Himes takes the noir vocabulary and translates it into the context of racial violence. His revision reveals noir's commitment to the logic of scapegoating, a logic at work on the streets of Los Angeles during the time of Himes's writing. Himes's portrayal of scapegoating is different in at least two ways from the scapegoating of white Hollywood noir. One, it renders the noir hero not a special isolated case but an Everyman who suffers from a collective problem. Two, Himes keeps Bob Jones alive at the end of the novel, shipped off to the army with two other dispossessed young men, two Chicano zoot-suiters. The racial war on the streets blends into the killing overseas. The violence stays uncontained.

Ironically, noir's logic of emotional containment doesn't work in *If He Hollers Let Him Go* precisely because of the black community's physical containment. During the war, the black population was bursting out of an increasingly overcrowded South Central Los Angeles. In the segregated city, however, there was nowhere else to go. Whether poor, well off, or in between, all black people had to stay in the same area and the same boat. Despite his good job, Jones is as vulnerable to racist attack as any other black man. Despite his ideal of detachment, Jones cannot stay detached from others' circumstances or his own intense feelings. He participates in the Los Angeles black community's shared psychology of disappointment.

The writer Arna Bontemps, who grew up in segregated black Los Angeles, explains its extreme containment and resulting mood. Like their white counterparts, African American migrants believed the Chamber of Commerce's idyllic visions. "Los Angeles in legend became 'Paradise West' to Negroes still languishing in the Egyptland of the South. . . . Even in a Negro section one might have a small front yard with a few flowers and a palm tree or maybe even a little vegetable garden in the rear." Gradually, the inhabitants of Mudtown—an early name for South Central Los Angeles—realized that their enclave was an inescapable ghetto. Bontemps conveys how hatred throws an invisible wall around a decent neighborhood and turns it into a ghetto. The "knowledge of restraining pressure from without" creates a containment zone of despair.

> Mudtown, with its hundred or so houses, with its migrants fresh from the South, and its across-the-tracks status, was on the verge of proving itself a wholesome and fertile community—when something hap-

pened. Mudtown and its extension known as Watts awakened to the fact that it was a ghetto and a slum. That was the end. All who could get away fled. Those who remained—trapped—sank to indifference and then despair. A crushing weight fell on the spirit of the neighborhood when Mudtown learned that it was hemmed in, that prejudice and malice had thrown a wall around it. As long as residence there seemed temporary and accidental, everything was fine, but the ghetto consciousness, the knowledge of restraining pressure from without, the awakening of children born in the community to the fact that they were rated as aliens and outsiders in the total life of the city and the state, was more than the vitality of any neighborhood—let alone Mudtown—could bear.[43]

The Detachable Description

Despite its ultimate failure, masculine detachment remains a significant ideal in *If He Hollers Let Him Go.* The novel's detachable descriptions emerge from noir fantasies of masculine solitude and universal access. As in *Double Indemnity,* the visual distancing of violence converges with the hero's attempt at emotional distance. Himes expertly practices the noir method of describing the urban landscape, creating "scenes which are hard-edged and durable like a footprint in cement."[44] Like Raymond Chandler, Himes creates sketches of Los Angeles so vivid and extractable from teller and plot, they could almost be sent as postcards. The noir novel is notable for this kind of descriptive set piece. Critic James Wolcott points out two important aspects of Raymond Chandler's descriptions: they have an oddly detachable quality, and they form the most memorable aspect of Chandler's work. According to Wolcott, "The beautiful, deep-dyed descriptive passages of buildings, botanical life, rainfall, and car drives at night which one remembers best from Chandler are almost detachable from the logistical labor of getting Marlowe from Point A to Point B."[45]

These detachable descriptions characterize not only Chandler's novels but noir writing in general. Indeed, the descriptive passages in Nathanael West's *Day of the Locust* can be extracted so painlessly from its characters and plot, historians like Carey McWilliams and Robert Fogelson quote them as objective pocket truths about Los Angeles. Chester Himes's use of the detachable description, however, marks his distance from other noir writers as clearly as it marks his kinship. Here, Himes makes a routine trip to work seem extraordinary.

It was a bright June morning. The sun was already high. If I'd been a white boy I might have enjoyed the scramble in the early morning sun, the tight competition for a twenty-foot lead on a thirty-mile highway. But to me it was racial. The huge industrial plants flanking the ribbon of road—shipyards, refineries, oil wells, steel mills, construction companies—the thousands of rushing workers, the low-hanging barrage balloons, the close hard roar of Diesel trucks and the distant drone of patrolling planes, the sharp, pungent smell of exhaust that used to send me driving clear across Ohio on a sunny summer morning, and the snow-capped mountains in the background, like picture postcards, didn't mean a thing to me. I didn't even see them; all I wanted in the world was to push my Buick Roadmaster over some peckerwood's face. (14)

Many elements mark this passage as typical of Los Angeles forties noir: the conjunction of danger and routine industry, the modernist desire to read the city through driving. However, something unique and extraordinary happens in this passage. Jones claims that he "didn't even see" a landscape he has just described in exhaustive—literally exhaustive—detail. This picture is detachable even from the person who describes it. He seems to tell us: this is what I would see, this is what I would enjoy, if I were white. We read the scene once through white eyes, then through black eyes, so we know what we're missing. Racial rage prevents all kinds of appreciation and knowledge. The African American hero cannot master the entire city.

Although Jones swaggers and tough-talks like a standard noir hero, his urban expertise becomes racialized, limited to his knowledge of the color line. For instance, Bob's approach on the Hotel Mohave sounds much like a Chandler hero's stakeout of a cheap downtown hotel. However, Bob's expertise lies specifically in his ability to read the city racially.

It was a narrow four-story building with a dry-cleaning joint on the first floor. The hotel entrance was to one side, a narrow stairway leading to the second floor with a round white dirty globe over the doorway. The neighborhood was spotted with vacant lots and cheap hotels, a stagnant part of town between the downtown section to the east and the residential district to the west. . . .

I knew these joints; if I walked in there dressed as I was, everybody who saw me would be hostile and curious; and the chances were somebody would call the police and have me arrested on general principles. (139)

Jones's intimate knowledge of "these joints" becomes one with his intimate knowledge of the racial hostility awaiting him. Expressing his desire for universal access despite the limitations of race, Jones maps out the city through driving directions. This tour-book mode of description is typical for Los Angeles noir. David Fine says of James M. Cain's *Double Indemnity,* "The novel is almost a gazetteer of L.A. street names, a grand auto tour of Southern California," while Graham Hodges calls *If He Hollers Let Him Go* "a Baedecker of high and low, white and black Angelino life during the 1940s."[46] This method of reading Los Angeles as a motorway became common during the city's first love affair with freeway building in the 1930s and 1940s.

Himes racializes this mode of description. Hatred and fear on the street and workplace contrast with safe black, middle-class enclaves, especially the refuge of Bob's car and the area where his squeaky-clean girlfriend, Alice Harrison, lives with her family: "It was a pleasant neighborhood, clean, quiet, well bred" (49). By giving driving directions and always letting us know whether we are on safe or dangerous turf, Bob points out the segregation of neighborhoods and implicitly argues for their reconnection. Himes contrasts the world of the new migrant-intruders with the world of Los Angeles's established black middle class. The novel always asserts the relationship among different kinds of black people, even when that relationship is uneasy.

> I glanced at my watch, saw that it was a quarter to, and hurried to the car. At Vernon I turned west to Normandie, driving straight into the sun; north on Normandie to Twenty-eighth Street, then west past Western. This was the West Side. When you asked a Negro where he lived, and he said on the West Side, that was supposed to mean he was better than the Negroes who lived on the South Side; it was like the white folks giving a Beverly Hills address. . . .
>
> Alice's folks lived in a modern two-story house in the middle of the block. I parked in front, strolled across the wet sidewalk to the little stone porch, and pushed the bell. Chimes sounded inside. The air smelled of freshly cut grass and gardenias in bloom. A car passed, leaving the smell of burnt gasoline. Some children were playing in the yard a couple of houses down, and all up and down the street people were working in their yards. I felt like an intruder and it made me slightly resentful. (49)

The world of the resolutely middle-class Harrison family starts to seem impossibly constricted, banal, and naive. Jones serves as a sociologist, delineating the differences between newcomers and old-timers in black Los Angeles. Here, the noir hero's prowess at description serves to assert Jones's authentic blackness. He comes into the neighborhood like "the smell of burnt gasoline." As in *Double Indemnity,* the extraordinary hero turns the peaceful enclave into a toxic impossibility. Jones's wisecrack humor also demonstrates his expert knowledge of racism. When the light-skinned Mrs. Harrison mentions "the few of us" who have gained white acceptance, Jones "started to say 'Maybe they think the few of you are white,' but thought better of it" (52). It is no accident that the straight men for Bob's race jokes are nearly always women. Asserting the reality of racism in the face of hypocrisy and naïveté, Jones claims a consistent masculine identity. He owns the superior knowledge of the noir hero, even if that knowledge is racialized.

Pushing It

Just as Walter Neff needs witnesses for his alibi, Bob Jones needs to be seen. Both Walter and Bob make themselves seen through acts of violence. To be violent is to belong in the city and thus to exist. Over and over, the novel's descriptions reveal Bob's urgent need to push himself upon the landscape, to impress his urban presence upon the bodies of white, southern, redneck Los Angeles.[47] Images of pushing, shoving, and driving govern Jones's sensibility throughout the novel. Here, he looks for his car the morning after a drinking bout: "It was parked across the street with the front wheels cut sharply up over the curb as if I'd started to drive into the people's house and had caught myself" (72). Similarly, Jones describes the workday on the ship. "Pushing it" corresponds to the muscular strength of the defense industry. The men are a working, fighting machine, and Jones likes it that way: "The noon whistle blew as I was weaving my way through the machine shop and I joined the densely packed, gouging, pushing, fighting crush leaving the ship, stepping on one another's feet, ramming the edges of our hard hats into one another's eyes. But it didn't bother me; I felt at peace with everybody. Anyway, I never minded the scramble nor the hard, hurried push, liked it, in fact" (162).

While Walter's trajectory involves plotting and mental intensity, Bob's trajectory involves this hard physical push against limits. Bob Jones is always pushing it: asking for a fight, testing the limits of his endurance and other people's patience. Jones makes the city his home by driving its invisible conflicts up to the surface. The wartime conjunction between beauty and intangible violence is driving him slowly crazy. He can belong in his surroundings only when he has made his internal fear and rage visible. If we analyze the placement of descriptive passages throughout the novel, a pattern emerges. Jones can see the landscape only after he has made himself visible, usually through an act of symbolic violence.

For example, a splendidly accurate description of Los Angeles at sundown ("Outside the setting sun slanted from the south with a yellowish, old-gold glow, and the air was warm and fragrant. It was the best part of the day in Los Angeles; the colors of flowers were more vivid, while the houses were less starkly white and the red–tiled roofs were weathered maroon") follows a rough sexual scuffle with Ella Mae, his married housemate ("I pushed her away roughly, almost knocking her down. 'Goddamnit, quit teasing me!' I snarled") (48–49).

"American violence is public life, it's a public way of life," Chester Himes once said,[48] and his protagonist joins the public through violence. As in forties Hollywood noir, the violent man makes a pact with the violent city. Bob's relief flows not from the literal act of violence but from the thought of it, the threat of death hanging in the air. Violence defines the atmosphere. A picture postcard follows the fantasy of violence, a postcard that resembles Charles Sheeler's sharp-edged modernist paintings of American factories. Once again, Jones can see the landscape only after an imaginative act of violence.

> I was going to kill him if they hung me for it, I thought pleasantly. A white man, a supreme being. Just the thought of it did something for me; just contemplating it. All the tightness that had been in my body, making my motions jerky, keeping my muscles taut, left me and I felt relaxed, confident, strong. I felt just like I thought a white boy oughta feel; I had never felt so strong in all my life. . . . Now I felt the heat of the day, saw the hard, bright California sunshine. It lay in the road like a white, frozen brilliance, hot but unshimmering, cutting the vision of my eyes into unwavering curves and stark unbroken angles. The shipyards had an impressive look, three-dimensional but infinite. Colors seemed brighter. Cranes were silhouetted against the grey-blue distance of sky.
>
> I felt the size of it, the immensity of the production. I felt the importance of it, the importance of the whole war. I'd never given a damn one way or the other about the war excepting wanting to keep out of it; and at first when I wanted the Japanese to win. And now I did; I was stirred as I had been when I was a little boy watching a parade, seeing the flag go by. That filled-up feeling of my country. I felt included in it all; I had never felt included before. It was a wonderful feeling. (38)

Jones is so detached in this fantasy, he can think about murder quite pleasantly. Paradoxically, violence also helps Jones overcome detachment. Once he's finally made up his mind to kill a white man, Jones feels a joyful surge of patriotism; he can join public life. Jones needs violence in order to overcome estrangement. The novel's oppositional politics lie in the hero's need for direct contact. This contact usually takes the form of hurt. As Chester Himes wrote in his autobiography, "Los Angeles hurt me racially as much as any city I have ever known—much more than any city I remember from the South."[49] Himes never overcomes noir's dependence on violence, but he achieves a direct expression of feeling very different from film noir's witty and stylized visual pleasure.

The Femme Fatale and the Noir Everyman

For white men, noir transforms the city into a place not to live in but only to work in; for black men noir transforms the city into a place not to work in but only to live in. *If He Hollers Let Him Go* concerns itself almost entirely with the world of work. Paradoxically, however, it also signals the end of work and the postwar mass unemployment of African Americans. Racism interferes with the black noir hero's ability to turn all space into intense work space. Instead, every space becomes a race war. Bob Jones's leaderman job is the pride and joy of his life, and yet his productive life is endlessly deferred. The novel becomes painful to read precisely because Jones never gets to work. Racist politics at the shipyard stop him from playing his supervisory role. "I knew the average overpatriotic American would have said a leaderman was justified in cursing out a white woman worker for refusing to do a job of work in a war industry in time of war—so long as the leaderman was white" (152). Then, Jones's own rage at racist politics causes him to leave the job over and over again in the middle of the day on sick passes. This deferral of production becomes not only nerve-wracking but also gendered. It takes the form of the femme fatale.

The femme fatale reveals both the acuteness of Himes's racial politics and the troublesome nature of his sexual politics. The noir hero's claim to "universal access" can extend to sexual violence. Bob Jones's link between contact and violence becomes especially problematic when it leads to fantasies of raping the femme fatale. On the other hand, the femme fatale also reveals Jones as Everyman, not in isolated splendor but in relation to every other black man in America. Himes takes the familiar noir figure of the femme fatale and uses it toward a deeper understanding of the black community.

Like *Double Indemnity*'s portrayal of Phyllis Dietrichson, Himes's portrayal of the femme fatale Madge exaggerates the artificiality of feminine looks. However, Himes fails to contain her in a perfect enclave. Her edges keep blearing and blurring. Her lips and her figure are not the right shape. Unlike Barbara Stanwyck in *Double Indemnity,* this femme fatale is not perfectly made up but overly made up. In contrast to Stanwyck's deceptively luminous face, Madge looks just as evil as she is and is just as evil as she looks. According to Bob's all-knowing description, she's one of the city's commodities. Like Walter Neff, Jones has all the expert details.

> She was a peroxide blonde with a large-featured, overly made-up face, and she had a large, bright-painted, fleshy mouth, kidney-shaped, thinner in the middle than at the ends. Her big blue babyish eyes were mascaraed like a burlesque queen's and there were tiny wrinkles in their corners and about the flare of her nostrils, calipering down about the edges of her mouth. She looked thirty and well sexed, rife but not quite rotten. She looked as if she might have worked half those years in a cat house, and if she hadn't she must have given a lot of it away. (19)

As in *Double Indemnity,* the femme fatale represents a threat to the world of honest work. Now, Bob Jones is not the first or last noir hero to meet destruction at the hands of a cheap blond. However, in creating the noir novel of racial protest, Chester Himes combines the figure of the femme fatale with another old American story of sexual danger: the myth of the black rapist as pretext for lynching. Bob Jones claims the right to the male gaze, but he can't use it with impunity. Himes uses Madge, the blond hussy, to bring all the novel's racial complexities to the surface. In his first exchange with Madge, Bob becomes the innocent victim of injustice. He asks her to do a piece of tack welding for one of his workers. She says she won't work for a nigger, Bob responds by calling her a "cracker bitch," and for this he loses his leaderman job while Madge goes unpunished. According to Josh Sides, members of the separate-and-unequal black shipyard union were "susceptible to punishment for small infractions . . . while white union members were not."[50]

Here, however, a noir vision of obsessive sexuality takes over. The genre often contains sadistic fantasies toward women like Faye in *The Day of the Locust* and Cora in *The Postman Always Rings Twice,* women who seem to have sexual power over men. Bob's tendency to "push it" culminates in his fantasies of rape. Thus he falls into Madge's exact stereotype of him. Like Walter Neff, he knows his actions are wrong and self-destructive, but he can't stop himself. Bob goes so far as to visit her at the Hotel Mohave and pin her down on the floor before coming to his senses. Finally, at the end of the novel, Madge causes Bob's downfall in a situation in which he is entirely innocent: she locks him in a cabin at work and cries rape. In a typical noir combination of the routine and the sinister, Bob gets carted off to jail and then the army at the most ordinary moment of his week, checking out a new work site for his crew. He meets his destruction when is just about to settle in and start working, at last.

Himes's novel takes noir's nameless dread and names it as racial injustice. As the subplot involving Madge becomes the main plot, Chester Himes reveals what can happen when the hero tries to give his nameless dread tangible form. Elizabeth Cowie writes that in noir sexual fantasy demands punishment, "for in the punishment the reality of the forbidden wish is acknowledged."[51] In Jim Crow America, the black man's free gaze also demands punishment. Bob's obsession with Madge, and his role as innocent victim, push the reality of racial conflict up to the surface. An unabashed Texas bigot, Madge states the rules of the game. It can be and is the way it looks. She says words like "lynching," "rape," and "nigger" out loud. She gives Bob a concrete home for his fears. She exposes the workings of the American system. "A white woman yelling 'Rape,' and a Negro caught locked in the room. The whole structure of American thought was against me" (187). When Chester Himes rewrites film noir from a black man's viewpoint, his plot almost inevitably returns to the punishment awaiting a black man's gaze.

By crying rape Madge can make him die at any moment. Despite his status as noir hero, Jones is as vulnerable as any other African American man. He cannot hold himself separate from his community. Bob is drawn to Madge because he already thinks he's about to die in a violent city and is tired of being alone with the thought. Because any white woman can condemn him to death at any time, Bob Jones's class status as a leader-man becomes irrelevant. By the end of the novel, running from the police, Jones says, "I felt pressed, cornered, black, as small and weak and helpless as any Negro sharecropper facing a white mob in Georgia" (194). Unlike its African American literary progenitor, *Native Son, If He Hollers Let Him Go* treats black problems within a context of relative prosperity. However, the peaceful black, middle-class enclave becomes an impossibility, given the force of racial prejudice. Hurt becomes Jones's way to declare his allegiance to the collectivity of black people.

Each in his or her way, both Bob and his impeccably bourgeois girlfriend, Alice Harrison, are grappling with the limitations of black, middle-class life. In the end, Bob decides he cannot accept the Harrisons' vision of success on segregated terms: "They hadn't stopped trying, I gave them that much; they'd keep trying, always would; but they had recognized their limit—a nigger limit" (151). In a better world, freed from racial injustice, Bob Jones could achieve his goal of emotional detachment. His rage, grief, and desire for revenge would not overtake his existence. As I have said, the noir narrative requires the sublimation of grief. The hero sublimates this grief not only through "a cool spirit of detachment" but, quite frequently, through alcohol. One morning after, Bob Jones tells us: "The hangover gave me a strange indifference, a weird sort of honesty, like a man about to die" (150). However, *If He Hollers Let Him Go* remains a powerful novel precisely because its hero cannot detach himself from the painful desire for freedom. As Bob Jones describes his drinking later that same morning: "I started off tryna kill my grief but I went along too" (157).

2 | Post-traumatic Fiction; or, The Suspiciously Impeccable Fifties Short Story

It was a rough commute from World War II into the eerie calm of the 1950s. As Gregory Peck says to Jennifer Jones in *The Man in the Gray Flannel Suit* (1956), "One day a man's catching the 8:26 and then suddenly he's killing people. And a few weeks later he's catching the 8:26 again."[1] The 1950s short story reflects this abrupt transfer into postwar existence. This chapter examines stories that both conceal and reveal the era's vexed gender relations and dislocated sense of place. Like the decade itself, fifties short stories have a smooth and polished surface belying their stressful underpinnings. The smoothness of fifties discourse reflects the psychic numbing that often accompanies post-traumatic stress disorder. We have to read underneath the surface to find postwar shock in structures of flashback and denial.

This chapter compares two profoundly different yet uncannily similar examples: Hisaye Yamamoto's "Wilshire Bus" (1950) and John Cheever's "The Country Husband" (1954). These stories do not primarily concern themselves with the trauma of World War II or the shock of postwar transition. Rather, they encapsulate the trauma into flashbacks, displace its truths from the content into the narrative structure, and use emotional containment to express uncontrollable emotions. Both stories call on readers to witness a submerged tale visible only to the main character. They resemble noir narrative in their emotional containment and the privileged sight granted to the protagonist.

Cheever and Yamamoto explore postwar shock through the perspectives of two opposed figures: the hipster versus the housewife. One figure moves toward masculine isolation, the other toward imagined community. Even though one protagonist is male and one female, both share a common symbolic status as war veterans, their truths cordoned off from the rest of society. A comparison between these two stories refutes the huge gender gap in fifties culture. Their similarity belies the prevalent notion of an absolute split between the wife who stayed home and "the veteran as a man apart." Judith Herman describes the quarantine of wartime memory:

> Too often, this view of the veteran as a man apart is shared by civilians, who are content to idealize or disparage his military service while avoiding detailed knowledge of what that service entailed. Social support for the telling of war stories, to the extent that it exists at all, is usually segregated among combat veterans. The war story is closely kept among men of a particular era, disconnected from the broader society that includes two sexes and many generations. Thus the fixation on the trauma—the sense of a moment frozen in time—may be perpetuated by social customs that foster the segregation of warriors from the rest of society.[2]

The short story form itself becomes a synecdoche for segregated wartime memory. A stylistic containment betrays the psychic numbing of the postwar era. Both Cheever and Yamamoto display the tidy understatement made famous by *New Yorker* fiction writers but ubiquitous in the 1950s. Cheever's and Yamamoto's stories share similar literary pleasures. Their sense of craft approaches perfection. Each paragraph, each story, rounds off with a satisfying resolution. However, this smooth artistry seems incongruous when the subject matter is rough and unresolved. As Herman writes, the telling of a war story sits uncomfortably on the smooth postwar surface. Post-traumatic memory remains disconnected and disintegrated.

On the surface, Yamamoto and Cheever have little in common. Hisaye Yamamoto is well known primarily in Asian American and feminist literary circles. Until her fiction was collected by Kitchen Table/Women of Color Press in *Seventeen Syllables and Other Stories* (1988), Yamamoto had written mostly for a regional Japanese American audience in Los Angeles community newspapers like *Rafu Shimpo.* By contrast, John Cheever was the preeminent postwar short story writer, nationally known and published constantly in the *New Yorker.* His stories have been collected repeatedly, starting with *The Housebreaker of Shady Hill and Other Stories* in1958. The authors' characters and settings are far apart. Yamamoto's "Wilshire Bus" takes place in downtown Los Angeles, while Cheever's "The Country Husband" takes place on the commuter corridor between New York City and a Connecticut bedroom town. Cheever's main character, Francis Weed, is a white male executive with a New York firm, while Yamamoto's Esther Kuroiwa is a Nisei bride recently released from the internment camps and "lucky enough to get a job as a secretary at the Community Chest."

Despite their differences, these two stories' similarities show the widespread nature of postwar shock. Trauma affected a much wider group than the already wide circle of returning veterans. The stories share the same muted, impeccable prose, and they also share a dislocated sense of place. This dislocation occurred across lines of race, gender, class, and region. Both stories literally concern "rough commutes"—one on a bus, one on a plane and a train—which can be read as emblems of uneasy postwar transition. In both tales, a routine trip provokes a sudden, extraordinary threat that reminds the protagonist of submerged past trauma. Each story renders absurd the widespread postwar optimism about limitless progress and upward mobility. The two protagonists get stuck in futile, lateral movement.

For both Yamamoto and Cheever, landscape plays a crucial role in repressing postwar unease. Although one story takes place in a city and the other mostly in a suburb, both places foster emotional containment. Like the fifties short story itself, the landscape becomes a smooth and polished capsule of almost-forgetting. City and suburb become concrete islands, holding themselves aloof from the flow of unfortunate memory. It seems impossible to read one's personal trauma back onto the landscape. Therefore, wartime trauma comes to seem a personal problem rather than a collective experience. By reading both stories together, we can see how trauma affected not just individuals but the entire postwar generation.

Housewife Discourse; or, The Pink Lampshade

Although Yamamoto and Cheever write about a shared postwar experience, they branch out in opposite directions. Their differences have a great deal to do with gender and race as well as personal temperament. Cheever's narrative reinforces the lone male isolation explored in the previous chapter; Yamamoto's narrative gravitates to collective experience. Her subtext the internment of all West Coast Japanese Americans during World War II, Yamamoto suggests that personal shock may grow and require response from an entire community's social conscience. She shows how women and entire communities can be war veterans along with individual men. Not coincidentally, Yamamoto has written stories about sexual harassment and domestic violence as well as wartime trauma. As Judith Herman writes in *Trauma and Recovery*, a battered woman and a male war veteran share the same combat fatigue. "It is now apparent also that the traumas of one are the traumas of the other. The hysteria of women and the combat neurosis of men are one. Recognizing the commonality of affliction may even make it possible at times to transcend the immense gulf that separates the public sphere of war and politics—the world of men—and the private sphere of domestic life—the world of women."[3]

However, Herman's assertion of commonality between men and women is a 1990s insight, not a 1950s one. Fifties discourse shows a yawning chasm between the domestic lives of women and the public lives of men, a split much bigger than it had been before the war. Cheever's and Yamamoto's stories reflect the great gender gap in fifties discourse, as if men and women spoke entirely different languages. Many fifties short stories anatomize the stresses and disappointments of postwar marriage. A happy marriage was supposed to be the great reward for the sacrifices young men and women endured in World War II. George Lipsitz writes, "In their songs, Ernest Tubb and Perry Como sang about the love of women as the ultimate postwar reward for men, a view encouraged at the highest levels of government."[4] The stories of Yamamoto and Cheever express the disappointing discovery that love wasn't all you had wanted or hoped for. In "Wilshire Bus" and "The Country Husband," a spouse waits as the final goal at the end of a rough commute. The stories' social satire lies in exaggerating everything that gets in the way of reunion, happiness, and being understood. Marriage becomes a dubious reward. Each story reflects a wider social malaise beyond the problems of one couple. Stereotypical gender roles make it impossible to talk about what happened during the day, much less during the war. Two people bury their memories within a superficial coupledom.

The problems of marriage seem akin to the suspiciously impeccable fifties story form. As Barbara Ehrenreich writes, postwar couples were supposed to marry young: "Maturity was not dull, but 'heroic,' a measured acceptance of the limits of one's private endeavors at a time when action on a broader political scale could only seem foolish—or suspect."[5] Similarly, Cheever and Yamamoto work their magic by accepting the tight confines of the short story form. They translate the broad social issues of the postwar era into small domestic upsets. However, they also allow readers to suspect and criticize the narrow limits placed on their characters' lives and to glimpse the wider worlds inside their minds. The reader understands what the spouse doesn't.

The gulf between men's and women's worlds shows up in fifties discourse as the conflict between two opposed figures: the hipster versus the housewife. Like many fictional suburban husbands, Cheever's hero is a would-be hipster. The hipster inherits the masculine detachment of the noir hero, with the added alienation of the existentialist, the beatnik, and the war vet. The hipster occupies a unique vantage point for social criticism: no one else in his world can see and satirize as sharply as he. He gains validity for his views because he is usually a war veteran who has tasted the reality of combat. Judith Herman describes the war veteran's superior vision as an outcome of his trauma. Like the noir hero, the veteran lives in a decadent yet enlightened world: "The veteran is isolated not only by the images of the horror that he has witnessed and perpetrated but also by his special status as an initiate in the cult of war. He imagines that no civilian, certainly no woman or child, can comprehend his confrontation with evil and death. He views the civilian with a mixture of idealization and contempt: she is at once innocent and ignorant. He views himself, by contrast, as at once superior and defiled."[6]

Like a war vet contemplating women and children, the hipster satirizes society's "innocence and ignorance" by mocking the voice of the housewife. The housewife seems complicit with the fifties' cheerful avoidance of reality. The aproned and exquisitely coiffed Mom represents mindless conformity, shallow consumerism, keeping up appearances, boredom, blandness, decor, and emotional cover-ups. To this day, the fifties housewife serves as the butt of satire. Like the hipster, the housewife is now a thoroughly commodified figure. As Thomas Frank observes in *Commodify Your Dissent,* recent consumer culture addresses the audience as if it was all hipsters using their purchase power in an "ever-more determined defiance of the repressive rules and mores of the American 1950s—rules and mores that by now we know only from movies."[7]

From a masculinist perspective, it takes a male hipster to enlighten a housewife, or even to understand the depths of her shallowness. In the 1998 neo-fifties film *Pleasantville,* it takes a Salinger-reading son to wake up his sitcom mom to the joys of colors and social rebellion. In the 1999 neo-fifties film *American Beauty,* the would-be hipster husband lambastes his suburban wife for her superficial materialism. He mocks her impeccable white sofa while his brand-new red sports car sits in the driveway. The fifties gave birth to the impeccable sitcom mom, but it also gave birth to the intense hostility toward her. Like many fifties male writers, John Cheever blames the housewife for postwar discontent. In the words of one admiring critic, Cheever's "country husband" is an "imaginative suburbanite in an unimaginative land."[8] Cheever portrays the housewife as the most oppressively unimaginative force in that land.

Not only in Cheever but all over fifties discourse, the housewife becomes a scapegoat for the ills of postwar conformity. She turns her men into obedient drones. In Barbara Ehrenreich's analysis, Mom provided a handy target at a time when criticizing capitalism or political ideology could lead to anti-Communist persecution. "But the less sophisticated gray flannel rebel needed a scapegoat, and if the corporate captains were out of the bounds of legitimate criticism in Cold War America, there was always another more accessible and acceptable villain—woman."[9] America's new status as center of corporate capitalism gave rise to this odd scapegoating. The job security of fifties corporate America seems hard to comprehend from our current perspective of downsizing, start-ups, and job shifts. In the fifties a college-educated white man could put on a gray flannel suit, sign on with a company, and stay there until he retired or died in his office chair. Meanwhile his wife stayed home and redecorated the living room—and no housewife satire is complete without a mockery of her obsessive decor. What Ehrenreich calls "gray flannel rebels" (like Cheever's hero) stayed in their jobs despite inner protest and discontent. Many social critics saw the corporate man as weak and effeminized. In a leading critique of corporate conformity, *The Organization Man* (1956), *Fortune* editor William H. Whyte complained that the man in the gray flannel suit had become weak, conformist, noncompetitive, and obedient to the will of others. "The pink lampshade" symbolizes the superficial and effeminate results of American prosperity: "The fruits of social revolution are always more desirable in anticipation than in fact, and the pink lampshade in the picture window can be a sore disappointment to those who dreamed that the emancipation of the worker might take a more spiritual turn."[10]

Hisaye Yamamoto's fifties short stories may seem modest in their scope and intention, but they fly in the face of hostility toward housewives. Yamamoto employs the soothing, practical, colloquial tones of housewife discourse to defy stereotypes about postwar women. Although the main character in "Wilshire Bus" has a secretarial job, she thinks in housewife discourse. Yamamoto herself has been a housewife and stay-at-home mother for much of her life. "Wilshire Bus" launches a critique of postwar culture as acute and powerful as any hipster's. Housewife discourse is neither innocent nor ignorant.

Yamamoto is far from alone in her use of housewife discourse for artistic effect and social critique. Housewife discourse plays an important literary role in Gwendolyn Brooks, Ann Bannon, Paule Marshall, and Sylvia Plath, whose novels are analyzed later in this book. As we shall see, housewife discourse also structured the anti–Cold War protests of Janice Smith and Mary Sharmat. And, like Yamamoto, Tillie Olsen and Grace Paley were housewives who published short stories in the 1950s. Their stories, like Yamamoto's, show the typical fifties combination of large issues contained in small spaces. The title of Grace Paley's 1959 short story collection, *The Little Disturbances of Man,* suggests how each story encapsulates a small piece of a big human trouble. Paley wrote in small capsules because she wrote around her children's school schedules, but the encapsulation also derives from her subject matter. Portraying women's sexual and financial vulnerabilities, each story could be seen as a "small drop of worried resentment and noble rage": "I was a woman writing at the early moment when small drops of worried resentment and noble rage were secretly, slowly building into the second wave of the women's movement. I didn't know my small-drop presence or usefulness in this accumulation."[11]

Paley's depiction of New York City centers on the disparaged world of the fifties wife and mother. In the story "An Interest in Life," Virginia's husband starts making his way toward leaving her after she becomes pregnant with their fourth child. "Later on he said, 'Oh, you make me so sick, you're so goddamn big and fat, you look like a goddamn brownstone, the way you're squared off in front.'"[12] Although men may denigrate its importance, the brownstone, the multifamily home full of women and children, is the central space in Grace Paley's New York. It is Paley's most fertile literary site.

Tillie Olsen also employs housewife discourse to talk about big issues in small ways. Included in *The Best American Short Stories of 1957,* Olsen's "I Stand Here Ironing" speaks in a housewife's voice from its title onward. The perfect roundness of its central metaphor marks it as a typically impeccable fifties short story. The housewife meditates on her daughter's wrenching history through many flashbacks over nineteen years. Contemplating her daughter's adolescent troubles, the housewife relates them to the troubles of the mid-twentieth century, from the depression and World War II to the atom bomb. Her domestic focus does not limit her biting social critique. "My wisdom came too late. She had much in her and probably nothing will come of it. She is a child of her age, of depression, of war, of fear." These wide-ranging meditations happen during the short space of time while the speaker irons a dress. The tight unity of time and place constricts the story's pain. As the dress under the iron becomes a metaphor for the daughter, Olsen rolls the story's tragedy into a bundle small enough so that the reader can bear it: "Let her be. So all that is in her will not bloom—but in how many does it? There is still enough left to live by. Only help her to believe—help make it so that there is cause for her to believe that she is more than this dress on the ironing board, helpless before the iron."[13]

The housewife remains mute in many discussions of fifties culture, as if she never spoke for herself. The reason for this continued silence is that American culture is still in rebellion against her. Wini Breines writes of herself and her fellow seventies feminists, "Our memories are imbued with the sense that the 1950s were not a good time for women because we learned to understand our lives as a flight from that time."[14] The fifties housewife comes off very poorly in retrospect, for reasons beyond her control. In 1963 Betty Friedan published *The Feminine Mystique,* a groundbreaking study of discontent among postwar housewives. She called their unease "the problem that has no name." Inadvertently, this phrasing dovetails all too well with the misogynist idea that housewives cannot articulate their own experiences: "The problem lay buried, unspoken, for many years in the minds of American women. It was a strange stirring, a sense of dissatisfaction, a yearning that women suffered in the middle of the twentieth century in the United States. Each suburban wife struggled with it alone. . . . In 1960, the problem that has no name burst like a boil through the image of the happy American housewife."[15]

Friedan speaks strongly in women's interests, and her book had liberating effects for many women. However, in misogynist discourse "the problem that has no name" has been turned against women's interests. Many writers still speak of housewives as if they need outside help to understand their own lives. Furthermore, the "buried, unspoken" nature of fifties women's oppression gets confused with the "buried, unspoken" effects of postwar shock. Women get blamed for the postwar repression of men's truths, along with their own.

Post-traumatic Fiction

Gender politics heavily influence the way Cheever and Yamamoto rewrite trauma. "Wilshire Bus" and "The Country Husband" are not autobiographical testimonies but highly polished fictions. Michael Lambek writes of memory, "The smoother the story, the more evident that it is the product of secondary reworking."[16] Looking at trauma in these fictions, we must ask several questions: What aspects of post-traumatic stress disorder does each author use? When trauma becomes a literary trope, what purposes does it serve? How do people use past trauma to gain more power or validity? As Kali Tal points out, traumatic stories do not enter the dominant culture value-free but rather come to serve a variety of agendas. Someone's hurt enters the wider culture in codified rather than direct form. The manner of its codification reflects a power struggle. "The work of the critic of the literature of trauma is both to identify and explicate literature by members of survivor groups, and to deconstruct the process by which the dominant culture codifies their traumatic experience. . . . Members of opposing interest groups will attempt to appropriate traumatic experiences while survivors will struggle to retain their control. The winner of this battle over meaning will determine the manner in which the experience is to be codified."[17]

As we shall see, Cheever and Yamamoto rework post-traumatic stress disorder to convey its importance in defining social space. They use two chief components of PTSD to help them describe the texture of life in the postwar era. These components are flashback and psychic numbing. In the fourth edition of the American Psychiatric Association's *Diagnostic and Statistical Manual* (*DSM-IV*), the official psychiatric definition of post-traumatic stress disorder describes flashback and psychic numbing in the following ways. Flashback is the "persistent reexperiencing of the traumatic event" through "images, thoughts, or perceptions," dreams, "acting or telling as if the traumatic event were recurring," or "intense psychological distress at exposure to internal or external cues that symbolize or resemble an aspect of the traumatic event." Psychic numbing involves "deliberate efforts to avoid thoughts, feelings, or conversations about the traumatic event. . . . This avoidance of reminders may include amnesia for an important aspect of the traumatic event. . . . Diminished responsiveness to the external world, referred to as 'psychic numbing' or 'emotional anesthesia,' usually begins soon after the traumatic event."[18]

The emotional containment of PTSD interlocks with the containment culture of the 1950s. As the clinical definitions show, both flashback and psychic numbing are essentially narrative symptoms, emerging from the compulsion to remember or to forget. These narrative symptoms translate well into fictional narrative. More specifically, they translate well into the emotional containment of the fifties short story. Psychic numbing is by nature a form of emotional containment, whether through avoidance of feeling, amnesia, or the inability to feel. We can detect psychic numbing in the inappropriate neutrality common to fifties discourse. Less obviously, flashback is also a form of emotional containment. Past trauma lives in the psyche as an encapsulated island, quarantined away from the rest of memory. Cathy Caruth calls it an "unclaimed experience."[19] In an analysis of flashback and amnesia, Caruth reveals a connection between emotional and geographic containment. This connection shaped fifties culture, providing the psychological "back story" for racial segregation and Cold War foreign policy.

> The ability to recover the past is thus closely and paradoxically tied up, in trauma, with the inability to have access to it. And this suggests that what returns in the flashback is not simply an overwhelming experience that has been obstructed by a later repression or amnesia, but an event that is itself constituted, in part, by its lack

of integration into consciousness. . . . The history that a flashback
tells—as psychiatry, psychoanalysis, and neurobiology equally suggest—is, therefore, a history that literally has no place, neither in
the past, in which it was not fully experienced, nor in the present,
in which its precise images and enactments are not fully understood.[20]

Pursuing this connection between emotional and geographic containment, fifties fiction writers transfer PTSD from the individual to the
landscape. They describe post-traumatic cities and suburbs in which
wartime memory "has no place." The community itself seems amnesiac,
even though individuals may want to remember. The "lack of integration
into consciousness" translates into greatly intensified racial segregation. As we shall see in Part II, fiction writers describe the Japanese
American and African American ghettos and the white suburb as encapsulated islands, carefully holding themselves aloof from each other for
fear of emotional meltdown.

The act of retelling or repressing trauma can itself be seen as a landscape. In "Landscapes of Memory" Lawrence Kirmayer defines trauma
as social space in ways highly useful for analyzing Cheever's and
Yamamoto's fiction. Kirmayer argues that, when telling is forbidden, individuals construct a virtual telling space that can be either social or asocial in nature.

In situations where telling and even thinking are forbidden, where
individuals are utterly alone (in prison, or the isolation of an abusive family), they still may construct a virtual space where their
story can be narrated. When this virtual space is imagined as a social
landscape, memory remains accessible. When the costs of recollection seem catastrophic for self or others, memory may be
sequestered in a virtual (mental) space that is asocial, a space
that closes in on itself through the conviction that no telling will
ever be possible. . . .

There is a crucial distinction between the social space in which
the trauma occurred and the contemporary space in which it is (or
is not) recalled. In the case of the dissociative disorder patient and
the Holocaust victim, the difference is between a public space of solidarity and a private space of shame. Trauma shared by a whole community creates a potential public space for retelling. If a community
agrees traumatic events occurred and weaves this fact into its identity, then collective memory survives and individual memory can
find a place (albeit transformed) within that landscape. If a family
or a community agrees that a trauma did not happen, then it vanishes

from collective memory and the possibility for individual memory is severely strained.[21]

Kirmayer illustrates a crucial difference between Cheever and Yamamoto. Although both writers construct trauma as social landscape, their protagonists and readers have very different relationships to that landscape. Yamamoto heads toward a "public space of solidarity," while Cheever heads toward a "private space of shame." By the end of "Wilshire Bus," Hisaye Yamamoto returns readers to the suppressed truth of trauma and calls on us to witness it together. She treats the Wilshire bus as a Petrie dish for growing an experimental new postwar community. As Judith Herman writes, "To hold traumatic reality in consciousness requires a social context that affirms and protects the victim and that joins victim and witness in a common alliance."[22] Although Yamamoto's protagonist lacks that affirming social context, the author brings in the reader as ally and witness.

By contrast, John Cheever's vision tends toward the asocial and individual. He presents the strain between a constricted social landscape and a lone, alienated man within that landscape. The trauma vanishes into the lone man's "private space of shame," represented by forbidden sexuality. Rather than forming a community alliance with the main character, the reader ultimately takes over his role as sardonic hipster.

World War II affected an entire generation, but it did not affect everyone in the same way or to the same degree. Some people got hurt more than others. What does it mean, then, to label a city, an era, or a fictional genre as post-traumatic? It is crucial to move carefully from personal experience to literary reworking. In *Post-traumatic Culture* Kirby Farrell writes, "Because not everybody in a given culture is likely to be neurologically afflicted, or affected the same way, trauma is always to some extent a trope."[23] However, trauma is always much more than a trope, because someone got hurt. As we have seen, PTSD is by nature a narrative distress. That narrative becomes figurative rather than literal, especially when the dominant culture appropriates it. As Kali Tal cautions, it is appropriate to make analogies between literature and real experience only if we acknowledge the power relations and agendas involved in literary reworking.

What agendas are at work in these two fictional reworkings of wartime trauma? John Cheever uses flashback to register the shock of moving into the postwar era and to describe the texture of postwar community. However, he also uses the war veteran's perspective to validate the scornful alienation, and sometimes the violence, of the lone man. Cheever scapegoats the housewife for co-opting the postwar man into fifties conformity.

Like Cheever, Yamamoto also seeks to convey postwar shock and the ambivalence of postwar community. However, she draws the reader into social witness rather than social alienation. Only the housewife acknowledges the racial hatred that caused great wartime trauma and still breaks out on postwar city streets. The Nisei housewife is herself a war veteran, of America's internal war against Japanese Americans. Nonetheless, Yamamoto resists the impulse to scapegoat, even though it is tempting for the trauma victim to close her eyes to others' traumatization.

Post-traumatic Cheever

> On Fifth Avenue, passing Atlas with his shoulders bent under the weight of the world, Francis thought of the strenuousness of containing his physicalness within the patterns he had chosen.[24]

John Cheever's "The Country Husband" (1954) presents a powerful allegory for the transition from wartime shock to postwar conformity. However, this transition disappears under the weight of its gender politics. Cheever translates the emotional containment of post-traumatic shock into two varieties of physical containment. One variety is geographic, the other sexual. The main character, Francis Weed, lives in the constricted world of the New York City commuter corridor and a Connecticut suburb called Shady Hill. Cheever critiques this world's narrow standards of acceptable mores. From inside the psyche of an alienated white man, the postwar suburbs' "economic and racial homogeneity" appears as moral and behavioral homogeneity.[25] Physical containment threatens suburban masculinity. The problem of uneasy postwar transition turns into the problem of male sexuality. The suburban husband blames the housewife for his emasculation, and he dreams of illicit romance to restore missing passion. The large cultural issue of emotional and physical containment appears within the small and perfect confines of marriage satire.

The anticlimactic plane crash at the beginning of "The Country Husband" can be read as allegory for a generation's experience. Like World War II, the emergency landing catches a wide cross section of people all at the same heightened moment. Their reactions vary, but each adult faces the reality of death. Cheever presents a trauma in miniature so we can see his characters' reactions. The official diagnostic manual for psychiatrists, *DSM-IV,* defines trauma as a set of responses to "an event that involves actual or threatened death of serious injury, or other threat to one's physical integrity."[26]

> Francis had been in heavy weather before, but he had never been shaken up so much. The man in the seat beside him pulled a flask

out of his pocket and took a drink. Francis smiled at his neighbor, but the man looked away; he wasn't sharing his pain killer with anyone. The plane began to drop and flounder wildly. A child was crying. The air in the cabin was overheated and stale, and Francis' left foot went to sleep. He read a little from a paper book that he had bought at the airport, but the violence of the storm divided his attention. It was black outside the ports. The exhaust fires blazed and shed sparks in the dark, and, inside, the shaded lights, the stuffiness, and the window curtains gave the cabin an atmosphere of intense and misplaced domesticity. Then the lights flickered and went out. "You know what I've always wanted to do?" the man beside Francis said suddenly. "I've always wanted to buy a farm in New Hampshire and raise beef cattle." The stewardess announced that they were going to make an emergency landing. All but the children saw in their minds the spreading wings of the Angel of Death. The pilot could be heard singing faintly, "I've got sixpence, jolly, jolly sixpence. I've got sixpence to last me all my life. . . ." There was no other sound. (325; ellipsis in original)

It is hard to imagine a better beginning for a short story. In one paragraph, Cheever tells an entire story in miniature, with a perfect arc from beginning to middle to end. Each detail, from the "jolly sixpence" to the Angel of Death, vividly conveys the heightened atmosphere. Within this perfect frame, however, Cheever places clues to a larger story outside the frame. The passengers react to the shock of turbulence the way a generation reacted to the shock of World War II. With his flask of "pain killer," Francis's seatmate tries emotional anesthesia, one form of psychic numbing. Meanwhile, Francis tries to read a book to distract himself from "violence," but the violence keeps intruding on the book we are reading. His seatmate's sudden confession sounds like a war buddy's confession in a bomber or a foxhole. Like many traumas, the plane crash represents an unprecedented shock. Francis "had never been shaken up so much."

Cheever explores the strange conjunction, so typical of the postwar era, between extraordinary circumstance and continued normality. "The exhaust fires blazed and shed sparks in the dark, and, inside, the shaded lights, the stuffiness, and the window curtains gave the cabin an atmosphere of intense and misplaced domesticity." This line seems to foreshadow Francis's eventual predicament. He finds himself swallowed up in a feminized suburban world of too much domestic drama, too much stuffy decor, too many window curtains. His emotional truths have no home in his house. Francis himself is misplaced, actually living not in

Shady Hill but in his mind and along the commuter corridor. Furthermore, the story itself misplaces domesticity. Shady Hill seems an artificial and forced place to live. Beyond this, the domestic becomes a red herring, distracting our attention away from the problem of postwar unease. "Intense and misplaced domesticity" describes not only Cheever's writing but much of postwar fiction as well, with its dislocated sense of place.

The plane's emergency landing turns out to be comically anticlimactic, just as one could view the 1950s as a giant anticlimax.

> Anxious for their lives, they filed out of the doors and scattered over the cornfield in all directions, praying that the thread would hold. It did. Nothing happened. When it was clear that the plane would not burn or explode, the crew and the stewardess gathered the passengers together and led them to the shelter of a barn. They were not far from Philadelphia, and in a little while a string of taxis took them into the city. "It's just like the Marne," someone said, but there was surprisingly little relaxation of that suspiciousness with which many Americans regard their fellow travelers.
>
> In Philadelphia, Francis Weed got a train to New York. At the end of that journey, he crossed the city and caught just as it was about to pull out the commuting train that he took five nights a week to his home in Shady Hill. (325–326)

It's oddly comic that Francis ends up on his usual commuter train after a plane crash. Cheever brilliantly violates the Aristotelian unity of place, moving Francis in a few lines from the cornfield to Philadelphia to New York to Shady Hill. Like his friends and family, the reader also can't comprehend all the places Francis has been. This abrupt yet strangely normal movement suggests the rough commute from wartime shock to postwar routine. The passage itself suggests an analogy with war; the string of taxis reminds one onlooker of Paris taxis driving out to the battlefront during the World War I Battle of the Marne.

Francis himself cannot articulate the relationship between his shock and his routine commuter existence. He tries to explain the crash to his seatmate on the commuter train. "Francis had no powers that would let him re-create a brush with death—particularly in the atmosphere of a commuting train, journeying through a sunny countryside where already, in the slum gardens, there were signs of harvest. Trace picked up his newspaper, and Francis was left alone with his thoughts" (326). As Lawrence Kirmayer writes, Francis's brush with death remains "asocial" because he has no space for telling. His culture offers him no language of reintegration, no objective correlative for his experience. It's sunny in New York.

To use Lawrence Langer's terms, the "common memory" shared with his seatmate bears no relationship to Francis's unspeakable "deep memory."[27] As Cheever describes Francis later in the story, "It was not his limitation at all to be unable to escape the past; it was perhaps his limitation that he had escaped it so successfully" (330). In Francis's exchange on the train with Trace, only the single word "slum" mediates between deep memory and common memory, suggesting a trouble beyond his suburb's "tacit claim . . . that there was no danger or trouble in the world" (331). Denied a social space of telling, Francis is "left alone with his thoughts." The story reinforces the image of the postwar man as a figure of loneliness and alienation.

The past disappears when Francis arrives home. At the exact moment Francis tries and fails to get an audience for his story, Cheever switches temporarily from past to present tense. Francis's past shock disappears into the present fracas of suburban family life.

> Nothing here was neglected; nothing had not been burnished. It was not the kind of household where, after prying open a stuck cigarette box, you would find an old shirt button and a tarnished nickel. The hearth was swept, the roses on the piano were reflected in the polish of the broad top, and there was an album of Schubert waltzes on the rack. . . . Francis, taking off his hat and putting down his paper, was not consciously pleased with the scene; he was not that reflective. It was his element, his creation, and he returned to it with that scene of lightness and strength with which any creature returns to his home. "Hi, everybody," he said. "The plane from Minneapolis . . ."
>
> Nine times out of ten, Francis would be greeted with affection, but tonight the children are absorbed in their own antagonisms. Francis had not finished his sentence before Henry plants a kick in Louisa's behind. (326–327)

The burnished and tranquil room seems akin to Cheever's perfectly polished short story. In form and content, we watch the shock disappear under a smooth and reworked surface. All this smoothness suggests its opposite, however, just as the children's hostilities complicate the impeccable home. In the phrase "nothing had not been burnished," the double negative suggests the not-burnished. Like the theory that art mirrors life, "the roses on the piano were reflected in the polish on the broad top." However, we know that these polished surfaces do not reflect Francis's deep memory. Francis "was not that reflective," and his surroundings do not reflect him. He does not mirror his home, nor does he have the words to articulate his vexed relationship to it. He gets cut off in mid-sentence. Francis doesn't fit in partly because he is an adult male. The room's excessive perfection summons up "the pink lampshade," men's fear that fifties middle-class life has become overfeminized.

Francis has had a shock he cannot integrate into the rest of his life. This problem gets subsumed into the problem of postwar marriage and sexuality. Francis contrasts his constrictive and emasculating wife with a teenage girl he imagines can reempower him and restore him to virility. This sexual fantasy will become the crux of "The Country Husband," as the problem of post-traumatic shock sinks slowly beneath the surface. The split between past and present lives gets conflated with the split between men's and women's experiences. The lone man dreams of other worlds, while the housewife accepts the inadequacy of her present existence. When Francis tries once again to tell the family about his day, the power of feminine emotion silences him.

> Francis says that that he must be understood; he was nearly killed in an airplane crash, and he doesn't like to come home every night to a battlefield. Now Julia is deeply concerned. Her voice trembles. He doesn't come home every night to a battlefield. The accusation is stupid and mean. Everything was tranquil until he arrived. She stops speaking, puts down her knife and fork, and looks into her plate as if it is a gulf. She begins to cry. (328)

Julia transforms her husband's shock into a routine household argument. She can't tell the difference between the normal and the extraordinary. Like other adultery-inclined men, Francis can say, "My wife doesn't understand me." Their mutual resentment is a gulf wider than the width of a dinner plate. The resentment grows from their rigidly defined roles as commuter husband and stay-at-home wife. Francis's declaration of feeling turns into an argument about Julia's feelings, and the narrative sides with the misunderstood Francis. As Julia converts Francis's distress into her own, she claims center stage for herself. This confusion between her feelings and his feelings reflects a fifties masculine fear of getting swallowed up in femininity. Wini Breines detects a similar fear in the writings of fifties male sociologists: "At the heart of their concerns was the unappealing image, for them, of a new feminized man who had lost his traditional manhood, a demasculinized husband and father unable to hold his own in the face of restless and demanding women."[28]

From here "The Country Husband" swings into a full-fledged critique of the pink lampshade. The story satirizes Julia's narrow-mindedness, love of appearances, and "self-deception" even more than it satirizes Francis's lustful midlife crisis. Cheever partially legitimates Francis's adulterous desire by portraying it as a rebellion against the housewife's power.

Francis pits his masculine physicality against actual pink lampshades. "He thought of Anne Murchison, and the physical need to express himself, instead of being restrained by the pink lamps of Julia's dressing table, engulfed him. He went to Julia's desk, took a piece of writing paper, and began to write on it. 'Dear Anne, I love you, I love you, I love you . . .' " (337). The narrative blames the housewife for masculine discontent. Francis's legitimate need to express himself, to connect his present with his past, disappears underneath the satire of Julia's conformity. Meanwhile, Julia's legitimate needs also disappear.

> "I've got to express my likes and dislikes."
>
> "You can conceal your dislikes. You don't have to meet everything head on, like a child. Unless you're anxious to be a social leper. It's no accident that we get asked out a great deal. It's no accident that Helen has so many friends. How would you like to spend your Saturday nights at the movies? How would you like to spend your Sundays raking up dead leaves? How would you like it if your daughter spent the assembly nights sitting at her window, listening to the music from the club? How would you like it—" He did something then that was, after all, not so unaccountable, since her words seemed to raise up between them a wall so deadening that he gagged. He struck her full in the face. (340)

Francis advocates free expression, while Julia advocates keeping up appearances. Ironically, however, his free expression shuts her up with a slap. Francis's blow seems natural and "not so unaccountable." The narrative does not register shock. Cheever brilliantly describes the wall between past and present, the wall between husband and wife. However, he blames Francis's action on "Julia's words." The narrative attributes Francis's discontent to Julia's obsession with conformity. Julia also gets a chance to express her discontent, but Francis's inner monologue undercuts her words.

> "What do you mean?"
>
> "I mean the way you leave your dirty clothes around in order to express your subconscious hatred of me."
>
> "I don't understand."
>
> "I mean your dirty socks and your dirty pajamas and your dirty underwear and your dirty shirts!" She rose from kneeling by the suitcase and faced him, her eyes blazing and her voice ringing with emotion. "I'm talking about the fact that you've never learned to hang up anything. You just leave your clothes all over the floor where they

drop, in order to humiliate me. You do it on purpose!" She fell on the bed, sobbing.

"Julia, darling!" he said, but when she felt his hand on her shoulder she got up.

"Leave me alone," she said. "I have to go." She brushed past him to the closet and came back with a dress. "I'm not taking any of the things you've given me," she said. "I'm leaving my pearls and the fur stole."

"Oh, Julia!" Her figure, so helpless in its self-deceptions, bent over the suitcase made him nearly sick with pity. (342)

Julia has thoroughly busted Francis. Francis not only doesn't realize it but also has the nerve to pity her. Julia's complaints are legitimate: Francis's slobbery is not only annoying but disrespectful, and he probably does hate her sometimes. However, Julia's psychobabble and dislike of everything "dirty" discredit her legitimate complaints. Francis sees her assertion of independence as self-deception, and Cheever validates his view by having her cave in at the end of the scene. Cheever's satire of Julia's speech mannerisms makes it seem as if the housewife cannot articulate her own experience, even though she's just done it.

In the fifties, as we have seen, the pink lampshade represented not just a trivial target of satire but a serious threat to masculinity. In reaction, male writers adopted the rebellious stance of the hipster. The hipster combined the superior yet defiled viewpoint of the war veteran with the privileged sight, expert detachment, and wisecracks of the noir hero. Of course, Francis is not a beatnik hipster, but he toys with anti-conformity. He's a "gray flannel rebel." He assumes a hipster stance to declare his independence from an emasculating housewife discourse. Satire of the housewife's voice grows particularly intense when Francis encounters the suburban socialite Mrs. Wrightson on the commuter train platform. Mrs. Wrightson represents all the social niceties Julia loves and Francis hates.

"Well, I guess you must be surprised to see me here the third morning in a row," she said, "but because of my window curtains I'm becoming a regular commuter. The curtains I bought on Monday I returned on Tuesday, and the curtains I bought Tuesday I'm returning today. On Monday, I got exactly what I wanted—it's a wool tapestry with roses and birds—but when I got them home, I found they were the wrong length. Well, I exchanged them yesterday, and when I got them home, I found they were still the wrong length. Now

I'm praying to high heaven that the decorator will have them in the right length, because you know my house, you *know* my living-room windows, and you can imagine what a problem they present. I don't know what to do with them."

"I know what to do with them," Francis said.

"What?"

"Paint them black on the inside, and shut up."

There was a gasp from Mrs. Wrightson, and Francis looked down at her to be sure that she knew he meant to be rude. She turned and walked away from him, so damaged in spirit that she limped. A wonderful feeling enveloped him, as if light were being shaken about him, and he thought again of Venus combing and combing her hair as she drifted through the Bronx. The realization of how many years had passed since he had enjoyed being deliberately impolite sobered him. Among his friends and neighbors, there were brilliant and gifted people—he saw that—but many of them, also, were bores and fools, and he had made the mistake of listening to them all with equal attention. (334)

Francis acquires the hipster's superior powers of discernment; suddenly he can distinguish between hips and squares. Mrs. Wrightson's long discourse on curtains makes her seem inane and entirely superficial. To know her is to know her living room windows. Even her decorator would probably long for her to shut up. Her triviality reinforces the idea that real troubles and real emotion have no place in Shady Hill, despite Mrs. Wrightson's own real emotion. The wounding of her spirit is vivid to the reader but irrelevant to Francis. As in Julia's case, the narrative deflects attention away from the housewife's pain and into Francis's inner monologue. The story respects the lone man's inner life above all. Francis sees his own rudeness as a liberation from boredom and hypocrisy. A fifties anticonformist audience might agree. Mrs. Wrightson might not seem like a tyrant to us, but she does to him and perhaps to other anti-matriarchal readers. Lawrence Jay Dessner points out that Francis's remark evokes blackout curtains, "an appurtenance of warfare"—and one particularly associated with World War II.[29] Cheever subtly contrasts the reality of war with the unreality of the suburban matron.

Francis's deliberate rudeness may seem adolescent, but his unspoken inner life lends his viewpoint special validity. Shortly before the scene with Mrs. Wrightson, Francis has relived a wartime memory no one else can understand. Why should he respect a social space that makes no room for his experiences? This scene presents the most explicit clue that "The Country Husband" is an allegory of postwar trauma. At a neighbors' dinner party, Francis recognizes their French maid from a wartime sojourn in Normandy. The French village's distinctive sense of place contrasts with Shady Hill's generic pleasantness.

> Francis realized where he had seen the woman before. It had been at the end of the war. He had left a replacement depot with some other men and taken a three-day pass in Trenon. On their second day, they had walked out to a crossroads to see the public chastisement of a young woman who had lived with the German commandant during the Occupation.
>
> It was a cool morning in the fall. The sky was overcast, and poured down onto the dirt crossroads a very discouraging light. They were on high land and could see how like one another the shapes of the clouds and the hills were as they stretched off toward the sea. The prisoner arrived sitting on a three-legged stool in a farm cart. She stood by the cart while the Mayor read the accusation and the sentence. Her head was bent and her face was set in that empty half smile behind which the whipped soul is suspended. . . . The round white face had aged a little, but there was no question but that the maid who passed his cocktails and later served Francis his dinner was the woman who had been punished at the crossroads.
>
> The war seemed now so distant and that world where the cost of partisanship had been death or torture so long ago. Francis had lost track of the men who had been with him in Vesey. He could not count on Julia's discretion. He could not tell anyone. And if he had told the story now, at the dinner table, it would have been a social as well as a human error. The people in the Farquarson's living room seemed united in their tacit claim that there had been no past, no war—that there was no danger or trouble in the world. In the recorded history of human arrangements, this extraordinary meeting would have fallen into place, but the atmosphere of Shady Hill made the memory unseemly and impolite. (330–331)

Again Cheever violates the unity of place to remind readers of postwar dislocation. It seems so unlikely that Francis would see the Frenchwoman again, in such a different context, that we question the link between the war and postwar eras. "This extraordinary meeting" sinks below the banal surface of the postwar suburb with its cocktails and polite dinner parties. Cheever becomes explicit here that the emotional containment of Shady Hill is a widespread cultural problem, not just a problem for Francis. The entire suburban community suffers from amnesia, acting as if "there had been no past, no war—that there was no danger or trouble in the world." Shady Hill's dislocated sense of place seems separate from all of human history. The community's psychic numbing becomes obvious when juxtaposed with Francis's vivid flashback. The incredibly precise detail of his memory marks its encapsulation and separation from the rest of his experience. We are suddenly there in Normandy, reliving the event, with no way of mediating between that unspeakable experience and the common experience of before-dinner cocktails.

Of course, the woman from Trenon is standing right there in the room and could provide mediation between deep memory and common memory. Although Shady Hill fails to provide a social space of telling, Francis could still create a space of solidarity with the French woman. After all, Francis seems to identify with her sexual transgression and her naked courage. An alliance could exist between victim and witness, an alliance Judith Herman calls necessary to healing and community building. However, Francis retreats into lonely masculinity instead. As Lawrence Jay Dessner points out, "The French woman does not have a place in the story's final parade in which 'everything comes together.' . . . The story's supposedly unifying structure leaves these escapes, these selves, out of the celebration."[30] The flashback remains an encapsulated and unclaimed experience, separate from the rest of memory.

As Judith Herman also points out, male war veterans and sexually victimized women suffer from the same combat fatigue. However, "The Country Husband" draws no such analogies across gender lines. It valorizes the unique and separate memory of the male veteran. The story's Normandy setting also lends it special validity, since Normandy was the site of the D-Day invasion. Cheever himself felt guilty at being transferred to noncombat duty while his former comrades in E Company died during the Normandy invasion.[31] Perhaps not coincidentally, Francis serves in Normandy but seems to survive unscathed. As it turns out, the war trauma Francis remembers was not his own. We get no clue that he himself survived personal trauma. The story keeps bringing up women's hurts only to dismiss and submerge them. The gender gulf remains in place, and Francis remains isolated. Ultimately, the story presents the woman from Trenon not as an interactive character but as a vehicle to explain Francis's loneliness.

The narrative immediately translates this wartime memory of sexual victimization into present-day sexual obsession. Francis falls in love with Anne, the babysitter, immediately after recognizing the French woman. Anne lives in a poor neighborhood and cries in front of Francis over her alcoholic father's treatment of her. She probably appeals to Francis because her troubles remind him of all the real-life shadows banished from Shady Hill. Again, emotion becomes geographic. "The street was dark, and, stirred by the grace and beauty of the troubled girl, he seemed, in turning into it, to have come into the deepest part of some submerged memory" (332). The story converts the problem of the submerged and unspeakable past into the bedroom farce of midlife crisis.

By deciding to see a psychiatrist at the end of the story, Francis abandons the "perfect loneliness" of the hipster. "To abdicate the perfect loneliness in which he had made his most vital decisions shattered his concept of character and left him now in a condition that felt like shock" (344). The narrative, however, does not abandon this solitary perspective. Instead, the angle shifts from Francis's viewpoint to omniscience. The reader adopts his hipster stance. The last scene is a detachable description with a panoramic view. Who speaks and who sees here, especially the famous last line? The reader keeps Francis's big dreams in mind, even though Francis himself seems to have abandoned them.

> It is a week or ten days later in Shady Hill. The seven-fourteen has come and gone, and here and there dinner is finished and the dishes are in the dish-washing machine. The village hangs, morally and economically, from a thread; but it hangs by its thread in the evening light. Donald Goslin has begun to worry the "Moonlight Sonata" again. Marcato ma sempre pianissimo! He seems to be wringing out a wet bath towel, but the housemaid does not heed him. She is writing a letter to Arthur Godfrey. In the cellar of his house, Francis Weed is building a coffee table. Dr. Herzog recommends woodwork as a therapy, and Francis finds some true consolation in the simple arithmetic involved and in the holy smell of new wood. Francis is happy. . . .
>
> Cutting the last of the roses in her garden, Julia hears old Mr. Nixon shouting at the squirrels in his bird-feeding station. "Rapscallions! Varmints! Avaunt and quit my sight!" A miserable cat wanders into the garden, sunk in spiritual and physical discomfort. Tied to its head is a small straw hat—a doll's hat—and it is securely buttoned into a doll's dress, from the skirts of which protrudes its long, hairy tail. As it walks, it shakes its feet, as if it had fallen into water.
>
> "Here, pussy, pussy, pussy!" Julia calls.
>
> "Here, pussy, here, poor pussy!" But the cat gives her a skeptical look and stumbles away in its skirts. The last to come is Jupiter. He prances through the tomato vines, holding in his generous mouth the remains of an evening slipper. Then it is dark; it is a night where kings in golden suits ride elephants over the mountains. (345–346)

Francis is no longer a king roaming freely where his imagination leads. The reader's last glimpse mocks Francis rather than forming an alliance with him. We see him now from the outside, as we see other satirized characters. His woodworking forms one of many sad, absurd suburban scenes in the final panorama. Francis seems to accept his own diminishment, blending into the feminine decor so completely that he's even building a coffee table. He contentedly measures out the constrictions of his own life. David Riesman's introduction to a 1956 sociological study claimed that only women live in the suburbs, while men are "visiting from the bush."[32] Francis, by contrast, has been tamed and domesticated. To be part of the suburbs is to be confined and to accept one's own confinement. Francis is like the phallic, hairy pussycat trapped in a doll's dress, except that Francis is no longer miserable. By now Cheever has taught us to suspect the story's too easy closure. We know that Shady Hill "hangs by a thread," just like the airplane in the storm. We know Francis Weed's odyssey raise more questions than it answers. By the end, however, Francis has become one of the absurd suburban figures he previously mocked. The reader takes on his perfect loneliness.

Hisaye Yamamoto's Concrete Island

In 1950 Hisaye Yamamoto wrote a short story called "Wilshire Bus," its main character a young Japanese American woman resettling in Los Angeles after the wartime internment camps. Like Cheever's "The Country Husband," Yamamoto's "Wilshire Bus" alternates between wartime flashback and the psychic numbing of the 1950s. Her female main character is a war veteran, too. Like Francis Weed, Esther Kuroiwa has a clear, if silent, vision of her world's flaws and dislocations. In this deceptively modest tale of a bus ride down Wilshire Boulevard, Yamamoto shows the strangeness of postwar optimism and redevelopment in the face of a difficult history. With irony and care, she exposes the city's racial complexities and the buried costs of World War II. Wilshire Boulevard's "recent stark architecture" obscures a recent past most city residents would rather forget. Nonetheless, Yamamoto calls on readers to witness this buried history.

Hisaye Yamamoto has sketched the lives of southern California's Japanese Americans through many decades of complex history. Born in Redondo Beach, California, in 1921, Yamamoto has published short stories, memoirs, and reportage steadily since her teenage years. Like all other West Coast Japanese, Yamamoto and her family were interned in a concentration camp during World War II. After the war, Yamamoto became one of the first Nisei writers to receive national attention, but her work appeared primarily in Los Angeles publications for a Japanese

American readership. Critics like Sau-Ling Wong, King-Kok Cheung, and Stan Yogi have assessed Yamamoto's importance within Asian American literature and have brilliantly analyzed her tales of prewar rural life.[33]

Here, however, I wish to concentrate on Hisaye Yamamoto as an urban writer, a chronicler of postwar Los Angeles. This chapter offers a reading of "Wilshire Bus" in the cultural context of Japanese Americans returning to Los Angeles after their wartime internment. Along with a different take on postwar life, Yamamoto also provides a new angle on the common literary image of Los Angeles as a "nowhere city," a place one "can't be from." Los Angeles fiction is different from other regional literatures in that alienated outsiders, not locals, have produced many of its best-known works. According to David Fine, outsider status has become intrinsic to Los Angeles fiction: "[Los Angeles fiction] is for the most part the product of newcomers, of outsiders, of writers born elsewhere, but who lived and worked for a time in the region. Most of them never felt at home in southern California, and it is their estrangement, their sense of displacement, that provides both theme and ambiance to their works and distinguishes the Los Angeles novel from novels of other regions."[34]

For Yamamoto, however, the estrangement reflects a specific postwar history rather than a literary tradition. Hisaye Yamamoto anatomizes displacement and estrangement, but in an entirely different vein than writers like Nathanael West and Alison Lurie. A native of the region, Yamamoto found herself literally displaced and rendered alien not by private despair but by forces of racism beyond her control. Esther Kuroiwa, Yamamoto's main character in "Wilshire Bus," traverses the city in the guise of a well-adjusted 1950s housewife. However, just below the surface lies "the infuriatingly helpless, insidiously sickening sensation of there being in the world nothing solid she could put her finger on, nothing solid she could come to grips with, nothing solid she could sink her teeth into, nothing solid."[35] Yamamoto's remarkable writing style, with its dramatic irony, competing layers, and unexplained shifts between compassion and detachment, corresponds to a wartime history her characters can neither entirely remember nor entirely forget.

In many ways, Yamamoto's writing speaks back in housewife discourse to the voice of the lone, alienated man. She uses many aspects of noir style, but ultimately toward the end of community building rather than alienation. Like a noir hero, the young woman protagonist of "Wilshire Bus" classifies the city and its inhabitants with ironic humor. In another kinship with noir, Yamamoto's narrative style struggles back and forth between grief and detachment. One marker of Yamamoto's style is the occasional intrusion of misplaced neutrality. This neutrality is a symptom of aftershock. It alerts our attention to the muted presence of psychic numbing.

The Significant Digression

"Wilshire Bus" begins with a deceptively objective description of Wilshire Boulevard in Los Angeles, rendered in the bland tones of a public television documentary or the AAA tour book. The paragraph could be omitted and the story would remain much the same. It is like a noir detachable description taken out of first person and rendered more neutral, more in tune with fifties pleasantries. This gratuitous beginning seems an odd choice for a careful craftswoman like Yamamoto. Nonetheless, we shall see how this seemingly misplaced paragraph interlocks perfectly with a story of buried trauma.

> Wilshire Boulevard begins somewhere near the heart of downtown Los Angeles and, except for a few digressions scarcely worth mentioning, goes straight out to the edge of the Pacific Ocean. It is a wide boulevard and traffic on it is fairly fast. For the most part, it is bordered on either side with examples of the recent stark architecture which favors a great deal of glass. As the boulevard approaches the sea, however, the landscape becomes a bit more pastoral, so that the university and the soldiers' home there give the appearance of being huge country estates.
>
> Esther Kuroiwa got to know this stretch of territory quite well while her husband Buro was in one of the hospitals at the soldiers' home. They had been married less than a year when his back, injured in the war, began troubling him again, and he was forced to take three months of treatments at Sawtelle before he was able to go back to work. During this time, Esther was permitted to visit him twice a week and she usually took the yellow bus out on Wednesdays because her friends were not able to take her except on Sundays. She always enjoyed the long bus ride very much because her seat companions usually turned out to be amiable, and if they did not, she took vicarious pleasure in gazing out at the almost unmitigated elegance along the fabulous street. (34)

A routine commute and an innocent way to begin. However, Yamamoto's characteristic irony appears in the phrase "except for a few digressions scarcely worth mentioning." Yamamoto equates Wilshire Boulevard with a narrative, and in her own narratives the core of the story often lies buried in the digressions. The parenthetical and the digressive resemble the encapsulation of traumatic memory. Yamamoto drops a quiet clue that the story's real issue is post-traumatic stress: an old injury begins to trouble the veteran again. Yamamoto will go on to make subtle analogies between the troubled postwar body and the troubled postwar conscience. As Stan Yogi has pointed out, her stories usually have two plot lines, one "manifest," the other "buried": "'Buried plots' are related to the common literary idea of the 'double plot.' Whereas double plots involve an explicit presentation of a secondary, albeit related plot in a story or play (for example, the Gloucester plot in *King Lear*), buried plots in Yamamoto's stories are not always clearly delineated. Often the reader must piece together a buried plot from clues garnered in the 'main' or 'surface plot.'"[36]

Even on the surface level, "Wilshire Bus" becomes the story of a buried story: the reader watches Esther Kuroiwa witness a racist incident and then bury it in silence. Underneath this, the story has another buried tale that the reader must unearth through scattered clues. Although it appears only once in a parenthesis, the wartime internment forms a buried but principal plot. On the Wilshire bus, Esther hears a drunken white man launch into a racist attack at an elderly Chinese couple. Esther's "acute discomfort" after this incident sounds a great deal like Criterion (B4) in the diagnosis of post-traumatic flashback: "intense psychological distress at exposure to internal or external cues that symbolize or resemble an aspect of the traumatic event."[37]

> Suddenly, the woman with the chrysanthemums jerked around to get a look at the speaker and Esther felt her giving him a quick but thorough examination before she turned back around.
>
> "So you don't like it?" the man inquired, and it was a moment before Esther realized that he was now directing his attention to her seat neighbor.
>
> "Well, if you don't like it," he continued, "why don't you get off this bus, why don't you go back where you came from? Why don't you go back to China?"
>
> Then, his voice growing jovial, as though he were certain of the support of the bus in this at least, he embroidered on this theme with a new eloquence. "Why don't you go back to China, where you can be coolies working in your bare feet out in the rice fields? You can let your pigtails grow and grow in China. Alla samee, mama, no tickee no shirtee. Ha, pretty good, no tickee no shirtee!"
>
> He chortled with delight and seemed to be looking around the bus for approval. Then some memory caused him to launch on a new

idea. "Or why don't you go back to Trinidad? They got Chinks running the whole she-bang in Trinidad. Every place you go in
Trinidad."(35–36)

It is probably no accident that this incident takes place on a bus, since
buses played an important role in World War II racial history. Upon being
released from camp, Japanese Americans received "a bus ticket and
twenty-five dollars."[38] Many members of Yamamoto's original Nisei
readership in the *Pacific Citizen* newspaper would have returned to
Los Angeles using those bus tickets. The setting of the bus would evoke
the difficulties of homecoming. However, Yamamoto focuses not on the
racist history but on the psychological and moral challenges of people
who survive racist attack. Yamamoto captures the radarlike ability of the
alcoholic to perceive and lash back at scrutiny. However, the narrative
dwells not on the white man's slurs but on Esther Kuroiwa's reaction.
Except for the strangely omniscient opening paragraph, Yamamoto, like
Cheever, keeps her perspective close to that of her main character.
Unlike Francis, however, Esther refuses to scapegoat someone else for her
own moral failings. Cheever takes it for granted that Francis will not identify with the hurts of women surrounding him. By contrast, Yamamoto
takes such failure of identification and makes it the crux of her narrative.
Yamamoto often depicts Japanese American women engaged in a complex dance of identifying with, and refusing to identify with, people of
other races, especially other people of color. Unlike many Nisei authors
who write "totally within the Japanese-American community," Yamamoto
"sees a world in interaction," as McDonald and Newman point out.[39]
Yamamoto's 1950s fiction records a multicultural city radically different from Cheever's encapsulated white world. Whites and Japanese play
only two of the parts. Yamamoto approaches with particular honesty those
internal moments when a good person fails to identify with another's suffering. Here in "Wilshire Bus," Esther Kuroiwa is "startled to realize . . .
she was gloating."

> She found herself wondering whether the man meant her in his exclu-
> sion order or whether she was identifiably Japanese. Of course, he
> was not sober enough to be interested in such fine distinctions, but
> it did matter, she decided, because she was Japanese, not Chinese,
> and therefore in the present case immune. Then she was startled to
> realize that what she was actually doing was gloating over the fact
> that the drunken man had specified the Chinese as the unwanted.
>   Briefly, there bobbled on her memory the face of an elderly
> Oriental man whom she had once seen from a streetcar on her way

home from work. (This was not long after she had returned to Los Angeles from the concentration camp in Arkansas and been lucky enough to get a clerical job with the Community Chest.) The old man was on a concrete island at Seventh and Broadway, waiting for his streetcar. She had looked down on him benignly as a fellow Oriental, from her seat by the window, then been suddenly thrown for a loop by the legend on a large lapel button on his jacket. I AM KOREAN, said the button.

Heat suddenly rising to her throat, she had felt angry, then desolate and betrayed. True, reason had returned to ask whether she might not, under the circumstances, have worn such a button herself. She had heard rumors of I AM CHINESE buttons. So it was true then; why not I AM KOREAN buttons, too? Wryly, she wished for an I AM JAPANESE button, just to be able to call the man's attention to it, "Look at me!" (36)

Yamamoto brings up the camp experience in the gentlest possible way. Throughout the story traumatic memory remains entirely encapsulated, like a beach ball—or a tumor. She uses a light, almost playful phrasing: the Korean man's face "bobbled on her memory." However, if this story only floats on the surface of memory, other stories must lie submerged underneath. The "I AM KOREAN" button is a small incident compared with everything Esther must have seen in and after the camps. Yamamoto concludes the anecdote with an absurd and housewifely joke, to round off the rage and make it bearable. The past, however, will not succumb to easy closure. Even though Esther's time in the camps appears only in a one-sentence parenthesis, the use of the strong term "concentration camp"—strong especially in 1950—belies its parenthetical status. Yamamoto refers to the alcoholic's slurs as his "exclusion order," as if Executive Order 9066 could be reactivated at any moment.

Throughout "Wilshire Bus," the past interrupts the busy onrush of progress. This dynamic appears in the story's controlling image: the metaphoric lump in the midst of an otherwise smooth flow. The image comes in several forms, for example, the parenthesis within the anecdote or the Korean man on a concrete island in the midst of traffic. The Wilshire Bus itself serves as a time capsule, carrying the racial politics of the war down the fast-moving lanes of the postwar boulevard. Sometimes the image retains the same shape but reverses its meaning. For instance, the image that "bobbled on the surface of her memory" captures in contained form a larger, angrier sea of past wrongs.

The desire to remember and blame contradicts an equally strong desire to fit in and forget. Esther shows a proper gratitude for the smooth resumption of her life in Los Angeles, thinking of herself as "lucky enough to get a clerical job with the Community Chest."[40] Even in small matters of word choice, "Wilshire Bus" contains a sharp dramatic irony, a conflict in perspective between a white public consensus and a private Nisei awareness of racial difference. The name "Community Chest" conveys the story's layered and contradictory realities. The Community Chest conjures up a benign sense of shared civic good. However, to Yamamoto's original Nisei audience in the *Pacific Citizen,* it would also provide an ironic reminder that the Japanese Americans had just experienced the fracture of their own community, the loss of savings and possessions, and exclusion from the community at large.

Rotating Scapegoats:
The Structure of Wartime Racism

Although "Wilshire Bus" addresses itself to a Japanese American audience, it also casts out threads to other communities. Esther Kuroiwa feels a guilty desire to assert the difference between Japanese and Chinese and thus her own immunity from persecution. However, the story emphasizes the arbitrary and rotating nature of bigotry. Yamamoto renders the ethnic-identity slogans on the buttons in capital letters, as if to magnify their absurdly interchangeable character: "I AM CHINESE . . . I AM KOREAN . . . I AM JAPANESE." Interchangeability also governs the drunk's last confused insult: "So clear out, all of you, and remember to take every last one of your slant-eyed pickaninnies with you!" (37). Yamamoto renders absurd the whole moral structure of scapegoating.

"Wilshire Bus" reflects the whirling turnabout quality of racist paranoia in Los Angeles during World War II. One scapegoat replaced another in rapid succession. After the internment of the Japanese, historian and activist Carey McWilliams wrote: "In Los Angeles, where fantasy is a way of life, it was a foregone conclusion that the Mexicans would be substituted as the major scapegoat group once the Japanese were removed."[41] From 1942 through 1943, the persecution of young Mexican Americans took place both in the courts (the Sleepy Lagoon murder trial) and in the streets (the mob violence of the Zoot Suit Riots).[42]

This variety of take-turns racism has a long history in southern California.[43] Fears of invasion and bombing during World War II only magnified a structure already in place. In describing African American migration to the city, Arna Bontemps and Jack Conroy emphasized the rotational aspect of Los Angeles racial politics.

> And the adjustment of this group to the community as a whole was perhaps better than that of any group of equal size in any other

American city. This despite the predominance of Southern whites in the population. Perhaps the Japanese and the Mexicans are to be thanked. They drew off much of the racial hostility which otherwise might have been concentrated on the Negroes. And when Japanese American citizens were removed from cities of the Coast to inland relocation camps following Pearl Harbor, their places were quickly filled by another wave of Negro migrants.[44]

Because one set of targets took the place of another, the nonwhite resident had to guard against rejoicing in others' misfortune. Esther's failure of compassion toward the elderly Chinese couple forms the moral center of "Wilshire Bus." Note that Esther uses the word *sin*. She judges herself according to her own value system, not an external standard for her behavior. She takes responsibility for her own actions: "It was on one of those Wednesday trips that Esther committed a grave sin of omission which caused her later to burst into tears and which caused her acute discomfort for a long time afterwards whenever something reminded her of it" (34).

Esther's trouble reflects a shifting postwar racial dynamic for Japanese Americans. Before the war, Japanese American farmers and produce merchants frequently occupied an economic "middleman" position beneath whites and above other races. In his history of the Japanese in Los Angeles, John Modell writes: "Members of the middle group may align themselves more with the top than with those below. On the whole, Los Angeles Japanese—particularly the immigrant generation—saw whites as their customers, and viewed Mexicans and Filipinos as employees. As long as these arrangements satisfied enough of their ambitions, they could comfortably adopt the assumptions of the dominant group about the worth of people, at least as operating values."[45]

Yamamoto's stories of prewar farm life show a separate and intact Japanese American world. She includes the disdain of Issei (first-generation Japanese American) farmers toward their Mexican and Filipino help: "'You look like a Filipino,' Mr. Hosoume said sternly, for it was another irrefutable fact among Japanese in general that Filipinos in general were a gaudy lot."[46] After the war, however, the Japanese could not afford to regard themselves as separate or superior. Anyone could be the next target. Esther Kuroiwa operates in a world where there are no irrefutable facts or comfortable assumptions.

Esther's concerns grow squarely out of wartime racial politics. After all, Japan and China were on opposite sides during World War II. The federal government persecuted Japanese Americans, not other Asians. In her encounters with both Chinese and Korean Americans, Esther goes back and forth between separation and solidarity. Communication on the Wilshire Bus remains indirect and incomplete, with lines drawn sketchily. For example, the reader cannot know why the Chinese woman fails to return friendly overtures. She may not share Esther's smile because she detects what Esther calls her own "moral shabbiness," or she may resent Japanese Americans because of Japan's occupation of China.

> Trying now to make up for her moral shabbiness, she turned towards the little woman and smiled at her across the chrysanthemums, shaking her head a little to get across her message (don't pay any attention to that stupid old drunk, he doesn't know what he's saying, let's take things like this in our stride). But the woman, in turn looking at her, presented a face so impassive yet cold, and eyes so expressionless yet hostile, that Esther's overture fell quite flat. (37)

Rotating scapegoats appear in other works of wartime Los Angeles literature, demonstrating the widespread nature of the issue. Bob Jones in *If He Hollers Let Him Go* (1945) identifies compassionately with the removal of the Japanese population. Drawn to the city by good wartime jobs, Jones does not assume that the removal of the Japanese furthers his opportunities. Quite the opposite: Jones assumes he could be the next target.

> Maybe it had started then, I'm not sure, or maybe it wasn't until I'd seen them send the Japanese away that I'd noticed it. Little Riki Oyana singing "God Bless America" and going to Santa Anita with his parents next day. It was taking a man up by the roots and locking him up without a chance. Without a trial. Without a charge. Without even giving him a chance to say one word. It was thinking about if they ever did that to me, Robert Jones, Mrs. Jones's dark son, that started me to getting scared. (3–4)

"Wilshire Bus" corroborates this view of extreme racial tension on the city's streets. However, racism appears more fundamental to the city's character in Himes than it does in Yamamoto. From Bob Jones's perspective, hatred pervades the wartime city so thoroughly that it becomes the substance people breathe all day: "that tight crazy feeling of race as thick in the street as gas fumes." Writing in the relative peace of the postwar era, Yamamoto asks more questions than she answers about the centrality of racism to the city. "Wilshire Bus" seems to inquire: Is racism a digression in the story, or is it the story itself?

Concepts of Community

Yamamoto plays with the idea of community, assembling representatives of various races on the bus and watching them interact. For instance, she includes not only the racism of the drunkard but also the opposing response from a bespectacled white man who shakes "his head mournfully in sympathy" and later makes a "clumsy speech": "'I want you to know,' he said, 'that we aren't all like that man. We don't all feel the way he does. We believe in an America that is a melting pot of all sorts of people. I'm originally Scotch and French myself'" (37). The bus is a full-fledged urban community, running the emotional spectrum from amiability to hatred. It contrasts dramatically with Cheever's emotionally and racially constricted suburbs. A network of glances, sounds, and gestures unites the passengers. Much of this communication happens without words, in exchanged looks or overdone mime, and often involves three parties rather than two. The bus offers a place to play out conflicts rather than bury them, and to draw moral inferences from witnessing those conflicts.

After her own community had been scattered, Yamamoto acquired a strong abstract interest in community. From 1953 to 1955 Yamamoto belonged to an experimental community, the Staten Island branch of the Catholic Worker. Since the 1930s, Catholic Workers have provided hospitality to the poor and practiced civil disobedience against war. Yamamoto's fiction parallels Catholic Worker concerns in several ways. Like Catholic Worker founders Dorothy Day and Peter Maurin, Yamamoto is interested in "creating a society where it is easier for people to be good." "Wilshire Bus" parallels the Worker belief that spiritual truth arises out of day-to-day contact with needy, often troublesome strangers. In fact, Yamamoto defines Esther's encounter as a spiritual struggle with sin.

However, while displaying a strong utopian bent, Yamamoto's writing gives a much more central voice to the troubling side of community. Yamamoto has declared, "I believe Dorothy Day is the most important person this country has ever produced." Nonetheless, in a 1987 interview Yamamoto also expressed disappointment in Dorothy Day's writing. "Well, it was a pretty good two years at the farm, even though I found out Dorothy Day never wrote about the darker aspects of living in community in her column, which had so enchanted me. . . . She said those aberrations were not the important thing, only incidentals."[47] This reminiscence raises a question integral to Yamamoto's own work: Are "the darker aspects of living in community" a central problem, or merely aberrations?

Exceptions to the Rule of Progress

Yamamoto's concern with digressions, aberrations, and exceptions to the rule takes place within the discourse of postwar optimism. Traumatic memory keeps bobbing insistently against the smooth surfaces of fifties culture. Two descriptions of postwar America, one by Nisei novelist John Okada and one by Miss America 1945, Bess Myerson, show a characteristic postwar line of thought. Like Yamamoto, both speakers stand outside the American mainstream because of their ethnic backgrounds. Nonetheless, both of them describe in longing detail the suburban, consumerist vision of the good life prevalent in the 1950s. Both believe in this version of the American dream even though they may be locked out of it. In this discourse, grief, injustice, and obstacles can only be discussed as exceptions to the general rule of progress.

Even John Okada's *No-No Boy* (1957), rejected by white and Japanese Americans alike for its bitter portrayal of the postwar Nisei experience, reflects a deep longing to participate in the American consensus. The protagonist, Ichiro, spends a great deal of the narrative blaming himself and his parents for his decision to refuse military service in World War II. When he witnesses discrimination against another, younger Nisei man, it suggests to him that racism and not his own refusal may explain his distance from the American Dream. Nonetheless, even a novel as ideologically brave as *No-No Boy* remains tentative in its conclusions. Ichiro wants to share in the consensus image of the postwar good life and is baffled by his own difference in perspective: "Where is that place with the clean, white cottages surrounding the new, red-brick church with the clean, white steeple, where the families all have two children, one boy and one girl, and a shining new car in the garage. . . . Surely it must be around here someplace, someplace in America. Or is it just that it's not for me? Maybe I dealt myself out, but what about that young lad on Burnside . . . ?"[48]

Similarly, Bess Myerson, the Jewish girl from the Bronx who became Miss America 1945, knew something about trying to live in two worlds at once. Nonetheless, she expresses very well the "exception-to-the-rule" problem: everyone was happy except those who had lost everything.

> Most people weren't thinking of the war's cost then. . . . They were just glad the war was over, that the boys were coming home, that red meat and nylon stockings and gas for the car would no longer be rationed. We heard that soon we would have antibiotics to cure every disease and splendid plastics and air conditioning and jet planes to travel by and television in the living room of every house. It was the happiest time I ever remember. . . . All the people were happy . . .

except for the people who had lost their sons in the war . . . except for the Jews, who had lost everything.[49]

In the post–World War II era, consensus had a negative, limiting quality. As Bess Myerson points out, it hushed all mention of "the war's cost" and imposed a false, materialistic sense of unity. On the other hand, the World War II period also brought a deeply felt, positive feeling of national unity unprecedented before or since. Everyone suffered from the restrictions of rationing and feared for someone at the front. According to historian Ronald Takaki, many people of color saw World War II as their first real chance to become full-fledged Americans. Everyone could participate and gain respect in the fight against fascism.

> Before the war, the many different racial and ethnic groups of American society had felt little in common, and they lacked a shared sense of national purpose. Then the war came, and Americans of all races found themselves fighting as one people against Nazism, bound by what Abraham Lincoln had described as the "mystic chords of memory" stretching from every battlefield and patriot grave to every "living heart and hearthstone" all over America. . . . W.E.B. Du Bois defined World War II as a "War for Racial Equality" and a struggle for "democracy not only for white folks but for yellow, brown, and black."[50]

Yamamoto works with both the positive and negative meanings of consensus. In "Wilshire Bus," the "mystic chords" of family bind not only Esther but also the elderly Chinese couple to the soldiers' home. The couple follow her off the bus, "most likely to visit a son who is an American veteran injured in the war," as King-Kok Cheung speculates.[51] In his appearance at the end of the story, Esther's husband, Buro, "looked around smugly at his roommates," as if sure of a consensus in attitude with his fellow veterans (38). However, Buro's smugness ironically echoes the smugness of the drunkard, who spews out racist insults, "his voice growing jovial, as though he were certain of the support of the bus in this at least" (35). This smugness reflects a "common memory" contradicting Esther's unspeakable "deep memory" of racial trauma.

Esther and Buro both do and do not participate in an American "common memory." As Takaki writes, the Nisei hoped "to be both Japanese and American." They sometimes exaggerated their own Americanness, emphasizing that they listened to swing music and read the *Saturday Evening Post* just like everybody else.[52] The Nisei children in Yamamoto's fiction are always busy reading the Sunday funnies and reciting the latest radio jingles. The desire to be hyper-American often shows up in the language of Nisei fiction. For example, Toshio Mori entitled his deeply contemplative prewar short story "The Woman Who Makes Swell Doughnuts." Yamamoto also relies a great deal on colloquial speech: "thrown for a loop," "it stuck in her craw," "that stupid old drunk." This highly American language refutes the "stupid old drunk"'s stereotypes of Asian speech ("Ha, pretty good, no tickee no shirtee!"). Esther speaks in the colloquial voice of a typical American housewife.

Esther and Buro both do and do not represent a typical postwar American couple. They are typical in their dislocation and detachment from extended family. Japanese Americans moved out of the ethnic ghetto in one generation, because that ghetto was evacuated. This movement has happened only gradually or in very small numbers to other communities of color. Furthermore, the Japanese resettled in isolated units, not in multigenerational families as before. This scattering completed a generational split that began in the internment camps.[53]

Often the Nisei departed for college or military service while their parents remained in camp. Many Nisei settled down permanently in brand-new areas of the country. Monica Sone concludes her 1953 autobiography *Nisei Daughter* with an upbeat description of her new life in the white Midwest, where she can achieve the goal of being Japanese and American at the same time: "I was returning to Wendell College with confidence and hope. I had discovered a deeper, stronger pulse in the American scene. I was going back into its main stream, still with my Oriental eyes, but with an entirely different outlook, for now I felt more like a whole person instead of a sadly split personality. The Japanese and the American parts of me were now blended into one."[54]

This process of dislocation and resettlement parallels in drastic and concentrated form the effects of modernity on Americans of all colors. For the first time after World War II, it became the norm for a veteran and his bride to uproot and relocate to a part of the country far from their parents. Taking advantage of new Federal Housing Authority loans, postwar prosperity, and the G.I. Bill for education, couples experienced an upward social mobility never before possible.[55] In "The Country Husband," Francis Weed struggles with prosperity and dislocation at the same time. Shady Hill takes him away from his past, literally and figuratively. Los Angeles was the city designed for such dislocated families, with its vast grid of roads leading to endlessly multiplying single-family suburban developments. Wilshire Boulevard played an integral role in the suburbanization process. The "Miracle Mile" of Wilshire was an early prototype for the shopping mall, with department stores not clustered downtown but laid out on a long strip accessible mainly by car.[56]

Nonetheless, a Nisei couple's relationship to the postwar landscape mirrors the experience of white Americans only in a bitterly ironic way. For instance, Cheever's characters get to choose their own dislocation, whereas Yamamoto's characters do not. Cheever makes it clear that Francis Weed has contained himself "within the patterns *he had chosen*" (emphasis added). By contrast, a Nisei couple had little choice in housing. It would have been nearly impossible for Esther and Buro to move into a suburb like Shady Hill, since housing covenants in many areas still prohibited nonwhite ownership. In *Asian Californians* Sucheng Chan writes: "Even in this era of good feeling, housing was still well-nigh impossible for Asians outside the ethnic ghettos."[57]

Many white Los Angeles residents supported segregated development because they wanted to live in a white capsule, not a multiracial community. A multiracial world reminded them too clearly of their own dislocation. White newcomers were moving to brand-new developments in a culturally diverse big city. Nonetheless, they wanted their homes to retain the homogeneity of New England or the Midwest. Racial segregation helped white newcomers straddle this paradox. The city would seem less alien if the neighbors looked like the folks back home. In Robert Fogelson's ironic phrasing, housing covenants excluded nonwhites so that the white "majority was able to maintain its untainted vision of an integrated community."[58] The literal or figurative walls around restricted developments hid not only a multiracial truth but also the fact that there was a truth to hide. Thus, the physical containment of segregation joined the emotional containment of post-traumatic memory.

After the war white American couples relocated by choice, seeking fresh opportunities, while Japanese Americans experienced a forced resettlement. Many came home to California to find that their houses and possessions had been lost, stolen, or auctioned away. "Japanese American . . . narratives on internment are about the *undoing* of home-founding," writes Sau-Ling Wong.[59] Wong differentiates between mobility in white mainstream American literature and in Asian American literature. Her analysis reveals the contrast between Yamamoto's collective vision and the despondent irony in film noir and Cheever's fiction.

> Though the conventional vocabulary of mobility has lost much of its exuberance in twentieth-century mainstream literature and is frequently subjected to ironic manipulation, this crisis of confidence is the direct result of a lengthy, actual national experiment: it is from *having had* the chance to realize the promises of mobility but coming up against its limitations that the nation has fallen into a somber mood, which in turn has given the modern literature of mobility a

defeatist cast. In Asian American literature, in contrast, there has from the beginning been a keen collective awareness of immobility as a historical given rather than a private frustration or temporary setback remediable by further ventures into virgin space.[60]

"Wilshire Bus" quietly lampoons the myth of mobility, both social and geographic. In contrast to the characters in *Double Indemnity* or *If He Hollers Let Him Go,* who race around Los Angeles in cars, Esther goes back and forth on the bus in static fashion while Buro lies flat on his back in the veterans' hospital. The notion of home, suburban or otherwise, seems noticeably absent from the story. While other literary depictions of Los Angeles often stress its lack of public space, in "Wilshire Bus" private space ceases to exist altogether. The sentence "the university and the soldiers' home there give the appearance of being huge country estates" only foregrounds their status not as homes but as institutions. An intimate conversation between husband and wife happens in public, as if the home had been emptied inside out. Whereas "The Country Husband" is claustrophobically domestic, "Wilshire Bus" is bereft of home.

The impersonal opening description of Wilshire Boulevard prevents readers from knowing where Esther lives. The bland voice of psychic numbing replaces personal information. She passes through town with no named starting point, and her pleasure in the stark elegance of Wilshire Boulevard is only "vicarious." In contrast to Esther's detachment, the drunkard's first subject for attack is "a figure in the local sporting world who had a nice fortune invested in several of the shining buildings the bus was just passing" (35).

The main character's detachment clearly results from postwar dislocation, since the city in "Wilshire Bus" contrasts sharply with Yamamoto's vision of prewar Los Angeles. In an autobiographical memoir of growing up in a strawberry-farming family in Redondo Beach in the 1920s, Yamamoto describes a different grid of the city in which Japanese American participation is anything but vicarious: "It must have been chilly January, too, when my father, with horse and plow, dug up the ground. After the earth was raked and leveled, he would pull after him the gigantic pegged ruler which marked off the ground for planting, first one way and then across, so that seen from the sky the fields would have been etched with a giant graph."[61]

Yamamoto's careful maps of Japanese California life seem responses to a fear that Wong has detected in other works of Asian American fiction: "a fear that, despite so much movement and activity, the group may end up leaving no mark whatsoever on a map of someone else's making."[62]

This was a reasonable fear in light of decades-old efforts to render the Japanese invisible. Long before World War II, the Japanese of Los Angeles crowded into Little Tokyo or onto odd-shaped farms—peripheral areas where land was left over from development reserved for whites only. The Yamamotos' family farm lay between the derricks in an oil field. Other Japanese farmed the land under utility poles. The Alien Land Laws of 1913 and 1920 prevented Japanese immigrants from owning California farmland or even from holding a lease on the same property for more than three years.[63]

Pushed out to the peripheries of white awareness, people of color almost inevitably reappeared during the tensions of World War II as the "spies / in your peripheral vision," as Mitsuye Yamada puts it.[64] One could see wartime racial tension in Los Angeles as a return of the city's repressed multiracial truth. In his book on the psychodynamics of racism in World War II Los Angeles, Mauricio Mazon offers the theory that Californians needed to create "an enemy in our midst" in order to participate in a distant and as yet intangible war. While Mazon defines scapegoating as a form of psychological displacement "in which aggression is transferred from one object to a more distant one," one might argue that the reverse took place in Los Angeles.[65] Californians brought the danger mentally closer to home. Instead of being marginal and invisible, suddenly the Japanese were right overhead.

What Esther Sees

In response to this fictive threat, the internment rendered Japanese Americans literally as well as culturally invisible. Sometimes the target of racism can internalize the desire to be invisible, because invisibility provides a cloak against attack. Jeanne Wakatsuki Houston has described this phenomenon in *Farewell to Manzanar* (1973): "In a way, nothing would have been nicer than for no one to see me. Although I couldn't have defined it at the time, I felt that if attention were drawn to me, people . . . wouldn't see me, they would see the slant-eyed face, the Oriental."[66]

However, something very different happens in "Wilshire Bus." Certainly the Chinese woman's public appearance on the bus opens her up for attack, allows her to be seen as an "Oriental" and nothing else. However, Yamamoto's narrative rejects the desire to become invisible. At one point Esther even wishes for a button that says "Look at me!" True, it is the concept of the Asian woman as an object-to-be-seen that propels the plot. Nonetheless, Yamamoto does not allow this concept to stay at the center. Rather than remaining a passive sight, the Asian woman in "Wilshire Bus" is by definition the one who actively sees—she witnesses, analyzes, chooses whether to look or not to look. The fifties housewife is fully capable of analysis and classification. At the drunk's first arrival, "Esther, somewhat amused and classifying him as a somatotonic, promptly forgot about him" (34–35). With Esther's ability to classify the city's inhabitants, Yamamoto reshapes and feminizes the voice of the hipster and the noir hero.

Yamamoto concerns herself primarily with Esther's judgments, not with other people's judgments of Esther. What matters about Esther's "Oriental eyes" is not how they look but how she sees through them. Even the Chinese woman draws fire not solely because of her Asian appearance but because she "thoroughly examines" the alcoholic. Women are subjects, not just objects, of the male gaze. Indeed, the complex pattern of sight lines, glances, smiles, and evaluations among bus passengers serves as a sign of civic health. As opposed to the complete removal of the Japanese, this contact happens very much face to face. Although Esther never breaks out of the witness role—no one ever speaks to her directly— at least she has the right to look. This is a crucial right to defend, since the excuse for internment was the fear that Japanese Americans might be spies. Furthermore, "Wilshire Bus" shows the crucial nature of the witness role in bringing forth the whole truth of trauma.

Esther may only have a "vicarious" relationship with Wilshire Boulevard, but she does participate in the difficult, fraught community of the Wilshire bus. "Wilshire Bus" contrasts community life with the narrow world of the postwar married couple. Esther's simultaneous participation in both worlds reveals the contrast between deep memory and common memory. The reader watches Esther's trauma disappear under the bland surface of fifties gender roles. At the same time, however, Yamamoto calls on the reader to hold that trauma in memory. Yamamoto creates an alliance of deep memory between Esther and the reader, even though Esther finds no such alliance in her own family life. When she finally arrives at the hospital, her husband cannot see her as the community member and fellow war veteran she actually is. He sees only the "gal waiting back home."

> When she reached Buro's room and caught sight of his welcoming face, she ran to his bed and broke into sobs that she could not control. Buro was amazed because it was hardly her first visit and she had never shown such weakness before, but solving the mystery handily, he patted her head, looked around smugly at his roommates, and asked tenderly, "What's the matter? You've been missing me a whole lot, huh?" And she, finally drying her eyes, sniffed and nod-

ded and bravely smiled and answered him with the question, yes, weren't women silly? (38)

The story's—and Buro's—false conclusion only highlights the after-image of the racism Esther has encountered. This ending maps the gulf between husband and wife, between common memory and deep memory. Within the context of suppressed truth, their domesticity seems "intense and misplaced," to use Cheever's words. Yamamoto often employs a dramatic irony in which the female main character has a secret relationship to a wider world. This structure appears not only in "Wilshire Bus" but in stories such as "Seventeen Syllables," "The Brown House," and "A Day in Little Tokyo." The Japanese American woman and the reader share an aspect of her life invisible to her family. This ethos reverses the usual structure of postwar fiction, in which a lone male has a relationship to a wider world invisible to his conventional family. In one sense, the double ending of "Wilshire Bus" signifies a gender gap between husband and wife. Such gaps in communication often appear in Yamamoto's writing—in "The Brown House," for instance, where a frustrated wife finally expresses herself to her husband: "You have no conception, Mr. Hattori!" she hissed. "You have absolutely no conception!"[67]

The final line in "Wilshire Bus"—"weren't women silly?"—evokes the stereotype of the pink lampshade only to destroy it. Esther says it because she knows Buro and his roommates will believe it. However, the reader knows it's not true. The reason behind Esther's sobs is anything but silly. The city would be a healthier place if everybody got upset about racism. By asking her question about women in general, not just herself, Esther makes the reader rethink prevailing views about women's triviality in general. She puts women's silliness in the form of a question so that we can question it.

Yamamoto may be playing with cultural difference as well as gender difference. If the Nisei hoped "to be both Japanese and American," the double plot marks the distance between Nisei and mainstream American realities. Esther's play-acting could be regarded as an effort to maintain dignity in front of outsiders. Racism becomes a secret matter to be discussed only in private or kept completely silent. Stan Yogi relates the buried plot in Yamamoto's work to feminist literary readings uncovering "the muted rebellion of women," but he also sees "forceful analogues in Japanese American culture," particularly the idea of *enryo*. "*Enryo* is difficult to define since it involves several different types of behavior including the denial of something proffered even though that item is wanted, the acceptance of a less desired object even if given a choice, and the hesitancy to ask questions or to make demands. . . . Linking the diverse behaviors associated with *enryo* is the idea that manifest actions do not always accurately reflect inner feelings."[68]

However, the story's conclusion suggests not only a specific Nisei reality but also efforts at an American consensus across racial lines. Buro speaks as a veteran, in an integrated ward full of other vets. Looking "around smugly at his roommates," Buro evokes a language of shared reality, as if any man would read the situation the same. His use of the proper cliché serves as an index of his Americanness: "What's the matter? You've been missing me a whole lot, huh?" While Esther eases down her rage with absurd humor, Buro eases down Esther's sobs with sentimentality. Their exchange sounds like dialogue from a World War II movie, complete with a wife smiling bravely through her tears. Like the war itself, their scene evokes a rhetoric of universally shared concerns.

Yamamoto uses understated irony to expose that consensus as false. Just as the glass-curtained buildings of Wilshire Boulevard seem to reflect everything there is to see, Buro thinks he can read Esther's face like a book. However, Esther's hidden experience belies the notion that facts are self-evident. Not everyone would read the story the same way. Here at the story's conclusion, the voices of author and protagonist separate: Yamamoto tells what Esther keeps silent. The question, "yes, weren't women silly?" reshapes the entire story as it is held in the reader's memory. To paraphrase Wong's comments on mobility, racism lingers in the reader's mind as a "historical given rather than a private frustration or temporary setback." Esther's perceptions are not silly. The exception to the rule of progress reshapes the rule itself.

While Cheever's ending moves the reader away from trauma and into postwar marriage satire, Yamamoto's concluding marriage satire loops the reader back into thoughts of trauma. Although "Wilshire Bus" describes the hatred that constrains community ideals, Yamamoto nonetheless draws the reader into an imagined community. Dori Laub has described the importance of the trauma survivor's finding a witness to his or her testimony: "Yet it is this very commitment to truth, in a dialogic context and with an authentic listener, which allows for a reconciliation with the broken promise, and which makes the resumption of life, in spite of the failed promise, at all possible."[69] In "Wilshire Bus" the postwar city continues the war's string of broken promises. Nonetheless, Yamamoto's dialogue with readers turns us into the authentic listeners the trauma survivor needs.

The Mellow Tones of Postwar Optimism

It is no accident that Yamamoto lays an example of continued racism at the feet of the shining new buildings on Wilshire Boulevard. She seems to question not only the costs of the war but also the costs of postwar progress. In her description of Wilshire Boulevard, Yamamoto writes: "For the most part, it is bordered on either side with examples of the recent stark architecture which favors a great deal of glass" (34). It is interesting to note that Yamamoto's vision of Wilshire Boulevard is a selective one. She does not mention Wilshire's outstanding landmarks from earlier eras: the Art Deco splendor of Bullocks Wilshire department store, for instance. She edits out the fancy furbelows and mythological figures from the 1920s and 1930s, focusing instead on the presence of brand-new glass-curtained office buildings.

Like the city itself, these buildings represent a world that both includes and excludes Esther. She can look through the windows to view bustling areas of commerce in which she plays no active role. On the other hand, the glass also reflects her own image back to herself. Similarly, racism in "Wilshire Bus" is both a self-reflective, individual problem and a structural problem involving complex groups.

Yamamoto uses two adjectives for Wilshire Boulevard's architecture, *recent* and *stark,* both of which indicate the shock of entry into the postwar era and its erasure of the past. *Recent* points to the story's sense of time: an eternal present, with scant traces of past and future. Esther and Buro exist in the separate bubbles of hospital and bus, transient worlds with only a temporary hold on their lives. Evoking the stillness of convalescence, the sense of time seems more cyclical than linear. As long as it remains separate from present experience, traumatic memory will replay on a continuous loop. Esther goes to the soldiers' home every Wednesday and Sunday; her sin of omission troubles her "whenever something reminded her of it." Even her Wednesday bus route back and forth along the Boulevard seems cyclical. Esther never reaches either end: we don't know where she gets on, and she exits before the bus reaches "the edge of the Pacific Ocean." Yamamoto seems at pains to avoid all edges and extremes. Buro's back trouble sounds routine, more like a job injury than a war wound. The avoidance of extremes seems deliberate on Yamamoto's part, since she would have been well aware of the war's ultimate costs. Her brother Johnny died at Livorno, Italy, in World War II.[70]

The architecture is also stark. In Yamamoto's version, Wilshire Boulevard stands not only for the present but also for the disappearance of the past. Glass can serve to wall up history rather than reflect it. From 1948 through the 1950s, an aggressive redevelopment campaign changed the face of Los Angeles in the name of high rises, "slum clearance," and adequate bomb shelters. As we shall see in Part II, such postwar redevelopment changed the face of cities all over America. In Los Angeles, redevelopment erased certain Los Angeles communities. In "'This Modern Marvel': Bunker Hill, Chavez Ravine, and the Politics of Modernism in Los Angeles," Don Parson shows how modernism did not benefit everyone. It probably would not benefit the Korean man downtown at Seventh and Broadway, standing on a small "concrete island" of safety in the midst of fast-moving traffic. Redevelopment pushed aside the downtown poor and elderly.

> Yet there were many people that would be adversely affected by the modernist vision of Los Angeles. The poor, the elderly, and minorities who lived downtown found themselves lost in the political shuffle and confronted by a progress that was clearly detrimental—even lethal—to their communities. . . . Opponents to the modernization strategies of Bunker Hill and Chavez Ravine were seen as obstructionists to the vision of modern Los Angeles.[71]

A photograph from 1959, reproduced in Parson's article, illustrates the distance between the modernist vision and the buried costs of the war. In order to build Dodger Stadium, the city of Los Angeles evicted the residents of Chavez Ravine, a low-income Mexican neighborhood that in 1943 had been a target of the Zoot Suit mob. Despite militant opposition from homeowners, the city reduced the district to rubble: another chapter in Los Angeles's history of bulldozing as a form of social policy.[72] The photograph shows a pile of rubble with a hand-painted, poorly lettered sign on top: "My Husband Died in World War Two to protect our Home."[73]

The sign indicates a betrayed faith that personal sacrifice in wartime would ensure personal freedom, security, and equality back home. Many Nisei veterans believed that their valor in combat would prove their loyalty and end prejudice against them once and for all. This viewpoint assumes a faith in the eventual rationality of white bigots, as if the problem were simply lack of evidence in a rational argument. One Nisei soldier wrote from the front, "My family and friends—they are the ones who will be able to back their arguments with facts. They are the ones who will be proud. In fact, it is better that we are sent to the front and that a few of us do not return, for the testimony will be stronger in favor of the folks back home."[74] This soldier's appeal to logic is so extreme, he transforms his living or dead body into a "fact" for use in his loved ones' reasoning. Psychic numbing indeed.

This faith in rationality conforms with ideas about racism prevalent in the late 1940s and early 1950s. Creating a model widely accepted in its day, Gunnar Myrdal's *An American Dilemma* (1944) stressed the irrational, personal aspects of bigotry rather than its economic and structural reasons for being. Better education and reasoned pleas for tolerance seemed the best solutions. Myrdal argued, "The American Negro problem is a problem in the heart of the American. It is there that the interracial tension has its focus. . . . Though our study includes economic, social and political race relations, at bottom our problem is the moral dilemma of the American. . . . Without any doubt there is also in the white man's concept of the Negro "race" an irrational element which cannot be expressed in terms of either biological or cultural differences. It is like the concept "unclean" in primitive religion."[75]

To an extent, "Wilshire Bus" confirms Myrdal's stress on individual morality and reason. Yamamoto certainly frames racism as a "moral dilemma" in the heart of Esther Kuroiwa. Yamamoto equates the irrationality of bigotry with the irrationality of drunkenness. The racist clearly appears as a clown and a fool. Furthermore, Esther Kuroiwa greatly values her own self-control and "saving detachment" (37). Esther occasionally sounds like a gently comic version of a Myrdalian social scientist, neatly classifying her fellow passengers as somatotonic or "probably Chinese." When she glimpses the elderly man with the "I AM KOREAN" button, she carefully reasons her way past her rage: "True, reason had returned to ask whether she might not, under the circumstances, have worn such a button herself" (36).

Yamamoto's housewife discourse plays into the discourse of reason but also undercuts it. Esther's soothing housewife voice makes life seem bearable and reasonable. Housewifely discourse joins *enryo* and "saving detachment" as an important coping mechanism. Yamamoto's style of writing cuts issues down to size in manners both soothing and sarcastic. The initial description of Wilshire Boulevard contains the soothing overstatement of women's magazines: "gazing out at the almost unmitigated elegance along the fabulous street." Esther uses a maternal inner monologue in responding to the Chinese woman—"(don't pay any attention to that stupid old drunk, he doesn't know what he's saying, let's take things like this in our stride)" (37). Esther mothers herself in a similar way after the upset of seeing the "I AM KOREAN" button. Yamamoto's housewifely style also contains a great deal of humor, a lilting absurdity that cuts through pretense. The final question "weren't women silly?" makes fun of a husband too dumb to see the truth. Yamamoto displays a keen awareness of the distance between domestic ideal and domestic reality. Her housewife discourse downplays psychological shock but never conceals or denies it. The story registers Esther's dilemma clearly, even when it appears in phrases like "thrown for a loop" and "stuck in her craw."

In Yamamoto as in Cheever, the smooth surface of postwar decor covers up continued problems. In Yamamoto, however, the housewife is not complicit with this cover-up, even when she speaks in soothing tones. Rather, she is the one who sees the problems when others can't. By the end of "Wilshire Bus" the issue of racism looms larger and larger, refusing to be cut down to size. In a deeper sense, Esther's experience of continued racism after the "War for Racial Equality" tests the limits of reason. Irrationality has its own truth and power: "there arose in her mind some words she had once read and let stick in her craw: People say, do not regard what he says, now he is in liquor. Perhaps it is the only time he ought to be regarded" (37). Hatred carries an element of the indeterminate and irreducible. In response to Esther's nonverbal plea for tolerance, the Chinese woman's face conveys a dislike impossible to alter or even interpret: "the woman, in turn looking at her, presented a face so impassive yet cold, and eyes so expressionless yet hostile, that Esther's overture fell quite flat" (37).

If racism can only be discussed in a reasonable tone of voice, many outrages go unspoken and unchallenged. Strong passion must sometimes counter the strength of bigotry. Esther's "sin of omission" that troubles her so greatly lies not in her loss of control but in her failure of compassion. In this sense, the moments of "saving detachment" in Yamamoto's writing seems less like sweet reason and more like clues to psychic numbing. King-Kok Cheung has questioned the brisk cheerfulness of the young Nisei main characters in another Yamamoto story, "The Legend of Miss Sasagawara" (1950). The legend of the title concerns a middle-aged dancer who apparently goes insane in the concentration camp. Cheung writes: "One begins to wonder whether the dancer—judged deviant for not behaving 'normally' under custody—is any more peculiar than Elsie and Kiku, who cherish their 'good old days' in camp."[76]

The distance between overt reason and buried emotion creates a tone problem that bifurcates the language of "Wilshire Bus." In 1976, Yamamoto described the repressed trauma of the internment in a way that helps explain her two-tiered narrative style: "The camp experience . . . is an episode in our collective life which wounded us more painfully than we realize. I didn't know myself what a lump it was in my subconscious until a few years ago when I watched one of the earlier television documentaries on the subject, narrated by the mellow voice of Walter Cronkite. To my surprise, I found the tears trickling down my cheeks and my voice squeaking out of control, as I tried to explain to my amazed husband and children why I was weeping."[77]

The oddly bland opening paragraph of "Wilshire Bus" sounds remarkably like "the mellow voice of Walter Cronkite." Yamamoto adopts the voice of consensus, the mellow tone of postwar optimism, and then pushes it until the voice sobs and "squeaks out of control." In this passage as in "Wilshire Bus," Yamamoto concludes with a question—"why I was weeping," "weren't women silly?"—which leads the reader back up into recent history to reevaluate its ultimate meaning.

In Wilshire Boulevard's straightforward modernist narrative, the concentration camp appears only as parenthesis or digression. "Wilshire Bus" has a very concrete, strangely still sense of location, with dislocation and relocation only implied. Monica Sone, another Nisei woman writer of the 1950s, renders the internment experience in conventional linear fashion: Before, During, and After. By contrast, Yamamoto presents an endless After picture in which During and Before appear only as "lumps in the subconscious," undetectable until a sudden jostling reminds the survivor. Yamamoto accurately describes how traumatic memory gets encapsulated and held apart from common memory. This encapsulation characterizes not only personal experience but the postwar city itself. The entire city of Los Angeles seems like a "concrete island," an island that holds itself separate and above the flow of unfortunate memory. The island is concrete in both senses: described with great particularity, and paved over in accordance with the demands of modernism. The story's fixed emphasis on the present contains an element of denial but also represents defiance. Yamamoto writes about the Nisei not only as if they were back and visible on the scene but as if they never left.

Cheung suggests that Yamamoto's understatement may be a form of internal censorship in a decade when the Nisei "wished to present a positive image to the larger society which had found reason to incarcerate them."[78] Whatever the cause, Yamamoto's layered technique approximates the actual experience of trying to forget. She realizes and acknowledges the patterns of unrealized and unacknowledged pain. Yamamoto's fifties fiction brings into words the liminal state between words and buried feeling. She records the disconcerting *almost* on a boulevard of "almost unmitigated elegance." She calls on the reader to witness the deep memory unspeakable in her own place and time.

The Segregated Imagination

3 American Novels before and after *Brown*

In postwar American cities, containment culture physically expressed itself through racial segregation. The concrete island turns into long and large concrete walls. With segregation, previous moments of encapsulation and enclave become systematic and permanent divisions. The G.I. Bill of 1944 extended Federal Housing Administration mortgage insurance to the 16 million World War II veterans. This remarkable program offered homeownership to Americans who never could have owned homes before the war. However, FHA policy guidelines also dictated a decisive split between poor nonwhite urban neighborhoods and new white suburbs. In one instance, a concrete wall literally went up between a black and a white neighborhood in Detroit in order to guarantee insurance.

> Occasionally, HA decisions were particularly bizarre and capricious. In the late 1930s, for example, as Detroit grew outward, white families began to settle near a black enclave adjacent to Eight Mile Road. By 1940 the blacks were surrounded, but neither they nor the whites could get HA insurance because of the proximity of an "inharmonious" racial group. So in 1941 an enterprising white developer built a concrete wall between white and black areas. The HA appraisers then took another look and approved mortgages on the white properties.[1]

How do these concrete walls take literary form? How can a city novel represent a physically divided city? Part II studies the segregated imagination in three otherwise very different novels: Gwendolyn Brooks's *Maud*

Martha (1953), John Okada's *No-No Boy* (1957), and Walker Percy's *The Moviegoer* (1961). The novels treated here share a segregated imagination, a veiled and indirect portrayal of concrete walls. Segregation translates into metaphoric neutral zones of brooding and contemplation. Each novel features a remarkably aware protagonist who reflects on his or her environs. These novels turn inward, just as segregation does. We live inside the main characters' heads just as they live inside segregated space. The novelist puts the character inside a small box, to show that the box is too small.

The inappropriately neutral voice discussed in the previous chapter becomes a neutral zone within the novels' sense of place. The neutral zone simultaneously represses and explores racial conflict. In some ways, these novels approach racial discord by making sure we all stay in our own communities and keep our hands to ourselves. This neutrality is a domestic version of the Korean War's Demilitarized Zone. In other ways, the neutral zone offers a nonviolent safe space for reaching across boundaries and contemplating future action. Just as the fifties short story both expresses and represses wartime trauma, these novels both critique and reflect segregation. This simultaneous opening-up and closing-down reflects the mingled optimism and constraint of fifties racial discourse. World War II gave rise to a new public embrace of racial justice. During the fight against Nazism, a multiracial philosophy went mainstream to a degree not seen again until the 1980s. The victory over fascism spurred a new commitment to racial justice, culminating in the *Brown v. Board of Education* desegregation order on May 17, 1954. As we have seen in regard to Japanese Americans, many nonwhite citizens saw wartime military service as a way to stake a claim for postwar racial equality. Agents of racial change took to city streets and transformed public space. As George Lipsitz writes in *Rainbow at Midnight: Labor and Culture in the 1940s*, "In the crucible of war mobilization and postwar reconversion, changing roles and expectations relating to ethnicity, race, age, and gender turned common and ordinary places like city buses, municipal parks, and housing projects into contested spaces where competing individuals and groups hammered out new ways of living."[2] In his study of resistance on segregated southern buses, Robin D. G. Kelley explains, "Wartime rhetoric unintentionally undermined the legitimacy of white supremacy. . . . African Americans, especially the youth, believed racism could no longer be justified on home soil, and those who were unwilling to tolerate it any longer exhibited greater militancy in public spaces such as busses, streetcars, or on city streets." Kelley retells "a popular African American joke during World War II":

A young soldier, in uniform, was seated in the front of a Birmingham bus, in the days when the white folks of that city had not yet gotten straightened out about civil rights. At the next stop a white man boarded the vehicle, paid his fare, and approached the ebony soldier. "I'll take that seat," he said imperiously. "You move to the back where you belong." The soldier didn't budge. "I have a question for you," he said, his voice low and even. "If we were on the battlefield, would you still want me to move to the back while *you* stayed up front?"[3]

Unfortunately, however, resegregation also transformed public space. Residential segregation increased dramatically after 1945. It was actively re-created and enhanced, not just continued, after the war.[4] Kenneth T. Jackson writes of the post-1945 period, "What was unusual in the new circumstances was not the presence of discrimination—Jews and Catholics as well as blacks had been excluded from certain neighborhoods for generations—but the thoroughness of the physical separation which it entailed."[5]

"The Segregated Imagination," Part II of this book, takes snapshots of the postwar city at three moments: just before the *Brown* decision, just after it, and at the start of its implementation. This process spans the 1950s. The argument assumes that segregation affects Americans of all races and neighborhoods, not just African Americans in inner cities. I analyze reactions to white oppression across several racial divides. Looking at separate enclaves together, we can imaginatively reintegrate the postwar city. The greatest difference between the novels is that Walker Percy writes from inside white privilege whereas John Okada and Gwendolyn Brooks write from outside it. Thus their problems with segregation are exactly opposite in many ways. For Brooks and Okada, segregation makes the world ugly, harsh, and violent; for Percy, segregation makes the world too pretty, too soft, and too banal. For Brooks and Okada, awareness leads to overwhelming rage or despair; for Percy, unawareness leads to spiritual malaise. Brooks's and Okada's characters desire access to the pretty, pleasant, and superficial side of the 1950s, while Percy's characters have so much postwar affluence they can afford to make fun of it.

There are great literary and regional differences between the novels as well. A prolific and distinguished poet, Gwendolyn Brooks wrote her only novel in lyrical fragments akin to modernist poetry. She also reacted to the African American "protest novel" tradition of Ann Petry, Richard Wright, and Chester Himes. Her housewife discourse resembles the fifties meditations of Hisaye Yamamoto and Anne Morrow Lindbergh's

Gift from the Sea (1955). Although *Maud Martha* "quietly went out of print," the novel inspired later black women novelists like Paule Marshall.[6] My analysis takes Brooks's fifties perspectives on their own terms, even though in 1967 she disavowed her earlier views as too assimilationist.[7]

No-No Boy, John Okada's lone published work, joins the "articulate silence" of the Nisei literature on internment and postwar return (Yamamoto, Monica Sone, Mitsuye Yamada, Jeanne Wakatsuki Houston). Other literary influences are postwar existentialism and American novels of generational conflict in immigrant families (Henry Roth, James T. Farrell, Anzia Yezierska). As the first Japanese American novel, *No-No Boy* is a foundational text of Asian American literature. However, the novel was out of print and ignored until excerpted in the groundbreaking *Aiiieeeee!: An Anthology of Asian American Writers* (1974).[8] *The Moviegoer* was Walker Percy's entree into the southern fictional tradition whose postwar company includes Flannery O'Connor, Eudora Welty, Carson McCullers, and Truman Capote. Perhaps influenced more by existentialism than by the likes of William Faulkner, he joined the famous postwar men's club of "great American novelists," including Saul Bellow, John Updike, Joseph Heller, and Norman Mailer. *The Moviegoer* was the first of five well-received novels.

Maud Martha, No-No Boy, and *The Moviegoer* portray three cities far apart in regional character, from the Midwest to the Pacific Northwest to the Deep South. *Maud Martha* takes place in the heart of Chicago, often the model American industrial city for sociologists. After 1945 it displayed the classic split of black inner city and white suburbs. Many American cities followed the urban renewal and suburbanization patterns of Chicago.[9] By contrast, neither Seattle or New Orleans appears as a classic American city in the public imagination. Perched on a forested peninsula over the Pacific Ocean, Seattle was hardly a city at all until the World War II defense industry boom. Asian Americans, not African Americans, were the principal minority population in a predominantly white city.[10] New Orleans's rich traditions seem typical of itself rather than emblematic of America. With its French Creole heritage, New Orleans seems a racially mixed and easygoing city—at the opposite pole from Chicago. On the surface the three novels have little in common except that they all take place in enclaves: the Southside of Chicago, Seattle's Japantown, and a middle-class suburb of New Orleans. Nonetheless, each novel reveals a similar postwar sense of place. These enclaves are not neighborhoods in the traditional sense. In his study of postwar fiction Carlo Rotella writes, "Neighborhood novels concern themselves with the local conjunction of people and place that makes up a lived urban order, attached to a particular piece of urban terrain."[11] However, these postwar works by Brooks, Okada, and Percy are not neighborhood novels. They take place in the neutral zone between the enclave and the trajectory, neither contained within the neighborhood nor bursting out of it. Although events happen on a particular piece of terrain, the narrative remains detached from it.

These novels display an abstract American sense of place that is not local in the prewar sense. After the war, many people imagined themselves living directly on American soil, with no regional mediation. This abstract, generalized sense of place has rebuilt the American landscape, providing the rationale for chain stores, freeways, and interchangeable housing developments. The characters in these books experiment with attachment to place and detachment from place against the background of urban renewal, suburban growth, and repressed wartime memory. All these factors militate against a local sense of place. Postwar America threatens these characters with the danger of becoming a nobody nowhere, as Walker Percy writes: "If a man travels lightly to a hundred strange cities and cares nothing for the risk he takes, he may find himself No one and Nowhere."[12]

Strong gender differences affect sense of place. John Okada and Walker Percy present the viewpoints of single, alienated men, while Gwendolyn Brooks presents a housewife and mother defiantly rooted in her community. Okada and Percy adopt the noir code of masculine detachment. They walk as strangers through their hometowns and accept their strangerhood as a philosophical position. Both have learned from existentialism. Unable to read themselves back onto the landscape, they use their estrangement to ask, "What have I done? What am I doing back here?" They see home as a trajectory rather than an address.

Both Okada and Percy fantasize about the suburbs as the solution to racial conflict, even though the suburbs were notoriously segregated. Bill Levitt, builder of the first subdivisions, declared in the early fifties: "As a company our position is simply this: We can solve a housing problem, or we can try to solve a racial problem but we cannot combine the two."[13] The young men in Okada and Percy see history as a kind of soiling incompatible with happiness. The clean, fresh start of suburbia offers everyone a desirable neutral ground. This need for neutrality bears the marks of post-traumatic stress disorder.

Both Okada and Percy explore the abstract American sense of place, while Brooks defies such abstraction. Her protagonist is a somebody somewhere, not a nobody nowhere. Brooks plants her characters down at one of the first intersections urban renewal destroyed in real life. Her almost exaggeratedly feminine metaphors of keeping house and hanging curtains show that her characters are here to stay, despite white opposition. She gently mocks the desire to rush off and be a hero somewhere else, when there's so much to do at home.

In a time of segregated roles for men and women, both these stances are gender-exaggerated. They need each other for completion. Without each other, Okada's and Percy's protagonists spend all their time roaming on buses, while Brooks's protagonist spends all her time in claustrophobic rooms. In fifties Chicago, the price of community is containment in an impossibly tight space. On the other hand, the price of masculine detachment is amnesia. To clear everyone out of the city and start fresh, one needs to segregate memory and yank up roots.

Since Gwendolyn Brooks has a stake in the continuity of black Chicago, her novel displays continuity of memory. She calls the reader to witness racial conflict hidden from most eyes. By contrast, Percy and Okada participate to differing degrees in a widespread social amnesia. Both repress the knowledge of white racism. Richard Dyer writes that whiteness itself ceased to be a racial category after World War II: "Before the middle of this century, few white people seem to have hesitated to call themselves white and to speak of belonging to the white race. This leaps out at one now, since in our time it is only extreme right and racist discourse that has an acknowledged and clear concept of a white race."[14] Both Percy and Okada fall silent about whiteness. Percy manages to write a novel of late fifties New Orleans without mentioning a massive civil rights conflict happening in the same years and locales. Okada represses the memory of internment, leaving his protagonist to wonder what has left Japantown so different and his soul so different.

Each novel, *Maud Martha* included, has a complex aesthetic of overlooking. Although Brooks reveals white oppression, her novel conveys the hidden violence of the era indirectly, through metaphors of containment. Each novelist builds formal structure around strategic silences. By nature, a segregated imagination cannot tell or show certain things. Instead, a blind spot, a cover-up, or a turning aside presents the telling detail. These novels reveal their historical moment in the shape of overlooking it.

4 | Hanging Curtains in Chicago

"The conflict over living space is an ever-present source of potential violence," St. Clair Drake and Horace R. Cayton wrote of Chicago in 1945.[1] Chicago's potential violence serves as subtext for Gwendolyn Brooks's seemingly peaceable novel *Maud Martha* (1953). Brooks's main characters live in the overcrowded conditions common in the postwar housing crisis and overwhelmingly common in black Chicago. During World War II, black southerners seeking defense industry work had poured into this city of arguably the most intense block-by-block segregation in the United States.[2] Approximately twenty-seven thousand new black residents arrived each year between 1940 and 1950.[3] Chicago was much more segregated in 1950 than it had been in 1940; by 1944 the segregation rate already stood at 90 percent.[4] The Black Belt of Chicago, only seven miles long and one and one-half miles wide, became massively overcrowded. Yet, when African Americans moved into white neighborhoods, they encountered "volatile and violent incidents all along the color line."[5] The siege lasted from 1944 through 1952, almost precisely the time period of *Maud Martha*'s writing.[6]

Maud Martha underplays the violent atmosphere of its making. Indeed, as Patricia and Vernon Lattin write, "The early Brooks has often been accused of failing to see racial oppression, and a superficial reader could use *Maud Martha* to support such a view of Brooks."[7] To the contrary, however, Chicago's postwar segregation influences the novel's spatial metaphors, philosophy, and narrative structure. *Maud Martha* reflects its historical moment even when it seems to sidestep that moment. Brooks uses housewife discourse to assert the dignity, anger, and staying power of black Chicagoans in the face of white violence. She rewrites the African American protest novel of the prewar and wartime eras. Her almost exaggeratedly feminine imagery provides a nonviolent resistance to racism very different from the masculine violence of Richard Wright's *Native Son* (1940) or Chester Himes's *If He Hollers Let Him Go* (1945).

Brooks maps the contours of emotional and physical containment. Her imagery repeatedly converts three dimensions into two. Black anger rushes forward and then suddenly dams itself up vertically, as if it has hit an invisible wall. This metaphoric wall repeats the structure of segregation yet also protects her characters from violence. Brooks portrays emotional containment as a problem but also as an important philosophical moment. Suppression of anger creates a nonviolent neutral zone where the quiet Maud Martha considers various responses to racism. However, the wall of dammed-up emotion holds fast only under tremendous pressure from both sides. As Maud Martha thinks in another context, "Leaning was a work."[8] Chester Himes and Richard Wright show how the dam of rage bursts forth in one grand violent outpouring. By contrast, Brooks explores small-scale, everyday resistance to racism. Building a wall also means drawing a personal boundary. In *Maud Martha,* each person draw that line in his or her own spot and way. The metaphoric walls have two seemingly contradictory purposes: to describe segregation and to help black Chicagoans resist uprooting.

The novel's containment of emotion reflects what Arnold Hirsch calls "an era of hidden violence."[9] Despite the conflicts of 1944–1952, the immediate postwar era is often regarded as a time of quiet between storms of the white Chicago race riots of 1919 and the black uprising of 1968. Brooks registers the era's quiet, invisible, but very real tension. Potential violence lurks within everyday transactions and the "grayness" of segregated life. Hirsch argues, "The ghetto existed before the riots, and it certainly persisted after they had ended. Yet that is precisely the point. The maintenance of the status quo was an act of great force. The preservation and expansion of Chicago's ghetto was due not to inertia but to the continuous application of old and new pressures."[10] The still, small world of *Maud Martha* results from the stasis of great pressure applied from both sides. Maud Martha lives in a kitchenette building, where larger apartments have been subdivided with beaverboard into small cubes. The sounds, smells, and emotions of too many neighbors push their way into her apartment:

She was becoming aware of an oddness in color and sound and smell of the kitchenette building. The color was gray, and the smell and sound had taken on a suggestion of the properties of color, and impressed one as gray, too. The sobbings, the frustrations, the small hates, the large and ugly hates, the little pushing-through love, the boredom, that came to her from behind those walls (some of them beaverboard) via speech and scream and sigh—all these were gray. And the smells of various types of sweat, and of bathing and bodily functions (the bathroom was always in use, someone was always in the bathroom) and of fresh or stale love-making, which rushed in thick fumes to your nostrils as you walked down the hall, or down the stairs—these were *gray.*

There was a whole lot of grayness here. (63–64)

During the novel's writing, black Chicago stood at an in-between moment. Like the overpopulated rooms of the kitchenette building, ghetto boundaries were bulging. However, these boundaries had not yet been recast in the concrete of urban renewal. Starting in 1952, the year Brooks finished *Maud Martha,* urban renewal began in Chicago on a massive scale. Two hallmarks were the groundbreaking of Lake Meadows, the first large housing project, and the demolition of the Mecca, a fabled, dilapidated apartment building Brooks would immortalize in *In the Mecca* (1968).[11] Indeed, *Maud Martha* takes place on a corner that became a major sticking point during urban renewal negotiations. The dispute reached its peak in 1950, while Brooks was writing the novel. Maud Martha lives on Thirty-fourth Street near Cottage Grove, a corner that no longer exists. The corner now forms part of the lawn around the Lake Meadows development. Since Lake Meadows had very low quotas for African American tenants, and since the plans called for the closing off of Cottage Grove Avenue, the corner and the project itself were hotly disputed during urban renewal hearings in 1950.[12] In setting her characters down on this very corner, Brooks asserts the black community's right to exist and persist.

Brooks wrote *Maud Martha* in an era of national as well as regional transition, when constraints still pressed hard on everyday black life but interacted with progress toward the Supreme Court's desegregation order in *Brown v. Board of Education* (1954). As Barbara Christian notes, African American writers in the late forties and early fifties lived between two worlds of "optimism and constraint."[13] World War II helped push the nation toward racial justice. However, the war also defined a politics of containment that characterized almost every aspect of postwar life—from Cold War foreign policy to the city of Chicago's housing policy.

This containment policy perpetuated the constraints of segregation. Fearful that the 1943 wartime race riots in Los Angeles, Detroit, and New York would also hit Chicago, city officials set up a Commission on Human Rights in 1943. The CHR embarked upon a policy of containment and silence. It hushed up the violence problem instead of solving it, building walls of police at racial borders and instituting a press blackout.[14] Chicago Urban League executive secretary Sidney Williams complained, "For too many years we Negro citizens have been plagued by the 'hush-hush' policy of our daily newspapers—a policy which was sponsored by a few of the 'responsible' human relations organizations."[15]

Thus Chicago officials missed their chance to reconceive the city as an integrated public space rather than a series of containment zones. CHR members congratulated themselves on their quarantine strategy. Thomas Wright, executive director of the CHR, explained, "These Commissions on Human Relations seek to quarantine the most explosive Human Relations elements and situations so that they will not and cannot infect the rest of the city."[16]

Brooks's novel reads like a parody of containment politics, with Maud Martha's adult life taking place in a series of impossibly tight rooms. Repeatedly Brooks invites the reader to witness a hidden conflict and then to watch the conflict papered over with some highly decorated surface. The narrative's sense of time also expresses a segregated sense of place. Maud Martha overcomes regret by "learning to love moments. To love moments for themselves" (78). Similarly, the novel teaches the reader to love moments for themselves. Each chapter of *Maud Martha* is a separate vignette, only loosely connected in time and theme to others. Each chapter is a segregated capsule, with no "public space" between scenes. Just as Maud Martha learns to love moments, readers learn to respect the inner lives of people within contained spaces.

Several critics have analyzed how Brooks uses domestic imagery "with a revisionist thrust."[17] Brooks also uses domesticity to revise the public discourse about segregation. Maud Martha confronts the wall of segregation and decorates it with floral prints. Despite its seeming frivolity, women's domesticity is a force powerful enough to push back at racial oppression. Maud Martha's youthful meditations on beauty mature into the ability to contemplate human weakness, face hard things directly, and make herself happy within constraints. Everywhere she goes, Maud Martha reconfigures public space, private space, and work space through the power of her imagination. She envisions nonviolent responses to the war overseas and to the racial battle zone at home. However, Maud

Martha's nonviolence is not the active organizing force of the civil rights movement to come. Rather, Maud Martha turns inward, expressing herself in daydream and metaphor, reflecting the latency of her era.

A characteristic image pattern emerges. Whenever something intrudes across her boundaries, a flat wall rises up to create a protective neutral zone. In "Anger So Flat," an article on Brooks's *Annie Allen* (1949), Claudia Tate makes a related point: "Annie represses all of her emotional responses and denies them expression by flattening them out until only her gratitude is perceptible." Tate argues that the poems of *Annie Allen* flatten anger out "into complex, static language. In this manner, Brooks supplies Annie and her readers with the missing anger."[18]

In *Maud Martha,* her next book, Brooks flattens the anger not into baroque language but into flatness itself. Maud Martha builds her adult racial politics out of her girlhood love for decorated surfaces: "It pleased her to dwell upon color and soft bready textures and light, on a complex beauty, on gemlike surfaces" (52). At seven, Maud Martha look at three-dimensional dandelions and sees two-dimensional fabric: "yellow jewels for everyday, studding the patched green dress of her backyard" (2). As she grows, her ways of handling racism seem to emerge from her "experiments in sewing" (144). Contrary to stereotype, a housewifely way of thinking provides an adequate and creative worldview for analyzing the most serious issues. Flat, decorated walls reshape the female public spaces, male public spaces, and kitchenettes of Maud Martha. The housewife hangs curtains in her south Chicago home to show that she and the African American community are here to stay.

Female Public Space

The novel has several scenes in feminine meeting grounds, including a hat shop, a beauty parlor, and a department store. To interpret these vignettes, one must understand the ambivalent contours of Chicago public space. As Cayton and Drake explained in 1945, "There are two areas in which the color line is tightly drawn—employment and housing." On the other hand, African Americans had freedom of movement in Chicago's public places. Maud Martha and her husband, Paul, feel scrutinized by whites in a downtown movie theater, but they are not refused admission or sent to a separate balcony, as they would have been in the Jim Crow South. "The retail stores of the city, too, as a general rule, treat Negroes like any other customers with money to spend. Negroes may handle the goods, try on hats, gloves, and shoes, and generally exercise the prerogatives of consumer choice."[19] This freedom within a climate of invisible violence creates the strange mystery of multiracial public space in Maud Martha. In the vignette "millinery," Maud Martha tries on hats and resists a hard sell from a white saleslady:

> "I've decided against the hat."
>   "What? Why, you told—But, you said—"
>   Maud Martha went out, tenderly closed the door.
>   "Black—oh, black—" said the hat woman to her hats—which, on the slender stands, shone pink and blue and white and lavender, showed off their tassels, their sleek satin ribbons, their flower coquettes. (156–157)

Their exchange reflects the hidden violence and transitional quality of the era. The saleslady can't refuse to serve Maud Martha, so her hatred and discomfort manifest themselves in fluttering overeagerness. The reader overhears the racial slur, but no direct confrontation happens. This need for neutrality grows from the high tension of the times: both Maud Martha and the hat store manager are walking on eggshells. Maud Martha closes the door "tenderly," as if the situation could blow up at any moment. But in this novel it never quite does. Brooks moves the target out of the way and redirects the abuse, absurdly, from "the hat woman to her hats."

This beautifully choreographed dance replicates the logic of containment. There is an invisible wall down the middle of the hat shop. At the moment of greatest conflict, each woman turns away. Brooks makes two parallel, symmetrical moves: Maud Martha closes the door, and the saleslady turns to the hats. Naming the hats with the wrong color emphasizes the displacement of the epithet. Brooks muffles the conflict in cloth for the participants, but not for the reader. The reader witnesses the muffled racism.

Why does the saleswoman calls pastel hats black? The extensive description of the hats seems an odd resolution to this charged moment, but it serves many purposes. It provides an object of contemplation, raises the issue of beauty standards, and asserts that important things happen in feminine space.

Like the false resolutions of Cheever's and Yamamoto's short stories, the hats provide a still object of contemplation so that the reader has time to assess what has just gone before. The racial conflict pops up and then sinks back down under a highly decorated surface. The description gives the reader time to watch the conflict submerge. The excessive decoration makes the cover-up more obvious.

Furthermore, the passage comments on 1950s standards of beauty. After the deprivations of the thirties and forties, fifties women's fashion emphasized hats, gloves, and the "New Look" of enormous skirts. With their veils, tassels, and pastels, the hats signal conventional femininity. Sleek, slender, coquettish show-offs, the hats are fashion models, and the writing style sounds like fashion magazine copy. They come in a set of pastels much closer to white skin tones that to the "Black—oh, black—" of the saleslady's epithet. We know from the rest of the novel that the dark-skinned Maud Martha endures a public opinion that does not see "black" as conventionally attractive. The hat woman and the hats themselves are trying to sell Maud Martha a look that doesn't suit her. She rightly rejects it, even as its exaggerated allure lingers in the reader's eye. Thus Brooks brings together the June Cleaver 1950s with an early assertion of "black is beautiful."

Yet the passage doesn't exactly make fun of the hats for their conventional beauty in an ugly moment. Maud Martha would like some conventional beauty in her world before she starts mocking it. Brooks contradicts a prevalent stereotype that fifties women were trivial. By contrast, Brooks asserts that real life happens in hat shops. Just because Maud Martha shops for a pretty hat doesn't mean she's superficial. The problem lies, rather, in the narrowness of her color choices: the oppressive pastels of the hat shop versus the grayness of the kitchenette building.

The vignette "the self-solace" also concerns a racial conflict between a white woman and a black woman in female retail space. The phrase "self-solace" seems to mean two things: pampering at the beauty parlor, and telling yourself it's OK not to speak out against racism. Again, racism blocks Maud Martha's access to the everyday treat of conventional beauty. Maud Martha is a young mother and keeps house in a kitchenette building; she tries to use the beauty parlor as a tiny vacation. Here Brooks reveals the psychology of refuge behind the hat passage and many other decorative passages in the novel.

> Maud Martha, waiting, was quiet. It was pleasant to let her mind go blank. And here in the beauty shop that was not a difficult thing to do. For the perfumes in the great jars, to be sold for twelve dollars and fifty cents an ounce and one dollar a dram, or seven dollars and fifty cents an ounce and one dollar a dram, the calendars, the bright signs extolling the virtues of Lily cologne (Made by the Management), the limp lengths of detached human hair, the pile of back-number Vogues and Bazaars, the earrings and clasps and beaded bags, white blouses—the "side line"—these things did not force themselves into the mind and make a disturbance there. One was and was not aware of them. Could sit here and think, or not think, of problems. Think, or not. One did not have to, if one wished not.

"If she burns me today—if she yanks at my hair—if she calls me
sweetheart or dahlin'—" (134–135)

Beauty and fashion create contemplative space. The wall of objects
helps Maud Martha resist mental intrusion. Like the devotional images
of religious meditation, the products help calm her mind into a quiet state
between thinking and not thinking. The reader witnesses the attempt to
escape from disturbance, but Brooks also foreshadows the disturbance.
Having her hair relaxed is far from relaxing. Underneath the need for quiet
is the subtext of pain: first, the everyday pain of hair straightening, and
later, the pain of another racist insult from another white saleswoman.

"People," confided Miss Ingram, "think this is a snap job. It ain't.
I work like a nigger to make a few pennies. A few lousy pennies."
Maud Martha's head shot up. She did not look at Miss Ingram.
She stared intently at Sonia Johnson. Sonia Johnson's sympathetic
smile remained. Her eyes turned, as if magnetized, toward Maud
Martha; but she forced her smile to stay on. Maud Martha went back
to *Vogue.* "For," she thought, "I must have been mistaken. I was afraid
I heard that woman say 'nigger.' Apparently not. Because of course
Mrs. Johnson wouldn't let her get away with it. In her own shop."
Maud Martha closed *Vogue.* She began to consider what she herself
might have said, had she been Sonia Johnson, and had the woman
really said "nigger." "I wouldn't curse. I wouldn't holler. I'll bet Mrs.
Johnson would do both those things. And I could understand her
wanting to, all right. I would be gentle in a cold way. I would give
her, not a return insult—directly, at any rate!—but information. I
would get it across that—" Maud Martha stretched. "But I wouldn't
insult her." Maud Martha began to take the hairpins out of her hair.
"I'm glad, though, that she didn't say it. She's pretty and pleasant.
If she had said it, I would feel all strained and tied up inside, and
I would feel that it was my duty to help Mrs. Johnson get it settled,
to help clear it up in some way. I'm too relaxed to fight today.
Sometimes fighting is interesting. Today, it would have been just plain
old ugly duty." (139–140)

Fighting is exhausting. It isn't always what you had in mind for the
day. But in postwar black Chicago, it's often what you get. Chicago's hidden violence happened sporadically, outside people's homes, all along
the color line. Racism in *Maud Martha* also happens in isolated bursts,
within homey places where one expected to feel safe. Like Yamamoto,
Brooks places emphasis not on the racist speaker but on the moral
response of the surprised listener. Brooks investigates the need for

"self-solace" in several ways. Maud Martha moves back and forth between wondering if she heard right, distracting herself with *Vogue,* and considering possible responses, from yelling to Myrdalesque "information." She retreats into prettiness: the prettiness of *Vogue,* the "pretty and pleasant" demeanor of Miss Ingram. Maud Martha and Sonia Johnson seem frozen in time, unable to react until they can take stock. The information Miss Ingram needs remains unsaid, replaced by the dash after "that—". The removal of hairpins substitutes for all the crucial things Miss Ingram doesn't understand. So much "information" needs to be conveyed, it becomes impossible to say anything at all. So much indignity intrudes, it is not necessary or wise for Maud Martha to repeat it to herself.

In this frozen zone, Maud Martha and Sonia Johnson become objects of contemplation for each other. Mrs. Johnson's "eyes turned, as if magnetized, toward Maud Martha." At the end of the vignette Maud Martha returns the stare, while Mrs. Johnson defends her own lack of response.

> "Sure, I could have got all hot and bothered, and told her to clear out of here, or cussed her daddy, or something like that. But what would be the point, when, like I say, that word 'nigger' can mean one of them just as fast as one of us, and in fact it don't mean us, and in fact we're just too sensitive and all? What would be the point? Why make enemies? Why go getting all hot and bothered all the time?"
>
> Maud Martha stared steadily into Sonia Johnson's irises. She said nothing. She kept on staring into Sonia Johnson's irises. (141–142)

Like the incident in the hat store, this vignette also concludes with still contemplation. As with Hisaye Yamamoto's short stories, the modesty and seeming irrelevance of the ending send the reader back to reevaluate what just happened. Next to Maud Martha's silence, Mrs. Johnson's speech seems blustering and inadequate. The use of "irises" instead of "eyes" evokes Maud Martha's childhood love of looking at flowers, one of the first things we learn about her: "She would have liked a lotus, or China asters or the Japanese Iris, or meadow lilies—yes, she would have liked meadow lilies, because the very word meadow made her breathe more deeply, and either fling her arms or want to fling her arms, depending on who was by, rapturously up to whatever was watching in the sky. But dandelions were what she chiefly saw" (1–2). Denied open, safe space, the adult Maud Martha uses childhood means of perception to create a refuge from the things that "force themselves into the mind and make a disturbance there." The contemplation she learned in childhood allows her not only to seek refuge but to stare directly at truth—even though she says nothing.

Although Maud Martha takes necessary retreats from conflict, she is no escapist. She considers what she'd do if she were Sonia Johnson, she walks out of the hat shop, and she taps into her anger, even if it remains invisible to the outside world. When a department store Santa Claus treats her daughter coldly, Maud Martha registers her own internal rage. As she does in the beauty shop, Maud Martha compares her own reaction to the imagined reactions of others—here, her sister Helen and her husband, Paul.

> Helen, she thought, would not have twitched, back there. Would not have yearned to jerk trimming scissors from purse and jab jab jab that evading eye. Would have gathered her fires, patted them, rolled them out, and blown on them. Because it really would not have made much difference to Helen. Paul would have twitched, twitched awfully, might have cursed, but after the first tough cough-up of rage would forget, or put off studious perusal indefinitely.
>
> She could neither resolve nor dismiss. There were these scraps of baffled hate in her, hate with no eyes, no smile and—this she especially regretted, called her hungriest lack—not much voice. (175–176)

Here Brooks says it directly: Maud Martha's lack of voice is a problem for her. Brooks comments directly on emotional containment and on the possibility of moving beyond containment. Again Maud Martha flattens her anger into a two-dimensional wall. Paul would have experienced a "tough cough-up" of rage: the flat motion of a chronic invalid, not the forward lunge of a stout defender. Similarly, twitching and jabbing are truncated motions. Both are vibrating movements made while standing in place—like the ripple of draperies.

Yet Brooks asks us to witness Maud Martha's strong reaction under her still surface. She describes a no-man's-land where forgetting is impossible but speaking out is painfully difficult. Nonetheless, the passage suggests subtly that Maud Martha could experiment with overt reactions just as she experiments with sewing. Although Maud Martha lacks the tool of a strong voice, she carries another tool: a pair of trimming scissors. "There were these scraps of baffled hate in her," Brooks writes. The phrase expresses Maud Martha's frustration and futility, but it also expresses the potential for assembling a future response. "Scraps of baffled hate" may seem impossibly repressed and fragmented. However, a housewife saves scraps in order to piece them together into something useful or beautiful. Maud Martha carries a tool for uniting scraps right in her purse. Trimming scissors complete the finishing touches of mending, embroidery or hand sewing. It is ludicrous to imagine jabbing Santa with such an ineffectual weapon. However, their presence hints that Maud Martha could assemble all those scraps of baffled hate into a full-scale emotional response, complete right down to the final trimmings. And in her response Maud Martha could remain just who she is, a quiet, meticulous craftswoman. She wouldn't have to turn into Bob Jones, Bigger Thomas, or anyone else.

Male Public Space

Maud Martha contemplates men in public space—her husband, Paul, and the men of the neighborhood—with her own antiheroic focus on small occurrences.

> The baby was getting darker all the time! She knew that he was tired of his wife, tired of his living quarters, tired of working at Sam's, tired of his two suits.
>
> He is ever so tired, she thought.
>
> He had no money, no car, no clothes, and he had not been put up for membership in the Foxy Cats Club.
>
> Something should happen. He was not on show. She knew that he believed he had been born to invade, to occur, to confront, to inspire the flapping of flags, to panic people. To wear, but carelessly, a crown. What could give him his chance, illuminate his gold?—be a happening?
>
> . . . She watched the little dreams of smoke as they spiraled about his hand, and she thought about happenings. She was afraid to suggest to him that, to most people, nothing at all "happens." That most people merely live from day to day until they die. (146–147; 149)

In this manifesto for everyday living, Brooks writes explicitly about the war but implicitly about the postwar era. When Brooks writes "born to invade, to occur, to confront, to inspire the flapping of flags, to panic people," the stated context is World War II, but the phrasing is just as well suited to the housing battle in postwar Chicago. Many white Chicagoans did interpret their new black neighbors as an invasion and a source of panic. Brooks directs attention away from the remote battle zone and back to the small struggles of everyday life. In stating that "most people merely live from day to day until they die," Maud Martha asserts the value of community. The desire for adventure can translate into escapism. She thinks her husband fantasizes about the war because he is tired of his commitment to a people and a place, to his wife, children, apartment, and job.

In Maud Martha's view, the masculine, dramatic brand of heroism reflects a desire to be more special than other people. Chester Himes defines heroism in these exceptional terms. His hero Bob Jones contrasts himself with his girlfriend's parents: "They hadn't stopped trying, I gave them that much; they'd keep trying, always would; but they had recognized their limit—a nigger limit. . . . But my mind kept rebelling against it" (151). Jones would rather destroy himself than live within Jim Crow. By contrast, Brooks's characters endure and survive. In *Maud Martha* there is no reason to call people names just because they live within limits. In the vignette "on Thirty-fourth Street," Brooks adopts Himes's disparaging voice just for a moment, labeling the men on the corner "tragic." She adopts the voice in order to contradict it.

> At the corner of Thirty-fourth and Cottage Grove, a middle-aged blind man on a three-legged stool picked at a scarred guitar. The five or six patched and middle-aged men around him sang in husky, low tones, which carried the higher tone—ungarnished, insistent, at once a question and an answer—of the instrument.
>
> Those men were going no further—and had gone nowhere. Tragedy.
>
> She considered that word. On the whole, she felt, life was more comedy than tragedy. Nearly everything that happened had its comic element, not too well buried, either. Sooner or later one could find something to laugh at in almost every situation. That was what, in the last analysis, could keep folks from going mad. The truth was, if you got a good Tragedy out of a lifetime, one good, ripping tragedy, thorough, unridiculous, bottom-scraping, not the issue of human stupidity, you were doing, she thought, very well, you were doing well. (164–165)

Ironically, these men *will* be "going further"—displaced from Thirty-fourth and Cottage Grove by the bulldozers of urban renewal. Hanging in there is heroism enough. Brooks asserts the beauty of street corner life just when the life of this very street corner was in dispute. The music and the people are worthwhile for their own sake, not as examples of social tragedy. Their constancy is notable in and of itself. The phrase "going no further—and had gone nowhere" runs these men up against the wall we have seen elsewhere in the novel: a limbo zone where forward motion stops. However, the lack of forward motion doesn't mean nothing happens. The battles in *Maud Martha* have more to do with everyday human stupidity than with the epic sweep of race war in Chester Himes or Richard Wright. You don't have to go far afield to be a hero. You can stay in the kitchenette building and fight your battles day by day.

Kitchenette Folks

The "kitchenette folks" portrayed in the novel were frequently labeled and disparaged in real life. In the mid-1940s Cayton and Drake interviewed a middle-class African American homeowner who feared the fate of the house next door: "I hear that the people who are buying the place are going to cut it up into kitchenettes. This will be terrible, but what can we do? I wish that we could petition and protest against their making kitchenettes here. Kitchenettes usually bring a lower class of people into the neighborhood. So many fine houses have been ruined by cutting them up into kitchenettes."[20] *Maud Martha* registers the impact of these stereotypes. In postwar Chicago's housing crisis, you are where you live. The vignette "we're the only colored people here" takes place at a downtown movie theater: "The white women looked at the Negro woman in her outfit with which no special fault could be found, but which made them think, somehow, of close rooms, and wee, close lives" (76). However, Brooks turns these stereotypes around. Maud Martha works just one day in the home of Mrs. Burns-Cooper, in the white suburb of Winnetka:

> "It's quite a kitchen, isn't it?" Maud Martha observed. "I mean, big."
>   Mrs. Burns-Cooper's brows raced up in amazement.
>   "Really? I hadn't thought so. I'll bet"—she twinkled indulgently— you're comparing it to your *own* little kitchen." And why do that, her light eyes laughed. Why talk of beautiful mountains and grains of alley sand in the same breath? (160)

Brooks turns the disparagement around by talking of the two households in the same breath. When the senior and junior Mrs. Burns-Coopers complain that Maud Martha peels potatoes incorrectly, a moment of tension ensues similar to those in the hat shop and the beauty parlor. Brooks details another moment of hidden violence on the racial borderline. The racism occurs, but both women turn away simultaneously from direct confrontation.

> The two of them, richly dressed, and each with that health in the face that bespeaks, or seems to bespeak, much milk drinking from earliest childhood, looked at Maud Martha. There was no remonstrance; no firing! They just looked. . . . As though she were a child, a ridiculous one, and one that ought to be given a little shaking, except that shaking was—not quite the thing, would not quite do. One held up one's finger (if one did anything), cocked one's head, was arch. As in the old song, one hinted, "Tut tut! now now! come come!" Metal rose, all built, in one's eye.

I'll never come back, Maud Martha assured herself, when she hung up her apron at eight in the evening. She knew Mrs. Burns-Cooper would be puzzled. The wages were very good. Indeed, what could be said in explanation? Perhaps that the hours were long. I couldn't explain *my* explanation, she thought.

One walked out from the almost perfect wall, spitting at the firing squad. What difference did it make whether the firing squad understood the manner of one's retaliation or why one had to retaliate?

Why, one was a human being. One wore clean nightgowns. One loved one's baby. One drank cocoa by the fire—or the gas range—come the evening, in the wintertime. (162–163)

Unlike the beauty parlor episode, Maud Martha expends no mental effort on making herself understood. She just walks away. Brooks shows the "almost perfect wall" of segregation from both sides. Emotional containment creates a protective zone where the white women's movements are exaggeratedly small and the black woman can spit at a firing squad and walk away unscathed. Brooks ends the vignette by evoking Maud Martha's decency, wisdom, and good motherhood. Again she hangs a protective wall of cloth, here a clean nightgown. Finally, Brooks defends the honor of kitchenette living. The gas stove of the kitchenette is a valid family hearth, like the fireplace of a more affluent home. The coziness of this image rehabilitates the dreadful reputation of the gas stove, one of the most notorious aspects of kitchenette buildings:

The threat of fire was another "constant and agonizing worry to thousands of Southside Negroes," especially those confined to the ubiquitous kitchenettes, according to the *Defender*. Divided by partitions that were often themselves flammable, the "rabbit warrens" that filled large old buildings made escape difficult, if not impossible, in time of emergency. Buildings packed with families and their furnishings, which often served as so much kindling, were also rendered vulnerable by the frequent lack of heat and cooking facilities. Gas stoves, routinely kept in closets, served as 24-hour-a-day kitchens and heaters in cold weather. One alderman consequently labeled the entire Black Belt a "gigantic fire trap." Between November 1946 and November 1947 at least 751 fires occurred between 26th and 59th Streets and Halsted and the lake.[21]

In the vignette "kitchenette folks," Brooks shows how Maud Martha's neighbors handle their daily constraints. Her sketches have strong links to the social realism of the prewar Chicago novelists (Dreiser, Farrell, Algren, Wright) and to the famed Chicago School of sociology (Park,

Burgess, Frazier, Drake and Cayton). However, her portrayal also makes important postwar innovations. In *Writing Chicago,* Carla Cappetti points out the similarities between prewar ethnography and prewar novels such as James T. Farrell's *Studs Lonigan* trilogy:

> Farrell's representation of the neighborhood as a self-enclosed "little world" is as much part of a literary tradition as it is part of a sociological one: a tradition that revolves around the theory that the city is a continent of little distinct worlds to be explored topographically and ethnographically. The empirically detailed character of Chicago in *Studs Lonigan* is inseparable from the theories and methods developed by the Chicago sociologists during the first decades of this century. The essence of the metropolis, [Robert] Park has explained, is to be composed of "cities within cities," to be a "mosaic of little worlds which touch but do not interpenetrate."[22]

On the one hand, Brooks also portrays the kitchenette building as an ethnographic "little world" unto itself, as she would do again with the Mecca building in *In the Mecca* (1968). In *Maud Martha,* many vignettes carry generic titles reminiscent of ethnography: "description of Maud Martha," "death of Grandmother," "a birth." Brooks's phrasing is sometimes indistinguishable from that of social scientists like Drake and Cayton in *Black Metropolis.* In "kitchenette folks," Brooks writes, "Little Clement's mother had grown listless after the desertion" (114). In "Lower Class: Sex and Family," Drake and Cayton write of Betty Lou and Slick: "The three months in the kitchenette started on a note of confidence and ended in tragedy" (573). Brooks presents heart-twisting fictional versions of the caseworker's psychosocial evaluation, showing how outside pressures impact families. A husband and father finally disappears because he can't stand to watch the effects of his shrinking wages on his family; Little Clement tends to himself because his single working mother is gone all day: "At eight Little Clement punched off the alarm, stretched, got up, washed, dressed, combed, brushed, ate his breakfast. It was quiet in the apartment. He hurried off to school" (115). Like the famous maps of Park, Burgess, and Frazier, Brooks takes a cross section of the building, only vertical instead of horizontal: like peeping into the rooms of a dollhouse.

However, this postwar "little world" also has aspects very different from the neighborhoods of prewar Chicago. This little world is not self-contained, because it has not achieved balance. It is subject to enormous pressure from inside and outside. Outside the building, the pressures of racism keep African Americans cinched within the Black Belt. Inside the building, it seems as if the walls will explode from overcrowding. Living within a maze of beaverboard, Maud Martha can hear every word of the same "very bad" popular song her next-door neighbor sings all day. Brooks describes Maud Martha's forced overhearing, and by extension her lack of privacy, as an overbearing pressure with nowhere to go.

> She didn't know whether she liked a little or a lot (a person could not always tell) the white woman married to a West Indian who lived in the third-floor kitchenette next Maud Martha's own. Through the day and night this woman, Eugena Banks, sang over and over again—varying the choruses, using what undoubtedly were her own improvisations, for they were very bad—the same popular song. Maud Martha had her own ideas about popular songs. "A popular song," thought she, "especially if it's one of the old, soft ones, is beautiful, sometimes, and seems to touch your mood exactly. But the touch is usually not full. You rise up with a popular song, but it isn't able to rise as high, once it has you started, as you are; by the time you've risen as high as it can take you you can't bear to stop, and you swell up and up and up till you're swelled to bursting. The popular music has long ago given up and left you." (112–113)

Maud Martha survives intolerable pressure by keeping her response flat, vertical, and bemused. The dam of emotion rises up high. Just as Maud Martha compares her own elevation level to the popular song's, each person in the building has his or her own emotional watermark for withstanding pressure. The day-to-day heroism of "kitchenette folks" lies in the effort to hold one's own line. The line is different for each person. Each vignette asks: What can you tolerate and still be happy? What are your tradeoffs? What are your benchmarks for happiness? How do you draw the line?

Binnie, "an insane youth of twenty," visits other apartments: "He opened a dresser drawer, took out a ruler. 'This is ni-ice—but I won't take it' (with a firm decision, noble virtue). 'I'll put it back' " (117, 119). Little Clement can stand his lonely routine because it transforms itself at the end of the day, when his mother appears and "his eyes lashed into brightness, his lips opened suddenly and became a smile, and his eyebrows climbed toward his hairline in relief and joy" (116). Oberto is "the happiest man, he argued, in his community," because he has a dainty, quiet, sexy wife—even if she is unfaithful and no housekeeper (110). Mrs. Teenie Thompson establishes a comparative benchmark for jiving between her herself and her white former employers: "They can't beat me jivin'. They'll have to jive much, to come anywhere *near* my mark in jivin' " (119).

Gwendolyn Brooks's portrayal of Maud Martha and other "kitchenette folks" shows how building a wall can also mean setting a limit and staking a claim. Maud Martha creates an imaginative safe zone for herself because she plans to stay in this neighborhood day after day, year after year, despite the opposition. She hangs metaphoric curtains because she's here to stay. A sign in her childhood schoolyard read: "PLEASE KEEP OFF THE GRASS—NEWLY SEEDED" (5). Similarly, Maud Martha draws limits so that she can put down roots. Postwar black Chicago expands and redefines itself against great opposition from white neighbors and redevelopers. However, Brooks's novel makes the community seem not so different from the prewar Black Belt of Maud Martha's childhood, where her father cherished an "almost desperate love for this old house" (37). The borders shift, and the housing deteriorates. Nonetheless, the roots keep growing, and the plants flower, pushing against constraining boundaries. "Maud Martha went east on Thirty-fourth Street, headed for Cottage Grove. It was August, and Thirty-fourth Street was all in bloom. The blooms, in their undershirts, sundresses and diapers, were hanging over porches and fence stiles and strollers, and were even bringing chairs out to the rims of the sidewalks" (164).

5 | Questioning Seattle

Nearly all the businesses and organizations in Nihon-machi met the needs of its Japanese residents. Grocery stores, drug stores, laundries, restaurants, banks, insurance agencies, hotels, churches, the Japanese language school, *ofuro* (public baths) were all located within walking distance of where most people lived. . . . Many Nisei described Nihon-machi as a little island, an ethnically homogeneous neighborhood. One explained, "the only white persons I ever saw were the mailman, the policeman and the delivery man since we owned a grocery store." Many Nisei called the prewar community a ghetto. . . . "To go outside of the Nikkei ghetto area, so-called ghetto area," Ichiro Matsuda said, "we knew that we could not rent or move into an apartment where it was predominantly white people. Even though there were 'For Rent' signs, as soon as you go in, they'd say, 'Oh it's been rented. Sorry I forgot to put the sign away.' It was common. That was a common experience."[1]

Like Chicago's Bronzeville, Seattle's Japantown (Nihon-machi) was a "little world" before the war. Yasuko Takezawa's interviews with Seattle Nisei show how segregation is not just a black-white issue. Like the residents interviewed above, the Nisei novelist John Okada also saw Japantown as a ghetto. His only published novel, *No-No Boy* (1957), is set in Seattle's Japantown, one of the oldest and largest Asian communities in the United States. The wartime evacuation of Japanese Americans prompts the novel's postwar questioning of community itself. Like Gwendolyn Brooks, John Okada details a liminal zone not contained within the prewar ghetto yet not bursting out of it. Also like Brooks, Okada's novel displays a mixture of optimism and constraint. The main character, Ichiro Yamada, dreams of future integration into the American mainstream. Meanwhile, the traumas of recent history constrain his present horizon. Although critics have not focused on the novel's landscapes, Ichiro's struggle has everything to do with sense of place: "And, as his heart mercifully stacked the blocks of hope into the pattern of an America which would someday hold an unquestioned place for him, his mind said no, it is not to be, and the castle tumbled and was swallowed up by the darkness of his soul, for time might cloud the memories of others but the trouble was inside of him and time would not soften that."[2]

Ichiro sees place as an inward moral problem, not an outward constraint. The novel's worldview grows from the trauma of internment; indeed, the novel is a journey through the postinternment worldview. Okada contrasts ideal and real senses of place. Trauma leaves Ichiro with an abstract longing for America and a concrete dislike of Seattle and Japantown. Despite their similarities, Brooks and Okada come to opposite conclusions about community. *Maud Martha* asserts the power of rooting in one's own neighborhood despite opposition, whereas *No-No Boy* expresses the desire to move out and move on. Okada embraces the postwar creeds of mobility and masculine detachment. His protagonist, Ichiro, wants to resolve alienation through modernist progress: a clean, fresh start in suburbia, the anonymity of the lone male, and a perfect alignment with an abstract, generically "American" sense of place. The internment has soiled Okada's vision of Seattle. Trauma causes a subtle amnesia: Ichiro cannot read his own history back onto the landscape. In order to move on, he represses his intimate knowledge of white racism. This repressed knowledge stains the landscape itself.

While Brooks and Percy imagine segregation from inside their own communities, John Okada has no such option. After the war, his protagonist has no intact community to be inside. The liminal zone is the only space available. This liminal zone offers the novel's truest sense of place. Caught between the ghetto and the suburb, Ichiro questions what it means to be American. He dreams of assimilation, but in the present moment he questions and searches. Like *Maud Martha* and *The Moviegoer, No-No Boy* opens up a contemplative space that leaves room for future action and future questions. However, the liminal zone of *No-No Boy* is not the "neutral zone" of Brooks and Percy. This zone doesn't feel neutral—it feels anguished. The novel's sense of place borders on despair.

Social Amnesia

No-No Boy speaks and remains silent about the internment in ways true to Nisei experience. "In the postwar years, the Nisei,
with a few exceptions, hardly discussed internment. Tetsuden Kashima
calls this phenomenon 'social amnesia,' defining it as 'a group phenomenon in which attempts are made to suppress feelings and memories of particular moments or extended time periods.' "[3] *No-No Boy*
registers the aftershocks of trauma while also disavowing it. In the
novel's first few pages, postwar trauma hits the reader in the face. By page
4, a Nisei war veteran has already spit on Ichiro, the protagonist. Ichiro's
alienation and self-hatred appear immediately.

> Two weeks after his twenty-fifth birthday, Ichiro got off a bus at
> Second and Main in Seattle. He had been gone four years, two in
> camp and two in prison.
>
> Walking down the street that autumn morning with a small,
> black suitcase, he felt like an intruder in a world to which he had
> no claim. It was just enough that he should feel that way, for, of his
> own free will, he had stood before the judge and said that he would
> not go in the army. At the time there was no other choice for him.
> That was when he was twenty-three, a man of twenty-three. Now,
> two years older, he was even more of a man.
>
> Christ, he thought to himself, just a goddamn kid is all I was.
> Didn't know enough to wipe my own nose. What the hell have I done?
> What am I doing back here? Best thing I can do would be to kill some
> son of a bitch and head back to prison. (1)

The narrative reproduces the main character's shock and amnesia.
Ichiro walks down the streets of his hometown as if he were a stranger.
Okada dumps Ichiro back into Seattle, denying him connection to the local
past. The passage evokes the evacuation of Seattle's Japanese Americans
and then disavows the connection. The Nikkei left Seattle on buses, bound
for a temporary assembly camp in Puyallup.[4] Ichiro finally returns on a
bus. Yet the novel hushes up the connection between the outbound and
return trips. Instead, Ichiro views his exile as the result of individual
choice. He may have left Seattle in a community group, but he comes back
alone. In response, he comes to celebrate his own strangerhood. He
takes on the noir mantle of the lone male walking through the city.
Indeed, the last line of the passage, "Best thing I can do would be to kill
some son of a bitch and head back to prison," sounds like noir tough-guy
talk. In the course of the novel, buses will come to represent a modernist
faith in moving on.

The text continues to have large gaps and silences. Okada represents the "four years, two in camp and two in prison" fleetingly and indirectly. Only one story about camp swims to the surface, when Ichiro faces a similarly difficult situation, and Ichiro occasionally mentions fellow prisoners. For the most part, "the trouble was inside of him." Okada renders Ichiro's trauma as private anguish and absence: his absence from Seattle and his absence from his own decision making. The novel also evokes and then disavows the charged words "no-no boy." Despite the novel's title, Okada never explains in the text what a no-no boy is. The U.S. government asked two questions of all draft-age men in the camps. Women and older men received different versions of the two questions.[5] Answering these questions tore friends and families apart. The questionnaire expected Japanese Americans to pledge allegiance to a nation that had just withdrawn its allegiance from them. Young men like Ichiro who answered "no" to both questions went to prison. In a context of forced answers to impossible questions, no wonder *No-No Boy* asks more questions than it answers.

> 27. Are you willing to serve in the Armed Forces of the United States on combat duty, wherever ordered?
> 28. Will you swear unqualified allegiance to the United States of America and faithfully defend the United States from any or all attack by foreign or domestic forces, and forswear any form of allegiance or obedience to the Japanese emperor, or any other foreign government, power, or organization?[6]

The novel takes place in a typically postwar zone of indecision. As sociologist Jere Takahashi writes, "For most Nisei of college age, the immediate postwar period was a difficult time. Many were unsure of their future course of action and experienced a period that University of California professor Paul Takagi, a Nisei college student then, referred to as 'drift.' "[7] Although the Nisei had their own specific and powerful obstacles, postwar young people of many races also felt this "drift." *No-No Boy* concerns not shocks but aftershocks. The trauma has already come and gone, while the main character remains in limbo. The story takes place after an important birthday, which ought to signal the transition from one phase of young manhood to another. As in many postwar novels, however, the transition has stalled. In *The Moviegoer*, Binx must face down his aunt's expectations in the week before his thirtieth birthday, while Ichiro returns home to his parents just after his twenty-fifth. At twenty-five and thirty, these young men face pressure to stop asking the basic questions and settle down at last. Ichiro, however, like others of his generation, is still asking, "What the hell have I done? What am I doing back here?"

Trauma prevents Ichiro's understanding of his place "back here." In the novel's vision, the war has decayed the city of Seattle in four short years. This decay comes from the repressed shame of internment. Many Nisei felt shame after the war, even though they had done nothing wrong. "Barbara Yamaguchi, like many other Nisei, equated the camp experience with rape: 'When a woman is raped, she does not want to talk, because she feels ashamed. In the same way, even though we did nothing wrong, there was a feeling of shame. We just assumed let's not talk about it.' "[8] *No-No Boy* displaces the shame onto the landscape. Ichiro's way of walking through the city as an alienated stranger allows him to hold himself aloof from the shame.

In his worst moments, however, Ichiro sees no future but slow decay. He regards himself as "one already dead but still alive and contemplating fifty or sixty years more of dead aliveness" (73). His friend Kenji's war wound is a physical version of the post-traumatic "sense of a foreshortened future."[9] The wound shortens his leg and his life. Kenji explains, "There's something rotten in my leg that's eating it away" (62). As the doctors carve away at the rottenness inch by inch, Kenji approaches his death.

Rottenness represents both postwar bodies and the postwar city. Okada calls Seattle "a dirty city" and, oddly, suggests that all the dirt has accumulated during the war's four years.

> Like the dirty clock tower of the depot, the filth of Jackson Street had increased. Ichiro paused momentarily at an alley and peered down the passage formed by the walls of two sagging buildings. There had been a door there at one time, a back door to a movie house which only charged a nickel. A nickel was a lot of money when he had been seven or nine or eleven. He wanted to go into the alley to see if the door was still there.
>
> He walked toward the railroad depot where the tower with the clocks on all four sides was. It was a dirty looking tower of ancient brick. It was a dirty city. Dirtier, certainly, than it had a right to be after only four years. . . .
>
> Being on Jackson Street with its familiar store fronts and taverns and restaurants, which were somehow different because the war had left its mark on them, was like trying to find one's way out of a dream that seemed real most of the time but wasn't really real because it was still only a dream. The war had wrought violent changes upon the people, and the people, in turn, working hard and living hard

and earning a lot of money and spending it on whatever was available, had distorted the profile of Jackson Street. The street had about it the air of a carnival without quite succeeding at becoming one. A shooting gallery stood where once had been a clothing store; fish and chips had replaced a jewelry shop; and a bunch of Negroes were horsing around raucously in front of a pool parlor. Everything looked older and dirtier and shabbier. (1, 4–5)

Trauma marks this seemingly objective description. Ichiro's dislocation makes familiar sights seem like a strange dream. He forgets what happened to make Japantown so different. He has no memory of the evacuation's marks on the community: the posting of evacuation dates and assembly areas, the disposal of homes and property, the removal itself. Because the actual memory is repressed, the trauma appears as soiling. The war has left its mark of shame, not only dirtying the city but "distorting its profile." In response to white racism, Japantown has lost the distinctive features of its face. Ichiro blames the war for the city's dirt, but his explanation isn't literally true. Seattle is and was a clean city on the whole. Jackson Street, center of Japantown's business district, declined before the war, owing to the depression of the 1930s and the Immigrant Act of 1924, which ceased all Japanese immigration. In 1939 sociologist S. Frank Miyamoto, a Seattle Nisei himself, described the pre-war Japantown:

> Almost directly to the southeast of Seattle's central business district in the gargantuan shadows of the Smith Tower are several streets of small shops occupied by busy little dark-skinned men. Here, near Fifth and Sixth avenues on Main and Jackson streets, is the business center of the Japanese district, consisting of a congeries of shops including everything from barber shops and restaurants to book stores and law offices. The business center is not today what it was in the heyday of the early nineteen-twenties, when Main Street really teemed with the life of incoming immigrants and prosperous farmers visiting town. Rather one is aware now that the depression has not dealt kindly with these shop-keepers; that the failure of the community's one bank, and the large movements of their population back to Japan, and even more to California, have drained a good part of the life-blood out of the community.[10]

Ichiro transfers this decay to the wartime era. He is, of course, right that "the war had wrought violent changes on the people." No wonder Ichiro sees the mark of war on every storefront; Japanese probably owned many of the enterprises now gone. In their place have come carnival-style businesses to attract the prosperity of defense workers. Before the war, during the depression, almost everyone had to make do with very little. When the war came along, suddenly everyone had a job and many had jobs with high wages. As a result, "everybody went a little wild," as my mother's cousin recently recalled.[11] This wildness accounts for the decadence Ichiro senses. As in Los Angeles, the war turned Seattle into a major city. Boeing Aircraft and other defense industries came of age and brought Seattle with them. Historian Quintard Taylor describes how this growth prompted a massive influx of workers.

> The Second World War generated profound changes in economic and social conditions in the Pacific Northwest, prompting historian Carlos Schwantes to describe the years 1941–1945 as the beginning of the modern era for the region. The Puget Sound area soon became a major center for ship and aircraft construction, which in turn stimulated other sectors of the economy. . . . By 1944, at the peak of wartime production, [the Boeing Airplane Company] employed nearly 50,000 workers in the Seattle area and amassed total sales of more than $600 million annually, sharply contrasting with the $70 million value of all Seattle manufacturing in 1939.[12]

The war made Seattle but destroyed Japantown. From a Nisei perspective, Okada sees "violent changes" rather than new prosperity. Ichiro internalizes the decay of the Asian ghetto, equating it with moral decay in Asian people. "The filth of Jackson Street" seems an odd way to begin a description of one's own home neighborhood. Ichiro sees filth as an intrinsic quality of Japantown, not a by-product of ghettoization. The young Nisei in *No-No Boy* see ethnic community as self-segregation. They overlook the external forces that perpetuate the ghetto. Kenji equates the reemerging Japanese quarter with the internment camps. For Kenji, to live among one's own kind isn't just risky—it's immoral. Note that he uses the word "shame": "It's a shame, a dirty rotten shame. Pretty soon it'll be just like it was before the war. A bunch of Japs with a fence around them, not the kind you can see, but it'll hurt them just as much. . . . They screamed because the government said they were Japs and, when they finally got out, they couldn't wait to rush together and prove that they were" (164).

Repressing the memory of white racism, both Kenji and Ichiro blame the Nikkei themselves for the barbed wire around them. Sense of place becomes personal moral choice without external constraints, even though the external constraints were severe. Japanese Americans met with fierce job and housing discrimination upon their return to Seattle. "Right after the war, the hostility toward Japanese Americans and discrimination against them were even more intense than before the war. Furthermore, the Nisei were more exposed to racism, having lost Japantown, their protective enclave."[13]

Many Nisei learned to distrust community while in camp. As Mo Nishioka recalled, "When we left camp, basically what they told us was not to come together, not to congregate, not to stick out. In that way, the way they told us was there was something bad about being Japanese."[14] *No-No Boy* presents a general distrust of ethnic-based community. Ichiro criticizes both Japantown and Chinatown, neighbors in Seattle's pan-ethnic International District. Ichiro and Kenji, along with most other Asian men in the novel, frequent a Chinatown bottle club called the Club Oriental. Although few places welcome the young men, the club's name represents the clannishness the young men associate with the old ethnic neighborhoods. Tellingly, the Club Oriental stands in the midst of urban dirt. In a rush of self-hatred, Okada sees the people as ugly because the street and buildings are ugly. The ghetto is a mentality, not just an address. Brooks's characters have dignity despite their address, but Okada's characters do not.

> They walked down the ugly street with the ugly buildings among the ugly people which was a part of America and, at the same time, would never be wholly America. The night was cool and dark.
>
> Halfway down an alley, among the forlorn stairways and innumerable trash cans, was the entrance to the Club Oriental. (71)

Lining Up with America

The Club Oriental sits on a street that is "part of America and, at the same time, would never be wholly America." Ichiro attempts to line up his personal sense of place with an abstract American sense of place. This concept of planting oneself directly in America, without regional affiliation, may be the war's most lasting legacy to the rest of the twentieth century. Superhighways, national chain stores, and interchangeable suburbs grow directly from this principle. It may seem odd to regard different American locales as "wholly American" or not "wholly American." However, the question "Does my neighborhood represent America?" was central to postwar culture. Americans began to imagine their houses not just situated in a town or state but situated directly in America. The distinction between American and un-American neighborhoods bears an obvious link to Joseph McCarthy's persecutions of supposed "un-American activities." However, the desire to imagine one's house in America comes most powerfully from World War II. Soldiers fought for an abstraction called American democracy. They made the abstraction worth defending by imagining a particular girl or house and then associating that girl or house with the nation.

An immensely popular wartime song articulated the link between house and nation. Frank Sinatra recorded "The House I Live In (That's America to Me)," on August 22, 1945, the week after Japan's surrender to the Allies. Originally composed in 1942 as a paean to American diversity and freedom of speech, the 1945 Sinatra recording seems to explain why America won the war. Lewis Allan's lyrics to "The House I Live In" establish a profoundly moving link between America in general and one plot of earth in particular. The song defines America as an integrated neighborhood. Its creed is explicitly multiracial: "The house I live in / My neighbors white or black / The people who just came here / Or generations back."[15]

This celebration of being at home in America was released just after the United States dropped atomic bombs on the Japanese cities of Hiroshima and Nagasaki. No wonder Ichiro has conceptual trouble feeling at home back in Japantown. The American creed seems to celebrate multiracial inclusion, but are his people the exception to the rule? Ichiro engages in a painful and deadly serious effort to line up neighborhood and nation again. Like children who write their addresses starting with the street number and ending with "the Solar System," Ichiro creates a mental chain from this "small span of concrete" to "the nation that is America." But the chain has been broken, and "the meaning got lost." The wartime linkage of home and patriotism didn't work for Japantown. When he answered "no-no," his local sense of place failed to provide him with the reasons to fight for America: "I remember a lot of people and a lot of things now as I walk confidently through the night over a small span of concrete which is part of the sidewalks which are part of the city which is part of the state and the country and the nation that is America. It is for this that I meant to fight, only the meaning got lost when I needed it most badly" (34).

Social amnesia prevents Ichiro from remembering that he didn't live in Japantown when he had to make his decision about military service. Instead, he was living in an internment camp. Ichiro couldn't fight for his home because his home didn't exist. Ichiro's friend Kenji questions him about absence, return, and memory. Kenji's questions strike at the heart of the novel's dilemma. The returning Nisei has no conceptual framework for understanding the changes in his life since he left Seattle. "You've probably been walking around the campus, trying to catch the same smells and sounds and the other things which you've been thinking about all the time the government kept you away from Seattle. Is it still the same? Can you start back to school tomorrow and pick up just where you left off?" (58). Ichiro may "walk confidently through the night," but he walks as a stranger.

Ichiro measures his current life against the greatest prewar symbol of his Americanness: his status as a college student at the University of Washington. The right to matriculate was culturally central for prewar Nisei and formed a large exception to the rule of segregation. "Unlike blacks and Chicanos, Japanese Americans had not been excluded from higher education. Although Nisei faced the problem of segregation in their primary schooling . . . [they] did have access, however, to higher education on the Pacific Coast at major schools such as the University of California, University of Washington, and Stanford University."[16] Like Bob Jones's Buick Roadmaster, Ichiro Yamada's slide rule is a shining symbol of his enfranchisement. In his prewar student life, Ichiro had a vivid, lyrical, and firm sense of place. His happiness depended very much on the everyday symbols of belonging.

> Not until the bus had traversed the business district and pointed itself toward the northeast did he realize that he was on the same bus which he used to take every morning as a university student. There had been such a time and he vividly brought to mind, with a hunger that he would never lose, the weighty volumes which he had carried against his side so that the cloth of his pants became thin and frayed, and the sandwiches in a brown grocery bag and the slide rule with the leather case which hung from his belt like the sword of learning which it was, for he was going to become an engineer and it had not mattered that Japan would soon be at war with America. To be a student in America was a wonderful thing. To be a student in America studying engineering was a beautiful life. That, in itself, was worth defending from anyone and anything which dared to threaten it with change or extinction. Where was the slide rule, he asked himself, where was the shaft of exacting and thrilling discovery when I needed it most? If only I had pictured it and felt it in my hands, I might well have made the right decision, for the seeing and feeling of it would have pushed out the bitterness with the greenness of the grass on the campus and the hardness of the chairs in the airy classrooms with the blackboards stretched wall-to-wall behind the professor, and the books and the sandwiches and the bus rides coming and going. I would have gone into the army for that and I would have shot and killed, and shot and killed some more, because I was happy when I was a student with the finely calculated white sword at my side. But I did not remember or could not remember because, when one is born in America and learning to love it more

and more everyday without thinking it, it is not an easy thing to discover suddenly that being American is a terribly incomplete thing if one's face is not white and one's parents are Japanese of the country Japan which attacked America. It is like being pulled asunder by a whirling tornado and one does not think of a slide rule though that may be the thing which will save one. (52–54)

Ichiro cannot compare wartime experience to his present life. He's trying to use a slide rule to measure a tornado. Seattle looms too close for Ichiro to see its edges; he cannot estimate how his time elsewhere has framed his choice. Ichiro tries to use the familiarity of the city and the greenness of the campus as the measure of his life. However, he can't make the equation work. Wartime displacement means that Ichiro must compare this place to other, less peaceful places. He cannot simply fold Seattle then against Seattle now. Ichiro muses that he couldn't picture the slide rule in his hands and therefore couldn't make the right decision. However, he suppresses the reason why the slide rule and classrooms seemed remote: he was in an internment camp when he answered, "no, no." Kenji says to him, "The government kept you from Seattle," but Ichiro seems unable to remember this fact.

The Joys of Modernism

The prewar Ichiro studied civil engineering; the postwar Ichiro finds hope for America in new roads and new buildings. Ichiro reroots himself by thinking like a civil engineer: a cultural insider, not an intruder. A civil engineer actually builds the landscapes where others will live. The future belongs to everyone, not just one race. While Brooks expresses hope through natural metaphors of roots and flowers, Okada expresses hope through metaphors of construction. As we have seen, Ichiro's trauma structures itself in imagery of rottenness. By contrast, clean new construction symbolizes social health. Despite his prison record, Ichiro receives a job offer from a firm in a new building. The offer gives Ichiro a moment of hope in the midst of despair, just as the city's new construction sits in the middle of age and decay. Why should Ichiro feel preservationist about an American history that made no place for him? "It was a short ride to the new, brick structure which had recently been constructed in an area, once residential, but now giving way to the demands of a growing city. Low, flat, modern clinics and store buildings intermingled with rambling, ugly apartment houses of wood and dirt-ridden brick" (147).

For Ichiro, rooting and mobility complement rather than contradict each other. He believes in the twin postwar creeds of new highways and new homeownership. He admires Issei who, unlike his parents, have shown their loyalty to America in twin ways: living in a nice home and offering up their sons for U.S. military service. He admires the Kumasakas because they cease to live above their Japantown shop and buy "a freshly painted frame house that was situated behind a neatly kept lawn . . . this home which he envied because it was like millions of other homes in America" (25–26). Even though this home is in Japantown, it claims an interchangeably American sense of place because its owners are patriotic. Kenji's father's house also represents the triumph of mobility over clannishness. The house looks out at vistas of fresh pavement, not Japantown or Seattle's famed shoreline. "It sat on the top of a steep, unpaved hill and commanded an uninspiring view of clean, gray concrete that was six lanes wide and an assortment of boxy, flat store buildings and spacious super gas-stations" (117). The house seems poised to tank up, get on the on-ramp, and hit the highways. It lines up with America. One of the Kannos' impressive new possessions is "a big television set with the radio and phonograph all built into one impressive blond console" (118). Everything stacks up inside the American ideal.

The Questioning Zone

Ichiro would like to build a life inside the impressive blond console of the suburbs. A hotel porter's offer to get Ichiro a girl makes him long for the clean, pale ideals of suburbia. Ichiro's vision of the suburbs looks just like an old-fashioned New England village, yet cleansed of all its exclusionary history. Like Main Street U.S.A. at Disneyland, constructed in the same time period, Ichiro's suburb re-creates the classic white American community so that anyone can come from there.[17] We can all be reborn as residents of Middletown, not Japantown. Like Maud Martha, however, Ichiro knows that the pictures in the "homey magazines" are not real life, even though they provide temporary refuge from it. Barriers against Nisei suburban homeownership broke down only in the late 1950s, well after the novel's writing in 1955.[18]

> "Filthy-minded old bastard," he muttered viciously under his breath. No wonder the world's such a rotten place, rotten and filthy and cheap and smelly. Where is that place they talk of and paint nice pictures of and describe in all the homey magazines? Where is that place with the clean, white cottages surrounding the new, red-brick church with the clean, white steeple, where the families all have two children, one boy and one girl, and a shiny new car in the garage and a dog and a cat and life is like living in the land of the happily-

ever-after? Surely it must be around here someplace, someplace in America. Or is it just that it's not for me? Maybe I dealt myself out, but what about that young kid on Burnside who was in the army and found it wasn't enough so that he has to keep proving it to every-one who comes in for a cup of coffee that he was fighting for his country like the button on his shirt says he did because the army didn't do anything about his face to make him look more American? And what about the poor niggers on Jackson Street who can't find anything better to do than spit on the sidewalk and show me the way to Tokyo? They're on the outside looking in, just like that kid and just like me and just like everybody else I've ever seen or known. Even Mr. Carrick. Why isn't he in? Why is he on the outside squan-dering his goodness on outcasts like me? Maybe the answer is that there is no in. Maybe the whole damned country is pushing and shov-ing and screaming to get into someplace that doesn't exist, because they don't know that the outside could be the inside if only they would stop all this pushing and shoving and realize that. That makes sense. I've got the answer all figured out, simple and neat and sensible.

And then he thought about Kenji in the hospital and of Emi in bed with a stranger who reminded her of her husband and of his mother waiting for the ship from Japan, and there was no more answer. (159)

The novel's strongest sense of place is not the ethnic ghetto or the imaginary suburbs but the zone of open searching. For every jibe at the past or idealization of the future, the novel offers a stunning, unan-swerable question about the present. Okada's phenomenally bold ques-tions reach out beyond the 1950s to the unsolved problems of our own day. Jinqi Ling describes "the space opened up by the novel": "Ichiro's ongoing confusion about his predicament also marks the political poten-tials of Okada's novel in the 1950s: it kept alive a marginal sensibility replete with Okada's moral anguish about racial oppression against Japanese Americans during World War II and with his yearning for social change which had not yet found its agents."[19]

Okada offers a far-ranging critique of the segregated imagination. He questions its very terms: "Maybe the whole damned country is pushing and shoving and screaming to get into someplace that doesn't exist." Ichiro's continued despair does not invalidate his search. Gayle K. Fujita Sato notes that by the novel's end "Ichiro has walked and talked his way through a dozen characters and situations."[20] Like a noir detective, he makes his way through strangers and questions them. Minor characters become a roster of witnesses for or against the proposition that postwar America is a livable place. Ichiro still walks as a stranger among strangers. However, the process of questioning allows for an "insinuation of promise" at the novel's end. Maybe Japantown can line up with America at last. Maybe a no-no boy's best gift is his ability to ask questions that don't have answers.

> He walked along, thinking, searching, thinking and probing, and, in the darkness of the alley of the community that was a tiny bit of America, he chased that faint and elusive insinuation of promise as it continued to take shape in mind and in heart. (251)

6 | Neutralizing New Orleans

New Orleans has never been segregated in the block-by-block manner of Chicago or Los Angeles, yet has its own history of racial division. In the American imaginary, New Orleans often ranks as the nation's most relaxed and racially mixed city. Nonetheless, the city fell under the U.S. southern system of segregation from the 1880s until the civil rights movement of the 1950s and 1960s.[1] During the highest pitch of the desegregation battle in New Orleans, Walker Percy wrote a first novel deeply rooted in the city's sense of place: "I sat down one day in New Orleans and began to write *The Moviegoer*."[2]

Despite the city's easygoing reputation, Percy's 1961 novel reflects a rigid separation between black and white worlds. Max Webb describes the main thrust of the novel very well: the narrator's effort "to assess the consequences of his sudden full awareness of being alive in a precise, historical moment."[3] It is astounding, then, that Percy overlooks the civil rights movement, an event of lasting historical significance taking place on the streets and buses where and when he sets his novel. Furthermore, Percy's critics also ignore this crucial historical moment.

I intend not to upbraid Percy for his blind spot but to show how much this blind spot tells us about the segregated white imagination. Percy offers a very true-to-life portrayal of what it feels like to operate within white privilege, to know and yet not know you aren't seeing everything there is to see. Like *Maud Martha, The Moviegoer* reflects its historical moment in the very ways it sidesteps that moment. Percy maps the contours of white privilege from the inside. In patrolling its borders, he reveals white culture's limitations. His main character's malaise and existential alienation come from running up against his culture's limits yet not being able to transcend them. Percy cannot imagine an integrated city, so he imagines a neutral zone. Like Ichiro Yamada, Percy's main character embraces masculine detachment and the suburbs' abstract sense of place as possible solutions to racial conflict. In many instances he resolves the conflict by eliminating people from the landscape altogether. At first I explore why Percy's blind spot is so surprising; I then analyze what we can learn from it about the segregated imagination.

A Blind Spot

During the era of segregation, a "race screen" was a board placed between "white" and "colored" sections on southern buses. In the city of New Orleans the race screens came down at midnight on Friday, May 30, 1958.[4] Walker Percy began *The Moviegoer* in early 1958, just a few months before the race screens came down. He completed the manuscript in the fall of 1960, as the battle to desegregate the public schools hit its frenzied peak.

The novel contains a powerful "race screen" of its own: a willed indifference to racial injustice. Like *No-No Boy, The Moviegoer* maintains a social amnesia toward white oppression. Percy sets his novel in the very spaces hotly contested by New Orleans segregationists and integrationists: the buses, the tramcars, the schools, the movie theaters, the suburbs, and the Mardi Gras. Percy writes about these spaces with an inappropriate neutrality reminiscent of Yamamoto and Cheever. Take, for instance, the casual reference to segregation on a New Orleans bus, written just as bus segregation ended. What's at stake in Percy's neutral presentation?

> It is a gloomy March day. The swamps are still burning at Chef Menteur and the sky over Gentilly is the color of ashes. The bus is crowded with shoppers, nearly all women. The windows are steamed. I sit on the lengthwise seat in front. Women sit beside me and stand above me. On the long back seat are five Negresses so black that the whole rear of the bus seems darkened. Directly next to me, on the first cross seat, is a very fine-looking girl. She is a strapping girl but by no means too big, done up head to toe in cellophane, the hood pushed back to show a helmet of glossy black hair. She is magnificent with her split tooth and her Prince Val bangs split on her forehead. Gray eyes and wide black brows, a good arm and a fine swell of calf above her cellophane boot. One of those solitary Amazons one sees on Fifty-seventh Street in New York or in Neiman Marcus in

Dallas. . . . What a tragedy it is that I do not know her, will probably never see her again. What good times we could have! This very afternoon we could go spinning along the Gulf Coast. What consideration and tenderness I could show her! If it were a movie, I would have only to wait. The bus would get lost or the city would be bombed and she and I would tend the wounded. As it is, I may as well stop thinking about her.[5]

The placement of the five women in the back of the bus seems entirely taken for granted. Unlike the bus rides in Yamamoto and Okada, Percy's narration contains no internal monologue about race relations. Yamamoto and Okada present the bus explicitly as an experiment in multiculturalism. They portray an individual bus rider trying to banish a racist incident from language and conscious memory. In Percy, however, the multiracial dimension surfaces and disappears too quickly to register in the bus rider's memory, beyond a brief visual impression on the retina. Percy does not usher the reader into witnessing the hidden racial conflict.

Instead, the narrator John Bickerson (Binx) Bolling channels his awareness away from the "Negresses" and into a self-parody of his own skirt chasing. He even imagines himself and the "solitary Amazon" tending the wounded in some overblown Hollywood disaster. In typical postwar thinking, he imagines the city as a place to be bombed. However, Binx misses the chance to heal the wounds of history presented right in front of him. The five African American women in back merely provide atmosphere. They are "local color," in line with the old picturesque tradition of New Orleans (touristic talk Binx himself hates). The five women form part of the scenery and natural order; they darken the rear of the bus in the same way the ashes of swamp-burning darken the sky. Binx doesn't question why the swamps are burning, nor does he question the phrase "the rear of the bus." The quiet melancholy of the scene suggests that everyday life may not be perfect, but it's not going to change, either.

Percy's neutral tone is strange given the settings he chooses, his public opposition to segregation, and the novel's philosophical commitment to seeing what is in front of one's eyes on the everyday landscape.

Percy sets *The Moviegoer* in nearly every key site of the New Orleans civil rights movement: buses and tramcars, schools, Mardi Gras, public entertainment facilities, and the segregated suburbs. The novel takes place over Mardi Gras week, from the preceding Wednesday to Ash Wednesday. By comparison, the writing of the novel fell within the era of antisegregation Mardi Gras boycotts in the springs of 1957 and 1960. Buses and Mardi Gras intertwine in Percy's novel and also in the civil rights movement: the 1957 Mardi Gras boycott was timed to coincide with the

Montgomery bus boycott in Alabama. Boycott sponsors published ads: "New Orleans Negroes Will Not Dance While Montgomery Negroes Walk."[6]

Public spaces like Mardi Gras and public transportation were racially and emotionally charged during the three years of *The Moviegoer*'s writing. Yet little of this charged emotion shows up in the novel. There is a remarkable contrast in tone between the segregationists' frenetic campaigns against integration and Percy's pleasantly detached observations of the same locales at the same time. Percy makes no reference to segregation or desegregation at all. Is Percy forward-thinking, or is he in denial?

The writing of *The Moviegoer* coincided precisely with the desegregation timetable in New Orleans, and, indeed, with Percy's own growing interest in civil rights outside the confines of the novel. White opposition coalesced soon after the *Brown v. Board of Education* decision on May 17, 1954. Judge J. Skelly Wright's 1956 order to desegregate the New Orleans public schools finally went into effect in fall 1960 and encountered massive, even terrorist, resistance until the fall of 1961, during the time when Percy was finishing the novel.[7] Archbishop Joseph F. Rummel ordered the desegregation of New Orleans Catholic schools in 1956, but this order did not go into effect until 1962, also because of white opposition.[8]

Percy saw the battle in front of his eyes. In the fall of 1957, Percy and his wife moved back into New Orleans from the outlying town of Covington and enrolled their elder daughter in the (segregated) Academy of the Sacred Heart near their new home on Milan Street.[9] In 1956–1957, Percy wrote a series of articles on desegregation from the viewpoint of a white southern Catholic. In "The Southern Moderate," written in fall 1957, just before he began *The Moviegoer,* Percy declares, "Segregation is sinful because, as Archbishop Rummel of New Orleans said, it is a denial of the unity and solidarity of the human race; it is sinful as openly practiced in the South; it is at least as sinful as covertly practiced in the North."[10] During the writing of *The Moviegoer,* "one of the few extramural involvements Percy allowed himself during his New Orleans months was a loose affiliation with a group of men who met from time to time to discuss civil rights issues."[11] This group occasionally included African American leaders as well as Father Louis Twomey, a Jesuit involved in civil rights and labor education.

If Percy the essayist and citizen concerned himself with civil rights, why not Percy the novelist? If the setting were incidental to the novel, the omission might be understandable. Quite the contrary holds true, however. The ability to register time and place serves as the novel's central theme. Here Binx, an avid moviegoer, describes one of his moviegoing moments: "There is a danger of slipping clean out of space and time. It is possible to become a ghost and not know whether one is in downtown Loews in Denver or suburban Bijou in Jacksonville. So it was with me" (64). Yet the movie theaters where Binx ponders space and time are themselves segregated spaces—a fact the novel fails to notice. Binx spends the entire novel observing small moments others ignore, moments that are strange in their very everydayness. Like Ichiro, he walks through a familiar landscape as if he were a stranger. Binx's mission in life is "the search," which he defines like this: "The search is what anyone would undertake if he were not sunk in the everydayness of his own life. This morning, for example, I felt as if I had come to myself on a strange island. And what does a castaway do? Why, he pokes around the neighborhood and he doesn't miss a trick" (18).

Ironically, Binx defines his search to the reader while he is still riding the bus, just after he has failed to notice the strangeness of segregation displayed before his eyes in his own neighborhood. Binx's attempts to make meaning from everyday reality, to shatter its "everydayness" and taken-for-grantedness, parallel African American strategies of resistance to segregation. In an essay Percy declared that "the peculiar virtue of New Orleans" may be "a talent for everyday life." Similarly, historian Robin D. G. Kelley has analyzed "the politics of the everyday" in black working people's resistance to southern segregation during and after World War II. Kelley's description of Birmingham buses as "moving theaters" is reminiscent of Binx's bus ride in New Orleans.

> An especially apt metaphor for understanding the character of domination and resistance on public transportation might be to view the interior spaces as "moving theaters." Theater can have two meanings: as a site of performance and as a site of military conflict. First, dramas of conflict, repression, and resistance are performed in which passengers witness, or participate in, a wide variety of "skirmishes" that shape their collective memory, illustrate the limitations as well as the possibilities of resistance to domination, and draw more passengers into the "performance." The design of streetcars and buses themselves—enclosed spaces with seats facing forward or towards the center aisle—lent a dramaturgical quality to everyday discursive and physical confrontations.[12]

With a crucial difference, Percy also represents public space as performance. Binx is an ardent moviegoer. On streets and buses, he transforms the people he meets into actors and actresses in his mental pictures. As in *Maud Martha* and *No-No Boy,* much of the action happens within the mind of the protagonist. Binx's imagination "lends a dra-

maturgical quality" to his observation of the "solitary Amazon" on the
bus. He writes a script for her in his head and stage-manages her exit.
However, Percy's bus is a moving theater only in the dramatic sense, not
as a "site of military conflict" in the desegregation battle. Binx's drama
pulls attention away from racial injustice, not toward it. With his precise eye for detail, Binx seems to tell us all we need to know, even
when he doesn't. Percy's sense of place is insulated and public at the same
time.

Percy's critics ignore the issue of race almost entirely.[13] His biogra-
phers raise the cultural context of civil rights and then dismiss it from
their discussion of the novel. After reassuring us that Percy had "compassion" for African Americans, biographer Patrick Samway notes in passing, "Curiously, the racial and political tensions prevalent throughout the
South seemed not to have had a direct impact on Walker's creative
imagination at this time."[14] Even more curiously, biographer Robert
Coles also fails to make the connection. An eminent psychiatrist, Coles
counseled the four black schoolchildren who were the first to desegregate New Orleans's public schools in 1960. He later wrote extensively
about the psychological effects of racial conflict in his well-respected
Children of Crisis book series. However, in his biography of Walker
Percy, even Dr. Coles fails to notice *The Moviegoer*'s silence about segregation. He begins his discussion of the novel declaring, "Sometimes,
however, a historical moment makes everyone's life 'different.' The
immanent is challenged directly and massively by the transcendent: in
our everyday lives a great ideal and its demands confront us. So it went
for Percy and those like him after the Supreme Court ruled school desegregation unconstitutional in 1954."[15] Coles then goes on to discuss every
possible aspect of the novel, except this "great ideal and its demands."
It is hard to believe that this silence has nothing to do with Percy's status as a white, upper-class southerner. The Percy family has been wealthy
and prominent in the politics and cultural life of the Deep South for two
centuries.[16] Just as publisher Alfred Knopf gave Walker Percy an extra fifty
dollars earnest money for the novel upon hearing that the author was a
man of independent means, critics seem to give Percy extra credit for not
being an overt racist.[17]

The Meaning of Silence

This critical silence reflects the invisibility of whiteness. Walker Percy had no public obligation to write a novel of social
protest, whereas a black novelist of the 1960s would have been criticized
in print for ignoring racial oppression. Percy's blind spot does not represent a personal moral failing but rather a fascinating symptom of

segregation. White fiction writers often have great difficulty imagining a multiracial world, even though we live in such a world. The "strange island" where Binx conducts his search is the limited enclave of white New Orleans, not New Orleans as a whole.

The critical silence reproduces the structure of the novel itself. Just as critics take Percy on his own terms, Percy takes white culture on its own terms. He documents the segregated imagination from inside. Like a moviegoer watching a 1950s Hollywood film, Binx can only see and critique what white culture is willing to show. The novel registers a wordless queasiness when Binx runs up against the limits of this narrow frame. Binx knows and yet can't articulate the fact that he's not seeing all there is to see. A member of the younger generation, Binx approaches southern tradition with a naïveté that is both true and false. Binx tries to work within white southern culture and in doing so exposes the limits of its explanations. His alienation, malaise, and boredom come from running up against limits yet not being able to surpass them.

A Commitment to Neutrality

Percy the novelist's neutrality on race comes from two sources: the southern conservatism of his past and the postwar existentialism of his present. On the conservative side, the logic of containment leads to neutrality. The pleasure of Percy's narration lies in Binx's ability to identify people as types and satirize them through reading their minds. This mastery over discourse relies on social types staying the same. Thus, it reflects a desire for stasis, for a world where white men remain in control enough to be ironic about the world. Percy's neutrality also reflects traditional southern politeness, in which it is considered gentlemanly or ladylike to overlook ugliness on the landscape. Furthermore, given Percy's cultural background, neutrality may seem a laudable option compared with the alternatives. At least Binx isn't Yamamoto's white racist yelling epithets on the bus. Since the heated rhetoric of desegregation came from white racists, it is understandable that Percy would choose a neutral tone as the best alternative.

If Binx noticed the black women's position at the back of the bus, it might force a political commitment out of him. He would have to get upset, and that would blow his cover as moviegoer, ironic observer, and postwar existentialist. Beyond cowardice or conservatism, there are important generational reasons why Binx remains neutral. Percy makes a commitment to a certain kind of intellectual modesty: he writes from a given cultural standpoint and only records what that character could see and know. Percy saw himself as representing in *The Moviegoer* a conflict between two options: not neutrality versus activist engagement but neutrality versus white paternalism. Percy commented that his first two novels concerned the differences between him and his uncle: "The whole thing is a dialectic between his attitudes and the attitudes of the two young men in these novels, a more detached, alienated point of view."[18] This detachment reflects the shared distaste among postwar intellectuals for rhetoric, ideology, and abstraction. Andrew Ross's description of beatnik alienation also applies to Percy, even though Percy was a very different sort of postwar American existentialist: "Between the time of the anti-bourgeois demimonde and the romantic pietism of Beat comes the period when intellectuals put themselves in the service of revolutionary movements, and when intellectual sponsorship of the masses was seen as a *responsibility,* and not as an act of free political will. This is why the existentialist *acte gratuite,* which Beat culture celebrated, represented something like a release or relief from that burden of responsibility."[19]

Binx cannot explain his existentialist "free acts" to his aunt, nor will he sign on to any particular program. Furthermore, as we have seen in chapter 2, neutrality characterizes the postwar era in another way. The post-traumatic avoidance of triggers leads to a neutral tone of voice. A Korean War veteran, Binx measures his current world against the heightened reality of war. The neutral zones of cliché, mass-culture banality, and suburban anonymity fascinate him. Underneath his fascination lies compassion for the need of shell-shocked people to avoid further shock. His interpretation of racial conflict grows from this urge to avoid shock.

In mapping out the white geography of *The Moviegoer,* we can differentiate between two kinds of segregated space: the neutral zone versus the containment zone. Both have the same slightly limited and deadened quality, but there are important distinctions between them. The neutral zone represents Percy's ideal of social harmony. It excludes conflict but does allow for movement across borders. This neutral zone exhibits a healthy balance between public and private space. While Binx still mocks the limitations of this world, he does so with restraint. This is the world of the suburbs, the middle class, his mother.

On the other hand, the containment zone is the glass bubble of upper-class New Orleans, the world of his aunt Emily. It has invisible but solid walls around it, and Binx satirizes it freely. Between them, Binx's mother's space and his aunt's space represent the spectrum of southern bourgeois whiteness. He uses their perspectives to map white space, and he takes pains to prove that neither world is better than the other. The customs of his fraternal aunt's patrician family, the Bollings, and the customs of his mother's middle-class family, the Smiths, both carry a sense of limitation so delicate and so unnameable, Binx can only characterize it by use of the word "pleasant"—that archetypal fifties adjective: "As a Bolling in Feliciana Parish, I became accustomed to sitting on the porch in the dark and talking of the size of the universe and the treachery of men; as a Smith on the Gulf Coast I have become accustomed to eating crabs and drinking beer under a hundred and fifty watt bulb—and one is as pleasant a way as the other of passing a summer night" (124).

The White Zone

On the first page of the novel, Percy stages a dialogue between the old southern paternalism and the new southern detachment.

> I remember when my older brother Scott died of pneumonia. I was eight years old. My aunt had charge of me and she took me for a walk behind the hospital. It was an interesting street. On one side were the power plant and blowers and incinerator of the hospital, all humming and blowing out a hot meaty smell. On the other side was a row of Negro houses. Children and old folks and dogs sat on the porches watching us. I noticed with pleasure that Aunt Emily seemed to have all the time in the world and was willing to talk about anything I wanted to talk about. Something extraordinary had happened all right. We walked slowly in step. "Jack," she said, squeezing me tight and smiling at the Negro shacks, "you and I have always been good buddies, haven't we?" "Yes ma'am." My heart gave a big pump and the back of my neck prickled like a dog's. "I've got bad news for you, son." She squeezed me tighter than ever. "Scotty is dead. Now it's all up to you. It's going to be difficult for you but I know you're going to act like a soldier." This was true. I could easily act like a soldier. Was that all I had to do? (11)

It is instructive to read this scene in tandem with a statement Percy made about race relations in one of his 1957 essays, "Stoicism in the South": "The fact is that neither the ethos nor the traditional worldview of the upper-class white Southerner is any longer adequate to the situation. No longer able to maintain a steadfast and temperate position, he finds himself caught up in violent and contradictory cross-movements. There is nothing atypical about Faulkner's crying the South's guilt to the high heavens one moment and the next condoning street fighting to perpetuate it."[20] The novel and the essay are talking about the same thing. In comforting her newly bereaved nephew, the aunt's worldview is clearly "inadequate to the situation." Her heavy-handed stoicism is something like the hospital's power plant, industriously processing raw human experience and "blowing out a hot meaty smell." But there is also an interesting contrast at work between the novel and the essay. While "Stoicism in the South" looks directly at desegregation, this scene from

mer) fiancé, urges Binx to rejoin the krewe of Neptune: " 'You may not agree with me, but in my opinion it is the best all-around krewe in Carnival. We're no upstarts and on the other hand we're not a bunch of old farts—and—' he adds hastily as he thinks of Uncle Jules, 'our older men are among the ten wealthiest and most prominent families in New Orleans.' Walter would never say 'rich'; and indeed the word 'wealthy,' as he says it, is redolent of a life spiced and sumptuous, a tapestry thick to the touch and shot through with the bright thread of freedom" (34).

Percy opposes Neptune's financial stability to Kate's emotional instability. A former queen of Neptune herself, Kate is the canary in the gold mine of wealthy New Orleans. Her unease with this year's Mardi Gras specifies vaguely that something unspecified is wrong here. As her stepmother, Aunt Emily, says, "Kate is afraid of a general catastrophe." Equating mental health with the ability to perform in one's social circle, Aunt Emily declares, "It is very important that she not come to the point where it becomes more and more difficult to meet people. . . . Now all in the world I want you to do is take her to the Lejiers and watch the parade from the front porch" (29–30). Her aunt's assertion of normality just doesn't work for Kate this year. Kate watches the Mardi Gras parade with Binx, but from an anonymous viewpoint on the street, not in the patrician circles of the Lejiers' porch. Furthermore, Binx and Kate watch the "wrong" part of the parade. They see the African American flambeau bearers and leave before Walter and the Neptune krewe approach.

> We are in time for the downtown swing of Neptune. The crowd has already moved from the lake side to the river side of St. Charles. It is quite dark now. The streetlights make golden spaces inside the wet leaves of the live oaks. A south wind carries the smell of coffee from the Tchoupitoulas docks. Mounted police shoulder the crowd over the curb. To the dark neutral ground come Negroes from Louisiana Avenue and Claiborne; some Negro men carry children astride their necks to see over the crowd.
>
> Here is the public service truck with its tower, measuring the clearance under the oak limbs and cutting some wet drooping branches. We wait to see the flambeaux bearers and now here they come, a vanguard of half a dozen extraordinary Negroes dressed in dirty Ku Klux Klan robes, each bearing aloft a brace of pink and white flares. The flambeaux create a sensation. The bearers stride swiftly along the very edge of the crowd, showering sparks on everyone. They look angrily at each other to keep abreast, their fierce black faces peeping sidewise from their soiled hoods. Kate laughs at them. The Negro onlookers find them funny, but their bold manner, their

contemptuous treatment of the crowd, excites them too. "Ah now!" they cry. "Look at him!" "Ain't he something though!"

The floats rumble along under the leaves. Some fathers have brought ladders with orange crates, big enough for three children, nailed to the top. These lucky ones gaze openmouthed at the maskers who pass them at eye level and almost within reach. The maskers look like crusaders with their nosepieces and their black eye sockets. Yet these specters are strangely good-natured, leaning forward and dropping whole bunches of necklaces and bracelets or sailing them over to the colored folk in the neutral ground. High school bands from North Louisiana and Texas follow the floats. Negro boys run along behind the crowd to keep up with the parade and catch the trinkets that sail too high.

The krewe captain and a duke come towards us on horseback.

I ask Kate whether she wants to see Walter.

"No."

"We'd better go then." (54–55)

From the public service truck to the segregation of onlookers, street space is carefully trimmed and controlled. Although Percy doesn't spell it out, he assumes we understand the crowd is segregated. African Americans stand in something called "the dark neutral ground" behind the sidewalks. The maskers have to "sail" the trinkets hard in order to reach black onlookers. White children are the "lucky ones" for whom the parade is "almost within reach." Like the moviegoer himself, these children gaze in wonder at everything they see. However, they also stay contained in their skyboxes of privilege. By contrast, African American boys run along the margins, behind the sidewalks.

The unspoken context of segregation helps to explain the otherwise inexplicable anger of the black flambeau bearers. Percy's description both expresses and controls the threat of black anger. From Binx's viewpoint, the black members of the crowd find the bearers both inspiring and funny. The robes of carnival derive from European Catholic custom, not from the Klan. However, Percy's flambeau bearers wear "Ku Klux Klan robes" while carrying torches, as if the tables had turned and the moment of payback for white racism had arrived. The bearers have "fierce black faces." They shower sparks on the white crowd. Strangely, these marginal participants in official Mardi Gras wear dirty costumes, even though the unofficial black Mardi Gras groups, the carnival Indians, are famous for the beauty, elaboration, and newness of their costumes every year.[23] These flambeau bearers, however, seem soiled by the history of southern white racism, as if one had to choose between history and joy. Like Okada, Percy will contrast the soiling of history with the cleanliness of new suburbs.

Percy contains the threat of black anger by portraying the flambeau bearers as local color. There is an awareness of hostility, but a controlled, picturesque awareness. Binx sees them as having an Old World charm he usually hates ("I can't stand the old-world atmosphere of the French Quarter or the genteel charm of the Garden District" [13]). The flambeau bearers' bold manner excites the black onlookers, but they are exciting in a touristic sense. These are "extraordinary Negroes," folkloric characters who do not reflect the frustrations and indignities of ordinary life. They are scary as Halloween costumes are scary.

Nonetheless, the novel displays a peripheral awareness of the difference between a soiled hood and Walter's "bright thread of freedom." This peripheral awareness shows in the way Binx and Kate move out into the "neutral ground" themselves. As in many white writers, the awareness of racial conflict causes an emptying-out of urban space. Kate escapes from the royal enclosure: she leaves her supper with the former queens "abruptly" to wander in the night (88). When Binx comes upon her, he thinks, "Thus she would a thousand times rather find herself in the middle of no man's land than at a family party or luncheon club" (91). If Binx and Kate have to choose between official celebration and no-man's-land, they choose no-man's-land. (Of course, they get to choose the neutral ground, whereas the black community doesn't.) Finally, the novel boycotts the Mardi Gras altogether. Percy cuts the carnival party scene and instead whisks Binx off on a business trip to Chicago over Fat Tuesday, with Kate in tow. By the time the novel returns to New Orleans, Mardi Gras is over, and only a no-man's-land remains. If Mardi Gras can't be integrated, it will cease to exist.

> Canal Street is dark and almost empty. The last parade, the Krewe of Comus, has long since disappeared down Royal Street with its shuddering floats and its blazing flambeaux. Street cleaners sweep confetti and finery into soggy heaps in the gutters. The cold mizzling rain smells of sour paper pulp. Only a few maskers remain abroad, tottering apes clad in Spanish moss, Frankenstein monsters with bolts through their necks, and a neighborhood gang or two making their way arm in arm, wheeling and whip-popping, back to their trucks. (172–173)

Like the far-flung trinkets in the flambeau bearers scene, only the stray remains are left behind. The lingering revelers represent the borderlines of human society: a vegetable ape, a Frankenstein monster, and a neighborhood gang. Just as Kate escaped the royal enclosure of former queens, the last parade "has long since disappeared down Royal Street." Comus, one of "the famous old krewes" of New Orleans (21), has faded away, the ancient regime replaced not by a multiracial society but by emptiness.

Suburbia

This strange, almost postnuclear emptiness also characterizes the suburban Catholic school next door to Binx's house. It seems Percy resolves conflict by eliminating people from the landscape altogether. Like the Mardi Gras, Percy takes another racially charged space and turns it into a desert zone of solitude and melancholy. *The Moviegoer* takes place primarily in Gentilly, the middle-class suburb where Binx lives. In the New Orleans of 1958–1962, suburban Catholic schools offered a redoubled opportunity for "white flight." The parochial schools resisted integration longer, while brand-new suburbs offered a second chance at segregation.[24]

Percy was completing the novel at the height of the schools crisis. "Daily, throughout November and December [1960], mobs of women met the children at Frantz and McDonogh 19 with screams, threats, and racial epithets as they walked into the schools. They also made death threats to NAACP leaders, to the parents of all the children, and to the white activists in Save Our Schools, who drove the white children to the schools for the first four weeks of the crisis. The school crisis became the 'Shame of New Orleans,' covered by national news media and splashed in headlines across the country."[25] Percy's tranquil description of a suburban school contrasts violently with "the Shame of New Orleans."

> Life in Gentilly is very peaceful. I manage a small branch office of my uncle's brokerage firm. My home is the basement apartment of a raised bungalow belonging to Mrs. Schexnaydre, the widow of a fireman. . . . Next door to Mrs. Schexnaydre is a brand new school. It is my custom on summer evenings after work to take a shower, put on shirt and pants and stroll over to the deserted playground and there sit on the ocean wave, spread out the movie page of the *Times-Picayune* on one side, phone book on the other, and a city map in my lap. After I have made my choice, plotted a route—often to some remote neighborhood like Algiers or St. Bernard—I stroll around the schoolyard in the last golden light of day and admire the building. Everything is so spick-and-span: the aluminum sashes fitted into the brick wall and gilded in the sunset, the pretty terrazzo floors and the desks molded like wings. Suspended by wires above the door is a schematic sort of bird, the Holy Ghost I suppose. It gives

me a pleasant sense of the goodness of creation to think of the brick and glass and the aluminum being extracted from common dirt—though no doubt it is less a religious sentiment than a financial one, since I own a few shares of Alcoa. How smooth and well-fitted and thrifty the aluminum feels! (16)

With the schools crisis in the background, this Gentilly school seems a fantasy of white flight. The "desks molded like wings" seem ready to take flight into the airy openness of Elysian Fields. The scene is both narrowly pretty and surprisingly beautiful. Percy has a great gift for describing the beauty of the everyday, the utilitarian, and the overlooked. The schoolyard is a desert in two senses: a landscape devoid of human society, and a contemplative retreat. This dual role influences the dual color of the window frames: the everyday silver of aluminum, and their transformational gilding in the sunset. As befits a neutral zone, the colors are mostly earth tones: brick, aluminum, glass. Like the clean, white cottages of Ichiro Yamada's imagination, everything in Percy's suburb "is so spick-and-span." All is in exaggeratedly good order. Brand-new, the school seems exempt from the troubles of history. Children encounter rocks and death threats on their way to Frantz and McDonogh 19 schools, but Binx can move freely between one part of town and another. Percy imagines a smooth unbroken movement from suburban schoolyard to the bus to a movie theater in a remote parish. Racial hatred denies African Americans these very spaces and this freedom of movement. Binx, on the other hand, can "make his choice" and plot a route to anywhere.

Yet Percy's tone is far from straightforward praise for the pleasures of white flight. Like his white southerners, Percy's suburb is "caught up in violent and even contradictory cross-movements." This passage displays Percy's uncanny gift for language that can be read straight and satirically at the same time. This scene is both a satire of white culture and an index of white culture's possibilities. A variety of contradictory attitudes appear in a sentence like "How smooth and well-fitted and thrifty the aluminum feels!" As a satirist, Percy fits himself neatly inside the confines of white custom to show that the fit is too snug for full humanity. Like Yamamoto, Okada, and Brooks, he employs housewifely terms such as "spick-and-span," "pretty," "thrifty," and, of course, "pleasant." These terms are complimentary but resolutely limited in scope. The terminology does not directly criticize suburban order. Rather, it draws attention to the narrowness of this world. As in Maud Martha's hat shop or No-No Boy's imaginary suburb, the extensive detail raises our suspicions that something far less tidy may be taking place outside the frame of the picture.

This style of portrayal relates directly to Binx's moviegoing habit. The movies of Binx's choice are all conventional 1950s Hollywood films, which means they depict white culture almost exclusively. What Binx really likes about the movies are the clichés. Clichés are limited and indirect representations of human truth, viewpoints that, like southern paternalism, are no longer adequate to the situation. Binx also loves the viewers' secret language of response to clichés: "the little touches we see in the movie, and in the seeing, know that the other sees—as when Clint Walker tells the saddle tramp in the softest easiest old Virginian voice: 'Mister, I don't believe I'd do that if I was you' " (116–117). The moviegoer cannot see what is outside the frame of the picture. Similarly, Binx only sees what is inside the confines of white culture. Nonetheless, he can question that culture's limitations by drawing attention to the frames themselves and praising how smoothly and tightly they fit.

Percy's too tidy style of narration also leads to the larger question of voice in postwar fiction. Percy's writing style is suspiciously impeccable, with a remarkably satisfying sense of closure and rightness. Like the stories of a minor character in *The Moviegoer,* Binx's anecdotes arouse "an appreciation so keen and pleasurable that it bordered on the irritable" (144). As we have seen, this satisfying and excessive closure characterizes the fifties short story. It also characterizes the postwar novels of Percy, Salinger, Roth, Plath, Ellison, Charles S. Wright, and countless others. Like him, they employ the pleasant voice of closure and satirize it at the same time. The postwar novel owes part of its phenomenal success to the combination of a deeply pleasurable narrative style with a cleansing bath of satirical truth.

Because Binx has a segregated consciousness, he cannot criticize his culture directly. His body answers instead. Kate responds to southern custom with suicidal depression; Binx responds with his "good nose for merde." He can't name the problem exactly, but he knows bullshit when he smells it. Binx lives inside a discourse of banality, cliché, hypocrisy, dogma, and other verbal shortcuts around human experience. Nearly always, he replies with the body instead of words. When his cousin Nell gushes about reading *The Prophet* aloud by the hi-fi to prove to him that life is not gloomy, Binx tells the reader, "A rumble has commenced in my descending bowel, heralding a tremendous defecation" (84). When people talk about the Cold War or even the civil rights movement, Binx responds not to the content but to the "deadness" of their voices: "At such times it seems that the conversation is spoken by automatons who have no choice in what they say. I hear myself or someone else saying things like 'In my opinion the Russian people are a great people, but—' or

'Yes, what you say about the hypocrisy of the North is unquestionably true. However—' and I think to myself: this is death. Lately it is all I can do to carry on such everyday conversations, because my cheek has developed a tendency to twitch of its own accord. Wednesday as I stood speaking to Eddie Lovell, I felt my eye closing in a broad wink" (83).

For the climax of the novel, Percy returns to the playground of the Catholic school, where Binx decides to marry Kate. Percy portrays the suburbs here with a strange but appropriate combination of blandness and violence. An apocalypse seems to be happening just outside Pleasantville. Binx knows nothing of its source, but he can see its effects. The flames aren't visible from Gentilly, but Binx can feel a hot wind blowing and sees the fallout of soot and malaise. Not only is the traditional worldview of the white southerner inadequate to the situation. Also inadequate are the answers of postwar affluence, popular psychology, newspaper surveys, television advertising, and modern social science. Typically, Binx speaks from inside the languages he hates rather than forging an alternative language.

> It is a gloomy day. Gentilly is swept fitfully by desire and by an east wind from the burning swamps at Chef Menteur.
>
> It is my thirtieth birthday and I sit on the ocean wave in the schoolyard and wait for Kate and think of nothing. Now in the thirty-first year of my dark pilgrimage on this earth and knowing less than I ever knew before, having learned only to recognize merde when I see it, having inherited no more from my father than a good nose for merde, for every species of shit that flies—my only talent—smelling merde from every quarter, living in fact in the very century of merde, the great shithouse of scientific humanism where needs are satisfied, everyone becomes an anyone, a warm and creative person, and prospers like a dung beetle, and one hundred percent of people are humanists and ninety-eight percent believe in God, and men are dead, dead, dead; and the malaise has settled like a fall-out and what people really fear is not that the bomb will fall but that the bomb will not fall—on this my thirtieth birthday, I know nothing and there is nothing to do but fall prey to desire. . . . A watery sunlight breaks through the smoke of the Chef and turns the sky yellow. Elysian Fields glistens like a vat of sulfur; the playground looks as if it alone had survived the end of the world. At last I spy Kate; her stiff little Plymouth comes nosing into my bus stop. There she sits like a bomber pilot, resting on her wheel and looking sideways at the children and not seeing, and she could be I myself, sooty eyed and nowhere.

> Is it possible that—For a long time I have secretly hoped for the end of the world and believed with Kate and my aunt and Sam Yerger and many other people that only after the end could the few who survive creep out of their holes and discover themselves to be themselves and live as merrily as children among the viny ruins. It is possible that—it is not too late?
>
> *Iii-oor* goes the ocean wave, its struts twinkling in the golden light, its skirt swaying to and fro like a young dancing girl. (180, 182–183)

Like many other young suburbanites, Binx grows impatient with boredom and blandness. He is like the teenage boy who lives in a nice neighborhood and makes bombs in his bedroom. Percy refers directly here to the threat of the nuclear bomb, but racial violence also lingers outside the scene as an unthinkable threat. Binx says of Kate, "She could be I myself, sooty eyed and nowhere." As John Edward Hardy has noticed, the black people in the novel "all are associated in one way and another with fire and ashes."[26] In this decisive moment, Percy associates soot with Binx and Kate. Perhaps Binx and Kate are sooty eyed because they can spot a fire happening at a great distance.

In a venerable American line of thought, Binx can only imagine social transformation through blowing the old society up and founding another. Of course, he sees himself as a Founding Father. Like Maud Martha's husband, Binx imagines that he and his loved ones will be immune from the effects of the blast. Conflict in one's immediate surroundings is simply too messy, too far outside one's own control, to imagine fixing it. One cannot have both history and happiness.

Nonetheless, this final schoolyard scene carries remote glimmers of social change. As a reminder of transformation, sunlight again turns the playground gold, and there are actually children playing there this time. What kind of utopia does Percy imagine in his postapocalyptic schoolyard? In his essays of the fifties and sixties, Percy makes a surprising case for the suburbs as the solution to the South's racial problems—despite the suburbs' exclusionism. Percy argues that white southerners oppose integration because they see public space as if it were their own living room. In Percy's view, the suburbs could create a neutral zone equally unfamiliar and thus equally open to blacks and whites. In his 1957 essay "The Southern Moderate," Percy writes:

> What must take place if we are ever to have interracial peace is a shrinkage of the zone of personal intercourse. No doubt, it would be preferable to achieve racial accord by an implementing of Christian teachings. But if men do not wish to love one another, then let them at least strive for neutrality. We must, for better or worse,

see the public school for what it is, a public place, as public as a post office or a department-store elevator. In spite of the physical intimacy of an elevator, the passengers do not feel they are sharing the same living space.

. . . The growing depersonalization of Southern life may not be such a bad thing, after all. God writes straight with crooked lines. If the shrinkage of social intercourse to patio and barbecue pit serves no other purpose, it might yet provide a truly public zone outside where people are free to move about in a kind of secure anonymity until the time comes when they might wish to be friends.[27]

This goal of "striving for neutrality" in public space has a strong postwar flavor. It sounds like Cold War liberals' rejection of ideology. By contrast, for instance, 1990s African American historian Robin Kelley sees segregated buses as significant precisely because they are "contested terrain" where conflicts can come up to the surface and move toward resolution: "the bitter struggles waged by black working people on public transportation . . . should force us to rethink the meaning of public space as a terrain of class, race, and gender conflict."[28] As a white moderate writing in the Cold War era, Percy sees no benefit in airing conflict. Rather, he imagines an end to racial hatred in neutral zones where conflicts simply won't surface. Like Gwendolyn Brooks, he imagines a zone of insulation. Percy's vision of racial harmony combines two postwar worldviews: a love of new construction with a post-traumatic avoidance of conflict. Paradoxically, the segregation of memory would lead to the desegregation of public space.

Like John Okada, Percy has a vision of suburbia at odds with common notions about its exclusionary and isolated nature. In many respects, Percy's Gentilly is the opposite of the separate world Robert Fishman describes in *Bourgeois Utopias: The Rise and Fall of Suburbia:* "From its origins, the suburban world of leisure, family life, and union with nature was based on the principle of exclusion. Work was excluded from the family residence; middle-class villas were segregated from working-class housing; the greenery of suburbia stood in contrast to a gray, polluted urban environment."[29]

By contrast, Binx emphasizes his suburbs' continuity with public space, the city, and the world of work. As if to counter the notion of an imaginary wall around suburbia, Percy draws the connecting lines between Binx's home and other parts of town. Like Binx himself, Percy plots routes. The novel begins with Binx riding on the bus from Gentilly into the Garden District of central New Orleans via the scenic route of the French Quarter. Binx even tells us he prefers buses to cars because a car is an isolated capsule while a bus is shared public space: "The truth is I dislike cars. Whenever I drive a car, I have the feeling I have become invisible. People on the street cannot see you; they only watch your rear fender until it is out of their way" (17). Counter to traditional notions of suburbia, Binx lives right down the street from his office. His description of a walk home from work at sunset is a small masterpiece. The tremendous openness of Gentilly conveys Percy's underlying optimism about the suburbs as a site for healing.

> The sun has set but the sky is luminous and clear and apple green in the east. Nothing is left of the smog but a thumb-smudge over Chef Menteur. Bullbats hawk the insects in the warm air next to the pavement. They dive and utter their thrumming skonk-skonk and go sculling up into the bright upper air. I stop at the corner of Elysian Fields to buy a paper from Ned Daigle. Ned is a former jockey and he looks quite a bit like Leo Carroll but older and more dried-up. "What seh, Jackie," he calls in his hoarse bass, as hoarse as the bullbats, and goes humping for the cars, snapping the papers into folds as he goes. He catches the boulevard traffic at the stoplight and often sells half a dozen papers before the light changes. . . .
>
> "Is it going to be clear for Carnival, Jackie?"
>
> We stand on the concrete island between the double streams of traffic. The light changes and off Ned goes again.
>
> Evening is the best time of day in Gentilly. There are not so many trees and the buildings are low and the world is all sky. The sky is a deep bright ocean full of light and life. A mare's tail of cirrus cloud stands in high from the Gulf. High above the Lake a broken vee of ibises points for the marshes; they go suddenly white as they fly into the tilting salient of sunlight. Swifts find a windy middle reach of sky and come twittering down so fast I think at first gnats have crossed my eyelids. In the last sector of apple green a Lockheed Connie lowers from Mobile, her running lights blinking in the dusk. Station wagons and Greyhounds and diesel rigs rumble towards the Gulf Coast, their fabulous tail-lights glowing like rubies in the darkening east. Most of the commercial buildings are empty except the filling stations where attendants hose down the concrete under the glowing discs and shells and stars. (62–63)

This scene is all about cross-movement rather than encapsulation. Binx sees the new American sense of place as a trajectory rather than a fixed address. Even the man who sells papers on the corner keeps flowing out into the boulevard. The old southern adherence to the land has given way to movement and flux. Like Kenji's father, Binx is glad to live near an on-ramp and a choice of gas stations. Cars head out for the Gulf Coast as freely as the bullbats and ibises soar. Traffic becomes streams flowing into the ocean of sky. Corporate logos become glowing sea creatures. Human society, even its prosaic and commercial elements, moves into an underwater realm where people move naturally. Just as Percy has emptied out the schoolyard and the Mardi Gras, Binx contemplates the modernist beauty of emptiness: wide pavement, treeless lots, and big skies.

Other transformations happen here. The borders disappear between racketeer and stockbroker, magic and banality, advertising logos and the bounty of creation. Like the connecting lines Percy draws between neighborhoods, Elysian Fields is a space of intersection. It sits between home and work. With its casual conversations and rich symbolic life, the boulevard represents the vital public space so many find lacking in the suburbs. Yet, in the middle of all this openness sits a concrete island of isolation. Percy's neutral zone represents freedom, but it also represents the desire to avoid human contact. Gentilly contains its share of isolated cubes. In fact, Binx lives in a rabidly segregated zone. He reports his landlady's racial hatred with disturbing nonchalance: "Her one fear in life is of Negroes. Although one seldom sees Negroes in this part of Gentilly, our small yard is enclosed by a hurricane fence eight feet high; every window is barred. Over the years she has acquired three dogs, each for the reason that it had been reputed to harbor a special dislike for Negroes. I have no particular objection to this trait in a dog—for all I know, Mrs. Schexnaydre's fears may be quite justified. However, these are miserable curs and to make matters worse, they also dislike me" (65).

It is hard to believe that Binx has a pleasant and tranquil existence inside this voluntary prison. Also suggestive of white segregation, the first movie theater Binx describes is an isolated pink cube (and "cube" is a word Percy loves). Percy makes no reference to the segregation of southern movie theaters, but the movies Binx attends often play in empty, estranged buildings: "It reminds me of a movie I saw last month out by Lake Pontchartrain. Linda and I went out to a theater in a new suburb. It was evident somebody had miscalculated, for the suburb had quit growing and here was the theater, a pink stucco cube, sitting out in a field all by itself" (12).

The theater sits in a field all by itself just as Binx sits in his apartment on Elysian Fields all by himself: "I switch on television and sit directly in front of it, bolt upright and hands on knees in my ladder-back chair" (66–67). Binx's preference for isolated viewing may point to the impulse underneath compulsive moviegoing: "One encounters chronic moviemania in rigid, inhibited types who feel exquisitely uncomfortable when forced into close interpersonal contact."[30] This diagnosis sounds close to Percy's recommendation that "interracial peace" will come only through "a shrinkage of the zone of personal intercourse." The desire for a neutral zone marks Percy's postwar generation. As we have seen, the avoidance of triggers characterizes post-traumatic stress disorder. In *The Moviegoer*, PTSD is not a literal psychological experience but rather the basis for a philosophical discourse shaping life in the postwar world.[31] New Orleans's "talent for everyday life" is also a good way to dwell on small things and thus avoid big triggers.

While Binx may satirize the clichés of white culture, he also has compassion for white people's need to limit their experience. He often feels this need himself. Binx evokes World War II and his own Korean War service in relation to "the canny management of the shocks of life." Binx calls one variety of moviegoing "repetition"—he sees a movie again after many years in order to feel the intervening stretch of time. But repetition is also a way to neutralize the shocks of history, just as Percy's narrative neutralizes the historical moment of the civil rights movement. Because the picture itself stays the same between viewings, "the events of the intervening twenty years were neutralized, the thirty million deaths, the countless torturings, uprootings and wanderings to and fro. . . . There remained only time itself, like a yard of smooth peanut brittle" (68). Repetition even has the power to neutralize the Holocaust and the ravages of war. Binx also makes analogies with the Holocaust when reflecting on his mother's use of clichés. "It is my mother's way to see life, past and present, in terms of a standard comic exaggeration. If she had spent four years in Buchenwald, she would recollect it so: 'So I said to him: listen, Mister, if you think I'm going to eat this stuff, you've got another think coming' " (122–123). In his comparative study of inadequate worldviews, Binx draws a relationship between trauma and cliché. His mother has already lost two sons to disease and is about to lose another. Binx both mocks and respects her use of triteness and joking to make maternal affection bearable. "Losing Duval, her favorite, confirmed her election of the ordinary. After Duval's death she has wanted everything colloquial and easy, even God" (116). "Her eyes brim with fondness, a fondness carefully guarded against the personal, the heartfelt, a fondness deliberately rendered trite" (128). Although the three boys die before reaching maturity, the cycle of deaths in one family reminds one of the nation's grief and exhaustion after World War II. Postwar events like the civil rights movement keep happening, even though some white people would prefer nothing major to happen ever again.

Binx himself is a war veteran, wounded during his service in Korea. His moment of reawakening after wounding serves as a constant touchstone, reminding him how it feels to be completely absorbed in one's historical moment. "Only once in my life was the grip of everydayness broken: when I lay bleeding in a ditch" (117–118). And yet the reality of the war remains disconnected from the reality of the late1950s. Binx describes war memory as "the sudden confrontation of a time past, a time so terrible and splendid in its arch-reality; and so lost—cut adrift like a great ship in the flood of years" (167). As it is for Cheever, Okada, and Yamamoto, wartime experience is a concrete island, adrift and segregated from the rest of life. Instead of teaching him how to live intensely in the here and now, Binx's past experience often cancels out the present. Despite its firm commitment to living in the moment, the novel neutralizes the historical moment in which it was written.

A moment of interracial contact in the suburbs closes the body of the novel. This last scene comes before an epilogue summarizing the characters' fates. Once again, Binx fails to see something clearly enough, but his acknowledgment of failure offers a modest redemption. Binx meets up with Kate and decides to marry her on Ash Wednesday, the end of carnival, the day after Mardi Gras. Rather than dwell on the happy couple, the novel ends with one last satirical vignette of a stranger. The scene presents an ambiguous clue about the conclusion of Binx's search. The two halves of the vignette bracket Binx and Kate's conclusive marriage dialogue.

> A florid new Mercury pulls up behind us and a Negro gets out and goes up into the church. He is more respectable than respectable; he is more middle-class than one could believe; his Archie Moore mustache, the way he turns and, seeing us see him, casts a weather eye at the sky: the way he plucks a handkerchief out of his rear pocket with a flurry of his coat tail and blows his nose in a magic placative gesture (you see, I have been here before: it is a routine matter).
>
> . . . The Negro has already come outside. His forehead is an ambiguous sienna color and pied: it is impossible to be sure he has received ashes. When he gets in his Mercury, he does not leave immediately but sits looking down at something on the seat beside him. A sample case? An insurance manual? I watch him closely in the rearview mirror. It is impossible to say why he is here. Is it part and parcel of the complex business of coming up in the world? Or is it because he believes that God himself is present here at the corner of Elysian Fields and Buns Enfants? Or is he here for both reasons: through some dim dazzling trick of grace, coming for the one and receiving the other as God's own importunate bonus?
>
> It is impossible to tell. (184–185; 185–186)

Percy again accompanies a black character with ashes, suggesting troubled social relations. Here, however, it's "impossible to be sure that he received ashes." Like Cinderella's fairy godmother, someone has magically made the ashes disappear. The man's affluence and routine presence at the suburban church gesture toward the end of racial inequality. However, Binx's staring and the man's "magic placative gesture" indicate remaining tension. This scene betrays two impulses underneath Walker Percy's neutrality: first, the hidden desire that someone will wave a magic wand and make racial turmoil disappear, without effort or attention on the writer's part; and second, the desire for neutrality as a positive virtue, a relinquishing of white mastery.

A notable change happens in the course of this scene. In the first half, Binx is a mocking, mind-reading know-it-all, as usual in his satirical vignettes. He inherits the wisecracking expertise of the noir detective. By the end of the novel, Binx admits he doesn't know. His detachment toward the stranger is a profound change from his savage mockery of Mercer, his aunt's butler, early in the novel: "I hate it when his vision of himself dissolves and he sees himself as neither, neither old retainer nor expert in current events. Then his eyes get muddy and his face runs together behind his mustache. Last Christmas I went looking for him in his rooms over the garage. He wasn't there but on his bed lay a well-thumbed volume put out by the Rosicrucians called How to Harness Your Secret Powers. The poor bastard" (26).

Binx contains the threat of Mercer's anger through condescension and satire. In the Ash Wednesday scene, by contrast, Binx renounces southern paternalism by admitting he cannot interpret the black man's appearance or behavior. After all, white southern traditionalists argued they knew black people so much better than the integrationists did. Like Mercer's face, the stranger's face also acquires an ambiguous and blurry color. However, this time Binx can sit with the ambiguity instead of hating it. The words "It is impossible to tell" close the body of the novel. Percy leaves the uncertainty flowing out into the suburbs, rather than containing it with excessive closure. Binx finally concedes there's something he can't see.

Percy substitutes the limited utopia of neutrality for the old southern paternalism. He cannot imagine a social space where racial conflict can be aired and resolved. But the very limitations of Percy's viewpoint tell us important things about postwar white America. *The Moviegoer* overlooks the civil rights movement, but this very overlooking serves as a marker of the historical moment. Percy writes from within the segregated white consciousness. Segregation is a turning inward, and Percy represents its inwardness. It is an odd aesthetic choice to represent racially charged urban space in a pleasant, detached, vaguely melancholic way. However, the choice is a fitting one, and to this day a common one in white bourgeois discourse. In his novel as opposed to his essays, Percy doesn't declare segregation wrong. However, he suggests its wrongness indirectly through a vague sense of malaise, banality, and limited horizons. To paraphrase the novel's epigraph from Kierkegaard, substituting whiteness for despair: "the specific character of whiteness is precisely this: it is unaware of being white."

PART III

The Open City

7

"A Ritual for Being Born Twice"

The Postwar Generation

Part III, "The Open City," describes postwar fiction's movements beyond containment culture. It follows a trajectory from hibernation to tentative recovery to the embrace of a more inclusive and joyous city vision. The concrete island becomes a cocoon for rebirth. American novels of the 1950s and early 1960s are nearly all coming-of-age novels, told through the eyes of the younger generation. These novels reveal several new urban geographies, including the open city, the subterranean city, camping out, and a diaspora sense of place. While these literary geographies reflect the uprooting and imperma- nence of the era, they also resist containment, amnesia, and urban dread. The postwar city—usually New York—appears most vibrantly in the cult novel, where the readership plays an imagined role in a new sub- cultural community. The subculture is still an enclave of its own, but its Open City vision holds the seeds of a liberating counternarrative.

Young adults or teens during the war, novelists inherited a postwar world of sudden and surreal prosperity. One American teenager recalled, "What I do remember clearly is the burst of consumption at the war's end. It seems to me that at the very moment we were banging pots and pans . . . there was an explosion of fresh cream and strawberries."[1] By and large, postwar novelists saw themselves in opposition to a prevailing climate of corporate blandness, upward mobility, urban renewal, and resegre- gation. They resisted a smooth and chipper move into conventional success, a move they assumed was theirs for the taking.

The postwar generation is often defined by its "alienation"; however, alienation can be a process of recovery rather than a permanent state. The alienated observer can hide within depression or can move out into creating new communities. The chapter's first section, "The Open City," looks at Jo Sinclair's novel *The Changelings* (1955) as a blueprint for the postwar generation's resistance to segregation and urban dread. The second section, "Hibernating," describes the shock of moving from the war into the postwar period and the invention of a new narrative style to register that shock. The last two sections analyze the novels of Charles S. Wright, Philip Roth, and Paule Marshall. Camping out and diaspora are methods of imagining city space that resist the destruction, amnesia, and resegregation of urban renewal.

The Open City

Jo Sinclair's 1955 novel *The Changelings* is a manifesto for the postwar generation. In it, a handful of young people imagine a city based on joy and interracial understanding rather than male violence, urban dread, and old griefs. *The Changelings* moves beyond the segregated imagination, taking difficult and tentative steps into a racially integrated world. The fourteen-year-old heroine, Judy Vincent (who prefers to be called Vincent), faces a moment when "her worlds had begun jumping out of their boundaries."² Sinclair sets her novel in a single-race enclave much like those discussed in Part II. A fictionalized version of Cleveland, Ohio, East 120th Street is a Jewish, Italian, and WASP neighborhood irrationally threatened by new black neighbors. Urban renewal's destruction of an African American area has caused black families to seek housing on East 120th Street.

Unlike the segregation novel, however, *The Changelings* attempts to transcend walls and map out a liminal, interracial space occupied by youth. A private world closed to parents, the Gully starts as a dividing line between black and white neighborhoods. "Negroes lived there, but the vastness of the Gully was like an ocean between them and East 120th" (2). However, the Gully quickly becomes an interracial zone where the younger generation experiments with new ways of life.

> The Gully could have been created for children. No matter how many adults walked there occasionally, it was a children's place, honeycombed with their ways of living. In winter, they slid down the shallows on sleds or sitting in discarded wash buckets. In spring, they searched as if for buried treasure for the partially burnt objects which came to the surface in certain muddy spots, through layers of old ashes. In summer—when the evenings were as open as the days—the gang unlocked its clubhouse, nailed tight the boards loosened by winter, and took over ownership. (2)

The Gully could symbolize the postwar novel and the postwar generation. While young people populate the postwar novel, children and teenagers occupy the Gully and fill it with their folkways. The postwar city's "camping out" ethos is a transient yet philosophically important sense of place. The Gully is a makeshift camp, yet important meanings reside there. Openness and free play replace the parents' old griefs: the children salvage "buried treasures" from the "old ashes" and play in the open from day until night. The Gully sounds like an ideal place for writers: "The vocabulary of the entire street was sparse, yet in this children's place of Gully, dream and emotion flowed like a rich language" (3). Similarly, creativity flows through the postwar novel despite Cold War repression.

Also like the postwar novel, the Gully serves as meeting ground for races and genders divided elsewhere. The Jewish girl Vincent and the African American girl Clara meet at the clubhouse. Like John Cheever and Hisaye Yamamoto, Gwendolyn Brooks and Walker Percy, Clara and Vincent mirror each other across racial lines: "For a fantastic second, it was like staring into a mirror—except for the brown color of the face" (22).

Confronting the male violence typical of postwar urban fiction, *The Changelings* seeks out other ways to portray city life. Through character development, Sinclair develops the image of a peaceable neighborhood. The interracial bond between two girls begins in opposition to male violence but doesn't end in a defensive posture. Clara lends Vincent a knife to defend herself against Dave; Dave has attacked Vincent to challenge her gang leadership. In the novel's first scene, the boys of the gang strip off Vincent's clothes. Violence threatens Vincent's world now that she has entered adolescence. The sadistic ritual suggests that the neighborhood may cascade toward violence, just as Vincent's friend Dave may inevitably become "like his father, his brothers—wounders and hurters of women" (67).

However, the attack symbolizes a turning point not only for Vincent but also for the neighborhood itself. "That forced stripping in the Gully on Friday somehow had left her mind naked, ready for a different kind of awareness" (103). Are Vincent's neighbors going to face their challenges with force or with "a different kind of awareness"? Is male violence built into city life? The novel questions whether violence is inevitable.

Sinclair finds alternatives to violence in "the changelings," the special young people in each family who want to break free of old suspicions. Like the boys of the gang, the parents also scan the street anxiously for potential dangers. Jewish and African American elders transfer their old traumas onto each other and thus regard each other as constant threats. With post-traumatic logic, Vincent's neighbor sees the appearance of a black man on East 120th as the first step toward another Holocaust: "Today was like the first bomb. Next is the crematorium" (266). Similarly, Clara's parents are always crouched and ready to spring at an unseen enemy: " 'Girl, you stay away from them white folks,' they keep saying. 'You colored, you stay with colored. Those white folks're waiting to get you. Take anything you got. Hurt you, kill you. Girl, you watch out!' So what do you do? Wherever you go, you got your fists all ready to let go" (137).

Attempting to break free of this post-traumatic worldview, the changelings want "to learn how to be braver than their parents" (33). They see integration as a conduit to joy, relaxation, and freedom. The seventeen-year-old Jules writes a Yiddish poem about black and white becoming each other: " 'It's got joy in it,' Jules had said. ' "A whole world dances and is full of joy" ' " (265). The new city is an open city, liberated from fear and grief. Vincent declares, "I'm going to be free, so I can go out in the world" (135).

Sinclair builds the new city on pacifist ideals. Although the younger generation's bond begins with a shared knife, it ends in reconciliation. Dave asks forgiveness for his attack against Vincent, and the two make the courageous gesture of helping a black man after he has been attacked on East 120th Street. This gesture emerges not from the world of adult ethics but from the childhood world of free play. To create a neighborhood where they can feel they belong, Vincent and Dave turn into their old selves running fast across the street. Childhood exhilaration in the face of danger becomes political courage.

> Then, suddenly, Dave was running across the street after Vincent, trying to unknot his boxing gloves with his teeth. He was on solid ground again; that first glimpse of Vincent running—the familiar figure in pants, the fast, daring leader of all the fighting and snitching years—was like knowing, for the first time since the break-up of the gang, where he belonged.
>
> When he got to Vincent she was kneeling beside the man, digging for her handkerchief, saying: "Hey, come on, get up. Come on, Mister, I'll help you get up."
>
> "Vincent!" Dave said, kneeling by her.
>
> They looked into each other's eyes intently, sharing a togetherness again that held all the old freedom and gladness of companionship, all the fiercely shared danger. (236)

Hibernating

The need to hibernate and heal creates another form of emotional containment yet also a pathway into an uncontained world. Most American novels after World War II catch their characters in a certain phase of life: what Jack Kerouac calls "the beat and evil days that come to guys in their middle twenties."[3] The action often concerns a period of withdrawal after injury. The narrative focuses on the second phase of aftershock, when everyone else starts thinking you really ought to be getting on with your life by now. Main characters often undergo a series of questions from girlfriends, elders, or mentors baffled by their refusals of conventional success. The protagonists can only reply with silence, distraction, or "I don't know." Sylvia Plath's main character in *The Bell Jar* is Esther Greenwood, a patient at a psychiatric hospital. Esther reflects on life after shock after she finishes a series of shock treatments. "There ought, I thought, to be a ritual for being born twice—patched, retreaded and approved for the road, I was trying to think of an appropriate one when Doctor Nolan appeared from nowhere and touched me on the shoulder."[4]

The postwar novel becomes just that, a ritual for being born twice. It provides the transitional moment for young people who are supposed to have fully transitioned already. Books like *The Catcher in the Rye, On the Road,* and *The Bell Jar* have inspired a fiercely loyal readership among young adults searching for their own truths in a world where everyone else seems certain of the correct path. Many postwar novels turn on a significant birthday that marks a delayed coming-of-age or a failure to come of age. In *Brown Girl, Brownstones, On the Road, The Subterraneans,* and *The Messenger,* the key age is twenty-nine going on thirty. In *No-No Boy* and *Goodbye, Columbus,* the significant birthdays are twenty-five and twenty-three. Concerned mentors and loved ones often refer to the character's age when asking their barrage of well-intentioned questions. In Walker Percy's *The Moviegoer,* Binx Bolling's aunt interrogates him as a warm-up to his thirtieth birthday. Characteristically, Binx refuses to explain or justify himself. His reply is ambiguous, or as he says, "lame." Like most veterans, he doesn't see the war as a cause for his current limbo. Instead, his refusal of conventional success seems a nameless, existentialist gesture for its own sake.

> "Of course!" she cries. "You're doing something every man used to do. When your father finished college, he had his Wanderjahr, a fine year's ramble up the Rhine and down the Loire, with a pretty girl on one arm and a good comrade on the other. What happened to you

when you finished college? War. And I'm so proud of you for that. But that's enough to take it out of any man."

Wanderjahr. My heart sinks. We do not understand each other after all. If I thought I'd spent the last four years as a Wanderjahr, before settling down, I'd shoot myself on the spot. . . .

"Now, I want you to make me a promise."

"Yes ma'am."

"Your birthday is one week from today."

"Is that right?"

"You will be thirty years old. Don't you think a thirty year old man ought to know what he wants to do with his life?"

"Yes."

"Will you tell me?"

"Then?"

"Yes. Next Wednesday afternoon. . . . I'll meet you here at this spot. Will you promise to come?"

"Yes ma'am." (49–50)

If we did not know that this ritual takes place in nearly every postwar novel, the exchange might seem characteristic only of a particular social class: the elder testing whether the young scion will assume his proper role in a patrician family. After all, Aunt Emily's breathless Eurocentrism marks her class background with exaggerated clarity. However, if we read across a wide spectrum of postwar novels, we see that this ritual is not individual but generational. Many young men and women were in limbo in ways they could not justify or explain.

World War II, of course, offers a compelling explanation. The younger generation viewed the postwar era with shock and skepticism. The transition was abrupt from the deprivations of depression and war to a postwar state of affluence and "everything's fine now." The Korean War made few dents in the eerie postwar optimism. The figure of the maladjusted veteran suggests a continued, if submerged, unease. His posttraumatic detachment lends him a kind of second sight. He acquires cult status because of his superior gifts at social observation. Toward the end of *Brown Girl, Brownstones,* Paule Marshall's young heroine meets Clive Springer, a classic example of the troubled yet insightful World War II veteran. Clive, too, is hibernating, watching life from the sidelines. "His tall slack body, under a worn bulky coat, gave the impression that it had once been full-fleshed and powerful—and this, along with his hooded eyes, made him somehow like an athlete who had been permanently injured in the heat of a rough game and now sat watching it without enthusiasm from the side lines. His gaze, distant yet piercing, transfixed

Selina now, baring her every defect, it seemed, but offering no comment, passing no judgment."[5]

Postwar novelists faced the artistic challenge of writing vivid stories about people who consider themselves numbed or deadened. They responded to this challenge by inventing a postdated narrative style, in which the story begins after the drama has ended. Discussing first-person narration in the postwar novel, Thomas Schaub notes, "One of the characteristic voices of this period is the voice of a narrator just getting over an unspecified mental illness."[6] In writers like Jack Kerouac and J. D. Salinger, the illness itself is scarcely mentioned; it simply provides a frame for the story of an aftermath.

This storytelling mode bears a concealed relationship to the war. Many novels concern a submerged mourning for a dead brother: for instance, *The Catcher in the Rye, Breakfast at Tiffany's,* and *Brown Girl, Brownstones.* Binx in *The Moviegoer* mourns not just one but three dead brothers and takes these losses as an unremarkable matter of course. The mourning is never the main point. Rather, grief becomes a culturally shared backdrop for stories. The period of recovery from shock becomes a predominant way to tell a story, even a story that has nothing to do with literal injury or death. Postwar classics like *The Catcher in the Rye* (1951) and *Invisible Man* (1952) are told as a series of shocks considered in retrospect. *The Catcher in the Rye* concerns a teenager recently kicked out of prep school, not a returning war veteran. In early short stories, however, *Catcher*'s main character, Holden Caulfield, originally appears as a soldier reported missing in action in World War II. Salinger began publishing these story-size fragments of the novel in 1945, even before he left the army.[7] His novel about a dazed and alienated young man in the second stages of mourning his younger brother's death must have had specific resonances for a nation mourning 292,000 war casualties.[8]

Ralph Ellison's *Invisible Man* also shows how World War II had resonances for a novel far removed from the war itself. A comparison with Chester Himes's *If He Hollers Let Him Go* (1945) reveals the distinctive characteristics of the postwar novel as opposed to the wartime novel. Himes and Ellison both conceived their novels in the same cultural context of war-related racism. Himes's novels deals directly with the pressures on African American defense workers, while Ellison explained in an essay: "During the historical moment when I was working out the concept of *Invisible Man* my people were involved in a terrific quarrel with the federal government over our not being allowed to participate in the war as combat personnel in the armed forces on an equal basis, and because we were not even being allowed to work in the war industries on an equal basis with other Americans. This quarrel led to my concern with the nature of leadership."[9]

Despite this shared context, Himes and Ellison tell a story in entirely different ways. In *If He Hollers Let Him Go,* the consequences of racism unfold moment by moment, in present tense. Rage and fear career at the reader like the car crashes in a Hollywood movie. By contrast, *Invisible Man* contemplates trauma in retrospect. From the safety of his underground hideout, the Invisible Man reflects on "all the shock-absorbing phrases that I had learned all my life."[10] He learns how to integrate a series of past shocks into his vision of the world and himself. "And now all past humiliations became precious parts of my experience, and for the first time, leaning against that stone wall in the sweltering night, I began to accept my past and, as I accepted it, I felt memories welling up within me" (496). Shock—as metaphor and physical reality—intrudes on every key episode in *Invisible Man.* In the battle royal, the young Invisible Man literally learns how to absorb shock:

> I lunged for a yellow coin lying on the blue design of the carpet, touching it and sending a surprised shriek to join those rising around me. I tried frantically to remove my hand but could not let go. A hot, violent force tore through my body, shaking me like a wet rat. The rug was electrified. The hair bristled up on my head as I shook myself free. My muscles jumped, my nerves jangled, writhed. . . . Ignoring the shock by laughing, as I brushed the coins off quickly, I discovered that I could contain the electricity—a contradiction, but it works. (27)

This passage serves as a microcosm of postwar containment culture. The issue becomes not the shock itself but how to contain the shock. "Call me Jack-the-Bear, for I am in a state of hibernation," says the Invisible Man (6). Like *The Bell Jar* and *The Catcher in the Rye, Invisible Man* is a set of tales told from within the perspective of an asylum. We can see the asylum—whether the crawl space underneath a suburban house, a psychiatric hospital, a fallout shelter, or the Invisible Man's basement hideout—as a powerful metaphor in postwar discourse. In 1961, sociologist Erving Goffman published *Asylums: Essays on the Social Situations of Mental Patients and Other Inmates.* In studying the adaptations of mental patients, Goffman compared the psychiatric hospital to that larger institution society itself. "The practice of reserving something of oneself from the clutch of an institution is very visible in mental hospitals and prisons but can be found in more benign and less totalistic institutions, too. I want to argue that this recalcitrance is not an incidental mechanism of defense but rather an essential constituent of the self. . . . Our status is backed by the solid buildings of the world, while our sense of personal identity often resides in the cracks."[11]

Camping Out

This opposition between the mainstream and the youthful margins was particularly evident in New York City, with its unique postwar status. New York simultaneously became the corporate capital of the world and the subcultural capital of the world. Postwar fiction usually defines itself as part of the subcultural world rather than the corporate-dominated consensus. The clash between two worldviews is particularly evident in New York City fiction, the focus of Part III. As in Goffman's architectural metaphor, the postwar novel proclaims itself from the cracks between corridors of gleaming high-rises. It's no accident that much of the action takes place in alleys. With their powerful series of refusals, postwar novels serve as a report from between the cracks. They express not only hibernation from society but the movement toward an alternative vision of society.

After World War II, New York City became the corporate, political, and financial capital of the Western world. Under urban renewal czar Robert Moses, New York acquired a shining new face to match its new status. Like other American cities, New York became much more divided by income and race.[12] Redevelopment cleared out poor nonwhites to build segregated housing for middle-class whites. Evicting nearly half a million people, disproportionately poor, black, and Puerto Rican, "'slum clearance' created new slums as fast as they were clearing the old."[13] Revisiting Harlem in 1960, James Baldwin commented first and foremost on the new low-income housing projects for those displaced and excluded from old neighborhoods and decent new housing.

> There is a housing project standing now where the house in which we grew up once stood, and one of those stunted city trees is snarling where our doorway used to be. . . . The projects in Harlem are hated. They are hated almost as much as policemen, and this is saying a great deal. And they are hated for the same reason: both reveal, unbearably, the real attitude of the white world, no matter how many liberal speeches are made, no matter how many lofty editorials are written, no matter how many civil-rights commissions are set up.[14]

Throughout the fifties, this inequity of development stayed hidden from most middle-class people. Protest remained "an underground movement" beneath the city's new corridors of gleaming corporate headquarters.[15] Therefore, the displacement shows up in fiction as a vague haunting or unease rather than a concrete fact. The mirror image to urban renewal's uprooting is postwar fiction's impermanent, nomadic sense of place. The trope of "the haunted brownstone" appears repeatedly in postwar novels, signaling the end of the human-scale buildings in New York's classic old neighborhoods. Main characters camp out in haunted brownstones in Truman Capote's *Breakfast at Tiffany's* (1958), Paule Marshall's *Brown Girl, Brownstones* (1959), and Charles S. Wright's *The Messenger* (1963). Wright's narrator, Charlie, muses, "This country has split open my head with a golden eagle's beak. Regardless of how I try, the parts won't come together. And this old midtown brownstone is waiting mutely for the demolition crew."[16] Novels suggest that something indefinably rotten is going on behind the city's shining new facades.

Wright's *The Messenger* provides an excellent example of literary marginality within postwar New York's corporate success. The novel chronicles a spring and summer in the life of Charlie Stevenson, who inhabits multiple marginal categories. Working at minimum wage for a Manhattan messenger service, he observes corporate environments as an outsider looking in. He lives in a condemned brownstone in Hell's Kitchen. He hangs out with drag queens, beatniks, and junkies. He is a bisexual, alcoholic, African American existentialist who occasionally turns tricks. Perhaps for these reasons, Wright's deft novel has never reappeared in print.[17] From his apartment window Charlie observes Goffman's "cracks," the islands of identity between straightforward lines of business.

> There is an open doorway between Pizza House and Tip Top Parking. It is deep and dark, almost the width of my narrow room. Men enter this dark, brooding tomb to urinate or to take long nips from a hip-pocket pint. The brilliant neon signs and street lights create only a gray haze there; it's a kind of island in evening fog. If you are not too particular and don't mind standing up, it is a fine place to have sex, and quite a number of people do just that. The people passing are locked in a dream world, their eyes focused elsewhere. The island is a safe and secret place. (100–101)

Although they have little else in common, Sylvia Plath and Charles S. Wright both view Manhattan as a haunted, repressed place where one must carve out one's own marginal sensibility. They create their own islands. Thus they show the common sensibility of their generation. Plath's novel *The Bell Jar* appeared in 1963, the same year as *The Messenger*. The two New Yorks, that of the underemployed, world-weary African American messenger and that of the up-and-coming, innocent German American college girl, are uncannily similar, like mirror images staring at each other across Central Park. Both novelists see the fashion world as the emblem of corporate New York's frightening unreality. Women's perfectly made-up bodies serve as markers of repressed trauma. Charlie comments on one of his messenger jobs: "And on this first day of May, everyone is talking labor. I am silent. I have just delivered several boxes of dresses to the garment district. How I hate that place. Laura Vee models in that gilded Buchenwald" (12).

In this glossy new environment, how can one see and register the scars of history, the violence of World War II, the Cold War, and redevelopment? The violence of both wars seems directly related to New York's sense of displacement. Plath's Esther Greenwood begins her story, "It was a queer, sultry summer, the summer they electrocuted the Rosenbergs, and I didn't know what I was doing in New York."[18] Plath never explains who the Rosenbergs were or that they were executed as Soviet spies in the classic case of Cold War hysteria. But the repetition of their name throughout the novel suggests that something is wrong in fifties New York and not just Esther herself. Like Wright, Plath associates atrocity with designer clothes and slick new facades. Esther's whole identity seems marginal and invisible before the glass boxes of Midtown.

> I knew something was wrong with me that summer, because all I could think about was the Rosenbergs and how stupid I'd been to buy all those uncomfortable, expensive clothes, hanging limp as fish in my closet, and how all the little successes I'd totted up so happily at college fizzled to nothing outside the slick marble and plate-glass fronts along Madison Avenue.
>
> I was supposed to be having the time of my life. (1–2)

Although the city looms and threatens, novelists can reinvent a new sense of place. Manhattan defeats Esther, and she leaves it for the suburbs and a suicidal depression. Charlie, by contrast, reworks Manhattan on his own terms. True enough, as Esther suggests, the destruction of neighborhoods has transformed the east side of Midtown into a corridor of "slick marble and plate-glass fronts."[19] Charlie sees the same new buildings; however, he reenvisions the neighborhood in terms of its wartime past and his own hustler's geography. Redevelopment may have eliminated buildings, but it cannot eliminate the city's subcultural communities. As we shall explore in subsequent chapters, subcultural fiction completely revised the postwar urban landscape.

> To score on the smart Eastside without good connections, you have to know the right bartenders in the right bars who will set Johns up for a cut. But male and female hustlers are always telling me in sad voices, "Gee, kid, you should have been around during World War II.

Or even the early fifties. Things jumped then. All you had to do was just walk down Third Avenue. You could even afford to be grand. Turn down tricks."

Now the scene has changed. Big new office and apartment buildings, bright new street lights, the cops clamping down like the great purge. Johns are also not as easy to come by. This is an age of elegance, stupidity, and fakery. (39)

Redevelopment cannot erase a multilayered history. Through their memories, hustlers resist their own erasure. This subculture isn't nostalgic for the good old days of small-town values but for the good old days of easy tricks. While Esther sees her New York self as a lone insignificant speck, Charlie sees New York together with his fellow hustlers.

Throughout the novel Charlie delights in revealing how hustlers use the new, cleaned-up, respectable New York for their own purposes. Disputing the idea of hustling as a lonely, horrific, and subterranean world, Wright's hustlers converge in ordinary public spaces like cafeterias, subways, and stores. Like any sorority, the con artists of Charlie's block hold regular meetings in a cafeteria: "old, sweet-voiced, motherly women, all of whom have a profitable con game. Their organization is a strict and exclusive one, run on the lines of the D.A.R. Not just anyone can get in. Their meetings are held in Horn and Hardart over tea and rolls, once a week, between two and four p.m." In Charlie's drag-queen circles, Miss Lena calls Bobby "Miss Subway" because he got busted for turning a trick there (89, 87). Miss Lena herself has made good use of Midtown:

Lena had discovered that there were good scores to be made in broad daylight between six and nine a.m. But this was usually on Saturdays. But it was on an early Sunday morning that Lena got busted in the doorway of a Fifth Avenue dress shop. The John said that Lena had cleaned him for a hundred and seventy-five dollars. Yet when the cops took her down, she only had ninety in her stockings. Lena never said what happened to the other eighty-five. (88)

This preservation of subcultural memory and space in the midst of corporate-driven redevelopment has important resonances with New York's more recent history. In 1993 artist Barbara Kruger lamented the current redevelopment and sanitizing of Times Square:

The problem posed: how to make Times Square safe for corporate capital, how to most efficiently erase the area's explicit sexualities and forthright mixing of black and white, poverty and big bucks, homeless New Yorkers and wide-eyed tourists, the Broadway theatuh and the choreographies of the street. If left to their own devices (which they almost always are), there's no doubt that the powers that be would handily convert Times Square into another tired stretch of boring behemoths which, bereft of advertising and commerce, would transform streetlevel (in the style of Park Avenue and the Avenue of the Americas) into merely another arid alley separating one CEO from another. . . . In other words, the "reclamation" of Times Square, while relieving the area of some of its most apparent difficulties, is engaged in the militant removal of all that is "unsightly," sweeping out of sight and under the rug the complex problems of an intense urban culture showered with both extraordinarily lustrous wealth and systemic poverty and disease.[20]

Kruger's statement helps illuminate the moral complexities of Charles S. Wright's New York, with its intersections of degradation and boredom. As we shall explore more fully in chapter 8, Times Square has long been a center of the sex trade and alternative sexualities. The influx of troops during World War II greatly expanded this role, and it continued in the postwar era. Certainly, the hustling subculture is far from an ideal world. *The Messenger* reveals how hustling goes together with drug abuse, violence, poverty, and depression. However, as Kruger notes, the solution is not a corporate cover-up transforming Midtown into "merely another arid alley." Redevelopment just sweeps problems under the rug. By tracing a hustler's geography onto Midtown, Wright attempts to resist the forces of cover-up. The novel's title might refer not only to Charlie's job description but also to the phrase "Don't shoot the messenger." Charlie can't be blamed for Manhattan's lifestyles; he just records what he sees.

As Kruger also notes, the "forthright mixing" of different peoples is a New York characteristic worth preserving. Charlie's perspective marks the beginning of a new urban vision more integrated than the segregated imagination explored in part 2. It forms part of an Open City evident in postwar cult novels. Charlie's friendships move back and forth between sexualities, classes, and races, and his work moves back and forth between street hustling and Wall Street. Well into the era of civil rights, Charlie sees himself excluded from conventional success not by racism but by his own emphatic resistance. Like many male writers of his day, he personifies conventional success as a domineering, frighteningly respectable middle-class woman. With classic postwar masculinism, his pornographic metaphor equates corporate success with sexual submission.

In comparing Goffman's *Asylums* to postwar corporate hegemony, Jackson Lears writes: "The only solution Goffman could imagine was an ironically detached acceptance of the fragmented self."²¹ This stance typifies postwar narrators like Charlie, gazing out his window with ironic detachment.

> I'm one of the boys, I'm as American as apple pie. But no. I cannot, simply cannot, don a mask and suck the c—— of that sweet, secure bitch, middle-class American life. Sometimes I sit in my fifth-floor window and watch the young Americans out on the town, healthy, laughing, contented as mother hens. Their faces indistinguishable as blades of grass. Look how happy they are! They are united and one. Yes, I could become one of the horde, despite the fact that I am Negro. (Remember the black dots on the great white field?) I could stop worrying about writing, about the corruption of this city, the world, and the fate of mankind. I could get a soft, safe, white-collar job, save the coins, marry, and all in the name of middle-class sanctity. (57)

For Charlie, stability would mean the loss of thinking for himself. His sense of place exemplifies the subcultural vision I call "camping out." Camping out both resists and mirrors the uprooting of urban renewal. In opposition to the wrecking and bulldozing of redevelopment, camping out rests on the city more lightly. Novelists describe the city's ephemeral beauty with great detail and affection. Their loving attachment to place, however, carries its own share of detachment. The transience of camping out reflects as well as resists the uprooting of urban renewal. Like many other postwar narrators, Charlie often repeats that he'll be leaving soon: "I am getting my possessions in order. Tonight there will be an auction in my pad. Everything will be sold, got rid of. And then I'll go away" (122). Like the protagonists in other postwar novels, notably William Burroughs's *Naked Lunch* (1959), Saul Bellow's *The Adventures of Augie March* (1953), and Truman Capote's *Breakfast at Tiffany's* (1958), Charlie plans on heading for Mexico.

Charlie's observations of city life outside his window are detached and attached at the same time. Always observed from the same vantage point, his landscapes are fixed as postcards, with a precise sense of place. He has a great eye for detail, describing commuter traffic and parking lots as if they were Renaissance art. He understands New York's combination of degradation and loveliness. Only a true lover of New York could capture and appreciate the rhythms of truck drivers' expletives.

> Nine-thirty a.m. A lusterless pearl sky, soft summer rain. The click-click, tap-tap, and shuffle of feet pressing jobward. The truck driver's four-letter morning song, "Get ya fuckin' ass in ge-aar." The

somnolent, suburban drivers creeping into Tip Top Parking. I look out the window at the bumper-to-bumper traffic blocked to Fifth Avenue. The cars are like a hem in the great cape of Rockefeller Center. The slender trees lining the street look like cheap corsages. Through the veil of rain, the Empire State building looks very lovely this morning. No sign of life at the Elmwood Hotel except the fourth-floor ash-blonde making her face with a hand mirror.

Afternoon. The staccato tone of rain. Indistinct street voices. The cool air has a touch of autumn. A neighbor comes in to tell me there's been a police raid. It doesn't interest me. At five o'clock, the darkening sky is like the early dusk of winter. The blaze of neon cuts the approaching darkness. I long for the end of summer, and going away. (77)

Despite its vivid particularity, the viewpoint expresses the transience of the traffic it describes. The gridlock, the commuters, and the parking lot below reflect the new world Robert Moses had just built, with its overclogged highways feeding commuters into Manhattan from new suburbs. Charlie's own longing for "going away" belies his seeming attachment to place and links him to the postwar city's constant movement. His hustler's geography cannot stop the endless changes.

A Diaspora Sense of Place

Postwar novelists did not just reflect or oppose urban renewal; they also moved beyond it to create new city visions. In developing a sense of place, these novelists faced two challenges. First, how do you write about your own heritage and history in the midst of displacement? In other words, how do you depict your roots when your roots keep moving? Second, how do you write about the interactions among different groups in a world of segregated enclaves?

One method of response is to develop a diaspora sense of place. The postwar generation acquired what certain immigrant groups have long possessed: a sense of "home" situated not in one place but triangulated among multiple sites. Since World War II more and more Americans have a diaspora sense of place, whether that diaspora consists of multiple inner cities, multiple Renaissance Fairs, or multiple research parks. Louis Chu's novel *Eat a Bowl of Tea* (1961) symbolizes how the postwar generation reappropriated a centuries-old diaspora sense of place. On the conspicuous level, the novel concerns the postwar generation's rebellion against the restrictive world of its elders (in this case, the aging bachelor society of New York's Chinatown). Like many other postwar couples, Ben Loy and Mei Oi move out west to San Francisco and find a happier life based on same-generation bonds with other war veterans and their wives.

> He liked San Francisco. With the passing of each day, the New York chapter of his life was pushed further back in his memory. New York represented parental supervision and the reckless mistakes of youth. Now all this was being replaced by new surroundings and new attitudes. The proverbial parental shackle had been cut. For the first time Ben Loy knew and enjoyed emancipation. New frontiers, new people, new times, new ideas unfolded. He had come to a new golden mountain.[22]

Yet on a subtler level, the novel relies on the traditional Chinese American diaspora. Ben Loy and Mei Oi do not move into America at large; rather, they move from New York's Chinatown to San Francisco's Chinatown. Between bicoastal Chinatowns, China's Kwangtung Province, and the China Pagoda Restaurant in Stanton, Connecticut, the novel's sense of place rests on multiple axes.

What happens when a writer tries to represent not just his or her own ethnic diaspora but multiple intersecting diasporas? By looking at parallels between two novels, we can see how separate enclaves form dialogues with each other. The postwar generation steps out from the neutral zone and makes an opening move toward interaction. Both published in 1959, Paule Marshall's *Brown Girl, Brownstones* and Philip Roth's *Goodbye, Columbus* document two different diasporas: Jews and Caribbean Americans in Greater New York. Like Plath's and Wright's characters poised on either side of Central Park, *Brown Girl, Brownstones* and *Goodbye, Columbus* tell parallel stories on either side of Manhattan. They speak to each other across two rivers.

Marshall traces the movements of an African diaspora from the Caribbean island of Barbados to Stuyvesant Heights, Brooklyn, and on to the posher Crown Heights. Roth follows the Jews of Newark out to the suburb of Short Hills. These novels concern typical postwar mobility from city to suburb. However, both young protagonists maintain a sense of home despite postwar abandonment. Both resist the idea of cities as sites of inevitable decay. Both attempt to love a ghost town.

If we look at these novels in tandem, we see a city vision moving beyond resistance into diaspora. The two novels step outside the segregated imagination to form a dialogue with each other as parallel stories. As cultural figures, the masculinist Philip Roth and the womanist Paule Marshall could scarcely be further apart. However, their first novels reflect the common concerns of their generation. Each tells a story of "my people" with a background awareness of other people. Thus they dispute

Carlo Rotella's diachronic model of postwar city fiction, in which a black community replaces a white one. Rather, the Jewish Americans in Roth and the Barbadian Americans in Marshall exist in the same time frame and follow the same trajectory. True, the groups lead parallel lives that scarcely touch; however, the novelists are aware of each other's realities. This awareness shows the postwar generation's desire to move beyond the segregated imagination.

The affinities between Marshall and Roth are both generational and regional. Otherwise, their literary reputations could hardly be further apart. Like John Updike, Saul Bellow, and Norman Mailer, Philip Roth was a celebrity, a conspicuously male postwar writer famous since the publication of his first book. His name is synonymous with postwar fiction. *Goodbye, Columbus* became a cult classic popular with college students. The paperback edition was reprinted eighteen times between 1959 and 1970, while *Brown Girl, Brownstones* was reprinted only once during those same years. Marshall's first novel went out of print between 1970 and the Feminist Press reprint in 1981. The author of many subsequent novels, Paule Marshall is now respected as a leader among African American and Caribbean American women writers. However, few critics place *Brown Girl, Brownstones* in its original fifties context.[23] Nonetheless, Roth and Marshall participate equally in their generation's worldview.

Roth and Marshall express their affinities in an uncanny shared trope. In both novels, the main character has premarital sex on a discarded sofa from the old neighborhood. In *Goodbye, Columbus,* the couple are Neil Klugman and his girlfriend, Brenda Patimkin. The encounter takes place in a storeroom in her parents' suburban home.

> "What is this?" I said.
> > "A storeroom. Our old furniture."
> > "How old?"
> > "From Newark," she said. "Come here."
> > . . . "Make love to me, Neil. Right now."
> > "Where?"
> > "Do it! Here. On this cruddy cruddy cruddy sofa."
> And I obeyed her.[24]

In *Brown Girl, Brownstones,* the encounter takes place between Selina Boyce and Clive Springer in a basement apartment his parents own.

> At first, she went to him nearly every day after school. He lived apart from his parents in a brownstone rooming house they owned, in the large basement kitchen which he had converted into a kind of

studio. . . . They were lying at either end of the long sofa, facing each other, their legs entwined. . . . "So home to Brooklyn!" he cried, pointing wildly. "Wolfe was wrong. You can go home again. But it costs. And he was right. Only the dead do know Brooklyn! So here I lie, surrounded by certain remnants: this sofa, which was so damn sacrosanct when I was a boy that I could never sit on it. . . . "I don't want to talk!" he suddenly shouted so that she started. Laughing, he leaned over and pulled her down on him. "I don't want to talk. I just want to forget inside you," he said softly against her mouth. "When we wake it'll be evening and we can take a drive before you go home." (241–244)

The young lover becomes the guardian of the parents' past. Paradoxically, Neil, Selina, and their partners rebel against family convention by communing with the family ghosts. Their acts lend new vigor and loyalty to superseded spaces—the storeroom for the Newark furniture, the rental unit left behind in the old neighborhood. Neil and Selina reject the idea of progress by moving backward and forward through the diaspora simultaneously. By making love on the sofa, they try to catch the family history in flight. They move forward into their own generation's rebellious sexuality. Their acts of unmarried sex are shocking in fifties households, "where sex was a commodity you traded for marriage."[25] Yet they also move backward in time, camping out in a history their parents have rejected. The sofa represents another "crack" of identity in the postwar status-driven world. Despite the cleanliness prosperity affords, young people immerse themselves in the filth of history.

Roth's and Marshall's young protagonists occupy a midway position between their own generation and the world of their hard-striving elders. On the one hand, Neil and Selina share the "numbness" and "swinging nothing style" of their peers. They question the materialism and conformity their parents celebrate. On the other hand, both feel tenderly toward elders who come from a heritage of oppression. Precisely because they honor their heritages, Neil and Selina feel tenderness for the cities their people are leaving. This tenderness complicates both novels' sense of place.

While their elders grappled with deprivation, postwar young adults grapple with prosperity. Neil and Selina face the moral complexity of war-generated money. A houseguest visiting from Newark, Neil Klugman casts ironic eyes on Brenda's family's wealth. Neil's description of their basement refrigerator makes the folkways of suburban New Jersey seem complex and strange. The old Newark appliances yield sudden abundance. Although most of the novel takes place in Short Hills, Roth always traces the routes of the diaspora. One can follow through food the route from city to suburb, modesty to affluence, Yiddishkeit to assimilation, herring in cream sauce to honeydew melons.

> Beside the freezer, incongruously, was a tall old refrigerator; its ancient presence was a reminder to me of the Patimkin roots in Newark. This same refrigerator had once stood in the kitchen of an apartment in some four-family house, probably in the same neighborhood where I had lived all my life, first with my parents and then, when the two of them went wheezing off to Arizona, with my aunt and uncle. After Pearl Harbor the refrigerator had made the move up to Short Hills; Patimkin Kitchen and Bathroom Sinks had gone to war: no new barracks was complete until it had a squad of Patimkin sinks lined up in its latrine.
>
> I opened the door of the old refrigerator; it was not empty. No longer did it hold butter, eggs, herring in cream sauce, ginger ale, tuna fish salad, an occasional corsage—rather it was heaped with fruit, shelves swelled with it, every color, every texture, and hidden within, every kind of pit. There were greengage plums, black plums, red plums, apricots, nectarines, peaches, long horns of grapes, black, yellow, red, and cherries, cherries flowing out of boxes and staining everything scarlet. And there were melons—cantaloupes and honeydews—and on the top shelf, half of a huge watermelon, a thin sheet of wax paper clinging to its bare red face like a wet lip. Oh Patimkin! Fruit grew in their refrigerator and sporting goods dropped from their trees! (30–31)

The Patimkin family fortunes came so directly from war, Roth makes it sound as if the refrigerator's move up to Short Hills were part of a troop deployment on the heels of Pearl Harbor. Postwar prosperity becomes an ambush of excess. To the naive eye, the fruits and sporting goods of the Patimkin Eden could occur naturally. We know better, since we know the distances traveled inch by inch and sink by sink. Neil resists amnesia. He reads the spare past into the juicy and abundant present. He's a walking reminder of the old neighborhood.

In *Brown Girl, Brownstones,* a more modest degree of prosperity also comes from war. Silla Boyce frightens her daughter Selina because she has no qualms about turning a profit from war any way she can. Selina even calls her mother "Hitler" because she turns Selina's unproductive father over to the INS for deportation (183–186). Marshall frequently compares Silla's power to the ferocity of World War II. The mother and the war keep going toe to toe. The novel's best-known line, addressed approvingly to Silla, comes straight from the wartime context: "Talk yuh talk, Silla! Be-Jees, in this white-man world you got to take yuh mouth and make a gun" (70). When Selina questions her mother's materialism, Silla defends herself fiercely. Selina opines, "Some people don't care about those things in store windows," and her mother responds, " 'Love! Give me a dollar in my hand any day!' she cried in a voice that was too loud to be convincing. 'Oh, I can see what you gon give, soul. I can see from the way you think now you ain gon amount to much. Scorning work and money like the father before you' " (103, 104–105). Compared with the relentless exploitation of the Barbadian sugarcane fields, American defense plant work is a true opportunity.

> The workers, white and colored, clustered and scurried around the machine-mass, trying, it seemed, to stave off the destruction it threatened. They had built it but, ironically, it had overreached them, so that now they were only small insignificant shapes against its overwhelming complexity. . . . Watching her, Selina felt the familiar grudging affection seep under her amazement. Only the mother's own formidable force could match that of the machines; only the mother could remain indifferent to the brutal noise. . . . Selina glanced up and away. A feeling nudged her and fled: the mother was like the machines, some larger form of life with an awesome beauty all her own. (99–101)

Silla sees the war in a diaspora context in which black women have traditionally represented oppressed labor. With her acute awareness of global power relations, Silla has no special allegiance or sentimentality. She has to be portable. She sees World War II as just "another white-man war" designed to make poor people suffer. (65, 69). Her daughter Selina sees the war as a machine of "overwhelming complexity." One of its complexities, of course, is its ability to bring money out of destruction. Only her mother is strong and ruthless enough to match the power of the war machine and wrestle success from it. Naturally, the younger generation isn't sure what to learn from elders so strong, so materialistic, so scarred, and so intent.

In both novels, young people cherish a ghost town abandoned by an older generation fixed on upward mobility. The abandonment of Stuyvesant Heights, the Brooklyn neighborhood depicted in *Brown Girl, Brownstones,* comes about through the inner resolve of Barbadians like Silla and the outer forces of urban renewal. The Barbadians try to keep one step ahead of the city's game. At the Barbadian Association, a neighbor "warned them of the city's plans to replace the brownstones around Fulton Park eventually with housing projects. 'Gone!' His short arm cut the air. 'All those houses we sweat so to buy and now, at last, making little money from gon soon be gone!'" (220). During the novel's writing, poor African Americans and Puerto Ricans crowded into Stuyvesant Heights, displaced from Manhattan to make room for whites-only high-rises. In the course of the fifties and sixties, middle-class Stuyvesant Heights became Bedford-Stuyvesant, one of the poorest and most dangerous areas of New York City.[26]

This knowledge of coming decay haunts the novel's sense of place. Even the book's beginning, set in the 1930s, portrays an intact community as if it were already a ghost town. Documenting a fading culture, Marshall spends the entire first page elaborately describing the brownstones of Stuyvesant Heights and the traditional look of an old Brooklyn neighborhood. The brownstones seem solid, permanent, yet already mourning their own doom. Like the Patimkin's refrigerator, the brownstones are troops ready to be deployed in the battle for prosperity—even if prosperity demands their destruction.

> In the somnolent July afternoon the unbroken line of brownstone houses down the long Brooklyn street resembled an army massed at attention. They were all one uniform red-brown stone. All with high massive stone stoops and black iron-grille fences staving off the sun. All draped in ivy as though mourning. . . . Many houses had bay windows or Gothic stonework; a few boasted turrets raised high above the other roofs. Yet they all shared the same brown monotony. All seemed doomed by the confusion in their design. (3)

Selina Boyce, like Gwendolyn Brooks's Maud Martha, resists the inevitable destruction through her own fierce attachment. Selina's love for the park across the street and the surrounding neighborhood runs counter to the values of urban renewal. New York's postwar zoning policy emphasized empty open space at the expense of pedestrians and neighborhoods.[27] By contrast, Selina at ten years old appreciates the noise, turbulence, and crowds of Brooklyn street life. Fulton Park and Fulton Street are so far from empty, even the sun and the grass emit loud noises. The park murmurs even at night.

> Chauncey Street languished in the afternoon heat, and across from it Fulton Park rose in a cool green wall. After the house, Selina loved the park. The thick trees, the grass—shrill-green in the sun—the statue of Robert Fulton and the pavilion where the lovers met and murmured at night formed, for her, the perfect boundary for her world; the park was the fitting buffer between Chauncey Street's gentility and Fulton Street's raucousness.

> The sun was always loud on Fulton Street. It hung low and dead
> to the pavement, searing the trolley tracks and store windows, bear-
> ing down until the street spun helplessly in an eddy of cars, voices,
> neon signs and trolleys. Selina responded to the turbulence, rush-
> ing and leaping in a dark streak through the crowd. (13)

The neighborhood is the perfect match for Selina. She corresponds
with it and it with her. Like a vigorous ten-year-old, it likes to spin, rush,
and make loud noises. A neighborhood that might seem out of control
to some people sets the perfect boundaries for her imagination. Even in
its decay at the end of the novel, Fulton Park provides the home for
Selina's important life experiences. At eighteen she loses her virginity
in the park with Clive Springer. Their murmurs join those of previous
generations and lend the neighborhood a temporary vigor.

> Giving her a sharp look, the man said, pointing to the statue of Robert
> Fulton, "I used to pride myself on being able to run around the ledge
> without falling as a boy."
> "Me too, and I never met you here?"
> "You were far too young."
> "How old are you?"
> "Twenty-nine."
> "Were you in the war?"
> . . . With a slight misgiving she followed him up the wide stone
> steps and amid the tall fluted columns and stone benches. "Come,
> let's sit in the caretaker's place. In these last dark days of neigh-
> borhood decline it's probably open. We might have to clean out a
> few winos though." But the small dark room with its warm smell of
> leaves was deserted. While she stood in the doorway he found a
> bench, then called, laughing, "You can come in. I promise not to talk
> about the war." (234, 236)

Most important, Clive and Selina share the same childhood memories of the park. By having sex there years later, they assert that the declin-
ing park is still home, because home is the place where new memories
continue to pile up on old memories. Although Clive is a troubled war
veteran, his alliance with Selina indicates the postwar generation's
desire for new laughter, new joy, and a new life that feeds something other
than destruction. The novel's ending counterpoises the new generation's vigor with ruin and departure. A ghostly beginning leads Stuyvesant
Heights inevitably to the blasting of urban renewal. Selina imagines the
inhabitants of the new housing project the way she used to imagine the

white ghosts of her house's previous occupants. As if conducting a funeral service, she remembers the strong women who would have occupied Fulton Park in the past. Yet the vigor of the new inhabitants seems to defy the postwar logic of constant dislocation: "As she passed, a man—silhouetted against a room where everything seemed poised for flight—burst into a fiercely sad song in Spanish" (309). Spring stirs despite the ruin, and lovers continue to murmur in the shadows. By contrast with Walker Percy, urban rubble does not indicate the disappearance of the city's population. Rather, new residents and new races come to take the place of the old. Selina surveys the new housing project amid the rubble of the old brownstones:

> The project receded and she was again the sole survivor amid the wreckage. And suddenly she turned away, unable to look any longer. For it was like seeing the bodies of all the people she had ever known broken, all the familiar voices that had ever sounded in those high-ceilinged rooms shattered—and the pieces piled into this giant cairn of stone and silence. She wanted, suddenly, to leave something with them. But she had nothing. She had left the mother and the meeting hall wearing only the gown and her spring coat. Then she remembered the two silver bangles she had always worn. She pushed up her coat sleeve and stretched one until it passed over her wrist, and, without turning, hurled it high over her shoulder. The bangle rose behind her, a bit of silver against the moon, then curved swiftly downward and struck a stone. A frail sound in that utter silence. (309–310)

Selina remains as a lone urban walker, a "sole survivor," but she is mournful rather than detached. She turns away because the destruction is too painful to observe, as if she gazed at familiar bodies rather than buildings. This is what it means to lose your home, to lose your familiar sights. Like many survivors, she feels a debt to those destroyed. The final tossing of the bangle constitutes a double reminder of diaspora. Since the beginning of the novel we have known that the bangles represent Selina's Caribbean heritage: "Slowly she raised her arm, thin and dark in the sun-haze, circled by two heavy silver bangles which had come from 'home' and which every Barbadian-American girl wore from birth" (5). The bangles move Selina forward and backward through the African diaspora. This symbol of "home" (Barbados) allows Selina to mourn and memorialize the loss of her literal home, Brooklyn. Through her mourning she moves backward against the prevailing currents of upward mobility, fixing her allegiance to one place. Yet in her mourning she throws part of her heritage away while retaining part of it. Like so many young protagonists, Selina will leave soon for a job on a Caribbean-bound ship, and the second bangle will accompany her "home."

Marshall's tale of the Barbadian diaspora takes place within a context of multiple diasporas. The Barbadians' relationship to New York Jews resists an urban-decay model of white ghosts giving way to black ghosts. Barbadians and Jews live parallel lives. The families in *Brown Girl, Brownstones* have a constant imaginary dialogue with an upwardly mobile Jewish community much like the one in Philip Roth's fiction. The constant identification of wealthier people as "the Jews" carries a double connotation. On the one hand, the labeling conveys hatred and anti-Semitism, playing into the old stereotype of Jewish people as stingy and sharp traders. On the other hand, the labeling identifies the Jews as a diaspora like us with lessons to teach us. At first, "the Jew" is a distrustful epithet meaning "the boss." "To scrub the Jew floor to make a penny" is an often-repeated synonym for hard labor (70). Selina imagines her mother and other housecleaners as a community of workers not far removed from the cane fields of Barbados. They bring home to their children not only cast-off clothes but lashing anger.

> What had she and the others who lived down in the gullies and up on the hills behind God's back done on Saturdays? She could never think of the mother alone. It was always the mother and the others, for they were alike—those watchful, wrathful women whose eyes seared and searched and laid bare, whose tongues lashed the world in unremitting distrust. Each morning they took the train to Flatbush and Sheepshead Bay to scrub floors. . . . They returned home laden with throw-offs: the old clothes which the Jews had given them. Whenever the mother forced her to wear them, Selina spent the day hating the unknown child to whom they belonged. (10–11)

It is hard to separate class hatred from racial antagonism. Like other Barbadians in her community, Selina has a imaginary relationship with Jews she hasn't even met. In the course of the novel, however, the community transforms the meaning of walking one step behind the Jews. Many Barbadians accept the stereotype of Jews as uniformly rich people who run the city. Their tone changes from anger at accepting "throw-offs" to learning lessons in success from an older immigrant group. The Barbadians aim to follow the Jews' footsteps into prosperity. The lessons they want to learn are the lessons of postwar modernism: freedom requires constant movement; oppression is staying in one place; success requires a failure to mourn the destruction of home. Across racial lines, the parents' generation shares common values.

"Who say I faulting the Jew? I lift my hat to him. He know how to make a dollar. He own all New York! . . . The white people thought they was gon keep us there but they din know what a Bajan does give. We here now and when they run we gon be right behind them. . . . Every West Indian out here taking a lesson from the Jew landlord and converting these old houses into rooming houses—making the closets-self into rooms some them! —and pulling down plenty-plenty money by the week. And now that the place is near overrun with roomers the Bajans getting out. They going! Every jack-man buying a swell house in dichty Crown Heights." (38–39, 173)

The elder generation finds no way to break the linkage between displacement and success. However, by emphasizing the similarities between the two diasporas, Marshall and Roth permit the younger generation to share a similar worldview across racial lines. Like *Brown Girl, Brownstones, Goodbye, Columbus* shows a strong attachment to neighborhood in spite of displacement. That attachment is poignant because the locality is Newark, New Jersey, rarely celebrated in story or song. Roth's description of Newark's Third Ward echoes Marshall's description of Stuyvesant Heights to an uncanny degree. The diaspora makes the same inevitable trek from city to suburb. In Roth as in Marshall, African Americans follow in the steps of the Jews. There is the same progression from struggling with poverty to struggling with success.

Patimkin Kitchen and Bathroom Sinks was in the heart of the Negro section of Newark. Years ago, at the time of the great immigration, it had been the Jewish section, and still one could see the little fish stores, the kosher delicatessens, the Turkish baths, where my grandparents had shopped and bathed at the beginning of the century. Even the smells had lingered: whitefish, corned beef, sour tomatoes—but now, on top of these, was the grander greasier smell of auto wrecking shops, the sour stink of a brewery, the burning odor from a leather factory; and on the street, instead of Yiddish, one heard the shouts of Negro children playing at Willie Mays with a broom handle and half a rubber ball. The neighborhood had changed: the old Jews like my grandparents had struggled and died, and their offspring had struggled and prospered, and moved further and further west, towards the edge of Newark, then out of it, and up the slope of the Orange Mountains, until they had reached the crest and started down the other side, pouring into Gentile territory as the Scotch-Irish had poured through the Cumberland Gap. Now, in fact, the Negroes were making the same migration, following the steps of the Jews, and those who remained in the Third Ward lived the most squalid of lives and dreamed in their fetid mattresses of the piny smell of Georgia nights. . . . Who would come after the Negroes? Who was left? No one, I thought, and someday these streets, where my grandmother drank hot tea from an old jahrzeit glass, would be empty and we would all of us have moved to the crest of the Orange Mountains, and wouldn't the dead stop kicking at the slats in their coffins then? (64–65)

Roth shares Marshall's awareness of ghosts. In Brooklyn, the lingering old-country smell is codfish, while in Newark it's whitefish, but it's the same haunting. The narrator retains a strong imaginative relationship with the Third Ward, picturing the sipping of hot tea and the dreams of its sleepers. Neil's grief over the abandonment is as active as Selina's. Neil refers to a jahrzeit glass, which commemorates the anniversary of a loved one's death. This brief mention indicates a still-fresh mourning. Yet Neil's narrative also brings immigrant history back to life. He links turn-of-the-century city dwellers to those of the present day and links both to the more celebrated rural pioneers. The immigrants of Newark are central rather than peripheral to the sweep of American history. Furthermore, he shows how the movements of blacks and Jews mirror each other.

Downtown Newark, where Neil works at the public library, is still a vigorous city center. Neil pauses at a park before the work day begins. The landscape itself argues against urban renewal and for the preservation of street life. Like Selina, Neil knows he is at home because he corresponds with his landscape.

Down Washington Street, behind me, was the Newark Museum—I could see it without even looking: two oriental vases in front like spittoons for a rajah, and next to it the little annex to which we had traveled on special buses as schoolchildren. The annex was a brick building, old and vine-covered, and always reminded me of New Jersey's link with the beginning of the country, with George Washington, who had trained his scrappy army—a little bronze tablet informed us children—in the very park where I now sat. At the far end of the park, beyond the Museum, was the bank building where I had gone to college. It had been converted some years before into an extension of Rutgers University; in fact, in what once had been the bank president's waiting room I had taken a course called Contemporary Moral Issues. . . . Sitting there in the park, I felt a deep knowledge of Newark, an attachment so rooted that it could not help but branch out into affection.

Suddenly it was nine o'clock and everything was scurrying. Wobbly-heeled girls revolved through the doors of the telephone building across the way, traffic honked desperately, policemen barked, whistled, and waved motorists to and fro. (21–22)

What is a sense of belonging? It isn't just love or affection. Love follows from "deep knowledge," from many varieties of roots sunk in the same place. Belonging is the ability to read your own history as well as regional history back onto the place, and to connect them with your present life. From one vantage point in the park, Neil can connect up his childhood, his adolescence, his college years, and his current employment to the history of New Jersey from George Washington forward. It's no accident that Neil works in the Newark Public Library, since he represents the fragile continuance of urban public space. Neil attempts to rewrite the story of decline so that Newark stands for something besides moving out and "there goes the neighborhood." This attempt reveals his cross-racial solidarity. Despite the censure of his co-workers, Neil defends the right of a small African American boy to look at an expensive art book in the public library.

> "Those are very expensive books."
> "Don't be so nervous, John. People are supposed to touch them."
> "There is touching," John said sententiously, "and there is touching. Someone should check on him. I was afraid to leave the desk here. You know the way they treat the housing projects we give them."
> "You give them?"
> "The city. Have you seen what they do at Seth Boyden? They throw beer bottles, those big ones, on the lawn. They're taking over the city."
> "Just the Negro sections."
> "It's easy to laugh, you don't live near them." (24)

The co-worker's bigotry makes it clear that multiracial public space is a fragile ideal. John ascribes to the common notion of the postwar city as a space where blacks crowd out whites. He blames the residents of new housing projects, not urban renewal policies, for the city's decline. White people are "we," responsible people to grant favors, while African Americans are "they," the interlopers. Roth disputes this bigotry by showing how well the African American youth belongs in the library. The boy's excitement and total absorption show that he's exactly the kind of person libraries were made to serve. Neil has just been contemplating what it means to belong in Newark; now the boy offers him another definition of belonging. "The lips were parted, the eyes wide, and even the ears seemed to have a heightened receptivity. . . . He lifted the book so I could see. It was an expensive large-sized edition of Gauguin reproductions. The page he had been looking at showed an $8\,^{1}/_{2} \times 11$ print, in color, of three native women standing knee-high in a rose-colored stream. It was a silent picture. He was right" (25).

Defying the logic of segregation, Roth seems to argue that Neil and the boy can and should occupy the same spaces. Neil sweats to preserve the library's relationship to the boy, keeping the Gauguin book away from another patron who requests it. Neil is fighting a losing battle, but a battle worth engaging. Young black males are often unwelcome in public places and needlessly regarded as threats. Most of the library staff assumes that an African American boy cannot coexist peaceably with fine art reproductions and staircases modeled after Versailles. The boy asserts not only his desire for the book but also his desire to pore over it in public: "I likes to come here. I likes them stairs" (43). Like Neil and Selina, he wants to have a solitary adventure downtown, to match himself against the city and see if he corresponds with it. Neil and the boy belong in the library at the same time.

Neil and the boy seem outwardly different but have many parallels. Like Neil's relatives, the boy has "a thick accent." Like Neil, the boy is remarkably receptive and curious. Both dream about exotic women. The boy loses and finds himself in the silent women of Tahiti, while Neil loses and finds himself in Brenda Patimkin of Short Hills. "I sat at the Information Desk thinking about Brenda and reminding myself that that evening I would have to get gas before I started up to Short Hills, which I could see now, in my mind's eye, at dusk, rose-colored, like a Gauguin stream" (27). In daydreaming about the suburbs, Neil seems to contemplate whether he, like Gauguin and the boy, could plunge into an environment where he is not a native. His encounters with the boy keep bringing up the concept of diaspora. Neil has a dream in which both he and the boy have to leave Newark:

> It had taken place on a ship, an old sailing ship like those you see in pirate movies. With me on the ship was the little colored kid from the library—I was the captain and he my mate, and we were the only crew members. For a while it was a pleasant dream; we were anchored in the harbor of an island in the Pacific and it was very sunny. Upon the beach there were beautiful bare-skinned Negresses, and none of them moved; but suddenly we were moving, our ship, out of the harbor, and the Negresses moved slowly down to the shore and began to throw leis at us and say, "Goodbye, Columbus . . . goodbye, Columbus . . . goodbye, Columbus . . . goodbye . . ." and though we did not want to go, the little boy and I, the boat was mov-

ing and there was nothing we could do about it, and he shouted at
me that it was my fault and I shouted it was his for not having a
library card, but we were wasting our breath, for we were further
and further from the island, and soon the natives were nothing at
all. (53)

The boy and Neil shout blame at each other, even though their
departure is a structural problem bigger than both of them. They cannot
stop the abandonment of the city. The dream satirizes the exoticist definition of a "native." In this definition, a native is not just a person born
and raised in Newark or Tahiti but a primitive life form made to be sur-
passed as civilization advances. Neil's and the boy's civilization is fragile. In order to succeed, Neil and the boy have to become pirates or
Columbus. They must conquer new terrain and sack new cities. Neil's
dream makes a wonderful wordplay on Columbus, since "goodbye,
Columbus" is a phrase from the voiceover on Ron Patimkin's Ohio State
graduation souvenir recording. It stands for everything fatuous about suburban values yet gains a wistful significance in the context of Gauguin's
island paintings and a small boy's love for them. Despite its pessimism,
the dream offers a literal version of Neil's and the boy's solidarity:
"We're all in the same boat."

Despite his dreams of Short Hills, Neil ultimately resists the suburban drift. As the novel ends, he leaves Brenda for good and returns to
spend the high holidays with his own family in Newark. The city remains
the site of living, continuing Jewish rituals beyond prayers for the dead.
"I did not look very much longer, but took a train that got me into
Newark just as the sun was rising on the first day of the Jewish New Year.
I was back in plenty of time for work" (97). Neil has presented an ironic
yet affectionate view of his family's rituals. Out in the coolness of suburbia, he thinks a few times of his aunt and uncle back in the airless city:
"I thought of my Aunt Gladys and Uncle Max, sharing a Mounds bar in
the cindery darkness of their alley, on beach chairs, each cool breeze sweet
to them as the promise of afterlife, and after a while I rolled onto the gravel
roads of the small park where Brenda was playing tennis. . . . For a while
I remained in the hall, bitten with the urge to slide quietly out of the house,
into my car, and back to Newark, where I might even sit in the alley and
break candy with my own" (6, 28). The breaking of candy sounds a lot
like the breaking of bread on Shabbat. An unkosher mitzvah is still a mitzvah. In contrast to the superabundance of the Patimkin paradise, the modest pleasure of a shared Mounds still carries intimations of the afterlife.
Neil and his family carve out habitable spaces in the cracks and alleys
of city life. The diaspora lingers in Newark.

The next chapter continues to explore postwar novelists' new city visions beyond segregation and decline. It focuses on the rise of new gay, Beat, and artistic subcultures after World War II. These subcultures contributed to postwar fiction a vision of the Open City based on joy, exuberance, and camping out. The action of the Open City takes place in a compelling here and now, leaving backdated storytelling behind.

8 | Camping Out in Cult Novels

"But New York was all right," said Paul.

"Yes," said the fat man. "New York was all right. One could find one's set. One could submerge and be ignored."

"Which is all wrong," said Paul, and Jim could see that he was angry, abstractly angry. "There should be no need to hide, to submerge in a big city; everything should be open and declared."[1]

This chapter sits at the intersection of two postwar events: the paperback cult novel and the subcultural city. After World War II, paperbacks presented new urban subcultures to a national audience of vicarious hipsters. New York was the main Subcultural City, home to the postwar artistic avant-garde, the Beat Generation, and rapidly expanding gay and lesbian communities. Readers of paperback cult novels could imagine themselves mingling in the underground scenes of Times Square and Greenwich Village. The Subcultural City is a funky and oppositional island in New York's new sea of glass-fronted corporate headquarters.

Does the subcultural city rely on the logic of segregation we have seen in previous chapters, or does it create a new, shared public space? I argue that subcultural writers take limited yet important steps toward desegregating the urban imagination. The subcultural city offers at least some awareness and contact across different races and sexualities. Characterized by alienation, postwar fiction nonetheless contains many beautiful, even ecstatic visions of urban community life. I call this positive vision the "Open City" variety of subcultural fiction. The Open City is the precursor to the best cultural features of today's American cities: creative freedom, racial diversity, and multiple, proliferating subcultures. The literary Open City of the twentieth century descends from Walt Whitman's literary Open City of the nineteenth. Even in an era when many people feared new influxes of population, the cult novel celebrates New York's diverse crowds—just as Whitman's *Leaves of Grass* celebrated them in a similarly fearful era.

> I am with you, you men and women of a generation, or ever
> so many generations hence,
> Just as you feel when you look on the river and sky, so I felt,
> Just as any of you is one of a living crowd, I was one of a
> crowd,
> Just as you are refresh'd by the gladness of the river and the
> bright flow, I was refresh'd,
> Just as you stand and lean on the rail, yet hurry with the swift
> current, I stood yet was hurried,
> Just as you look on the numberless masts of ships and the
> thick-stemm'd pipes of steamboats, I look'd.[2]

The postwar cult novel shares Whitman's exultant gaze on the city and its people. However, the twentieth-century Open City has its limitations. It depends on an ethos of "camping out," a sense of place that is fresh, exhilarating, yet impermanent. This transient sense of place mimics the uprooting of urban renewal, even though the counterculture may seem exactly opposite to the culture of planners, corporations, and other power brokers. Furthermore, the subcultural city is an enclave still dependent on binary oppositions: hipsters versus squares, youth versus everyone else, men versus women, straights versus gays. Cult novels both resist and exploit the binary oppositions of Us versus Them. Finally, the free and joyous expression of the Open City navigates a larger context of homophobic and sexist violence.

My approach widens the definitions of postwar bohemia by studying women's subcultural involvement along with men's. I pay careful attention to Paule Marshall's first novel *Brown Girl, Brownstones* (1959), in which the young heroine "goes arty," and to young women's discovery of the Greenwich Village gay scene in Ann Bannon's lesbian pulp novels *I Am a Woman* (1959), *Women in the Shadows* (1959), and *Beebo Brinker* (1962).

Women hipsters have remained largely invisible.[3] Stridently masculinist writers like Jack Kerouac, William Burroughs, and Philip Roth still define the cult novel and the era. For instance, Thomas Schaub writes in *American Fiction in the Cold War* (1991): "Perhaps inevitably, the discourses of strong, democratic individualism and sexual freedom that were essentially gender-neutral often produced a male-dominated rhetoric, in which society (totalitarianism, conformity) was associated with an emasculating femininity, and the rebel was always a man."[4] Like earlier sections on Hisaye Yamamoto and Gwendolyn Brooks, this chapter reintegrates women's voices into the postwar literary canon. The New York City of two renowned postwar novels, *Invisible Man* (1952) and *The Catcher in the Rye* (1951), looks very different after one reads the subcultural clues of lesbian pulp fiction. The Beat Generation writers also look very different from the viewpoint of Paule Marshall's Caribbean American women characters.

A female perspective undoes the common binary opposition between fifties hipster and fifties housewife. Male Beat writers often directed their own rebellion against everything the fifties woman supposedly represented: marriage, suburbia, respectability, the squelching of joy and freedom.[5] As hipster patriarch William Burroughs wrote in his cult novel *Naked Lunch* (1959), "God damned matriarchy. All matriarchies anti-homosexual, conformist and prosaic. Find yourself in a matriarchy walk don't run to the nearest frontier."[6] The beatnik plays the free-roaming Huck Finn to the matriarch's restrictive conformity.

Paule Marshall and Ann Bannon complicate this neat split between hipster and housewife. Their novels feature young women active in Manhattan subcultures, yet housewife discourse also plays important roles. Marshall's *Brown Girl, Brownstones* focuses on the interplay between young Selina Boyce and her mother, the formidable matriarch Silla Boyce. Although Selina lives in constant rebellion against her mother's conventional definitions of success, she comes to see their kinship in the long chain of black women's history. Ann Bannon (a pseudonym) was herself a fifties housewife, writing lesbian pulp novels on the sly and visiting Greenwich Village when her husband was away on business. She used her housewifely invisibility as a clever disguise: "everyone in my daily life thought that I was just a very nice, young conventional wife and mother. They really didn't know what was going on in my head or my emotions and that was sort of how I got away with it."[7]

While reading female hipsters as the often invisible doubles of male hipsters, I also read gay subcultures as the often invisible doubles of straight subcultures. Just as the civil rights movement informs Walker Percy's *The Moviegoer* by its absence, gay culture informs straight culture by its absence. I examine how "homosexuality always shadows heterosexuality."[8] Most of the cult novels under study here were written in the late fifties and early sixties, when a closeted gay sensibility cast a long shadow over mass culture (for instance, the movies *Pillow Talk* [1959], *Suddenly, Last Summer* [1959], *Cat on a Hot Tin Roof* [1961],

Breakfast at Tiffany's [1961], and *The Children's Hour* [1962]). Cult novels like Jack Kerouac's *On the Road* (1957) and Truman Capote's *Breakfast at Tiffany's* (1958) work "to exploit homosexuality by making it disappear," as David van Leer has written in another context.[9] In both books, a gay or bisexual community passes for a straight community. This passing allows the novelists to deny the context of homophobic and sexist violence. Thus they remain free to explore all the exhilaration and joy of the Open City. Capote, Kerouac, and even Paule Marshall rely on straight privilege to make the city safe for bohemians.

In the novels depicting openly gay characters, different logics operate. These novels include Hubert Selby Jr.'s *Last Exit to Brooklyn* (1964), William Burroughs's *Naked Lunch* (1959), Charles S. Wright's *The Messenger* (1963), and Ann Bannon's novels. These works entered a culture that generally regarded gays and lesbians as doomed, sad, and tortured people. Cold War homophobia projected masochism onto homosexuals. Masochism appeared not as a sexual role-play but as the homosexual way of life, as if the victims of hatred chose degradation. The counterpoint to this projection of masochism, sadism characterized the era's homophobic violence. Leslie Feinberg's autobiographical novel *Stone Butch Blues* (1993) describes the working-class Buffalo bar scene of the early sixties, which strictly observed distinctions between butch and femme lesbians. Cops and other men repeatedly rape and assault butches with a sadism designed to "school" them: "You think you're a guy, huh? You think you can take it like a guy?"[10] Like the noir City of Dread, this homophobic picture of the gay community leads inevitably toward violence.

Sadism characterizes depictions of gay life in two revered cult classics, *Last Exit to Brooklyn* and *Naked Lunch.* As Kali Tal points out, it is important to notice "how dominant culture codifies the traumatic experience."[11] Selby and Burroughs codify sadistic violence by transforming it into masochism chosen by the gay man himself. This is not the only choice for navigating a particularly homophobic era, however. To gain acceptance by mainstream publishers, Charles S. Wright and Ann Bannon adopt the codes of masochism to some extent. However, the depressive, fatalistic vision of gay life vies with two happier alternatives: the camp aesthetic and the Open City.

"Camping out" carries two intertwined meanings: the Open City's transient sense of place and the many uses of camp in cult novels. In Bannon, Capote, Selby, and Wright, camp offers a safety zone akin to the neutral zone between desegregation and segregation. Camp occupies the middle ground between the Open City and the Subterranean City, two competing countercultural models. The subterranean city model depicts subcultures as closed and self-protective enclaves. Fifties subcultures have usually been described in these sheltered, underground terms. Jack Kerouac used Allen Ginsberg's term *The Subterraneans* as the title for a 1958 novel about bohemians.[12] In his memoir *Down and In: Life in the Underground,* Ronald Sukenick describes fifties bohemia as a segregated enclave, making an analogy with ghettos. "But in Greenwich Village at the time there was a strong sense of alternative identity. In the underground of Greenwich Village you not only knew who They were, you also knew who We were. America was one thing and Greenwich Village another. Village people might go uptown but it was a kind of slumming in reverse."[13]

Despite common use of the "underground" metaphor, however, the counterculture occupies public space to a surprising degree in postwar novels. At moments, the Open City vision vanquishes the subterranean vision and the discourse of sadomasochistic violence. Novelists imagine the whole city as safe subcultural space. It is as if all the straights had deserted New York City and the hipsters had come aboveground to occupy its streets, bars, parks, and apartments. Obviously, the degree of openness depends partly on the degree of public safety a subculture enjoys.

This section's literary readings describe the space between the open and the subterranean, just as Part II described the neutral zone between desegregation and segregation. In ways analogous to the racial housing politics of the era, the fifties showed extraordinary contradictions in the politics surrounding homosexuality. After the war, newly thriving gay and lesbian communities created spaces of freedom within intense oppression. Paradoxically, the fifties represented the severest repression of lesbians and gay men in U.S. history as well as the starting point of the gay liberation movement.[14] Within a context of gay-bashing, police harassment, military witch-hunts, conflation of gay people with dreaded Communists, and constant fear of job loss, it took great bravery to label city space as queer space. Nonetheless, gay and lesbian communities emerged and grew, especially in Greenwich Village. Historian Lillian Faderman writes of fifties femme lesbians, "They braved the night alone to go out to gay bars to meet butches while straight women had not yet attempted to 'take back the night' and wander the streets for their own pleasure and purpose."[15] Faderman summarizes the postwar "mixed legacy" of oppression and liberation. She sees the Open City and the Subterranean City expanding at the same time.

> Lesbians inherited a mixed legacy from the 1950s, when lesbianism came to mean, much more than it had earlier, not only a choice of

sexual orientation, but a social orientation as well, though usually lived covertly. While the war and the migration afterward of masses of women, who often ended up in urban centers, meant that various lesbian subcultures could be established or expanded, these years were a most unfortunate time for such establishment and expansion. Suddenly there were large numbers of women who could become a part of a lesbian subculture, yet also suddenly there were more reasons than ever for the subculture to stay underground.[16]

This chapter's four themes of hipster versus housewife, gay culture as double for straight culture, camp performance, and the Open City versus the Subterranean City come together in political protests staged in New York from 1959 to 1961 by straight femme housewives. Many cult novels first appeared in the same era, the late fifties through the early sixties. I offer a reading of these protests as an appetizer to the chapter and a microcosm of its themes.

The Ladies of City Hall Park

In three annual protests against civil defense policy and the threat of nuclear war, two Manhattan housewives and their cohort appropriated the camp performance usually associated with gay male culture. Historian Dee Garrison's wonderful 1994 article " 'Our Skirts Gave Them Courage' " recovers a lost chapter of women's political action and refutes stereotypes of the fifties housewife as suburban, apolitical, and conformist.[17] While Garrison focuses on women's unrecognized activism, I focus on these protests as camp performance and as realization of the Open City vision. Janice Smith, Mary Sharmat, and the women's community they mobilized refused to abandon New York City to lone, expert, violent men. Straight women appropriated camp to mediate between open political expression and the hidden threat of violence. Their performance reveals concretely how gay culture serves as the marginalized other to straight culture.

In part 1's reading of film noir, I argued that wartime fears of bombing translated into a city vision dependent on containment and male expertise. Federal officials adopted similar strategies in response to postwar fears of nuclear bombing. Initiated in 1954, the air raid drills of Operation Alert depicted nuclear bombing of U.S. cities as a containable threat if only citizens would obey the experts (204). Once each year, the law required Americans to go underground into bomb shelters until the "all clear" signal. Obviously, the word *underground* had multiple resonances in the postwar era, as a synonym for subcultures and as the embodiment of nuclear fear. By remaining aboveground, New York City protesters exposed the absurdity of containment logic. Garrison writes, "This civil defense drill seemed ridiculous to Janice Smith and Mary Sharmat, who felt that in the event of nuclear war most of New York would be incinerated" (201).

The Open City of protesters grew from a handful in 1959 to 500 in City Hall Park in 1960 to 2,500 in the park in 1961 (210, 216, 217). These events not only brought down a bad law; they also presented a fresh, oppositional view of city life. The choice of City Hall Park staked a claim for the pacifist community as a new civic ideal. Reversing the wartime meaning of *underground* as a unit of political resistance, the conformist citizens went underground while the protesters stayed up in the park to claim the city symbolically as their own. Sharmat, Smith, and their co-workers built a community based on housewifely ties and discourses. They recruited other mothers at playgrounds in Central Park, a traditional meeting ground for subcultures of all persuasions (211). The city of pacifist housewives was a very different place than the noir city of lone, intent, violent men. Sharmat's written account of the protests reflects the exhilarating power of finding community. Sharmat represents the group as a complete village or an extended family. With its borrowed babies, this happy scene replays Cheever's "misplaced domesticity" from the perspective of the housewife rather than the disgruntled husband.

> I was not alone, Janice was not alone, the two mothers from the Grand Concourse in the Bronx were not alone. Over five hundred friends gathered at City Hall Park. Many men came down. Our skirts gave them courage. We loaned out extra babies to bachelors who had the misfortune to be childless. Dozens of children played in an area designated "Stay Off the Grass." Some of the students brought their musical instruments and softly played folk songs such as "We Shall Overcome" and "We Shall Not be Moved." . . . The sirens sounded. We stood. Mothers with children, fathers with mutual deep concerns, bachelors who had hopes and a borrowed baby, maiden aunts who had no children but were taking care of the rest of us. We stood. There was dead silence throughout the park. (215–216)

The protesters personify the members of an extended family. Smith and Sharmat took a new approach to protest by performing exaggerated versions of their real-life roles. Their exaggerated femininity owes much to the cross-dressing of male drag. These women did not reject the stereotype of "the pink lampshade"—they worked it hard. Specifically, they performed their identities as irreproachably respectable middle-class housewives and mothers. "Two weeks before the 1960 Operation Alert drill, Sharmat and Smith's group, assisted by the Metro chapter [of the

Women's International League of Peace and Freedom] had collected
pledges to join the protest from almost three hundred mother-with-
children volunteers. Mary Sharmat was an aspiring actress with a sure
sense of costume and dramatic effect. She instructed the women volunteers
to be polite to the police and to dress carefully for the protest in their best
dress and hose; no one could suspect them of being 'beatniks' " (213–214).
Sharmat herself wore "a large white hat trimmed in lace" (216). A photograph from the protest shows an impeccably coiffed and lipsticked
young mother of two, her white-gloved hands holding on to boy and girl
preschoolers. Both mother and daughter wear pale, elegantly tailored
spring coats (213). After a few protesters were arrested, "for the next five
days, until the protesters were released, scores picketed the Women's
House of Detention. The newspapers featured pictures of the picket
line. Many finely dressed women wearing white gloves and hats marched
with baby carriages and strollers. One woman pushed her shopping cart
around the line before continuing on to the market" (216).

The late fifties and early sixties saw the emergence of the camp sensibility into a wide cultural marketplace. Susan Sontag's essay "Notes on
Camp" (1964) is a milestone, since it expresses the need to explain
camp to a wider world. Andrew Ross calls camp "a *cultural economy* at
work from the time of the early 60s."[18] By appropriating camp, the protesters brought together two seemingly opposite languages: serious political engagement and fifties housewife discourse. Smith told the police,
"All this drill does is frighten children and birds. I will not raise my children to go underground" (210). Smith's indignation sounds like a mother
scolding a neighborhood bully or a big bad monster hiding under the bed.
The flyer publicizing the 1960 protest also exaggerated the housewife
voice: "The leaflet stressed that the only purpose of civil defense was 'to
frighten children and to fool the public into thinking there is protection
against an H-bomb' " (214–215). This campy tone is very different from
the sincere voices of the older pacifists. The Catholic Workers' Dorothy
Day distributed a pamphlet that read: "We know this drill to be a military act in a cold war to instill fear, to prepare the collective mind for war"
(207). While Catholic Workers denounced the serious threat of nuclear
war, Sharmat and Smith's group satirized the absurdity of "preparedness."
Although protesting war, Smith and Sharmat's tones banish high seriousness. The Open City vision impels us to speak "as if": as if we were
already freed from fear and violence; as if we had room to play.

I am drawing an analogy here between housewives' responses and
gay men's responses to their own trivialization. Indeed, the language of
postwar sexism often equated housewives and gay men, criticizing both
groups as effeminate and effeminizing.[19] Scott Long argues that camp arises

from an oppressive context in which the seriousness of gay men's lives has been misread as laughable. Camp turns the laughter around: "Camp assaults a society that presumes it knows what is serious and what is not."[20] The thinking of fifties housewives was also misread as trivial. Sharmat and Smith used their seeming triviality to point out the serious threat of nuclear war and to turn the laughter from themselves to the hyperserious experts. Garrison writes, "In his *Rules for Radicals,* the famed organizer Saul Alinsky taught that effective political protest must go beyond the expectations of the opposed authority and encourage public laughter at that authority. The Smith-Sharmat team with their baby carriages and tricycles did just that" (218–219). Camp can be seen as a "double conversation."[21] The exaggerated costuming was an in-joke for protesters who had fun tripping up the cops with trikes and high heels, but it also let them speak as sincere, indignant mothers to the general public. In her writings on the 1959 protest, Sharmat turns her own housewifely ordinariness into the ultimate weapon.

> Another Civil Defense man came over to argue sense to me and he screamed over the sirens and I just kept repeating, "This is wrong. I refuse to take cover." He was terrified of me and I of him. . . . I gave Jimmy his bottle but nothing would stop his crying. Then a policeman got out of his car. He walked over and said, "Lady, we are going to give you a ticket." I said, "Give me a ticket." That was the least of my worries. He threw up his hands and got back into his car. Both he and the other policeman waved and smiled at me. The Civil Defense men were furious. . . . [They] ran and took cover. Jimmy cried and I sat. The "all-clear" signal sounded. Commerce commenced and people continued their interrupted shopping. I picked up a pair of shoes at the repair shop and ran a few other errands and then went home. My husband was surprised to see us. He had anticipated a call from the jail. He went up to the bank and returned the bail money to our savings account. I unpacked the overnight case and put back the extra diapers and baby foods. Jimmy fell asleep in his crib. (211)

Sharmat can afford to be understated and funny about antinuclear protest because the Open City is safe space for women and children. Sharmat frays the men's tempers and defeats their expertise just by going on about her business. As the bail money goes back into the bank and the extra diapers back into the nursery, Sharmat makes brilliant use of anticlimax. Her city is quite relaxed, with easy movement between political, commercial, and private space. What happened to the intent, masculine expertise noir told us we needed in order to survive city life?

Sharmat's description minimizes the split between home and city. In this era, New York planners and developers aggressively built highways and increased the split between the gray-flannel city and the housewifely suburb. A journalist observed in 1955, "Two great developments arising from sources far beyond the city's ability to control them have interlocked. One is the fantastic growth of the suburban belt . . . , the second is the development of superhighways to deliver the suburbanite to the city by car."[22] However, Sharmat acknowledges no such geographic split. She acts in public city space, does a little shopping, and, in a role reversal, goes smoothly home to a supportive waiting husband.

Of course, Sharmat and Smith had husbands to ensure their respectability. The civil defense protests sparked an opposition strong enough to finish off Operation Alert. However, their success depended on the heterosexual status of its housewife-protagonists. Although they performed their identities ironically, they could also rely on those identities. Straight white middle-class privilege allowed them to be heard and stay safe. At the 1960 protest, "the police made twenty-six token arrests, deliberately singling out men—and women in slacks" (216). The women in dresses went untouched because they were women in dresses, not men in dresses or stone butches in trousers. In a Cold War context of persecution, the protesters relied on their difference from black civil rights activists, beatniks, lesbians, and Communists. They had to declare vehemently that they would not go "underground" as in "bohemian." This same mix of openness and concealment structures the era's cult novels. Truman Capote's Holly Golightly and Ann Bannon's lesbian love tales also use camp to walk the line between safety and danger.

The Postwar City and the Paperback Novel

My analysis of postwar cult novels falls into three sections. First I analyze the discourse of sadomasochistic violence in four novels featuring openly gay men: *Naked Lunch, Last Exit to Brooklyn, The City and the Pillar,* and *The Messenger.* Second, I show how Truman Capote's *Breakfast at Tiffany's* and Ann Bannon's Beebo Brinker novels use camp to negotiate this homophobic climate. Finally, I see how the hipster and the housewife fare in Jack Kerouac's and Paule Marshall's Open Cities.

I begin by situating these novels in the context of postwar publishing and postwar New York City. World War II brought sweeping changes to New York, including the city's new status as the political, financial, and artistic capital of the non-Communist world; the invention of the modern paperback book industry; and the rise of New York City as the home of multiple overlapping subcultures, including gays and lesbians, beatniks, and avant-garde artists. Marketing links all these trends. In the new culture capital, New York publishers figured out how to market its subcultures to the rest of the nation.

In 1943 Times Square was declared "the most densely populated place in the world at night." By 1956 *Business Week* called New York "the capital of the modern business age."[23] Observers found many ways to dub New York the capital of the Free World. The city became the headquarters for the United Nations, the new multinational corporate economy, and world finance.[24] Furthermore, New York became the international headquarters for the arts. Abstract expressionism was the dominant painting style among "an American avant-garde, which in the space of a few years succeeded in shifting the cultural center of the West from Paris to New York."[25] New cultural centers followed the artists and the money.

> Museums expanded, as did the Museum of Modern Art; relocated to midtown, as did the Whitney Museum of American Art; or erected striking new structures, as did the Guggenheim Museum, which opened its circular building, designed by Frank Lloyd Wright, at Fifth Avenue and Eighty-eighth Street in 1959. Lincoln Center, a complex built in the West Sixties, became the home of the Metropolitan Opera and the New York City Ballet. New York had become, as its artists and writers portrayed it in a range of striking expressions, a capital of the world.[26]

The subcultural scene of Greenwich Village expanded as rapidly as the official culture centers uptown and midtown. The postwar bohemia was fecund because it brought together many elements and brought together many elements because it was fecund. Poet Audre Lorde remembered "the Village gay-girl scene" as exceptionally racially integrated. "Lesbians were probably the only Black and white women in New York City in the fifties who were making any real attempt to communicate with each other; we learned lessons from each other, the values of which were not lessened by what we did not learn."

Many Village sites could symbolize the community building Lorde describes: "We tried to build a community of sorts where we could, at the very least, survive within a world we correctly perceived to be hostile to us."[27] One such site, the San Remo bar at the corner of Bleecker and MacDougal, was integrated in a different way. The San Remo "was one of the great gay-straight meeting grounds of the fifties" and a favorite hangout for writers, dancers, composers, activists, dramatists, and the Beat and gay male subcultures in general.[28] Jack Kerouac and Gore Vidal met and began a romantic interlude at the San Remo.[29] The recollection of one patron, Jack Dowling, epitomizes the difference between the Open City and the Subterranean City—even though Allen Ginsberg called San Remo regulars "the subterraneans": "It was all glass, a big long rectangular room and one whole wall of windows looking out on Bleecker Street. It was not the kind of bar you went into to hide because you were open to the world. It was wonderful in the winter watching the snow come down."[30]

In the last century or so many cities have seen the rise and fall of various bohemias. However, the gay and lesbian communities created during and after World War II were unprecedented and astonishing. Their impact has endured. As recent historians have shown, World War II was a watershed moment in gay history and "created something of a nationwide coming out experience."[31] Historians Lillian Faderman and Charles Kaiser tell parallel stories of community building during the war.

> The war and especially military life fostered some tolerance regarding lesbianism among young women who, perhaps for the first time in their lives, came in contact with sexuality between women in the close confines of the barracks. Even women who did not identify themselves as lesbians in the military tended to treat lesbianism, which became a familiar phenomenon, with a "who cares?" attitude. It may be that such a relative tolerance toward homosexuality was also promoted by the social upheaval of the war, which threw off balance various areas of American life.[32]

> Nothing would have a greater impact on the future shape of gay life in America than the explosive growth of the United States Army during World War II. Six months after the Japanese attack on Pearl Harbor, 14,000 men were entering 250 different training centers every day. The wartime draft pulled all kinds of men together from every hamlet and metropolis. The army then acted like a giant centrifuge, creating the largest concentration of gay men inside a single institution in American history. . . .

> The combination of friendship and discrimination experienced by homosexuals in uniform created one of the great ironies of gay history: this mixture made the United States Army a secret, powerful, and unwitting engine of gay liberation in America. The roots formed by this experience would nourish the movement that finally made its first public appearance in Manhattan twenty-four years after the war was over.[33]

These gay and lesbian military communities reshaped American cities. Historian George Chauncey puts it succinctly: "Many recruits saw the sort of gay life they could lead in large cities and chose to stay in those cities after the war."³⁴ During the war, the influx of military personnel meant that New York City finally had the population and cash to support gay and lesbian bars. These places provided the base for expanding postwar communities. "Back in Manhattan, the steady influx of thousands of men and women in uniform created scores of new locales with homoerotic undertones. . . . In the late 1940s, thousands of lesbian and gay soldiers who had poured through New York City on their way to Europe settled in Manhattan, bolstering what was already the largest gay community in America."³⁵ Lillian Faderman explains how the lesbian bar scene was not explicitly political yet did provide a growing sense of shared identity. The repression of the fifties replaced the tolerance of the forties, but some gains held. Even repression could offer ironic benefits, as in the federal financing of urban migration through the "queer ships."

> Ironically, the military also contributed to the establishment of a larger lesbian subculture when it became less lenient in its policy towards homosexuals once the war was over. Thousands of homosexual personnel were loaded on "queer ships" and sent with "undesirable" discharges to the nearest U.S. port. Many of them believed that they could not go home again. They simply stayed where they were disembarked, and their numbers helped to form the large homosexual enclaves that were beginning to develop in port cities such as New York, San Francisco, Los Angeles, and Boston. Historian Allan Berube wryly remarks, "The government sponsored a migration of the gay community."³⁶

The armed forces also fostered the rise of another postwar phenomenon, the paperback book industry. Michael Warner has pointed out how "in the lesbian and gay movement, to a much greater degree than in any comparable movement, the institutions of culture-building have been market-mediated: bars, discos, special services, newspapers, magazines, phone lines, resorts, urban commercial districts."³⁷ Similarly, the relationships between urban subcultures and the nation at large have been market-mediated as well. In the fifties this mediation came through the paperback cult novel. Pocket Books launched the mass-market paperback in 1939. Print runs soared from 3 million in 1939 to 214 million in 1950. World War II created a generation of American paperback readers. Between 1943 and 1947, the U.S. military distributed nearly 123 million paperbacks in special Armed Services Editions. In *Two-Bit Culture: The Paperbacking of America*, Kenneth C. Davis describes how Armed Services Editions created very literal "reading communities."

It would be impossible to judge which titles were actually most read by the men because the books were passed on until they literally fell apart or, as was often the case, were deliberately pulled apart. According to one veteran of the war in the South Pacific, a plane-load of men was flying toward a parachute drop, all hunched on the floor because the seats had been removed. They had with them a single Armed Services Edition and so, to kill time, it was passed around, page by page, with the faster readers urging the slower readers to hurry up.[38]

Paperbacks blurred the distinction between literary and popular culture, the mainstream and the offbeat. Postwar novelists wrote for the mass market as well as the cultural elite; their novels swiftly became Hollywood movies and required high school texts. A new literary style emerged. The postwar fiction literati were hardly ever high modernists with arcane vocabularies. They spoke directly and conversationally to readers. The famous second-person address opening J. D. Salinger's *The Catcher in the Rye* (1951), one of the first cult novels, exemplifies the close relationship between postwar author and reader: "If you really want to hear about it, the first thing you'll probably want to know is where I was born, and what my lousy childhood was like, and how my parents were occupied and all before they had me, and all that David Copperfield kind of crap, but I don't feel like going into it, if you want to know the truth."[39]

The assumption of outsider identity was an important part of reading cult novels as well as writing them. Critic Thomas Schaub sees the common turn from third to first person as a political move by writers "who conceived of themselves as minorities and outsiders."[40] Speaking directly, casually, and conversationally, writers also constructed their readers as outsiders. The paperback readership became an imagined community, a vicarious subculture. The children of World War II veterans were also devoted to paperbacks, and their shared reading helped create the sixties counterculture. As Kenneth Davis writes,

> Paperback books and the baby boomers were made for each other, a mass medium for a mass generation. . . . And they had their own favorite authors, such as J.D. Salinger and Kurt Vonnegut, whose resistance to orthodoxy seemed to travel best in paperback. . . . But two novelists seemed to capture this growing separation between the old generation and the new better than anyone else. . . . They were J.D. Salinger and Jack Kerouac, and they became two of the first authors deserving of a label coined years later, the "paperback

literati." . . . The notion of "cult books" and "cult writers" entered the realm of publishing.[41]

Cult novels' portrayal of New York City walks a fine line between imagined community and virtual tourism. Nearly all postwar cult novels were published by mainstream presses and expected to achieve commercial success. Paperback covers and blurbs sensationalized books in ways far removed from their actual content; however, the novels themselves also present city life with a commercially appealing mixture of voyeurism and insiderhood. The protagonist becomes an excellent tour guide, offering a privileged view of normally hidden scenes.

Always a remarkably perceptive and articulate young person, the protagonist helps the reader comprehend what others can't. As Barbara Ehrenreich writes, "By the end of the fifties, the beatnik had even come to rival the psychiatrist as an imagined watcher—a critical vantage point from which it might be possible to judge what something '*really* means.' "[42] Satirical vignettes crowd postwar fiction, and they owe their prevalence to the narrators' talents as social watchers. Like the noir detective, the postwar narrator is an expert witness. Walking down the street, *The Moviegoer*'s Binx Bolling can read minds at twenty paces: "It takes two seconds to size up the couple. They are twenty, twenty-one, and on their honeymoon. . . . They are not really happy. He is afraid their honeymoon is too conventional, that they are just another honeymoon couple."[43] From *The Catcher in the Rye* through *The Bell Jar,* cult novels see through phonies. The narrators show us people who, like Civil Defense men, take themselves very seriously while their absurdity is clear to us. Published twelve years apart, *The Catcher in the Rye* and *The Messenger* both contain vignettes of powerful men picking their noses.

> Sometimes I act a lot older than I am—I really do—but people never notice it. People never notice anything.
>
> Old Spencer started nodding again. He also started picking his nose. He made out like he was only pinching it, but he was really getting the old thumb right in there. I guess he thought it was all right to do because it was only me that was in the room. I didn't *care,* except that it's pretty disgusting to watch somebody pick their nose.
>
> Then he said, "I had the privilege of meeting your mother and dad when they had their little chat with Dr. Thurmer some weeks ago. They're grand people."
>
> "Yes, they are. They're very nice."

> Grand. That's a word I really hate. It's a phony. I could puke every time I hear it. (12)

> After the biggest drop since the Twenty-Nine harakiri, the stock market is rallying. Tuesday, May 30, 1962 at exactly a quarter of six in the evening.
> Three young and one gruff middle aged brokers are quite publicly picking their noses. Nervousness? Relief from tension? Only one broker has the sanitary turn-of-mind to use his handkerchief. This is the Park Avenue branch office of a Wall Street firm. I am here waiting to take stocks and bonds downtown. But the tickertape hasn't closed yet. Everyone is tensely excited. All I want to do is deliver the stuff and go home. The sudden change of fortune has no effect on me.[44]

While the people who surround him are too self-absorbed to notice anything, the postwar narrator pays attention. He remains aloof and observant. Despite the depth and accuracy of its social critique, the narrator's viewpoint can verge on voyeurism—as in this scene from *The Catcher in the Rye.* The narrator, Holden Caulfield, looks into windows like an inadvertent peeping tom. Salinger trades here on New York's wartime and postwar reputation as a haven for alternative sexualities. The figure of the man in drag appears in this straight-identified text as a marker of urban "perversion."

> I looked out the window for a while, with my coat on and all. I didn't have anything else to do. You'd be surprised what was going on on the other side of the hotel. They didn't even bother to pull their shades down. I saw one guy, a gray-haired, very distinguished-looking guy with only his shorts on, do something you wouldn't believe me if I told you. First he put his suitcase on the bed. Then he took out all these women's clothes, and put them on. Real women's clothes—silk stockings, high-heeled shoes, brassiere, and one of those corsets with the straps hanging down and all. Then he put on this very tight black evening dress. I swear to God. Then he started walking up and down the room, taking these very small steps, the way a woman does, and smoking a cigarette and looking at himself in the mirror. He was all alone, too. Unless somebody was in the bathroom—I couldn't see that much. . . . I'm not kidding, that hotel was lousy with perverts. I was probably the only normal bastard in the whole place—and that isn't saying much. (58)

This perspective resembles the peephole views on paperback jackets. Even the greatest literary classics often featured sensationalistic paintings. The original cover of *The Catcher in the Rye* was quite classy, but Salinger detested it all the same.[45] It showed young Holden Caufield in a touristic pose, carrying his suitcase down a New York City street. The viewer stands in the shoes of another sidewalk pedestrian, looking over Holden's shoulders at a heavily made-up blonde lighting a cigarette and at posters of big-busted blondes advertising a girlie show. A box on the front cover addresses the reader directly, appealing to the tourist looking for a vicarious shock and also to the cult novel reader changed forever by a special book. "This unusual book may shock you, will make you laugh, and may break your heart—but you will never forget it."

The original paperback cover for Ralph Ellison's *Invisible Man,* also by Signet/NAL star artist James Avati, offers the same mixture of community involvement and shock tourism.[46] A young man, presumably the Invisible Man, stands with his back to the viewer in the middle of a Harlem street. He stares at the frenetic activity on the sidewalk, while we stare over his shoulder. Every possible kind of street life happens on one corner: juvenile delinquency, old age, hard work, young love, prostitution, and grocery shopping. By having us share the Invisible Man's viewpoint, Avati clearly wants to evoke the narrator's complex observations on African American life in twentieth century America. However, the street scene he paints is also an easily consumable stereotype of ghetto vigor and squalor.

Novels originally published by straight-to-paperback "pulp fiction" imprints like Gold Medal, Crest, and Ace featured much more sensational covers. Subcultural authors like William Burroughs and Ann Bannon found an uneasy home in pulp paperback. The original covers of Burroughs's *Junkie* and Bannon's *Odd Girl Out* both spotlight conventionally attractive blonds with impossibly perky breasts—a social type not prominent in either author's work.[47] In the illustrations both blonds are plunging toward danger—one toward a hypodermic needle, the other toward her college roommate. Like the classier Avati covers, these book jackets offer the reader a marketable blend of familiar looks and exotic situations.

The front covers aside, cult novel readers are more than tourists—they are also community insiders who read with special involvement. As Ann Bannon reminisces about the lurid covers of lesbian novels: "The difficult part was to screw up one's courage to carry a pile of these spicy titles and unmistakable illustrations to a drugstore counter. . . . Despite all their editorially imposed quirks, the covers provided links among members of a wide-flung and incohesive community; a community that did not even think of itself as one and that, therefore, valued all the more any connection with others whose experience paralleled their own."[48]

Although distant and alienated from other characters, the protagonist of the cult novel shares a great intimacy with readers. This intimacy fuels the power of novels like *On The Road, The Moviegoer, The Catcher in the Rye,* and *I Am a Woman.* It makes us like characters who are smart-alecky, alcoholic, or otherwise unlikeable. The in-jokes of cult novels turn the reader into the narrator's best friend. Philip Roth's *Goodbye, Columbus* is a treasure trove of countercultural satire. The narrator, Neil, repeatedly scores jokes off his girlfriend's hypernormal brother Ron, with whom he temporarily shares a bathroom. "Behind me I could see Ron's jock straps hanging out to dry on the Hot and Cold knobs of the shower. Nobody ever questioned their tastefulness as adornment, and after a few nights I didn't even notice them."[49] *The Messenger*'s African American narrator Charlie describes a conspiratorial subway ride with his white friend Troy, a ride designed to mess with people's minds. This friendship grows within the close-knit, share-and-share-alike community of Greenwich Village and differentiates itself from the hardworking serious world of the squares. The reader gets to share in the joke and the Open City vision. Troy and Charlie baffle their fellow passengers by playing when they ought to be commuting and by reading racially inappropriate newspapers. Their silliness and their friendship are forms of mental desegregation.

> I met Troy four years ago at the White Horse Tavern. Those were lean, desperate days, and if Troy had a dollar, I certainly had half of it. Often we shared the same cigarette, divided a hard, buttered roll, split a container of black coffee. Neither of us had a steady job, though Troy received a spasmodic pittance from home. He was studying at N.Y.U., philosophy and anthropology. Ah, those days! Sometimes we rode the subway with the work-bound passengers. Troy would read a French or Chinese newspaper; I'd read the *Jewish Daily Forward.* It really upset the passengers; perhaps they thought they were still in bed, having nightmares.[50]

Many cult novels capitalize on their ability to shock. As Capote's Holly Golightly says, "Leave it to me: I'm always top banana in the shock department."[51] In the late fifties and early sixties, a marketing of shock entered popular culture and has since come to dominate it. While other postwar fictions treat shock as a component of personal trauma, cult novels also treat shock as a commodity. The narrator's hipster-cool often depends on the ability to remain unshocked while describing shocking events. This cool tone of voice seems related to the inappropriate neutrality discussed in earlier chapters. Here, however, inappropriate neutrality becomes an index of hipness. The narrative asks: Are you a tourist-reader on a day trip from the suburbs, shocked by everything and loving it? Or are you one of us, a hipster-reader, a vicarious insider shocked by nothing?

Naked Lunch presents an extreme case of the hipster-reader versus the tourist-reader. In its first scenes, William Burroughs imagines the New York City underground against the backdrop of suburban conformity: "Into the Interior: a vast subdivision, antennae of television to the meaningless sky. In lifeproof houses they hover over the young, sop up a little of what they shut out. Only the young bring anything in, and they are not young very long." The novel's first satirical vignette immediately presents the bad choice, the tourist-reader, eager to sop up some urban vice.

> Young, good looking, crew cut, Ivy League, advertising exec type fruit holds the door back for me. I am evidently his idea of a character. You know the type comes on with bartenders and cab drivers, talking about right hooks and the Dodgers, call the counterman in Nedick's by his first name. A real asshole. . . .
>
> A square wants to come on hip. . . . Talks about "pod," and smoke it now and then, and keeps some around to offer the fast Hollywood types.
>
> "Thanks, kid," I say, "I can see you're one of our own." His face lights up like a pinball machine, with stupid, pink effect.
>
> "Grassed on me he did," I said morosely. (Note: Grass is English thief slang for inform.) I drew closer and laid my dirty junky fingers on his sharkskin sleeve. "And us blood brothers in the same dirty needle. I can tell you in confidence he is due for a hot shot." (Note: This is a cap of poison junk sold to addict for liquidation purposes. Often given to informers. Usually the hot shot is strychnine since it tastes and looks like junk.)[52]

Burroughs's satire flatters us as good hipster-readers, letting us in on the jokes and even defining subcultural slang. We get to be insiders rather than "assholes." With its junkie onrush of slang and anecdotes, *Naked Lunch* tells how things *really* are in city parks and shooting galleries. The novel's reality claim centers on "the hot shot," on violence, as the ultimate truth of cities. The close readings that follow trace the interplay between peaceful openness and sadistic violence in subcultural New York.

9 The Discourse of Sadomasochistic Violence

Throughout its chapters, this book questions a dominant postwar narrative in which city living inevitably produces violence. This particular section analyzes a subset of that narrative: cult novels' linkage of sadomasochistic violence to gay culture. The book's closing arguments, comparing Ann Bannon with Truman Capote and Paule Marshall with Jack Kerouac, depend upon our understanding the sadomasochistic context. Whether gay or straight, male or female, all subcultural city novelists had to negotiate or censor this discourse of violence. By "sadomasochistic violence" I do not mean S&M as a form of fantasy in sex play. Rather, I mean an acceptance of physical assault as the inevitable outcome of homosexuality, a world in which a gay person only has two life choices: victimizer or victimized. In postwar literature, as Catharine Stimpson points out, anal sex often serves as an emblem of sadomasochistic violence. In this formulation, the "bottom" invites his own brutalization. Furthermore, his victimhood renders him womanly, effeminate: "Male homosexuals could also deploy that sexual grammar in which one lover is male and active, the other female and passive. In Beat writing, sodomy vividly emblemizes such a coupling. The sodomizer is dominant, powerful, potentially cruel, and masculine; the sodomized submissive, powerless, potentially a victim, and feminine."[1]

This section looks at four cult novels that feature openly gay men characters: Gore Vidal's *The City and the Pillar* (1948), William S. Burroughs's *Naked Lunch* (1959), Charles S. Wright's *The Messenger* (1963), and Hubert Selby Jr.'s *Last Exit to Brooklyn* (1964). These books' cult novel status goes hand in glove with the discourse of sadomasochistic violence.

Cult novels appeal to readers because they serve as tour guides to startling new worlds. These books let readers in on the slang, practices, and worldviews of New York City subcultures. Novels like *Last Exit to Brooklyn* and *Naked Lunch* make their readers engage with them in vicarious sadomasochistic violence. Like sadists, the novels assault the readers' sensibility, teaching them how to be cool and withstand the assault. Thus the reader comes to identify with the masochist. However, the reader also identifies with the sadist, deriving pleasure from elaborate rituals of violence. Masculinity means a "realistic" acceptance of violence as the city's essential nature. The ability to consume violence becomes an index of the reader's hipness.

To get published during the Cold War, novels seemingly had to show homosexuality meeting a tragic fate. However, subcultural city fiction also offers powerful alternatives to sadomasochistic violence. In Vidal, Selby, and Wright, we find varying traces of a liberating counternarrative. An oppositional Open City discourse appears in all three writers, competing with sadomasochistic violence. Camp speech provides self-defense in threatening contexts. A matter-of-fact, open portrayal of gay life argues for its own health. We shall see even more of the Open City in the pulp fiction of Ann Bannon.

Among the four writers discussed here, only William Burroughs offers no liberating counternarrative whatsoever. Vidal, Selby, and Wright explore the trauma of gay-bashing and the emotional costs of surviving it. Burroughs, on the other hand, identifies only with the perpetrators of abuse. He portrays rape as a pleasurable fantasy for the rapist. Ironically but perhaps not coincidentally, the other three novels went out of print for decades, while *Naked Lunch* has been permanently enshrined as the ultimate cult novel and the epitome of hipness.

Naked Lunch is the locus classicus for the postwar discourse of sadomasochistic violence. A fantasia of junkie surrealism, *Naked Lunch* makes its way in and out through hundreds of characters, scenes, and places, like Hieronymus Bosch's picture of Hell. The violence always asserts itself as the default mode in the narrator's stream of consciousness. At the novel's opening, the narrator impresses a would-be hipster by casually weaving gay-bashing together with the lingo of junkies and con men. The junkies charge money to let others watch the death of an informer through a one-way mirror. Similarly, the cult novelist sets up a "tasty" homophobic murder for readers' voyeuristic consumption. Witnessing these hate crimes helps readers lose their subcultural virginity.

> "Ever see a hot shot hit, kid? I saw the Gimp catch one in Philly. We
> rigged his room with a one-way whorehouse mirror and charged a

sawski to watch it. He never got the needle out of his arm. They don't
if the shot is right. That's the way they find them, dropper full of
clotted blood hanging out of a blue arm. The look in his eyes when
it hit—Kid, it was tasty. . . .

"Recollect when I am traveling with the Vigilante, best Shake Man
in the industry. Out in Chi. . . . We is working the fags in Lincoln
Park. So one night the Vigilante turns up for work in cowboy boots
and a black vest with a hunka tin on it and a lariat slung over his
shoulder.

"So I says: 'What's with you? You wig already?'

"He just looks at me and says, 'Fill your hand stranger' and
hauls out an old rusty six shooter and I take off across Lincoln
Park, bullets cutting all around me. And he hangs three fags before
the fuzz nail him. I mean the Vigilante earned his moniker. . . .

"Ever notice how many expressions carry over from queers to con
men? Like 'raise,' letting someone know you are in the same line?" (4)

In Burroughs's novel, drug-induced paranoia converges with Cold War
paranoia, and both paranoias intermingle with the discourse of sadomasochistic violence. As Robert Corber explains, the U.S. government
fired many gay employees for fear their sexual orientation would subject them to blackmail by Soviet spies.[2] In this paranoid worldview, by
its very nature being gay meant potential victimhood. Burroughs also links
Cold War expertise to sadomasochistic violence. One of the novel's fantasy sequences features Dr. Benway, "an expert on all phases of interro-
gation, brainwashing and control" (20). Dr. Benway is a classic Cold War
paranoid scientist, straight from the days of *Dr. Strangelove* and "Spy vs.
Spy." However, he is also a classic sadist.

"The Interrogator can gain complete hypnotic control—the subject
will come at his whistle, shit on the floor if he but say Open Sesame.
Needless to say, the sex humiliation angle is contraindicated for overt
homosexuals. (I mean let's keep our eye on the ball here and remember the old party line . . . never know who's listening in.) I recall this
one kid, I condition him to shit at the sight of me. Then I wash his
ass and screw him. It was real tasty. And he was a lovely fellah too.
And sometimes a subject will burst into boyish tears because he can't
keep from ejaculate when you screw him. Well, as you can plainly
see, the possibilities are endless like meandering paths in a great big
beautiful garden." (26–27)

This purported lecture on Dr. Benway's area of expertise is really a
common pornographic device: forcing another person not just to have sex

with you but to desire you as well. In fantasies of domination, the rape victim often enjoys being forced against his or her will. In Dr. Benway's stories, being the bottom in anal sex means being humiliated, victimized, and tricked. It reduces "the subject" to "boyish tears" (that is, to womanhood). *Naked Lunch* takes the Beat Generation's sacred pursuit of "kicks" and brings them in line with the severest forms of male domination. Burroughs dwells in the subterranean city rather than the Open City. The Open City assumes that fun is shared—clearly not the assumption in *Naked Lunch*. In Burroughs's novel, what's fun for one man is clearly not fun for the other.

Gore Vidal, by contrast, allows some of the Open City to emerge while sharing Burroughs's focus on violence. Writing as early as 1948, Vidal seems less bound by the sadomasochistic violence that would come to dominate Cold War portrayals of gay life. To be sure, Vidal portrays some gay men as effeminate or masochistic. For instance, the patrons of a gay bar "sat at the bar or at tables demurely, like young maidens prepared for rape."[3] However, victimhood is not universal or inevitable. Indeed, at moments the novel serves as prototype for gay liberation, decades before the Stonewall Rebellion of 1969.[4] The main character Jim's inner monologue expresses the minority opinion that homosexuality is natural. Anticipating 1970s thought, he imagines a collective coming-out leading to a more honest world for everyone. This new Open City of gay culture "would be the end of the submerged world."

> He wanted to come out and tell them what he was and defy them; to fight them if they dared be horrified. He wondered what would happen if he were to be honest and natural; if every man like himself were to be natural and honest. It would be the end of the submerged world and it would make a better beginning for others not yet born: to be born into a world where sex was natural and not fearsome, where men could love men naturally, they way they were meant to, as well as to love women naturally, the way they were meant to. (287)

Unfortunately, however, Vidal's novel also participates in the myth that homosexuality leads to a violent fate. The novel concludes with Jim's murder of Bob, his high school friend and first love, when the two men meet again as adults and Bob rejects him. Tellingly, the murder takes place not in their small hometown but in New York City. Homosexuality and the postwar city both tend toward violence, perhaps because the two are linked. As Bob says, puzzled, "I guess that *is* New York. There're a lot of queers here" (303). However, it is the novel's small-town beginning that decrees its violent end. When Bob and Jim wrestle as high school boys, violence seems the only way to resolve a forbidden desire. "Somehow the violence released Jim from certain emotions and he wrestled furiously with Bob, made free, for the time, by violence" (40). In the absence of true freedom, Jim cannot bend the course of his life. Therefore, violence steps in not only for emotional release but to resolve an unresolvable narrative.

Although violence prevails in *The City and the Pillar,* sadomasochistic violence does not. By the early sixties, however, the discourse of sadomasochistic violence had come into full dominance. It structures two novels published close together, Charles S. Wright's *The Messenger* (1963) and Hubert Selby Jr.'s *Last Exit to Brooklyn* (1964). Nonetheless, brief moments of joy and ease in each book point us toward the subcultural utopia of the Open City.

"After the Shock Subsides": ### *Charles S. Wright*

The discourse of sadomasochistic violence deeply informs *The Messenger.* Its main character, Charlie, experiences almost everything in the language of sexual trauma. Charlie's description of being raped when he was a runaway teenager is only the most tangible of his victimizations.

> I fell asleep and then, in the half-world of sleep and consciousness, I discovered something was happening to the lower part of my body. I was too afraid to scream, but I twisted and turned on that large bed, a Hollywood bed with an imitation ivory-and-leather headboard and with brass nails. I felt as though I were dying. Silently I prayed to God to let whatever was happening end. And then it was over. The man said, "Here, kid, take this two dollars and get the hell out of here. My wife will be home soon." (47)

This rape becomes the model for Charlie's adult experiences. He describes southern racism as if it, too, were a rape: "The wounds of my Missouri childhood were no worse than a sudden, sharp pain" (80). He regards the glitz and glamour of postwar New York with suspicion and disdain, as if it were the imitation headboard on his rapist's bed. Charlie learns to routinize pain, to hang in there silently until it ends, and to anesthetize himself. An alcoholic in adulthood, Charlie calls booze his "man-killer." "'This is a groove,' I said happily. 'Quick girl! Give me a shot of that man-killer.' I've discovered that drinking and jazz go hand in hand. A wonderful tranquilizer. Problems do not get less, but I can see them more clearly, or think I can" (119). Booze kills the man along with the pain. The root cause of pain is sexual trauma—after all, a "man-killer" is a fatal seductress. When turning tricks, Charlie also uses the post-traumatic lessons he's learned about numbing himself to shock: "He pushed me up against the wall roughly. I stared up at the ivory ceiling and stiffened and it was over" (63).

Charlie's ability to stiffen himself against shock provides the link between the subcultural world and the cult novel's circle of more conventional readers. *The Messenger*'s narrative of personal trauma participates in the marketing of shock. In its Fawcett Crest paperback edition, the novel sits between literature and pulp fiction. Like other Fawcett imprints, the Crest line had established itself with lesbian pulp fiction and other sensationalist titles. By 1963, however, Fawcett Crest attempted to upgrade its image by publishing works both literary and sensational, like Vladimir Nabokov's *Lolita*.[5] Crest sought titles that combined quality and shockability, and *The Messenger* fits the bill. On the one hand, *The Messenger* comes with impeccable literary pedigrees. Farrar, Straus is the hardcover publisher, and the front cover sports a blurb from James Baldwin. On the other hand, the book is about junkies, drag queens, male prostitutes, and other hustlers. Wright clearly understands the cult novel's imperative to shock the reader and to serve as unshockable tour guide through urban subcultures. From his apartment window Charlie observes the naive suburban viewer of shocking city life.

> The diners at the *Steak de Paris* have a wonderful vignette: a gypsy baby standing on the elegant rear of a Cadillac, stark naked, eating an orange. The baby's mother does a little hop and skipping dance, laughing, her huge, cat-shaped eyes zero in on an approaching sailor. The sailor in stiff white passes, placing his right hand over his crotch.
>
> There is no air. I watch the paralysis of mummified Americans waiting for their cars to take them back to suburbia. (43)

Such vignettes construct the reader simultaneously as hip and urban and as naive and suburban. Cult novel readers can flatter themselves that they must be hipper than the "mummified" diners at the Steak de Paris with its wonderfully pseudosophisticated name. The gypsy hustlers constitute the everyday life of Charlie's block. They certainly don't shock him. The hip reader can enjoy the irony of random street life rearranged as tourist spectacle. In another way, however, the reader is the diner at the Steak de Paris, observing Wright's carefully staged vignette. In one condensed moment, readers get to see sexual solicitation, stark contrasts of wealth and poverty, and the desecration of motherhood. The actual experience of sidewalk life usually offers just fragments of a full story. Here, by contrast, we get the full story, with Charlie the tour guide filling in the details.

Charlie also portrays his own life as if he were a tour guide through subterranean decadence. "And thus the country boy began to move through the subterranean junkie world where there is no day or night but an endless golden dusk if you are 'on'" (50). Throughout the novel he describes his own appeal as a fetish object to consumers. His face plays an important role in the worlds of hustling and heroin. "A slick young man with a pock-marked face picked me up in a drugstore. I thought he was queer, but discovered later that he was junkie-prone. (It was in Korea that I realized that my large, brown, dazed eyes gave me that junkie look.) Pimps would point their slender fingers at me and ask what my kick was" (49). "You'd be surprised how my color helps business. Though I've missed out several times because, of course, I just wasn't dark enough" (61). By extension, Charlie also markets his appeal to consumers of fiction. A close-up photograph of a young man who matches Charlie's description appears on the front cover of the Fawcett paperback. He appeals directly to the viewer with those large, brown, dazed eyes.

Charlie's ability to shock without being shocked moves far beyond marketing, however. It also means the chance to create a more tolerant world. Charlie describes his friendships with drag queens in a matter-of-fact way, beyond subterranean sensationalism: "I was in Claudia's pad today. Claudia, the Grand Duchess, is a fabulous Negro drag queen who lives down the street from me. He is my friend and is nothing much to speak of as a man, but he makes a swinging broad. Often, after getting dolled up in female attire, Claudia cruises the street, rides the subways and buses, getting picked up by straight men who, after the shock subsides, often accompany him home" (37).

Claudia travels openly and safely through public space. Wright promises that the utopian space of the Open City will be fun "after the shock subsides." The world of gay men isn't based on sex alone but on friendship as well. Telling your friend about sex is just as important as the sex itself. Claudia's campy speech reflects the fun and excitement of the postwar gay community. Wright reproduces the language of African American drag queens that only became a staple of mass culture thirty years later. We get whiffs of a genuine subculture, not just scenes staged for tourists: "Oh honey. Let me tell you. I brought this number home, and . . . Miss Thing! I had to put him through, put him through in the name. What? Oh please, Miss Thing. Built. Great, Greek muscles. Muscles, just gushing. Oh honey, quite facial. We had one old ball. I was so unlovely when I woke up. Not a curl in my head" (37–38).

The Inevitability of Violence:
Hubert Selby Jr.

Hubert Selby Jr. defines the city as fundamentally violent yet allows occasional glimpses of alternative possibilities. Like the novels of Wright and Capote, *Last Exit to Brooklyn* concerns the New York demimonde of straight and gay hustlers. By 1964 the drag queen was a visible public figure, appearing in *Last Exit* at neighborhood weddings, the union hall, and the local bar. This cult novel displays the drag queen as urban local color. Despite this open presentation, however, Selby's book extends the threat of male violence if a man or woman displays sexuality too openly. Women and gay men "get what's coming to them" as their inevitable fate. Although Selby ultimately denies the possibility of nonviolent city life, he offers a few glimpses of the Open City along the way. Drag queens use camp speech to keep themselves safe in very dangerous bars and situations. Gay men discover moments of happiness and ease in the company of other gay men.

Selby juxtaposes gay subcultures with a working-class Brooklyn neighborhood. Gay men are protagonists in two of *Last Exit*'s interconnected sections. "The Queen is Dead" features Georgette, a Brooklyn drag queen, while "Strike" concerns Harry, a buffoonishly macho union steward desperately concealing his homosexuality. Both come from the same poor white Brooklyn neighborhood near the East River. Both men have the same antagonist, leading man, and opposite number: Vinnie, who hangs out at the Greeks diner with his gang. Vinnie and friends represent the violent men who inhabit the city, its natural predators who will get you in the end. With his phonetic spellings of Brooklyn speech, Selby attempts to present an authentic slice of working-class life. If Selby's novel comes across as "real," then the reader must accept violence as the city's fundamental reality. The reader undergoes a sadomasochistic initiation ritual. While Georgette and Harry submit to violence, the reader gets jumped into the gang.

"Another Day Another Dollar," the novel's opening section, sets up violence as the city's basic reality. It introduces the brutal leitmotif to which the novel constantly returns. Violence is routine play, as routine as the boredom of hanging out in the same diner all the time. "They sprawled along the counter and on the chairs. Another night. Another drag of a night in the Greeks, a beatup all night diner near the Brooklyn Armybase."[6] Similar to Beat writing's onrush of language, Selby's page-long sentences present violence as the city's stream of consciousness.

> They formed a circle and kicked. He tried to roll over on his stomach and cover his face with his arms, but as he got to his side he was

kicked in the groin and stomped on the ear and he screamed, cried, started pleading then just cried as a foot cracked his mouth, Ya fuckin cottonpickin punk, and a hard kick in the ribs turned him slightly and he tried to raise himself on one knee and someone took a short step forward and kicked him in the solarplexus and he fell on his side, his knees up, arms folded across his abdomen, gasping for air and the blood in his mouth gurgled as he tried to scream, rolled down his chin then spumed forth as he vomited violently and someone stomped his face into the pool of vomit and the blood whirled slightly in arcs and a few bubbles gurgled in the puke as he panted and gasped and their shoes thudded into the shiteatinbastards kidneys and ribs and he groaned and his head rolled in the puke breaking the arching patterns of blood. (17)

This choreography is like *West Side Story* without the songs. It attempts to correct any sentimental version of New York street life. Along the way, however, it ritualizes and fetishizes violence. This isn't a fair fight but a sacred circle cast for a sadistic ritual. They literally kick the scapegoat when he's down, in excessive, baroque, and loving detail. Like Burroughs's scenes of violence, the vignette is aestheticized, stylized, and "tasty" if you like this sort of thing. The ritual of violence stabilizes the neighborhood, establishes who is at home here, and replaces the ritual of work. Vinnie and the gang end their day as it began, at the Greeks diner, washing up from the fight like men washing up from the workday. The section's title, "Another Day Another Dollar," emphasizes the nonshocking workaday nature of gang violence. The violence seems inevitable because the story ends at the Greeks, where it began, and the gang lives to fight another day. Violence is the neighborhood's steady state. Selby reinforces the routine by replaying this same conclusion over and over again. "Strike," for example, ends almost exactly like "Another Day Another Dollar," with the boys washing up and regrouping after a sadistic ritual: "The guys washed up in the Greeks, drying their hands with toilet paper and tossing the wet wads at each other, laughing. It was the first real kick since blowing up the trucks. The first good rumble since they dumped that doggy. They sprawled at the counter and at the tables and ordered coffeeand" (228).

Because we've seen these violent endings before, we know what will happen to Harry in "Strike" after he displays his desire for men. When Harry goes mad and solicits a neighborhood boy, Vinnie and the gang literally crucify him. They perform another sadistic ritual described in lavish detail. Harry's life becomes a predetermined Passion Play, each moment of his death as stylized as the Stations of the Cross. Indeed, the scene follows the Gospels closely, from the capital letters accusing the victim to the ritual blows and the descent from the cross.

> A minute later Joey, Vinnie and Sal and the rest of the guys from the Greeks came running down 2nd avenue to the lot. Harry was almost standing, holding on to the billboard, when they reached him. THERE HE IS. THERE HE IS. THE SONOFABITCH TRIED TA SUCK ME OFF. Harry let go of the billboard and started to extend his arms when Vinnie hit him on the cheek. Ya fuckin freak. Someone else hit him on the back of the neck and Harry fell to the ground and they kicked and stomped him, Joey squeezing in between to kick him too, and Harry barely moved, barely made a sound beyond a whimpering. A couple of the guys picked him up and stretched his arms across and around one of the crossbars of the sign and hung on his arms with all their weight and strength until Harrys arms were straining at their shoulder sockets, threatening to snap, and they took turns punching his stomach and chest and face until both eyes were drowned with blood, then a few of the guys joined the two pulling on his arms and they all tugged until they heard a snap and then they twisted his arms behind him almost tying them in a knot and when they let go he continued to hang from the bar then slowly started to slide down and to one side until one arm jerked around the bar and flopped back and forth like a snapped twig held only by a thin piece of bark and his shoulder jerked up until it was almost on a level with the top of his head and the guys watched Harry Black as he slowly descended from the billboard, his arms flapping back and forth until his jacket got caught on a splinter and the other arm spun around and he hung, impaled, and they hit and kicked him until the splinter snapped and Harry descended to the ground. (226–227)

The analogies with the Crucifixion make ritual scapegoating seem culturally necessary, as if violence had some higher reason. The victim has his necessary role. This sadism has its interlocking counterpart in the openly gay man's masochism. Masochism "asks for" and thus legitimates violence. In "The Queen Is Dead," the drag queen Georgette sees Vinnie as "rough trade," the fifties term for a supposedly straight working-class man who nonetheless accepts sexual favors from gay men. Masochistically, Georgette continues to pursue and idealize Vinnie even after he knifes her and has sex with her friend in the next room. With a switchblade or a penis, all acts of penetration seem equally wounding and humiliating. Thus, the penetrated is by nature a masochist. Georgette uses benzedrine-induced clouds of romance to deny Vinnie's violence. The likelihood of violence disappears neatly and matter-of-factly into her stream of consciousness. "It wasn't fear of being rebuked or hit by him (that could be developed in her mind into a lovers quarrel ending in a beautiful reconciliation) that restrained her, but she knew if done in the presence of his friends (who tolerated more than accepted her, or used her as a means to get high when broke or for amusement when bored) his pride would force him to abjure her completely and then there would not only be no hope, but, perhaps no dream" (25).

In "The Queen Is Dead"'s concluding moment of ritual subjugation, Georgette denies the olfactory evidence that Vinnie had another man before having her. The section ends with the words "O God no!!! Vinnie loves me. He loves me. It. Wasn't. Shit" (79). Georgette's effeminacy in a hypermasculine world marks her out as "the pink lampshade," the target for derision and abuse. Her fluttering and fussing prevent her from seeing what's in front of her eyes and thus make her deserving of humiliation.

Nonetheless, *Last Exit to Brooklyn* has liberating moments despite its violent conclusions. Georgette isn't only a foil and target for hipsters. She is a hipster herself. Her extravagant outness clears queer space. "Georgette was a hip queer. She (he) didnt try to disguise or conceal it with marriage and mans talk" (24). Although Georgette's defiance puts her at risk, it also makes the Subterranean City fall back before the Open City. Georgette uses camp speech as self-defense in her dangerous neighborhood: "Georgette was smart and could snow them under with words" (28). Georgette camps it up safely even at the Greeks, center of masculine violence. Her choreography serves as powerful counterpoint to Vinnie's choreography of violence.

> Some of the others in the Greeks clapped in time to the music and yelled, Go Georgette, Go! She put her hands behind her head, ellipsed her pelvis slowly and—bumped—up to one of the girls who was laughing at her and *threw* her hip in her face. Heres one for you, you big bitch. When the music stopped she sat on a stool at the counter, finished her coffee, spun around a few times on the stool, stopped, stood up holding her hands delicately in front of her in the dramatic manner of a concert singer and sang *un bel di* in a wavering falsetto. Someone laughed and said she should go on the stage. You have a nice voice, Georgie. Yeah, from the same girl, fa callin hogs. Georgette turned, put her hands on her hips, leaned her head to one side and looked at her disdainfully. What would you know about opera Miss Cocksucker? She *threw* her head back and sauntered out to the street in her finest regal fashion. (25)

"Strike" also offers a liberating counternarrative of safety and pleasure. In his everyday Brooklyn life, Harry is a petty tyrant who intimidates factory co-workers and slaps his wife around. However, even Harry gains temporary release when he allows himself sojourns at a Manhattan gay bar. Although we sense his tale will end horribly, these scenes do not feel doomed or overshadowed. Rather, they seem exempt from the inevitability of violence, as if they were intrusions from a happier story.

At first Harry is a tourist, enjoying the bar's sensationalism: "He stared at everyone as they moved and talked, never certain of their sex, but enjoying watching them and enjoying too the thrill and excitement he felt at being in such a weird place" (188). The bar is completely different from the predictable masculinity of his Brooklyn neighborhood. Soon, Harry moves beyond tourism to friendship, finding a temporary refuge in the gay community that—except for the hustling and benzedrine—borders on wholesomeness. His new world even allows him to cut loose from the city's iron grip. He falls into a state of pleasant inattention possible only when you've found your own crowd. "As summer passed, and the pleasant autumn weather followed, Harry joined his new friends when they went for a drive in the country . . . and Harry sat in the back, saying little, not minding the music or their screeching over a bunch of leaves, not noticing much of anything, but happy to be with them" (203–204). When Harry has sex with a man, he is purely and simply happy for the first time in his life—happy without violence, threats, or alcohol.

> Actually it was this feeling of happiness that bothered Harry more than anything else at the immediate moment he sat in the bed and looked at Alberta and remembered, with pleasure, the night before. He knew he felt good, yet he couldnt define his feeling. He couldnt say, I'm happy. He had nothing with which to compare his feeling. He felt good when he was telling wilson off; he felt good when he was with the guys having a drink; at those times he told himself he was happy, but his feeling now went so much beyond that that it was incomprehensible. He didnt realize that he had never been happy, this happy, before. (196–197)

Harry tries to compare his Brooklyn life to his Manhattan life and fails. Similarly, Selby intersperses Harry's comfortable happiness with scenes of tension, violence, and conventional masculinity at a Brooklyn strike. The world of the drag queens, not the world of the factory, unquestionably offers more chances for joy and true selfhood. These open-souled moments linger in the mind despite the story's violent conclusion. As we shall see, Ann Bannon and Truman Capote expand the Open City's pleasures much further, by denying the inevitability of violence.

10 | Sidestepping Assault
Ann Bannon and Truman Capote

Truman Capote's *Breakfast at Tiffany's* (1958) and Ann Bannon's lesbian pulp novels (1957–1962) emerge from New York's gay urban culture yet resist the discourse of sado-masochistic violence. While moody, "realistic" novels tend inevitably toward violence, these lighter works sidestep violence. Capote writes farce, while Bannon writes pulp melodrama. Bannon's soap operas sit at the intersection point between housewife discourse and the camp aesthetic usually associated with gay men. Capote's camp aesthetic blends with "camping out" to produce one of postwar fiction's most exhilarating portraits of the Open City. Both Bannon and Capote use the pop culture forms of camp and melodrama to clear safe subcultural space in a violently homophobic climate.

Both Bannon and Capote travel safely in disguise. To achieve mainstream success, Capote dresses up gay New York in heterosexual drag. Capote domesticates and desexualizes hustlers and bohemians so that they charm rather than alarm. Bannon's novels are "rituals for being born twice," explorations of young women's sexuality as compelling as coming-of-age novels like *The Catcher in the Rye* and *The Bell Jar*. However, she cloaks serious literature in melodrama, thus circumventing the discourse of sadomasochistic violence.

Ann Bannon: "Joyous, Crazy, Deep as Her Soul"
Ann Bannon's novels might seem like the last place to look for the Open City's joyful self-expression. Certainly, the shame

and masochism common in fifties homosexual discourse run through her fiction's stream of consciousness. Two main characters, Beebo Brinker and Jack Mann, are raging alcoholics; another, Laura Landon, seems to suffer from borderline personality disorder. Bannon's text confuses these two illnesses with that peculiar postwar disease gay melancholy. Bannon litters the narrative with phrases like "imprisoned in her homosexuality," "the whole discouraging mess of homosexual life," and "the heartbreak of the homosexual world."[1] Ultimately, however, Bannon uses the discourses of shame, heartbreak, and imprisonment to move beyond them. Through melodrama, she stage-manages her characters into natural and open lesbian lives.

Free pleasure contests fatalism in Bannon's fiction.[2] Lillian Faderman explains this contest by reference to the U.S. government's Cold War censorship of lesbian writing. To be published, lesbian writers had to disguise lesbian community within homophobic morality plays. Lesbians read between the lines. It wasn't ideal, but it was some form of community.

> That pulp novels with lesbian subject matter should have been permitted to proliferate during this period is not as surprising as it may seem at first glance, since they were generally cautionary tales: "moral" literature that warned females that lesbianism was sick or evil and that if a woman dared to love another woman she would end up lonely and suicidal. On the surface, at least, they seemed to confirm social prejudices about homosexuality. But despite that, lesbians read those novels avidly.
>
> The pulps, with their lurid covers featuring two women exchanging erotic gazes or locked in an embrace, could be picked up at newsstands and corner drugstores, even in small towns, and they helped spread the word about lesbian lifestyles to women who might have been too sheltered otherwise to know that such things existed. Lesbians bought those books with relish because they learned to read between the lines and get whatever nurturance they needed from them. Where else could one find public images of women loving women?[3]

Faderman concentrates on the ways pulp fiction cloaks reality and inhibits liberation. Ironically, however, pulp fiction can also make more imaginative room for female liberation than the serious, literary cult novels of the postwar era.[4] Like other forms of popular culture, pulp fiction is ambivalent in its liberating power. On the one hand, the sensationalism and moralizing of lesbian pulp prohibited honesty. On the other hand, as I shall argue, it is the melodrama of Bannon's fiction that resists the discourse of sadomasochistic violence common in other cult novels. The novels' most preposterous and grotesque moments pave the way for the Open City. Bannon's writing often veers close to camp, and as Scott Long writes, camp "zeroes in on moments when [texts] devote the most energy to stylizing and beautifying unassimilatable realities of power or pain."[5] Like the pearl in an oyster, Bannon's melodrama stylizes and beautifies the unassimilatable reality of homophobic violence.

When she wrote these novels, Ann Bannon was a housewife and young mother, occasionally visiting New York City from her home in Philadelphia.[6] Like the women protesters of City Hall Park, she uses the worldview and discourse of the white, middle-class housewife to claim protection in city space. Bannon uses soap opera, a form familiar to fifties housewives and very adaptable for use by gay writers. Like other cult novels, her books serve as tour guides to urban subcultures. However, Bannon's tourism reveals a signal difference based on gender. She opposes housewife-tourism to the more common tourism of the male gaze. This housewife-tourism grounds itself in the intertwined relationships of melodrama and women's community.

Bannon personifies male tourism through Jack Mann, a gay man who plays a strangely central role in these lesbian novels. As Michele Barale notes, Bannon uses "Jack as a site of narrative access. . . . Bannon makes use of the male's franchise on gazing."[7] Jack is the urban tour guide familiar to readers of *The Catcher in the Rye, The Adventures of Augie March,* or *Naked Lunch.* Indeed, he is that most familiar postwar figure, the war veteran rendered impervious to shock and blessed with second sight. Like the noir detective, the hipster, and other postwar male narrators, Jack can size people up at a glance: "Jack Mann had seen enough in his life to swear off surprise forever. He had seen the ports of the Pacific from the deck of a Navy hospital ship during World War II. He had helped patch the endless cut and bloodied bodies. . . . His emotional differentness had given Jack a good eye for people, a knack for sizing them up fast" (591–592). When Beebo Brinker and then Laura Landon come to town as naive young women, it is Jack, not a woman, who gives them (and readers) the gay vocabulary, the "tour of the bars," and even the news that they are lesbians: "Jack drank another shot. Then he put this glass down and leaned toward her over the table, his face serious. 'You're gay, Laura.'" "He would have to go slowly with [Beebo], teach her gently what she was, and teach her not to hate the word for it: Lesbian" (623, 242, 610).

Once Jack has ushered readers into Greenwich Village life, Bannon introduces a powerful housewife-tourism based on melodrama. When Jack takes Laura to her first gay bar, Bannon counterpoises a woman's reaction to the male gaze. In *I Am a Woman* (1959), Jack not only tour-guides but invites a straight male friend to join him in tour-guiding:

> "Doesn't anyone tell you anything, Mother? Burr, what's the matter with you? She's a tourist. Make with the old travelogue, boy."
>
> Burr laughed. "I thought you didn't get it, Laura." He smiled. "They're all queer." (226)

However, Bannon's Village thrives not on men's bemused observation but on women's sexual involvement. Sex, not travelogues, turns a woman into a Village insider. Unlike the tourism of male subcultural novels, Bannon doesn't dwell on picturesque or satirical vignettes. The bar scenes always lead right to Laura's enmeshment in sexual melodrama. Laura's and Beebo's lives become a soapy parody of the feminist "web of relationships." In her first bar visit, Laura immediately begins to imagine herself in dialogue with other patrons: "They looked at her—her own kind—from the bar and from the tables, and didn't recognize her. And Laura looked around at them and thought, I'm one of you. Help me" (226). She is drawn to Beebo at first sight, automatically and helplessly. "She pulled the comb hard through her hair, afraid to look into the mirror. She knew she would meet the eyes of the girl in the black pants" (229–230).

If Jack is the tour guide, then Laura occupies a halfway point between the tourist and the lesbian insider. Laura takes on the closeted persona of the imagined reader—or the author herself. Laura lives out the dream of many middle-class women when she escapes from her "confinement in luxury" at the start of *I Am a Woman.* Although not yet a housewife, she must break free from Betty Friedan's "feminine mystique": "It was a year of confinement in luxury, of tightly controlled resentment, of soul-searching. And one rainy night when he was out at a press dinner, she packed a small bag and went to Union Station. She bought a ticket to New York City. She could never be free from herself, but she could be free from her father, and at the moment that mattered the most" (195–196).

However, this escape to New York is not exactly the coming-out narrative it seems to be. Throughout the New York novels featuring Laura, she remains somehow confined and invisible within the gay community. While exploring lesbian life in the Village, Laura nonetheless remains the identification point for closeted readers. In *I Am a Woman* she leads a double life, commuting to the Village at night while juggling a job and a straight cover story uptown. This double life makes her anxious, always late, and fearful of discovery. She hides her emotions. She looks at her straight roommate: "Laura suddenly wanted to scream at her. It was so wrong, so false; so agonizing to have your lips sealed when you wanted to shout the truth" (230). Laura is invisible in the gay community: "It was as if she were a child of civilization, reared among the savages, who suddenly found herself among the civilized. She recognized them as her own. And yet she had adopted the habits of another race and she was embarrassed and lost with her own kind" (226).

In *Women in the Shadows* (1959), Laura lives as a confined housewife first with Beebo and then with Jack. Beebo has become hard-drinking and abusive. Even though living openly as a lesbian in the Village, Laura resides in a claustrophobic, violent home. She locks up her feelings in a diary kept in a steel strongbox: "She wrote in it only when she was alone, in the evenings before Beebo got home from work. Beebo had never read it—or seen it, in fact. It was Laura's own, Laura's aches and pains verbalized" (417). Laura becomes a figure of Bannon herself, writing down feelings and experiences kept hidden from her family and the outside world. As Bannon has described herself, "Everyone in my daily life thought that I was just a very nice, young conventional wife and mother. They really didn't know what was going on in my head or my emotions and that was sort of how I got away with it."[8] Finally, Laura ends up in a sexless marriage with Jack, becoming a sheltered housewife uptown. "Laura was naturally mild and yielding; Jack, efficient and good-humored and terribly proud of her" (517). In the marriage as well, Laura's feelings remain invisible: "There were times when Laura couldn't share her feelings, when she just hugged them to herself and brooded" (522).

Bannon never lets readers forget how it feels to be physically and emotionally confined. This confinement feeds into the dominant discourse of gay melancholy. However, confinement also allows Laura and her readers to burst forth into full enjoyment of the sexual Open City. When it comes to sex, Laura is anything but "mild and yielding." Laura may be unhappy, but she is also safely hidden from danger. Her confinement serves as a springboard for her joyous leaps into lesbian sex. "That's all the Village is, honey, just one crazy little soap opera after another," says Beebo, quoting tour guide Jack (275). However, Bannon finds the freeing potential within soap opera's shame and entrapment. Melodrama clears room for ever-repeating sexual pleasure despite "heartbreak." Indeed, the release from intense confinement determines the novel's intense erotics. For Bannon, sex itself is always exempt from shame, heartbreak, and entrapment, whatever the surrounding circumstances. Sex is the Open City itself, the home of natural expression and the soul's own truth. "Her hands explored, caressed, felt Beebo all over, while her own body responded with violent spasms—joyous, crazy, deep as her soul" (283).

Amazing for the repressive fifties context, Bannon associates lesbian sex not with the subterranean world of The Cellar bar but with the openness of the streets. She transforms the meaning of the woman on the street at night. In this era, a lesbian woman's presence on the nighttime street was itself subversive. Historian Charles Kaiser quotes the recollections of Joan Nestle: "Just going to the bar meant taking on fifties America. It meant being a woman who was different from the protected woman, the domesticated woman. It felt subversive just going out in the streets at two o'clock in the morning, knowing that I was going to a place that was illegal." Even the streets themselves seemed more shadowy and sinister. "New York at night looked more forbidding than it does today. Before high-intensity streetlights were installed as an anticrime measure during John Lindsay's administration at the end of the sixties, side streets were often steeped in shadows."[9] As in the title of one of Ann Bannon's books, lesbians were often called "women in the shadows," a designation meant to evoke shame and marginality. However, Bannon takes the signifier "shadows" and spins it around. The meaning of dark doorways changes from shame to pure sexual happiness.

> "Laura, darling." Beebo put an arm around her and led her away as she had before, and suddenly, strangely, Laura felt like running. She felt like running with all her strength until they reached Beebo's apartment. For there was no doubt about it any longer, that was where they were going.
>
> She wanted her arms around Beebo, their hot bare bodies pressed together as before. Almost without realizing it she began to speed up and then to run. Instantly Beebo was after her, then beside her, laughing that pagan laugh of hers. She caught a handful of Laura's streaming hair, silver in the street light, and pulled her to a stop, whirling her around. In almost the same gesture she swept her into a dark doorway and kissed her, still laughing. (326)

Running with all your might down city streets is the classic Open City trope, a signifier of joy and youthful abandon. If only for a moment, the subculture owns the streets. Usually tight and tense, Laura lets go. If Laura can turn into "somebody entirely different," so can the reader. The two women mix their adult desire with childlike game playing, a "wild race" and "a little shriek of unbearable excitement." This game breaks through the walls of shame and melancholy. The laughing excitement of young passion argues for its own wholesomeness. Lesbianism can't be "unnatural" when the desire is this wild, this uncontrollable, this much fun. Sex and laughter burst out together. Laura is inviting Beebo to capture her, but she is inviting sex, not violence.

Laura eluded her, moving just a little faster each time, until they were running again, and Laura felt the laughter coming out of her, soft and light at first, but growing wilder, uncontrollable. She fled, inches from Beebo's hands, into the dark hallway, and scrambled up the stairs, losing her footing, and nearly losing her freedom, twice. Beebo was so close behind her at the top that she could hear her breath. With a little shriek of unbearable excitement, she fell against Beebo's door, and felt within a second Beebo's weight come hard against her. The laughter burst out of her again until Beebo got the door open and they almost fell into the living room. (327–328)

If Laura is the housewife-spectator who comes into Village knowledge, Beebo Brinker is the spectacle. The narrative just can't keep its eyes off Beebo's butch beauty. It describes her looks over and over and over, in classic pulp style. Sequels in a pulp novel series need to repeat information, but pulp tends toward excess anyway. Why describe handsomeness once when you can do it again and again? The novels describe Beebo variously as "shockingly boyish," "the handsome boyish girl," "handsome, like a young boy of fourteen," and "uncommonly handsome," with "a startlingly handsome face gazing down at her: black hair, pure blue eyes, a slight smile that widened a little when Laura turned her face up" (230, 259, 273, 594, 261). There is something uncanny about Beebo's looks. Her presence is unintentionally provocative: "There was an air of self-confidence and sensual promise about Beebo that she couldn't help" (646). This presentation of Beebo's appearance falls into the pulp mode of instant attraction and instant passion.

Because she is so conspicuously butch, however, Beebo belongs to a social group that frequently gets attacked and raped. Within the discourse of sadomasochistic violence, Beebo is "asking for it." (Laura, by contrast, is a college-girl "kiki" who easily passes for straight.)[10] Thus, Bannon's melodrama works overtime to protect Beebo from violence. Preposterous soap opera plotting distracts attention from real-life power relationships and social trauma. Let's look at two particularly outlandish episodes: Beebo's "hectic affair with a fantastically difficult actress" named, of all things, Venus Bogardus (791); and Beebo's beating herself up and claiming she has been attacked by homophobic thugs, in order to get Laura's attention.

The start of *Beebo Brinker* (1962) presents us with the real-life homophobic context before floating off into fantasy. The Village has recently endured a rash of police raids against gay bars—according to historians, a constant occurrence from the 1930s through the 1960s.[11] By 1962, the Village has been gentrified before the term *gentrification* was coined. As

Beebo Brinker reports, the Village is home not just to bohemians but also to "ambitious businessmen with wives and families, who played hob with the local bohemia. A rash of raids was in progress on the homosexual bar hangouts at the moment, with cops rousting respectable beards-and-sandals off their favorite park benches; hustling old dykes, who were Village fixtures for eons, off the streets so they wouldn't offend the deodorized young middle-class wives" (592). Bannon turns the problem around, using the housewifely familiarity of soap opera to make the streets safe for butch lesbians.

The most absurd episode in Bannon's novels is Beebo's sojourn in Hollywood, where she serves as stable "boy" and lover to famous actress Venus Bogardus until the scandal breaks in the gossip columns. With a name like a newly discovered sex organ, Venus Bogardus is obviously (too obviously) modeled on Mae West. She shares West's combination of overt sexuality and aging grotesque. Beebo first thinks, "I never liked Venus Bogardus. . . . I read somewhere that her curves are built into her clothes. She's about as sexy as a hatrack under the finery—and a cool forty-eight years old" (672). Bowled over by Venus's charms, Beebo soon changes her tune: "With a thrill of recognition, Beebo suddenly saw her. She was wearing a scarlet, silk-jersey dress. When she moved, she proved there was nothing beneath it. The hatrack story lay down and died" (674). Va-va-va-voom.

To quote Scott Long, this campy episode stylizes and beautifies "unassimilatable realities of power or pain." Beebo accepts Venus's invitation to Hollywood in response to the threat of male violence. She suddenly decides to go when her boss, Pete, attacks her. Pete represents the subtext of sadomasochistic violence. Pete wants to teach Beebo a sadistic sexual lesson, and he believes she has it coming to her. His response grows with seeming inevitability from his first gaze at her. From their first meeting, Beebo has been "aware of his eyes on her face and body" (615). However, Bannon neatly sidetracks the "inevitable" march of violence.

> And with one abrupt movement he reached her side and threw her hard against the door of the truck, pulling her left arm up high in the back in a wrenchingly painful hammer lock. Beebo gave a gasp of shock and tried to break free. But for all her size and strength, she was still a girl, and no match for an angry, jealous man who had been wanting her and wanting to hurt her since he first saw her.
>
> He forced his mouth on hers and when she struggled he bit her. She tried to knee him, and he pulled her arm up so hard they both thought for a moment he had broken it. Beebo went white with the pain, and leaned weakly against the door. Pete kissed her again,

taking his time and not trying to unhinge her arm any more. The rough scratch of his whiskers, and smell of his winy breath, the push of his hard hips, almost made her faint.

"Now why do you make me hurt you, Beebo? Why do you do that?" he said in a tense whisper, as if it were all her fault. . . .

"Maybe Mona was right," he said, his voice getting thin and mean. "Maybe you need a lesson before you learn what's good for you."

"I don't need any from you," Beebo spat at him. "I'm getting out of here right now, and you'll never see me again."

"I'll catch up with you one of these days," he said. "No matter where you go."

"The hell you will. You're not going to chase me all the way to California just to kick my can," Beebo said hotly. (729–731)

Pete may believe in the discourse of sadomasochistic violence, but Beebo does not. Beebo is no masochist; she doesn't go weak-kneed at Pete's sadism. Thus she can resist his meanness and leave. Bannon deeroticizes violence. She makes it clear that wanting Beebo and wanting to hurt her are not the same thing. The preposterous Hollywood episode airlifts Beebo out of male violence, whether in the form of police harassment or sexual assault by a private individual.

Women in the Shadows (1959) also contains an episode of grotesque melodrama that evokes the discourse of sadomasochistic violence only to dismiss it. As in *Beebo Brinker,* the novel begins by presenting a real-life danger to lesbians. Soap operas are famous for inconsistency of character, and Bannon's soaps are no exception. In *Women in the Shadows,* Beebo has become a severe alcoholic, and her live-in lover, Laura, fears Beebo's erratic behavior. Beebo's drinking combined with her butch appearance places her at high risk. "It was true that Laura was ashamed to go anywhere out of Greenwich Village with her . . . Beebo, nearly six feet of her, with her hair cropped short and her strange clothes and her gruff voice. And when she flirted with the [store] clerks! Laura had been afraid more than once that they would call the police and drag Beebo off to jail" (441–442). The genuine threat to Beebo's safety emerges, although veiled in Laura's language of shame.

Since Laura's fears have alerted readers to the threat of danger, it comes as no surprise when Laura comes home to find Beebo bruised and half-naked on their bedroom floor. For the first time in the series, Bannon lets us know that assault happens to butches all the time. The "old story" of violence runs underneath Bannon's tales of wild sex and self-discovery.

"It's an old story," Beebo said, her voice tired and bitter, but curiously resigned. "I don't know why it didn't happen to me years sooner. Nearly every butch I know gets it one way or another. Sooner or later they catch up with you."

"Who catches up with you?"

"The goddam sonofabitch toughs who think it's smart to pick fights with Lesbians. They ask you who the hell do you think you are, going around in pants all the time. They say if you're going to wear pants and act like a man you can damn well fight like a man. And they jump you for laughs . . . God." (465)

This intrusion of realism is shocking in the midst of Beebo and Laura's baroque sexual intrigues. Beebo's acceptance of her fate is even more unnerving. Beebo seems resigned to violence. As in the case of Pete, the "old story" of violence lurks out there waiting to happen "sooner or later." Beebo even seems to accept that assault is fundamental to a butch's existence, an "occupational hazard." She takes on that risk as routinely as she puts on her pants. She is certainly realistic about the judicial system's indifference to the rape of a lesbian. In a context of seemingly irreparable injustice, no wonder Beebo drinks.

"*Prosecute*?" Beebo stared at her and then she gave a short, sharp laugh. "Are you kidding? Who's going to mourn for the lost virtue of a Lesbian? What lawyer is going to make a case for a poor queer gone wrong? Everybody will think I got what I deserved. . . .

"No thanks, baby," Beebo said, her voice suddenly tired. "I've got enough trouble in the world without advertising that I'm gay. I always knew this would happen and I always knew what I'd do about it . . . just exactly nothing. Because there's nothing I *can* do. It's part of the crazy life I live. A sort of occupational hazard, you might say." (467)

Thus, Bannon faces a still-central issue: the problem of hate crimes and their prosecution. But Bannon doesn't face the problem directly for long. Again, she uses melodrama to airlift Beebo out of the homophobic climate. The story has another twist. Beebo's elaborate political analysis is just a cover story. Beebo's friend Lili reveals to Laura that Beebo attacked herself and killed her own dog in order to recapture Laura's roving attention (Laura had just begun an affair with an exotic modern dancer named Tris). Serious exploration of real violence gives way to melodrama's "frustrated love." We know we're back in soap opera land with the sudden proliferation of characters involved: Lili, Laura, Tris, Beebo, and even Nix the dog. Another signal of soap opera is the deceit in the name of passionate obsession.

"Did anyone . . . really . . . beat her up?" Laura said, her breath betraying her and making her gasp. "Or did she make up the hoodlums, too—like Nix?" And she covered her face to cry while Lili answered her.

"She did that to herself. After she killed Nix. I don't know why she did it. I hate to admit it, but I guess she did it out of frustrated love. I tried to make her explain it when she told me about it—and believe me, she wouldn't have if she hadn't been fried—and she just said, "Laura hated him. I thought she might stay with me longer if he was gone." After she did it she beat herself. I don't know how. I don't know with what. She didn't say. Maybe she just whacked at herself with her fists. Maybe she used something heavy. Anyway, she did it while she was hysterical. At least, that's what I think. I don't see how she could have hurt herself that much if she hadn't been half crazy. She was mourning for Nix and she was afraid of losing you." (557)

This image of Beebo "whacking at herself" is tragic and absurd at the same time. Scott Long writes that since gay tragedy is already misperceived as funny, camp "imitates the oppressive mechanism only to expose it by forcing it to its extremes."[12] Beebo's self-administered beating imitates the oppressive mechanism of male violence but takes it way over the top. In a deeply ambivalent way, Bannon both mimics and exposes the discourse of sadomasochistic violence. This scene nods to homophobic discourse while also defying it. In one perspective, Beebo's masochism confirms homophobic prejudices. Why should we fight to stop hate crimes if women lie about attacks and bring trouble on themselves? If Beebo beats herself up, why shouldn't others beat her, too? Beebo's auto-abuse mirrors fifties homophobia. A leading gay-bashing "expert" of the times castigated lesbians for their "self-created trouble-making."[13] Beebo's beating herself up mimics this oppressive discourse to an absurd degree.

In another perspective, Beebo's melodrama opens the door to imaginative liberation, to having your fun "in the most natural way imaginable." Bannon breaks through the wall of sadomasochistic violence. At one moment, Bannon brings home the danger of gay-bashing. At another moment, she refutes the notion that assault is a lesbian's inevitable fate. Although Beebo claims that male violence is inevitable, she is lying. The attack lying in wait for every butch has never happened to her. Beebo's masochism, like Bannon's work in general, concerns strange domestic relationships among women, not the external threats of men. "The heartbreak of the homosexual world" turns out to be the synthetic and bearable heartbreak of soap opera. This sidestepping is not an ideal narrative solution, but Bannon does her best in a cold climate. Her characters live on to embarrass themselves another day.

Bannon strains factual credulity in order to make the reader believe in the world of lesbian pleasure and fantasy. Bannon makes the Village safe enough for Beebo, despite her unconcealable butchness, bravery, and swagger. The Open City has to embrace her because Beebo has no choice but openness. "Beebo saw her own doubts reflected in Paula's eyes. But she saw desire there, too; desire so big that it had to be brave: it hadn't any place to hide" (664).

Bannon's unnatural plot lines permit Beebo to experience the natural pleasures of lesbian life. On one of Beebo's first trips to a women's bar, she feels the exhilaration of the Open City. Encountering her proper context at last, Beebo finds that her face and frame provoke desire and friendly interest, not violence. Anticipating the 1970s, Bannon shows how community engenders pride. In line with postwar subcultural thought, Bannon also shows how community engenders excitement.

> It excited Beebo intensely—all that femininity. She was silent, studying the girls at the table while Jack talked with them. When she shook hands with them, a new feeling gripped her. For the first time in her life she was proud of her size, proud of her strength, even proud of her oddly boyish face. She could see interest, even admiration on the faces of the girls. She was not used to that kind of reaction in people, and it exhilarated her. . . .
>
> The music was rhythmic and popular. The floor was jammed with a mass of couples . . . a mass of girls, dancing, arms locked around each other, bodies pressed close and warm. Their cheeks were touching. Quick light kisses were exchanged. And they were all girls, every one of them: young and lovely and infatuated with each other. They touched one another with gentle caresses, they kissed, they smiled and laughed and whispered while they turned and moved together.
>
> There was no shame, no shock, no self-consciousness about it at all. They were enjoying themselves. They were having fun in the most natural way imaginable. (625)

Camping Out with Truman Capote

Among the postwar cult novels, *Breakfast at Tiffany's* most clearly illustrates the link between camping out and the camp aesthetic. Capote's main character, Holly Golightly, rests lightly on the city in two ways. She avoids putting down deep roots, and she lightens up the city with her frothy wit. Being subcultural means being on the run, but it also means having fun with your own transience.

Breakfast at Tiffany's describes the colorful tenants of an old brownstone apartment building in New York's East Seventies and the growing friendship between Holly Golightly and an unnamed, strangely invisible male narrator. (The Hollywood screen version rewrote this narrator as a romantic lead, played by George Peppard.) If we read between the lines, we know Holly is an uptown call girl who inhabits a queer subculture. Her world of hustlers, artists, and bohemians is only a social class away from the demimondes of Hubert Selby Jr. and Charles S. Wright. The crucial twist is that Capote's subculture passes for straight, and that change makes all the difference.[14] Capote's masquerade permitted *Breakfast at Tiffany's* to sell like hotcakes when serialized in *Esquire,* to succeed in book form, and to become one of Hollywood's best-loved films.[15] The masking also frees Capote from the discourse of sado-masochistic violence and liberates his Open City. Tiffany's jewelry store symbolizes the safety zone releasing Holly from the potential threats of depression, poverty, and male violence: "What I've found does the most good is just to get into a taxi and go to Tiffany's. It calms me down right away, the quietness and the proud look of it; nothing very bad could happen to you there, not with those kind men in their nice suits, and that lovely smell of silver and alligator wallets. If I could find a real-life place like Tiffany's, then I'd buy some furniture and give the cat a name."[16]

The novella as a whole also represents a safety zone, sheltered from real-life dangers. Holly boasts, "Leave it to me: I'm always top banana in the shock department" (51). However, her shocks aren't really very shocking. The book yields more charm than alarm. Even though he's writing about a hustler and her free-living friends, Capote suppresses sex altogether and thus sexual danger. Only occasionally does Holly's vulnerability peek through. When Holly explains why she'd rather skip town than testify against a gangster friend, her rationale betrays her knowledge of New York's hustler's geography. She knows just where she fits on a hierarchy of "escorts" that starts at "21" and runs all the way down to Forty-second Street.

> Tilting her compact mirror above her face, smoothing her lipstick with a crooked pinkie, she said: "And to be honest, that isn't all. Certain shades of limelight wreck a girl's complexion. Even if a jury gave me the Purple Heart, this neighborhood holds no future: they'd still have up every rope from LaRue to Perona's Bar and Grill—take my word, I'd be about as welcome as Mr. Frank E. Campbell. And if you lived off my particular talents, Cookie, you'd understand

the kind of bankruptcy I'm describing. Uh, uh, I don't just fancy a fade-out that finds me belly-bumping around Roseland with a pack of West Side hillbillies." (80)

Holly smoothes the mask of makeup on her face at the very moment she lets her hustler's mask slip. The line "Certain shades of limelight wreck a girl's complexion" sounds very much like the camp speech of hustler–drag queens in Selby or Wright. In describing how various gay male authors "repress [their]debt to camp," David van Leer notes, "It is [Holly's] language that most clearly links her to gay male culture. . . . Holly speaks in the epigrammatic style of domesticated camp."[17] Capote makes her a heterosexual character, however. Armed in straight privilege, Holly can confess breezily to sexual feelings that would fill Ann Bannon's characters with all the requisite shame. "I'd settle for Garbo any day. Why not? A person ought to able to marry men or women or—listen, if you came to me and said you wanted to hitch up with Man o' War, I'd respect your feeling" (66). "Of course people couldn't help but think I must be a bit of a dyke myself. And of course I am. Everyone is: a bit. So what? That never discouraged a man yet, in fact it seems to goad them on" (23). On the whole, Holly comes across more like a drag queen than a lesbian. Her camp mannerisms stylize and beautify moments of shock and pain. When Holly receives a rejection letter from her fiancé, she doesn't take the news barefaced.

> The instant she saw the letter she squinted her eyes and bent her lips in a tough tiny smile that advanced her age immeasurably. "Darling," she instructed me, "would you reach in the drawer there and give me my purse. A girl doesn't read this sort of thing without her lipstick."
>
> Guided by a compact mirror, she powdered, painted every vestige of twelve-year-old out of her face. She shaped her lips with one tube, colored her cheeks from another. She penciled the rims of her eyes, blued the lids, sprinkled her neck with 4711; attached pearls to her ears and donned her dark glasses; thus armored, and after a displeased appraisal of her manicure's shabby condition, she ripped open the letter and let her eyes race through it while her stony small smile grew smaller and harder. (77)

Holly's masking is far from trivial; it armors her for the undeniable shocks of life. With comic exaggeration, Capote builds a face for Holly so elaborate that it becomes a mask. Her face hardens as if it were made of plaster. The novella masks itself in the same way, elaborately and wittily disguising controversial topics. The narrator himself seems "infuriatingly left out" of the story, perhaps because Holly serves as his ego in drag. He reveals very little of his own history. "Never mind why, but once I walked from New Orleans to Nancy's Landing, Mississippi, just under five hundred miles" (82). The words "never mind why" mark the limits of his self-disclosure, but he also leaves a tiny clue, a double entendre called "Nancy's Landing."[18]

Indeed, the entire story seems to take place in a gay subculture passing for straight. It is difficult to keep in mind that Holly's roommate, Mag Wildwood, is supposed to be a woman and not a drag queen. Mag sails into a party wagging her finger and reproaching Holly for "hogging all these simply riveting men!" (38). Mag herself seems rather like an exceptionally riveting man. She uses her "ugly" masculine features as a paradoxical form of bewitching artifice.

> She was a triumph over ugliness, so often more beguiling than real beauty, if only because it contains paradox. In this case, as opposed to the scrupulous method of plain good taste and scientific grooming, the trick had been worked by exaggerating defects; she'd made them ornamental by admitting them boldly. Heels that emphasized her height, so steep her ankles trembled; a flat tight bodice that indicated she could go to a beach in bathing trunks; hair that was pulled straight back, accentuating the spareness, the starvation of her fashion-model face. (38–39)

Mag "works her tricks" one way; Holly works them another. Holly frequently escorts a wealthy man named Rusty Trawler. She explains to the narrator that Rusty seems babyish because he won't admit he's gay. But Rusty's childishness also suits Holly's purposes. It provides one of many ways for the novella to sidestep sexual danger. When Holly gets stabbed, it's only with a butter knife. Rusty feels safer in diapers the same way Holly feels safer in Tiffany's, but Capote never explains what the danger might be. Throughout the book, being childlike allows the characters to feel safe and free: "Use your head. Can't you see it's just that Rusty feels safer in diapers than he would in a skirt? Which is really the choice, only he's awfully touchy about it. He tried to stab me with a butter knife because I told him to grow up and face the issue, settle down and play house with a nice fatherly truck driver" (37).

Capote shows Holly fending off aggressive men, but he uses her winsome charm to distract our attention from the threat of violence. Holly appears on the narrator's fire escape one night, wearing nothing but a bathrobe. She has escaped from a "date" who is "terrifying" and a "beast." She shows off his bite marks on her skin. But Capote plays the scene not as sexual assault but as a bedroom farce. Holly's audacity and fluent chatter distract our attention from her vulnerability. The longer she rattles on, the less we worry about the drunk downstairs. Her camp speech lightens the moment: the man isn't "a beast" but "quel beast!"

> "I've got the most terrifying man downstairs," she said, stepping off the fire escape into the room. "I mean he's sweet when he isn't drunk, but let him start lapping up the vino, and oh God quel beast! If there's one thing I loathe, it's men who bite." She loosened a gray flannel robe off her shoulder to show me evidence of what happens if a man bites. The robe was all she was wearing. "I'm sorry if I frightened you. But when the beast got so tiresome I just went out the window."
> (19)

Holly's good taste and good timing ward off grotesquerie and keep her coolly in control. Capote's style is so deft, we forget she's a call girl subject to the whims of repulsive and potentially violent men. Holly seems so cool, trim, and together, it's hard to imagine anything defeating her. Her grace triumphs; she simply steps out of the way and lets her opponents trip on their own weight. The narrator first glimpses Holly in the hallway of their apartment building, accompanied by a most unattractive date: "When they reached her door she rummaged her purse in search of a key, and took no notice of the fact that his thick lips were nuzzling the nape of her neck" (17). Similarly, the reader learns to take no notice of oily men's advances and focuses on Holly's grace instead. Holly's cool beauty translates perfectly into the casting of Audrey Hepburn in the movie role. "It was a warm evening, nearly summer, and she wore a slim cool black dress, black sandals, a pearl choker. For all her chic thinness, she had an almost breakfast-cereal air of health, a soap and lemon cleanness, a rough pink darkening in the cheeks" (16). The narrator serves as a hidden camera, able to "see without being seen." Thus, the viewer can fetishize Holly's looks without turning into one of her creepy suitors.

Capote's masking of physical threat allows for one of postwar fiction's best depictions of the Open City. Holly and the narrator clasp hands and run giddily all over New York. Their sense of fun is always retrospective, however; the narrator is fondly recalling his "hither and yonning days with Holly" (46). The story happens during the early days of World War II. It begins, "I am always drawn back to places where I have lived, the houses and their neighborhoods. For instance, there is a brownstone in the East Seventies where, during the early years of the war, I had my first New York apartment" (9). This beginning sets up the novel's affectionate yet transient sense of place. The story will unfold in the golden days of first adulthood. The two friends' intense enjoyment of city life may reflect a deeroticized version of New York's role as playground for gay culture during World War II. The story's end marks the end of their lighthearted friendship, the end of the war and the coming of the postwar era. The narrator is "moving out of the brownstone because it was haunted" (85). During urban renewal, many old brownstones seemed haunted and doomed.

The friends' free play in New York City depends on masking. During their first shoplifting venture, they steal masks and wear them "all the way home." This is one of the few places where "home" appears unambivalently. Apparently they require their masks to ease into a comfortable sense of place. As we have seen, Capote hints at masquerade all the way through the story. Like the nuns in this scene, Holly and the narrator are in costume even before they get to the store. Just as the cult novel presents urban subcultures to a mass readership, the two friends perform their high jinks before "a pressure of eyes."

> Passing a Woolworth's, she gripped my arm: "Let's steal something," she said, pulling me into the store, where at once there seemed a pressure of eyes, as though we were already under suspicion. "Come on. Don't be chicken." She scouted a counter piled with paper pumpkins and Halloween masks. The saleslady was occupied with a group of nuns who were trying on masks. Holly picked up a mask and slipped it over her face; she chose another and put it on mine; then she took my hand and we walked away. It was a simple as that. Outside, we ran a few blocks, I think to make it more dramatic; but also because, as I'd discovered, successful theft exhilarates. I wondered if she'd often stolen. "I used to," she said. "I mean I had to. If I wanted anything. But I still do it every now and then, sort of to keep my hand in."
>
> We wore the masks all the way home. (46)

The Open City depends on strong bonds between members of the same generation, and the bonding starts here. The narrator experiences a delayed adolescence, learning to shoplift from an older and cooler kid. Like kids, they hold hands, run down the street, and take something fun and useless. This scene shows the childlike innocence of the Open City, with a hint of naughtiness. The whole city becomes childlike; even the nuns are trying on Halloween masks. This scene puts masks on top of masks. It renders poverty and criminality as no more serious than minor shoplifting, shoplifting where you don't get caught. The clerks look at them as though they were "already under suspicion," when in fact Holly really is under suspicion by the FBI for consorting with mobsters. Holly also masks the poverty of her upbringing. In Ralph Ellison or Charles S. Wright, this glancing reference to southern poverty would prompt a grim flashback. Holly isn't about to get that serious, but she does suggest that poverty still threatens. However, the two friends' happiness makes them immune from all dangers.

Holly and the narrator even appropriate the war for their own pleasure. Unlike the brooding, dread-filled city of film noir, Capote's wartime city is full of fanfare and fresh beginnings. Here, the two friends celebrate the sale of the narrator's first short story. The friendship has hit the point where they can spend endless hours wandering in perfect amity.

> That Monday in October, 1943. A beautiful day with the buoyancy of a bird. To start, we had Manhattans at Joe Bell's; and, when he heard of my good luck, champagne cocktails on the house. Later, we wandered toward Fifth Avenue, where there was a parade. The flags in the wind, the thump of military bands and military feet, seemed to have nothing to do with war, but to be, rather, a fanfare arranged in my personal honor.
>
> We ate lunch at the cafeteria in the park. Afterwards, avoiding the zoo (Holly said she couldn't bear to see anything in a cage), we giggled, ran, sang along the paths toward the old wooden boathouse, now gone. Leaves floated on the lake; on the shore, a parkman was fanning a bonfire of them, and the smoke, rising like Indian signals, was the only smudge on the quivering air. Aprils have never meant much to me, autumns seem that season of beginning, spring; which is how I felt sitting with Holly on the railings of the boathouse porch. (45)

Everyone should get to have a day like this: a day of perfect friendship, a day that seems arranged just for you. Even the bartender is your friend and buys you drinks on the house. Even the flags fly in your honor. Capote raises but then dismisses the possibility of war, the possibility of cages. His language is delightful: "a beautiful day with the buoyancy of a bird." Everyone seems to float through the air, from flags to birds to leaves to people. The city seems so safe that even children (or childlike adults) can wander in perfect freedom. Holly and the narrator are completely at ease, whether singing on the paths or perching on the railings.

This ease depends not only on camp masquerade but also on camping out. The two friends wander freely out in the open, but their freedom relies on a transitory sense of place. Shoplifting becomes a metaphor for urban life. Holly loves the city, but it doesn't belong to her; therefore, she steals little pieces of it. The narrator describes another outing when

Holly's sober Brazilian fiancé is out of town. The city appears as a set of pocketable objects: a box of joss sticks, a postcard view.

> Those final weeks, spanning end of summer and the beginning of another autumn, are blurred in memory, perhaps because our understanding of each other had reached that sweet depth where two people communicate more often in silence than in words: an affectionate quietness replaces the tensions, the unrelaxed chatter and chasing about that produce a friendship's more showy, more, in the surface sense, dramatic moments. Frequently, when he was out of town (I'd developed hostile attitudes toward *him,* and seldom used his name) we spent entire evenings together during which we exchanged less than a hundred words; once, we walked all the way to Chinatown, ate a chow-mein supper, bought some paper lanterns and stole a box of joss sticks, then moseyed across the Brooklyn Bridge, and on the bridge, as we watched seaward-moving ships pass between the cliffs of burning skyline, she said: "years from now, years and years, one of those ships will bring me back, me and my nine Brazilian brats. Because yes, they *must* see this, these lights, the river—I love New York, even though it isn't mine, the way something has to be, a tree or a street or a house, something, anyway, that belongs to me because I belong to it." (67)

Capote suggests the ease of urban movement along with the ease of this mature friendship. The corny cowboy word "mosey" suggests their childlike happiness along with their comfortable rambling. This is a New York without hassles and without borders. Despite New York's congestion, it is a common pleasure to wander from one neighborhood to another and to take a stroll across the bridge from Manhattan to Brooklyn. However, this friendship hits its ripening just at the parting point. The narrator's perspective is nostalgic recollection: "Those final weeks . . . are blurred in memory." Holly is acutely aware of the city's beauty precisely because she plans to leave soon and doesn't feel she belongs there. Her vision of an open and playful city depends on departure. The joss sticks suggest the festivity and ceremony of this friendship, but also its ephemeral nature.

The narrator describes Holly's apartment: "Her bedroom was consistent with her parlor: it perpetuated the same camping-out atmosphere; crates and suitcases, everything packed and ready to go, like the belongings of a criminal who feels the law not far behind" (44). Capote's camp wit distracts us from the truth that Holly lives very close to the criminal world and finally ends up on the lam. Capote stylizes and beautifies the difficult realities of New York's hustling and gay subcultures.

Holly's "camping out" both mirrors and defies the threat of homophobic violence. Camping out resembles the transience of New York's gay bars, building a subcultural community while forced to live on the run. As historian George Chauncey writes, "From the 1930s through the 1960s, most gay bars lasted only a few months or years before the police closed them and forced their patrons to move on to some other locale."[19] Like many subcultural denizens, Holly makes fun out of necessity.

11 | Hipster Meets Housewife
Paule Marshall and Jack Kerouac

The Manhattan subcultural scene offers new lives to the young protagonists of Jack Kerouac's *On the Road* (1957) and Paule Marshall's *Brown Girl, Brownstones* (1959). Both main characters live with relatives in Greater New York—Sal Paradise with his aunt in Paterson, New Jersey, and Selina Boyce with her mother in Brooklyn. The past weighs heavily on both immigrant families, the French Canadian and the Barbadian American. By contrast, the Open City vision frees young people into joy and out of past grief. As Diane Di Prima wrote in *Memoirs of a Beatnik,* living in Greenwich Village meant "one's blood running strong and red in one's own veins, not drawn to feed the ineradicable grief of the preceding generations."[1] Marshall and Kerouac share common imagery of young bohemians possessing the city streets through their camaraderie, art, and exhilaration. The underground comes above ground, pulsing with life. Both writers share what Catharine Stimpson calls the Beat "ethos of personal exposure."[2] Openness leads to vulnerability, however, especially if you are engaged in alternative practices others despise. For Selina Boyce the danger comes from interracial friendships and from the fundamental problem of walking as a black woman through a white-dominated world. Sal Paradise's circle, on the other hand, enjoys white privilege but indulges in drug use and joyriding and flirts with bisexuality. The question remains the same for both novels: How do you keep yourself safe and maintain your joy when you're living on the edge? Jack Kerouac portrays the Open City and the open road as innocent, joyful places because he suppresses the threat of homophobia and the pull of his elders, especially mother figures. For Kerouac, Mom represents everything the men of the Beat Generation rebel against; however, she also shadows him constantly.

Paule Marshall, on the other hand, cannot write as if violence and motherhood do not exist. The realities of racism intrude on (but do not defeat) the innocence of the Open City. Ultimately, as a black woman, Selina Boyce cannot repress past generations and set Mom up as the shockable, conventional other to her bohemianism. As Selina eventually learns, Mom is inside her in spite of herself. Thus, Marshall presents a young vigorous generation nonetheless linked in a long chain with the griefs of previous generations. Kerouac and Marshall share a similar Open City philosophy, but they come down on opposite sides of a central question: Can the younger generation start fresh? Kerouac answers yes, but Marshall answers no.

Jack Kerouac's *On the Road* injects new life into masculine detachment. If postwar displacement is inevitable, Kerouac shows readers how to love it. Among the Beats, masculine detachment is not for tense, isolated men but instead creates a relaxed, joyful male community. Sal Paradise loves his insane, delinquent friend Dean Moriarty because Dean shows him how to move beyond grief and numbness. Sal suppresses information about his immediate history, but his story upon meeting Dean nonetheless has far-reaching resonances. A war veteran, Sal is still drifting and depressed: "I first met Dean not long after my wife and I split up. I had just gotten over a serious illness that I won't bother to talk about, except that it had something to do with the miserable weary split-up and my feeling that everything was dead."[3] Sal's repeated sense of Dean as a "long-lost brother" is a wish fulfillment for a generation that had lost so many brothers and friends. Kerouac himself deeply mourned the deaths of his brother Gerard in childhood and his closest friend, Sammy Sampas, in World War II.[4]

Connecting with Dean, Sal finds a way to recapture lost brotherhood and move into "Natural Joy." Despite his glaring flaws, Dean's magic is that he "*cared about everything on principle*" (155). Dean's detachment from any particular place (or any particular wife) is not a numbed alienation but a fun, if temporary, absorption. In one of the novel's priceless lines, Dean's friend Carlo Marx says, "I have finally taught Dean that he can do anything he wants, become mayor of Denver, marry a millionairess, or become the greatest poet since Rimbaud. But he keeps rushing out to see the midget auto races" (37). The detached man is wildly vigorous, as Dean argues: "Sheeit, and you've got to look out for your boy. He ain't a man less he's a jumpin man—do what the doctor say. I'll tell you, Sal, straight, no matter where I live, my trunk's always sticking out from under the bed, I'm ready to leave or get thrown out" (206). The beautiful onrush of Kerouac's prose echoes the sound of Dean's jumping and rushing.

Kerouac's novel-length hymn to impermanence reflects the postwar era, but it also continues a long tradition in American culture. *On the Road* is a conspicuously American novel. Sal and Dean's road trips from East Coast to West Coast fall into the tradition of westward expansion. It's no accident Sal befriends a westerner like Dean and fetishizes him as a Denver cowboy. Richard Dyer writes, "The body of the white male . . . lean, sinewy, hard, taut, the cowboy as white male ego ideal. These figures in the landscape are intrinsic to the appeal of the Western."[5] The freedom to start fresh requires the suppression of certain attachments and certain griefs. This emotional suppression renders Sal unable to identify how leaving feels. He can only register a vague wistfulness as he hits the road. Griefs and attachments must not interfere with the process of moving. One generation must move aside to make room for the next: "What is that feeling when you're driving away from people and they recede on the plain till you see their specks dispersing?—it's the too-huge world vaulting us, and it's good-by. But we lean forward to the next crazy venture beneath the skies" (130).

To keep detachment joyful, Kerouac must suppress his relationship to past generations. The ascendancy of the Beat Generation matters most. For Kerouac, as we shall see, the crucial loss is leaving the world of the mothers rather than the world of the fathers. Suppressed bonds with women, ignored betrayals of women, form the novel's subtext. Furthermore, the ability to camp out while remaining safe requires the suppression of other content as well: homoeroticism, violence, the war's legacy.

On the Road takes place among young men at loose ends in the immediate postwar period. Curiously, then, the novel suppresses war history altogether. It is as if Sal Paradise were born again on meeting Dean Moriarty. The war's legacy, in the form of G.I. benefits, becomes just another way to start fresh. Like the postwar "queer ships," Sal's is a government-sponsored relocation. Financed by liquid capital, Sal never has to endure the humiliation and poverty of trying to support himself along the road. Each transcontinental road trip begins when Sal cashes in more postwar pay: "In the month of July 1947, having saved about fifty dollars from old veteran benefits, I was ready to go to the West Coast." "We got ready to cross the groaning continent again. I drew my GI check and gave Dean eighteen dollars to mail to his wife; she was waiting for him to come home and she was broke." "I never saw such crazy musicians. Everybody in Frisco blew. It was the end of the continent; they didn't give a damn. Dean and I goofed around San Francisco in this manner until I got my next GI check and got ready to go back home." "In the spring of 1949 I had a few dollars saved from my GI education checks and I went to Denver, thinking of settling down there. I saw myself in Middle America, a patriarch. I was lonesome" (11, 107, 147, 148).

On the Road's innocent bliss also requires a disconnection between gay subcultures and Beat subcultures—two overlapping worlds in real life. In fifties discourse, as I have discussed earlier, the open presentation of homosexuality met inevitably with violence. By contrast, as Barbara Ehrenreich notes, Kerouac's writing is "singularly, even unrealistically, devoid of violence."[6] To defend the peace, Kerouac suppresses a strong homoeroticism. In the novel Sal and Dean are compulsively heterosexual. Kerouac himself was defensive about his own heterosexuality despite the nights he spent with writers Gore Vidal and Allen Ginsberg.[7] "I am not a fool! a queer! I am not! He-he, understand?"[8] Nonetheless, Sal's first glimpse of Dean in *On the Road* marks him as an object of deep desire. Sal fetishizes Dean's clinging clothes and muscular sweat.

> He reminded me of some long-lost brother; the sight of his suffering bony face with the long sideburns and his straining muscular sweating neck made me remember my boyhood in those dye-dumps and swim holes and riversides of Paterson and the Passaic. His dirty workclothes clung to him so gracefully, as though you couldn't buy a better fit from a custom tailor but only earn it from the Natural Tailor of Natural Joy, as Dean had, in his stresses. And in his excited way of speaking I heard again the voices of old companions and brothers under the bridge, among the motorcycles, along the wash-lined neighborhood and drowsy doorsteps of afternoon where boys played guitars while their older brothers worked in the mills. (10)

With its eroticized proletarianism, Sal's portrait of Dean falls into the iconography of "rough trade" common in fifties gay male discourse. "Rough trade" refers to apparently straight working-class men who allow gay men to have sex with them. Throughout the novel, Sal chases after the impossible Dean the way the drag queens in Hubert Selby chase after Brooklyn hoodlums. Kerouac's description of "brothers under the bridge" sounds like a paradise made for one sex alone. However, this brothers' paradise must stay free of sex if it is to remain free of violence. Kerouac stays wholesome even when describing a hoodlums' and gay hustlers' bar in Times Square. The passage conveys the wildness of the wartime social scene in New York. Ritzy's Bar is both a gay and straight world, but it is definitely a boys' world. In a classic moment of homosocial bonding, Dean uses the context of a gay bar to propose that Sal sleep with his wife.

Finally he came out with it: he wanted me to work Marylou. I didn't ask him why because I knew he wanted to see what Marylou was like with another man. We were sitting in Ritzy's Bar when he proposed the idea; we'd spent an hour walking Times Square, looking for Hassel. Ritzy's Bar is the hoodlum bar of the streets around Times Square; it changes names every year. You walk in there and you don't see a single girl, even in the booths, just a great mob of young men dressed in all varieties of hoodlum cloth, from red shirts to zoot suits. It is also the hustlers' bar—the boys who make a living among the sad old homos of the Eighth Avenue night. Dean walked in there with his eyes slitted to see every single face. There were wild Negro queers, sullen guys with guns, shiv-packing seamen, thin, non-committal junkies, and an occasional well-dressed middle-aged detective, posing as a bookie and hanging around half for interest and half for duty. It was the typical place for Dean to put down his request. All kinds of evil plans are hatched in Ritzy's Bar— you can sense it in the air—and all kinds of mad sexual routines are initiated to go with them. The safecracker proposes not only a certain loft on 14th Street to the hoodlum, but that they sleep together. Kinsey spent a lot of time in Ritzy's Bar, interviewing some of the boys; I was there the night his assistant came, in 1945. Hassel and Carlo were interviewed. (108–109)

Despite all the "evil plans" at work, including Dean's own, Kerouac keeps the scene wholesome by describing the bar in touristic terms. The intended audience is cult novel readers, outsiders to New York City up for a little titillation. Kerouac, our tour guide, presents Ritzy's as a nationally known stop on the perversions tour. Why, this bar is so famous, Alfred Kinsey even interviewed the patrons! Sal remains detached from the action, merely serving as lecturer. We don't see any "mad sexual routines"—just a gallery of social types. Kerouac distinguishes himself from the gay subculture while distinguishing himself as subcultural expert.

One of the novel's most famous passages gains its exuberance at the cost of suppressing homoeroticism. This scene is postwar fiction's best-known description of the Open City. Like much of Beat writing, *On the Road* is a roman à clef, each character and scene corresponding to a friend and event in Kerouac's real life. Dean Moriarty and Carlo Marx are fictional counterparts to Kerouac's friends Neal Cassady and Allen Ginsberg. In real life, Neal and Allen became lovers shortly after Kerouac introduced them.[9] They remained lovers during several of the episodes recalled in the novel. However, in the novel they only engage in endless talk.

Considering the sexual subtext, no wonder the fictional Sal Paradise feels like a fifth wheel when his two friends find each other.

> A tremendous thing happened when Dean met Carlo Marx. Two keen minds that they are, they took to each other at the drop of a hat. Two piercing eyes glanced into two piercing eyes—the holy con-man with the shining mind, and the sorrowful poetic con-man with the dark mind that is Carlo Marx. From that moment on I saw very little of Dean, and I was a little sorry too. Their energies met head-on, I was a lout compared, I couldn't keep up with them. The whole mad swirl of everything that was to come began then; it would mix up all my friends and all I had left of my family in a big dust cloud over the American Night. . . . They rushed down the street together, digging everything in the early way they had, which later became so much sadder and perceptive and blank. But then they danced down the streets like dingledodies, and I shambled after as I've been doing all my life after people who interest me, because the only people for me are the mad ones, the ones who are mad to live, mad to talk, mad to be saved, desirous of everything at the same time, the ones who never yawn or say a commonplace thing, but burn, burn, burn like fabulous yellow roman candles exploding like spiders across the stars and in the middle you see the blue centerlight pop and everybody goes "Awww!" (8–9)

By suppressing the gay subtext, Kerouac has the freedom to let the Open City philosophy emerge. His characters don't have to be subterranean; they can roam the open streets without fear of homophobic violence. Kerouac's formulation does not focus on personal regret over two friends who become a pair and leave a third person out. Rather, Kerouac transcends the particulars to offer a manifesto for the Beat Generation. The Beats are a diaspora of "unknown people" all over America who are destined to meet. They are capable of deep affinity, absurdity, and spontaneous combustion. And, as the wild life in Kerouac's prose reveals, their blood burns for its own sake and not to feed the grief of past generations. The vitality rather than the destructiveness of this brotherhood is Kerouac's touchstone, even though the brotherhood eventually "would mix up all my friends and all I had left of my family in a big dust cloud over the American Night."

Kerouac's frequent use of the phrase "the American Night" is telling, for his writing epitomizes the abstract American sense of place. *On the Road* is one of few American novels written about America as a whole rather than somewhere in particular. Kerouac's incisive descriptions of multiple cities along the road make readers feel welcome and at home everywhere in America. As Dean exclaims, "Furthermore we know America, we're at home; I can go anywhere in America and get what I want because it's the same in every corner, I know the people, I know what they do. We give and take and go in the incredibly complicated sweet-ness zigzagging every side" (100). On a bus Sal sings a little song to him-self about being at home everywhere and nowhere at the same time:

> Home in Missoula,
> Home in Truckee,
> Home in Opelousas,
> Ain't no home for me.
> Home in old Medora,
> Home in Wounded Knee,
> Home in Ogallala,
> Home I'll never be.

Sal rejects emotional detachment in favor of passionate spontaneity. Nonetheless, his abstract sense of place relies on masculine detach-ment—with emphasis on masculine. Being at home everywhere also means being at home nowhere. Home becomes impossible because women represent home. Wandering the streets of San Francisco, Sal has an ecstatic vision of being everywhere at the same time. When a woman in a fish and chips shop shoots him "a terrified look," Sal has a guilt-ridden hallucination. A tremendous sense of guilt toward the abstract mother accompanies his abstract sense of place.

> I stopped, frozen with ecstasy on the sidewalk. I looked down Market Street. I didn't know whether it was that or Canal Street in New Orleans: it led to water, ambiguous, universal water, just as 42nd Street, New York, leads to water and you never know where you are. I thought of Ed Dunkel's ghost on Times Square. I was delirious. I wanted to go back and leer at my strange Dickensian mother in the hash joint. I tingled all over from head to foot. It seemed I had a whole host of memories leading back to 1750 in England and that I was in San Francisco now only in another life and in another body. "No," that woman seemed to say with that terrified glance, "don't come back and plague your honest, hard-working mother. You are no longer like a son to me—and like your father, my first husband. 'Ere this kindly Greek took pity on me." (The proprietor was a Greek with hairy arms.) "You are no good, inclined to drunkenness and routs and final disgraceful robbery of the fruits of my 'umble labors in the hashery. O son! did you not ever go on your knees and pray for deliv-erance for all your sins and scoundrel's acts?" (143)

Kerouac's ecstasies of place are always geographically accurate. Market Street in San Francisco, Canal Street in New Orleans, and Forty-second Street in New York City do share the awareness of invisible water where the pavement ends. Kerouac's "ambiguous, universal water" links all three places and also links them to the amniotic fluid of the universal mother. The mother's speech exaggerates every guilt-inducing lecture a mother ever directed at a child. The guilt seems to emerge from the mother's and son's different ways of experiencing place. The mother is stuck at hard labor in a particular place. By contrast, the son is free to experience three particular places at the same time without getting stuck in any one.

This guilt toward the abandoned mother is partly class guilt: the woman is stuck in one place because of her poverty, while the son has portable capital. This class guilt also characterizes Sal's romance with a Chicana woman named Terry, a California migrant laborer. Again, Sal can have an abstract sense of place because he is a middle-class man. His description of the California grape fields is characteristically vivid and welcoming, as if we all belonged there. However, it is also a voyeuristic glimpse into someone else's family. Sal enjoys the family's food and picturesque poverty as much as he enjoys Terry's lovemaking. Terry nurtures him while he observes her life from a distance.

> In California you chew the juice out of grapes and spit the skin away, a real luxury. Nightfall came. Terry went home for supper and came to the barn at nine o'clock with delicious tortillas and mashed beans. I lit a woodfire on the cement floor of the barn to make light. We made love on the crates. Terry got up and cut right back to the shack. Her father was yelling at her; I could hear him from the barn. She'd left me a cape to keep warm; I threw it over my shoulder and skulked through the moonlit vineyard to see what was going on. I crept to the end of a row and knelt in the warm dirt. Her five brothers were singing melodious songs in Spanish. The stars bent over the little roof; smoke poked from the stovepipe chimney. I smelled mashed beans and chili. The old man growled. The brothers kept right on yodeling. The mother was silent. Johnny and the kids were giggling in the bedroom. A California home; I hid in the grapevines, digging it all. I felt like a million dollars; I was adventuring in the crazy American night. (84)

The vitality of Sal's description comes partly from its abstraction. His affection for Terry is another regretful view from the rearview mirror. A shadowy yet omnipresent mother figure, Sal's aunt, provides a source of cash to supplement his GI checks. The Central Valley can be very picturesque if you don't rely on it financially. When Sal needs money, suddenly he is from somewhere rather than nowhere. Suddenly there is a "my own life" in contrast to life on the road: "I was through with my chores in the cottonfield. I could feel the pull of my own life calling me back. I shot my aunt a penny postcard across the land and asked for another fifty. . . . I walked down the highway to Sabinal, eating black walnuts from the walnut tree. I went on the SP tracks and balanced along the rail. I passed a watertower and a factory. This was the end of something. I went to the telegraph office of the railroad for my money order from New York. It was closed. I swore and sat on the steps to wait. The ticket master got back and invited me in. The money was in; my aunt had saved my lazy butt again" (83, 85).

Kerouac's suppression of homoeroticism and the mother reflect not only his personal psychology but also the spirit of the times. He wrote in a fifties climate of homophobia and hyperconventional family ideals. Kerouac had to suppress these elements in order to protect and defend his Open City vision of intensity and wildness. The vision Kerouac defends is essential to postwar urban fiction, since it rewrites the city as safe, joyful, and free.

. Paule Marshall shares the Beat principle of defeating past grief through joy. Like Kerouac, she wins this joy by separating the artistic bohemia from the gay subculture. *Brown Girl, Brownstones* ascribes to a common fifties theory that conformity in work and marriage emasculated young men and made them homosexual. Marshall puts her heroine Selina's refusal of conventional success in homophobic terms: "Prim, pious, pretentious pack! She noted the girls' tightly closed legs, the skirts dropping well over their knees, the hands folded decorously in their laps. No boy's hand had ever gained access to those breasts or succeeded in prying apart those clenched knees. Her cold glance swept the young men: Queers!" (226). For Marshall, then, to be bohemian is to be lustily, defiantly heterosexual. Selina experiences new ideas and feelings with an intense physicality. Her racial and emotional coming of age parallels her physical coming of age. It makes sense that modern dance is her art form. She throws her body into dance with sincere and utter authenticity.

On the other hand, Marshall's feminist rewriting of Beat culture allows suppressed elements of race and gender to emerge. She reunites hipster with housewife. Whether a white racist or an upright Barbadian, the middle-aged mother is always the figure who shocks bohemia with a needed dose of repressed truth. In a trope that almost seems a direct response to Jack Kerouac, Mom embodies the return of the repressed. Thus Marshall avoids presenting bohemia in cult novel terms as a touristic commodity designed to shock and titillate. Rather, the middle-aged mothers expose the naïveté and shockability of bohemia itself.

Selina requires the subcultural ethos of detachment and camping out to achieve spiritual growth. However, Marshall shifts the Beat focus from a single generation to a multigenerational perspective. Ultimately the novel connects Selina's coming of age to a long chain of generations. But first Selina must learn to avoid being the vessel of her parents' post-traumatic stress disorder. Both her parents frequently reexperience traumas of racism and poverty from their native Barbados. They structure their family lives around past trauma, designing their present lives to avoid previous troubles while also inviting their children to reexperience trauma with them. Indeed, Selina sometimes hates her mother because her life seems to prove that pain is woman's fate. Selina's mother's "eyes narrowed as she traveled back to that time and was that child again, feeling the sun on her back and the whip cutting her legs. More than that, she became the collective voice of all Bajan women, the vehicle through which their former suffering found utterance. . . . Selina listened. For always the mother's voice was a net flung wide, ensnaring all within its reach. She swayed helpless now within its hold, loving its rich color, loving and hating the mother for the pain of her childhood" (45–46)

Selina's father also suffers from flashbacks. "He studied the policeman's face and in his shattered mind it became the white faces in the stores of Bridgetown long ago" (182). Her parents' shocks reverberate through Selina's body, and she continuously fights off the resulting numbness. She must learn to avoid fusing with her parents' grief. She must feel her own heartbeat. " 'My father only beat me once. Long ago. I can't even remember why now.' What she could remember was that after the first blow she had been strangely numb to the others. Instead she had been aware only of his body against hers, his muscles moving smoothly under his skin as he flailed her, and his heaving chest crushed against hers. She had been fused with him; not only had he breathed for her but his heart had beaten for them both" (59).

Selina's bohemianism allows her to defeat these old griefs. The Open City ushers her into adult joy. After her sojourns in Times Square, "she would be free of the numbness." The destructive potential of Times Square excites her because it helps her destroy the past. Unlike Sal Paradise, Selina is looking for violence rather than avoiding it. *On the Road* and *Brown Girl, Brownstones* picture Times Square as a gallery of social types. However, Selina's experience is more direct and less touristically detached. She embodies Times Square. The jazz, swagger, and soul reverberate through her body. Unlike the boys-only space of *On the*

Road, her Times Square forms part of a giant, bejeweled woman's body. Selina corresponds to the city entirely, her body echoing its own.

> Evenings always found her striding, head up, tam askew, through Times Square, that bejeweled navel in the city's long sinuous form. To Selina it was a new constellation, the myriad lights hot stars bursting from chaos into their own vivid life, shooting, streaking, wheeling in the night void, then expiring, but only to burst again—and the concatenation of traffic and voices like the roar from the depth of a maelstrom—an irresistible call to destruction.
>
> She loved it, for its chaos echoed her inner chaos; each bedizened window, each gaudy empty display evoked something in her that loved and understood the gaudy, the emptiness defined her own emptiness and that in the faces flitting past her. She walked with a swagger here, gazing boldly into those faces, always hoping to happen upon some violence, or to be involved in some spectacular brawl. For hours she stood outside the Metropole, listening to the jazz that poured through the open doors in a thick guttural flow that churned the air into a pulsating mass; sometimes the music was thin and reedy, sometimes brassy and jarring, yet often soulful, and always expressing the chaos in the street. She would shift amid the crowd for a glimpse of the sailors strung along the bar, the brilliant streak of a woman's blond hair in the dimness and smoke, a gleam of silver on the drum, the pomaded head of a Negro musician. Standing there with her books stacked on the ground between her legs, her fists plunged in her pockets and her lean body absorbing each note, she would feel sucked into that roaring center, the lights exploding inside her, and she would be free of the numbness. (213–214)

Kerouac's image of city people as fireworks "exploding like spiders across the stars" resembles Marshall's image of city lights as "hot stars bursting from chaos into their own vivid life." With her "tam askew," Selina is a comrade to *On the Road*'s "dingledodies" dancing down the street. Marshall's description is another Open City manifesto. Times Square, like jazz, permits the full expression of the soul. Chaos is a happy state. As in Capote as well as Kerouac, the vitality of the wartime scene allows the true self to emerge. Akin to Kerouac's, Marshall's prose bursts forth into spontaneous combustion. It swings. Selina takes her own detachment and transforms it from numbness into syncopation. Her boy friend, Clive, loves her "swinging nothing style" (240).

Like Dean's, Selina's swinging nothing style involves total absorption rather than alienation. After she joins the Modern Dance Club at college, Selina forgets to go home on time. Clive makes fun of her because only beatnik women wear leotards and tights on the street. Both Kerouac and Marshall like to write about tight garments. Dean and Selina are so full of vigor, they're almost bursting out of their clothes.

> That next week Selina went with her to the club and became so absorbed that she forgot the time and had to rush to the subway wearing the long black tights under her clothes. When she reached Clive's it was nearly dark. He was sitting thoughtfully at the easel, the fading light picking out the white crescents of his eyes and the canvas. For a time he peered at her in the black tights, then throwing back his head, he laughed; his long arms lifted dramatically. "All is lost!" he intoned. "She's gone arty." (251)

Marshall, however, does not suppress the potential violence haunting the Open City. Here the violence is racial. The only African American in the dance troupe, Selina experiences "the sudden awareness of danger that made her hastily scan the room, a momentary desire to leave and thus spare them her unsettling dark presence; then, just as strong, the determination to remain" (252). Her free expression through modern dance is worth the risks of interracial collaboration. Selina's complete involvement in the dance goes hand in hand with her awareness of a racist subtext. It's worth it to Selina because her new artiness channels the girlish energy that had no place in the conventional world.

> Spring had ended. Coming up the subway stairs onto Fulton Street Selina saw the sun lingering late above the roofs and smelled a summer redolence in the air. A sinuous breeze wound her bare legs and, laughing, she gave a small joyous leap, her body still fluid and toned from the long afternoon rehearsal with the dance group. She was on her way home to eat before going to Clive's and she moved swiftly through the crowd—a slender dark girl with supple legs, a strong graceful lift to her head and back, and an almost irrepressible vitality in her stride, in each cutting swing of her arms. She might at any moment, it seemed, burst into a wild spin or execute another exuberant leap there on the street. (256)

Dean is a jumping man, and Selina is a leaping woman. Finding her own generation, Selina also finds a correspondence to the street's energy she once knew as a child. As a dancer, the grown woman can still have the child's vigor. Selina's first solo dance links her with "a single will" to her own rebellious generation, to her boyfriend, Clive, and her dancer friend Rachel Fine. However, her dance also speaks across generations, not just to her own generation. As a member of her own tribe, she dances beyond numbness into exuberance. However, she also dances a whole life cycle from birth to old age. She retains "the memory and scar of that other life"—her mother's life, in all its sadness.

> But as the light cascaded down and formed a protective ring around her, as the piano sounded and her body instinctively responded, she thought of Clive first, and then of Rachel—how she and Rachel had danced the night before as if guided by a single will, as if, indeed, they were simply reflections of each other. At this, her nervousness subsided, and she rose—sure, lithe, controlled; her head with its coarse hair lifting gracefully; the huge eyes in her dark face absorbed yet passionate, old as they had been old even when she was a child, suggesting always that she had lived before and had retained, deep within her, the memory and scar of that other life. Her slender arm boldly hailed the audience now, and their hushed suspense, palpable on the air, made them suddenly harmless.
>
> And she danced well, expressing with deft movements the life cycle, capturing its beauty and exceeding sadness. (281)

Marshall is realistic about the mingling of racism and camaraderie in the new interracial bohemia. This realism makes it necessary to link Selina's generation to previous generations in the African diaspora. By contrast, Jack Kerouac is famously naive about race, imagining all sorts of racial border crossings without factoring in the loss of white privilege. Kerouac imagines much of his novel *The Subterraneans* (1958) through the eyes of Mardou, an African American woman who roams freely and sometimes nakedly through San Francisco encountering only ecstasy and warm welcomes. She is the Open City, with her "out and open face." Although Mardou bears scars, just as Marshall's women do, Kerouac pulls her out of sorrow into complete safety and joy.

> Downtown around Market where our tattered holy Negro Joan of Arc wandered hosannahing in her brown borrowed-from-night skin and heart, flutters of betting sheets at corner newsstands, watchers at nude magazines, the flowers on the corner in baskets and the old Italian in his apron with the newspapers kneeling to water, and the Chinese father in tight ecstatic suit wheeling the basket-carriaged baby down Powell with his pink-spot-cheeked wife of glitter brown eyes in her new bonnet rippling to flap in sun, there stands Mardou smiling intensely and strangely and the old eccentric lady not any more conscious of her Negroness than the kind cripple of the store and because of her out and open face now, the clear indications of a troubled pure innocent spirit just risen from a pit in pockmarked earth and by own broken hands self-pulled to safety and salvation.[10]

Mardou's freedom to wander with an "out and open face" depends on a color-blindness rare in American society.

In *On the Road*'s most notorious passage about race, Sal imagines himself moving effortlessly through differently raced bodies with a remarkable naïveté. The minstrel show stereotype of the happy and innocent darky becomes a fetish object for Sal's ecstasy. "I was only myself, Sal Paradise, sad, strolling in this violet dark, this unbearably sweet night, wishing I could exchange worlds with the happy, true-hearted, ecstatic Negroes of America. . . . There was excitement and the air was filled with the vibration of really joyous life that knows nothing of disappointment and 'white sorrows' and all that" (148–149). By contrast, Marshall counts the Open City's costs. Almost immediately after her artistic triumph, Selina comes into her first full awareness of American racism. A mother figure steps in to dash cold truth on youthful hipsterism. Right after the dance performance, the troupe charges forth to occupy the Open City.

> The night was not vast enough, nor the towering college and the imposing apartment buildings around it substantial enough to withstand their brash voices. The buildings slid back, it seemed, to give them room. The evening sky with its noxious pall of smog lifted higher above the coldly glittering city. And even the city's pulse— that low, tremulous hum of chaos—was stilled.
>
> They trooped in bold formation down the street, spanning the entire sidewalk and spilling into the gutter. The wind snatched at the frothy costumes under their open coats and then scooted ahead, carrying their exhilaration in a warning to the other pedestrians. Selina, Rachel and the blond girl, Margaret Benton, were in the vanguard, and they made a startling trio—Selina, in the black leotard, her coat flaring wide, resembling somewhat a cavalier; Rachel a fabulous sprite and Margaret, her hair catching each passing light, a full-blown Wagnerian heroine. (282–283)

The uncontainable joy of the young women spills out into the streets. Their exhilaration serves "a warning to the other pedestrians" because it means something beyond itself. Exhilaration is the calling card of a new generation. The dancers take up the whole sidewalk and conquer the city. It must give way before their noise. Moving together as "one huge body," women from Jewish, WASP, and African backgrounds present the city with an interracial utopia. Marshall has no illusions about the ease of utopia, however. Immediately after this scene, Margaret's racist mother gives Selina her first real experience of being belittled, patronized, and rendered invisible. "But when she looked up and saw her reflection in those pale eyes, she knew that the woman saw one thing above all else.

Those eyes were a well-lighted mirror in which, for the first time, Selina truly saw—with a sharp and shattering clarity—the full meaning of her black skin" (289).

For better or worse, trauma never belongs to a single generation. Selina's boyfriend, Clive, does not attribute his scarring to his war experience alone: "you can't blame the war. That would be much too simple" (235). Similarly, Selina's shock links her to the racial trauma of her women elders. It makes her reinterpret her mother's behavior in light of the traumatic legacy. Finally linking cause to effect, Selina suddenly understands her mother's post-traumatic outbursts of rage.

> And she was one of them: the mother and the Bajan women, who had lived each day what she had come to know. How had the mother endured, she who had not chosen death by water? She remembered the mother striding home through Fulton Park each late afternoon, bearing the throw-offs under her arm as she must have borne the day's humiliations inside. How had the mother contained her swift rage?—and then she remembered those sudden, uncalled-for outbursts that would so stun them and split the serenity of the house. (292–293)

Nonetheless, the reality of shock cannot defeat the Open City vision. In regard to Selina's awakening, Joyce Pettis writes, "The exuberance of the evening can perhaps be blamed for her innocent expectations when she is summoned apart from the other girls for a chat with the hostess's mother."[11] For Selina's crowd, however, exuberance cannot become a target of blame. Selina's is a willed, defiant innocence typical of her generation. Neither Marshall nor Kerouac will allow a bad history to defeat joy.

Selina confines her bohemianism to her uptown dance troupe; only one scene takes place in Greenwich Village among the Beats. This scene comes across as a deliberate satire of Kerouac and company, ecstatically male-bonding while guiltily dependent on Mom. Marshall's version is a triumphant return of the repressed. In this scene Clive recalls how the Village became his "ritual for being born twice," his first confused stop upon his return from war. In Clive's tale of his Village interlude, the Barbadian mother shows up at the beatnik pad like the Ghost of Christmas Past.

> "So I had my cold-water flat where the light was bad, my weird friends and an income from Uncle Sam. I went back to college, but just to get the money and keep peace with my mother. I was even painting. . . . It was one of those intellectual bacchanalias—with

everybody on the floor talking at once, shoes off, the Chianti flowing—that my mother dropped by. God only knows how she found
the place! But there she was, in the doorway." His hooded eyes shifted
suddenly from her rapt face to the doorway but mirrored nothing.
Only his mouth tightened around the cigarette. " . . . All unstrung
from the subway ride and awed by those white weird faces. But not
awed enough not to say in raw-raw Bajan: 'But c'dear, Clive, where
this bunch come outta, nuh?' I got to the door fast and said something which I've very conveniently forgotten, but to the effect of 'get
the hell out.' " He broke off, his eyes sweeping back to Selina, alive
now with pain. "Try to see her," he said urgently, his body tense.
"She's the small hard dry type of West Indian who lives endlessly
and endures all. And she endured that. For a moment anyway, and
then left."

Selina averted her face, shaken by the same paroxysm of anguish
that seized him, cowering helplessly for a moment as he cowered
as though about to be struck. Gradually he fell back limp amid the
cushions, his eyes emptying, but the small muscle at his mouth still
pulsed.

He said casually, "As you can imagine my days there were num-
bered. The disgrace of one's mother stalking one down! But what the
hell, I had been planning to leave anyway." (242–243)

The beatniks' claim to hipness must be fragile if one mother can
destroy it. While Clive tells the story with earnest, twitching anguish, it
is also pretty funny to think of an entire Open City of chattering bohemians falling back before one small, dry, long-suffering Barbadian. The Open
City will collapse unless it incorporates and resolves past grief rather than
suppressing it. A truly Open City needs room for all kinds of people, from
hipster men to immigrant mothers.

Conclusion

This book juxtaposes the segregation of space with the segregation of memory. The capsule of trauma, unintegrated with the rest of the psyche, resembles the capsule of the segregated neighborhood. *Uncontained* reconnects separate literary areas and separate geographic areas. Its analysis of Cold War containment culture reveals an atmosphere of hidden violence. In postwar fiction, the styles of storytelling contain the trauma. The campy, resolute cheerfulness of fifties discourse is easy to satirize, but it covers up a deep and painful story—and the contours of the cover-up are fascinating in themselves.

Even a "just war" like World War II left its legacy of often invisible trauma. In his book *The Greatest Generation* Tom Brokaw lauds those who came of age during World War II: "They were mature beyond their years, tempered by what they had been through, disciplined by their military training and sacrifices. . . . At every stage of their lives they were part of historic challenges and achievements of a magnitude the world had never before witnessed." Nonetheless, the "greatest generation" was also a generation shaken by radical shocks. War disciplines, but it also destroys. When Brokaw interviewed veterans, "their stories did not come easily."[1] The war remained a quiet, painful presence.

Other forms of hushed-up violence, including racial conflict and gay-bashing, also left their scars on the city landscape. We inherit the post-war city's legacy of hidden violence, since we still live amid hate crimes and a casual acceptance of militarism. Whether in a city or a soul, a quarantined trauma always leaks out of its containment zone to alter the shape of the whole. If there is no telling space for certain memories, this deficiency warps the landscape itself. In other words, there is no such thing as a marginal experience. Cultural diversity constitutes the very nature of American life and literature. The scars of war and injustice are not exceptions to the rule of American progress; rather, they reshape the rule. Only by reintegrating the separate capsules of memory and place can we glimpse a peaceable community.

Throughout the works analyzed here, violence sinks beneath the smooth surface of postwar prosperity, leaving mere traces behind. This book studies those traces to find their deeper implications. The legacy of violence announces itself indirectly, through the aesthetics of fiction. One must look for the submerged history in the shape of denial or the shape of overlooking. The two principal markers of post-traumatic stress disorder, amnesia and flashback, often determine the shape of fictional narrative. By reading different parts of the literary canon and different parts of the city against each other, we can discern the larger shape of the historical moment. Sometimes hidden violence reappears not in an individual neighborhood or work but on the borderline between works and neighborhoods.

Along with the legacy of trauma, the postwar city offers a legacy of joy, freedom, and interchange among different ways of life. Many liberating counterstories challenge the containment logic prevalent in Cold War thought. For example, gay and Beat subcultural novels burst forth into a new Open City. We glimpse the postwar generation's larger vision if we read across a broad spectrum of famous and forgotten works by men and women of various ethnic and literary traditions. This vision moves beyond containment into healing and reimagining city life.

Sometimes it is hard to see this healing from within individual works. The postwar novel and short story often seem laden with alienation and malaise. A fogbank settles over the prose, and readers dwell too far inside the heads of Holden Caulfield, Esther Greenwood, Francis Weed, or the Invisible Man. It makes sense that high schools often assign postwar fiction, for its self-absorption resembles teenage angst. One is tempted to read each novel inside its own isolated capsule. However, if we integrate these literary capsules into a shared pattern, we begin to see how they portray a generational experience beyond their own self-absorption. Alienation and malaise come to seem not timeless existential states but symptoms of a particular historical moment. Personal trauma is a collective experience.

To place individual malaise in historical context is to reveal its racial and sexual politics. For instance, Ann Bannon and Gore Vidal made their characters seem masochistic or depressed at times so they could depict openly gay communities in a repressive era. What Bannon melodramatically calls "the heartbreak of homosexual life" is not a burden that automatically comes with being gay but rather the burden that comes with an oppressive history. Hidden sources of violence reveal themselves if we place the city's segregated neighborhoods into a shared pattern. Taken on its own terms, for instance, Walker Percy's *The Moviegoer* meditates on malaise as if it were a timeless existential state and a fundamental part of the human condition. The picture changes, however, when we realize the novel takes place against the unspoken backdrop of the civil rights movement. The suppressed historical context suddenly gives the malaise a racial cast. White privilege manifests itself as a wordless queasiness within individual souls. Like Percy, John Cheever, Philip Roth, and J. D. Salinger also satirize the alienation of living within an airtight world of privilege.

This book concerns not the lived experience of trauma but its fictional representation. Therefore it is necessary to examine what agendas fiction writers pursue when they rework historical trauma. Their reworkings always take place within preexisting power relations. However, the power relations can be difficult to see in a postwar era of cover-up, closeting, and containment. These fictions record the silencing and disappearance of trauma more than they record its conspicuous presence. How, then, to find the power relations among these texts? My solution has been to connect them by reading them geographically. I have researched the histories of specific neighborhoods portrayed in fiction and analyzed which elements authors choose to stress or ignore. This juxtaposition of material and literary histories brings new elements into the foreground. For instance, *Maud Martha*'s affectionate portrait of Thirty-fourth Avenue and Cottage Grove in Chicago's South Side takes on a militant cast when we learn that this intersection was the flashpoint for racially charged urban renewal debates during the novel's writing. If we know how radically the removal of all Japanese Americans changed downtown Seattle, the absence of these changes in *No-No Boy* starts to look like post-traumatic amnesia. And if we understand midcentury New York's vibrant subcultures, we can read *Breakfast at Tiffany's* as a refraction of the wartime gay community.

In reassembling lost pieces of the urban story, I challenge the predominant postwar story in which city living inevitably produces violence. Postwar fiction both tells and refutes this story of violence. Constant, subtle threats of harm reveal themselves in the vague urban dread of film noir and the carefully guarded inwardness of the segregation novel. Cult novels both express and resist the discourse of sado-masochistic violence, the belief that gay desire invites assault. Camp style, satire, and passing for straight provide fictional means for subcultures to refute the discourse of inevitable violence and to clear safe urban space for themselves.

Postwar fiction witnesses a phenomenon still growing and active in mass culture: the consumption of urban violence not as lived experience but as visual and narrative pleasure. A recent movie like *The Matrix* inherits film noir's elegant stylization of violence, while a hip-hop musician like Eminem inherits William Burroughs's ability to describe gay-bashing with bemused detachment. The stylization of violence has its own sadomasochism. The story takes the role of the sadist, schooling the consumer to withstand sensual assault without flinching. Meanwhile the consumer also becomes a sadist, enjoying spectacles of transgression and punishment. The city must lead inevitably to violence so that there will be something to watch.

Masculinity and femininity strongly affect the depiction of urban violence. The ability to consume violence becomes a marker of hipness, and beyond this, a marker of masculine hipness. Only a certain kind of detached man can contend with the violent "reality" of city life. To prefer peace or public safety is to be weak, effeminate, or unrealistic. It is no accident that women protesters against Cold War militarism went to City Hall Park in their best hats and gloves, exaggerating their own femininity on the urban landscape and linking it to their pacifism.

This book traces the violent city's principal hero, the lone, alienated man, through many manifestations, from the war veteran to the noir detective, the ironic suburbanite, and the Beat hipster. As counterpoints to the lone man of postwar fiction, *Uncontained* pays special attention to feminine and effeminate characters. The drag queens in Hubert Selby Jr. and Charles S. Wright use high style to make homophobic space habitable. Camp discourse emerged strongly in the late fifties and early sixties, raising the question: What is urban realism? Not despite but thanks to their lack of realism, the most outrageous and preposterous moments in Ann Bannon and Truman Capote may give the most realistic picture of postwar subcultures' exhilarating freedom. Moreover, fifties housewives defy ridiculous stereotypes to speak powerfully for themselves in postwar fiction. Their insights into postwar readjustment prove that men were not the only war veterans.

Postwar fiction's sense of humor also gestures toward new community and undercuts urban dread. With writers like Roth, Salinger, Heller, Percy, and Vonnegut in the canon, postwar fiction boasts some of American literature's best satire. The narrator and reader collude with each other to mock society at large and in doing so create new imagined communities. In the paperback cult novel the narrator addresses readers with astonishing directness and charm. Readers participate vicariously in the urban subcultures described.

Many cult novels push back at violence, creating a safety zone for city living. Over and over, fictional heroes and heroines display a kind of willed innocence. Their deliberate naïveté allows them to re-create a new society together with others of their generation. Holden Caulfield's famous daydream of himself as "the catcher in the rye" displays this willed innocence: "Anyway, I keep picturing all these little kids playing some game in this big field of rye and all. Thousands of little kids, and nobody's around—nobody big, I mean—except me. And I'm standing on the edge of some crazy cliff. What I have to do, I have to catch everybody if they start to go over the cliff—I mean if they're running and they don't look where they're going I have to come out from somewhere and *catch* them. That's all I'd do all day" (156).

Holden sees the threat of harm, yet he imagines a limited safety zone where thousands of youngsters play. In the postwar city, this zone is the urban subculture. Beat writers and other rebels seem to declare: we can't save society from evil, but we can save ourselves and each other. Willed innocence liberates a zone where playing becomes possible. Like Holden's "big field of rye," the Open City frees young people from the numbness of grief.

The postwar generation shares this open vision across lines of sexuality, race, and gender. If cultural diversity is the essence of American life and literature, postwar fiction offers an excellent spot to test this assumption. The Cold War years present such tremendous cultural contradictions; they force us to redefine a multicultural society and a multicultural literary reading. Postwar society was "multicultural" long before the term was coined, yet it was also terribly white-bread and repressive. This era saw the simultaneous birth of *Ozzie and Harriet,* Cold War paranoia, the lesbian bar, and the civil rights movement.

World War II created many of these contradictions. The war toppled one social barrier after another. Defense industries eliminated job discrimination, the modern gay community began, and antifascist rhetoric undermined white racism. On the other hand, hatred burst forth in multiple manifestations, from race riots to federal policy. The U.S. government interned all Japanese Americans. After the war, gay employees and other "subversives" lost their jobs. Housing discrimination created a huge racial split between city and suburb. Postwar segregation led John Cheever to describe suburbanites as living unawares in a completely insulated world: "The people in the Farquarson's living room seemed united in their tacit claim that there had been no past, no war—that there was no danger or trouble in the world. In the recorded history of human arrangements, this extraordinary meeting would have fallen into place, but the atmosphere of Shady Hill made the memory unseemly and impolite" (330–331).

These contradictions make postwar fiction a particularly interesting and challenging topic for a multicultural reading. Diversity goes through a process of becoming invisible, yet its traces remain visible all along. Many observers see the postwar city in terms of violence, racial division, and postindustrial decline. Decay and division certainly form major parts of the story. Nonetheless, with its diversity, its freedom of thought, movement, and association, the postwar city also represents much that is best about American life. While noting the tight boundaries of containment culture, one can also observe the way those boundaries could and did become uncontained.

This book challenges the logic of segregation across multiple axes of race, gender, sexuality, and genre. In literary study it is easy to reproduce structures of segregation while contesting them. Separatism has its place, of course. Specifically, it is crucial to identify the submerged literary traditions of oppressed peoples. Indeed, this book relies on previous scholars' tracing the separate strands of African American, Asian American, Anglo, Jewish, masculinist, feminist, gay, and lesbian literatures. However, the synchronic approach is just as important as the diachronic identification of separate traditions. Scholarship lacks a complete understanding of a given literary period if we cannot picture how diverse voices placed themselves in a dialogue with one another.

Many novels out of print for decades have returned to public attention in their roles as forebears to specific groups' literary traditions. However, novelists like Chester Himes, John Okada, and Paule Marshall did not speak only to their own groups. Especially in the assimilationist 1950s, novelists of many backgrounds positioned themselves in response to a shared American tradition. Juxtaposing canonical with recently recognized authors allows us to see American culture as fundamentally rather than incidentally diverse.

At stake here is an effort to challenge multiple structures of privilege: racial, masculine, economic, heterosexual. Privilege is invisible from within a privileged culture. This invisibility means that oppression comes to seem the problem of the oppressed only. By contrast, my analysis shows how the intensified postwar black ghetto and the internment of Japanese Americans share and reflect American culture as a whole. Since World War II, the ghetto and the suburb increasingly seem to speak separate languages. However, both discourses form part of the same interdependent dialogue. I repeatedly place a hegemonic discourse up against its long-repressed opposite. This method creates a fuller picture of the literary era and reveals moments of privilege often left unchallenged.

We are all on the same bus. The back of the bus mirrors the front of the bus, the suburban housewife mirrors the urban hipster, and the gay community mirrors the straight subculture. Violence against lesbians in Ann Bannon's pulp fiction reveals how Jack Kerouac and Truman Capote must suppress overt homosexual content in order to grant their characters full freedom of thought and movement. The long-ignored housewife discourse of Hisaye Yamamoto and Gwendolyn Brooks reveals how literary masculinism scapegoats women for postwar malaise. The explicit blackness of *If He Hollers Let Him Go* reveals the unstated whiteness of *Double Indemnity*. Like the urban fictions of our own era, postwar fiction separates out the lone, alienated man from his surrounding community and identifies the city exclusively with him. By placing the lone man in a wider context, we avoid the impulse to glorify, vilify, or commodify him. We see him as one of many choices, thus challenging the masculinism associated with postwar literature.

Memory and forgetting change dramatically depending on one's standpoint. For instance, the affluent white suburbanites of postwar fiction have a stake in amnesia, forgetting an unjust history that benefits them. Meanwhile, urban ethnic communities have a stake in the continuity of memory. The families in Brooks, Himes, Yamamoto, Roth, and Marshall struggle to keep their roots despite urban renewal, racism, and other forms of cultural erasure. This stake in memory aids their ability to picture urban community. In their works, racial memory includes not only memorials to atrocities like lynching, internment, and the Holocaust but also the smaller histories of one's neighbors, playing in a certain park, or the creaking of a certain stairway.

The postwar split between different neighborhoods may seem irrelevant now that suburbs are desegregated and the middle class is moving back into town. I would argue, however, that the invisible walls remain even though they have shifted. We still have much to learn from the postwar era's politics of overlooking. I lived for many years in Oakland, California. Even in this remarkably interracial city, sense of place is still segregated, and the segregation goes largely unremarked. One often sees a comfortable, mostly white neighborhood, where the cheaper houses sell for half a million dollars, sitting next to a poor black, Latino, and Vietnamese neighborhood where the local elementary school can't afford a crossing guard. Two adjoining neighborhoods, two separate realities. I began this book to understand the history behind such radical splits.

Postwar American culture was a laboratory of diversity. World War II brought a new discourse of shared Americanness and an unprecedented cultural mixing. Indeed, the fifties' intensified racial segregation and other repressions of difference should be seen as a desperate and futile effort to contain the new diversity. By emphasizing the ways Cold War logic shuts down diversity of thought, studies of containment culture can end up reproducing the containment of culture. By placing wildly disparate texts together, it becomes possible to see how segregation looks from both sides of the wall—and thus to detect movements beyond containment.

Notes

INTRODUCTION

1. Quote from James Naremore, *More Than Night: Film Noir in Its Contexts* (Berkeley and Los Angeles: University of California Press, 1998), 50.
2. Wini Breines, *Young, White, and Miserable: Growing Up Female in the Fifties* (Boston: Beacon Press, 1992), 10.
3. Thomas Schaub, *American Fiction in the Cold War* (Madison: University of Wisconsin Press, 1991), 154.
4. Carlo Rotella, *October Cities: The Redevelopment of Urban Literature* (Berkeley and Los Angeles: University of California Press, 1998), 15.
5. See King-Kok Cheung, *Articulate Silences: Hisaye Yamamoto, Maxine Hong Kingston, Joy Kogawa* (Ithaca, N.Y.: Cornell University Press, 1993).
6. Charles S. Wright's *The Messenger* remains out of print.
7. Gavin Jones, "'The Sea Ain't Got No Back Door': The Problems of Black Consciousness in Paule Marshall's *Brown Girl, Brownstones*," *African American Review* 32, no. 4 (1998): 602.
8. William H. Whyte, *The Organization Man* (New York: Simon and Schuster, 1956), 310.
9. Grace Paley, "Two Ears, Three Lucks," in *The Collected Stories* (New York: Farrar, Straus, and Giroux, 1994), ix, x.
10. Thomas Frank, "Why Johnny Can't Dissent," in *Commodify Your Dissent,* ed. by Thomas Frank and Matt Weiland (New York: Norton, 1997), 32.
11. Joanne Meyerowitz, ed., *Not June Cleaver: Women and Gender in Postwar America, 1945–1960* (Philadelphia: Temple University Press, 1994).
12. Daniel Boyarin, *Unheroic Conduct: The Rise of Heterosexuality and the Invention of the Jewish Man* (Berkeley and Los Angeles: University of California Press, 1997), 19.
13. Alan Nadel, *Containment Culture: American Narratives, Postmodernism, and the Atomic Age* (Durham, N.C.: Duke University Press, 1995), 2–3, 5.
14. Schaub, *American Fiction in the Cold War,* 92. For other ideological readings of containment culture, see Andrew Ross, *No Respect: Intellectuals and Popular Culture* (New York: Routledge, 1988); Robert Corber, *In the Name of National Security: Hitchcock, Homophobia, and the Political Construction*

of Gender in Postwar America (Durham, N.C.: Duke University Press, 1993); and Nadel, *Containment Culture.*

15. Charles Kaiser, *The Gay Metropolis: The Landmark History of Gay Life in America since World War II* (San Diego: Harcourt Brace, 1997), 27.

16. Many thanks to Ian Duncan for this suggestion.

17. Quoted in Arnold R. Hirsch, *Making the Second Ghetto: Race and Housing in Chicago, 1940–1960* (New York: Cambridge University Press, 1983), 153.

18. Ibid., 253.

19. Kenneth T. Jackson, *Crabgrass Frontier: The Suburbanization of the United States* (New York: Oxford University Press, 1985), 209.

20. Ross, *No Respect,* 43–45.

21. Quoted in Hirsch, *Making the Second Ghetto,* 40. The phrase "an era of hidden violence" is Hirsch's (40).

22. Robert Jay Lifton, *Death in Life: Survivors of Hiroshima* (New York: Random House, 1967), 509.

23. Henry Krystal, M.D., ed., *Massive Psychic Trauma* (New York: International Universities Press, 1968), 327.

24. Judith Herman, *Trauma and Recovery* (New York: Basic Books, 1992), 26.

25. Lawrence L. Langer, *Holocaust Testimonies: The Ruins of Memory* (New Haven: Yale University Press, 1991), 5–6.

26. Walker Percy, *The Moviegoer* (New York: Avon, 1961), 167.

27. Hisaye Yamamoto, " . . . I Still Carry It Around," *RIKKA* 3, no. 4 (1976): 11.

28. John Okada, *No-No Boy* (1957; reprint, Seattle: University of Washington Press, 1976), 159.

29. Gwendolyn Brooks, *Maud Martha* (New York: Harper & Brothers, 1953), 9.

30. Percy, *Moviegoer,* 18.

31. John Cheever, "The Country Husband," in *The Stories of John Cheever* (New York: Knopf, 1978), 325.

32. Sylvia Plath, *The Bell Jar* (1963; New York: Bantam, 1971), 199.

33. Kali Tal, *Worlds of Hurt: Reading the Literatures of Trauma* (New York: Cambridge University Press, 1996), 18–19.

34. The phrase is Benedict Anderson's: Benedict Anderson, *Imagined Communities: Reflections on the Origins and Spread of Nationalism* (New York: Verso, 1983; 2d ed., New York: Verso, 1991).

35. Khachig Tölölyan, "Rethinking *Diaspora*(s): Stateless Power in the Transnational Moment," *Diaspora* 5, no. 1 (1996): 13.

36. Audre Lorde, *Zami: A New Spelling of My Name: A Biomythography* (Trumansburg, N.Y.: Crossing Press, 1982), 179.

CHAPTER 1. THE LONE VIOLENT MAN

1. Naremore, *More Than Night,* 50.

2. For a good treatment of race in film noir, see James Naremore, "The Other Side of the Street," in ibid., 220–253. Manthia Diawara and Justus J. Nieland have written on 1990s African American neo-noir: see Manthia Diawara, "Noir by *Noirs,*" in *Shades of Noir,* ed. Joan Copjec (London: Verso, 1993), 261–278, and Justus J. Nieland, "Race-ing *Noir* and Re-placing History: The Mulatta and Memory in *One False Move* and *Devil in a Blue Dress,*" *Velvet Light Trap* 43 (Spring 1999): 63–77.

3. Mike Davis, "The *Noirs,*" in *City of Quartz* (New York: Vintage Books, 1992), 36–46.

4. Naremore, *More Than Night,* 81.

5. Dean MacCannell, "Democracy's Turn: On Homeless *Noir,*" in Copjec, *Shades of Noir,* 287.

6. Joseph E. Stevens, *Hoover Dam: An American Adventure* (Norman: University of Oklahoma Press, 1988), 259–260.

7. See C.L.R. James et al., *Fighting Racism in World War II* (New York: Monad/Pathfinder, 1980), 243.

8. Ronald Takaki, *A Different Mirror: A History of Multicultural America* (Boston: Little, Brown, 1993), 397.

9. Josh Sides, "Battle on the Home Front: African American Shipyard Workers in World War II Los Angeles," *California History* 75 (Fall 1996): 252.

10. From 55,114 to 118,888. Gerald Horne, *The Fire This Time: The Watts Uprising and the 1960s* (Charlottesville: University Press of Virginia, 1995).

11. Robert M. Fogelson, *The Fragmented Metropolis: Los Angeles, 1850–1930* (Berkeley and Los Angeles: University of California Press, 1967), 200.

12. Sides, "Battle on the Home Front," 253.

13. Chester Himes, *If He Hollers Let Him Go* (1945; reprint, New York: Thunder's Mouth Press, 1986), 4. Subsequent page references appear in the text.

14. See Mauricio Mazon, *The Zoot-Suit Riots: The Psychology of Symbolic Annihilation* (Austin: University of Texas Press, 1984).

15. Vivian Sobchack, "Lounge Time: Postwar Crises and the Chronotope of Film Noir," in *Refiguring American Film Genres: History and Theory,* ed. Nick Browne (Berkeley and Los Angeles: University of California Press, 1998), 159–160.

16. Raymond Chandler, "The Simple Art of Murder," in *The Simple Art of Murder* (New York: Norton, 1968), 533.

17. Mike Davis locates the origins of noir in the "Depression-crazed Middle-Classes of Southern California," in Davis, *City of Quartz,* 37.

18. James Naremore makes this point: *More Than Night,* 44, 55–56, 66.

19. Richard Schickel, *Double Indemnity* (London: British Film Institute, 1992), 10.

20. As Vivian Sobchack writes, "The intimacy and security of home and the integrity and solidity of the home front are lost to wartime and postwar America and to those films we associate at both the core and periphery of that cinematic grouping we circumscribe as noir." Sobchack, "Lounge Time," 146.

21. Davis, *City of Quartz,* 38.

22. Richard T. Ford uses the term "horizontal vertigo" to describe the urban sprawl of Los Angeles. Ford, "Spaced Out in L.A.: Race, Real Estate, and Politics in the City of Fallen Angels," *Transition,* no. 61 (New York: Oxford University Press, 1993), 88.

23. Herman, *Trauma and Recovery,* 66, 38.

24. James M. Cain, *Double Indemnity* (New York: Vintage Books, 1936), 24.

25. For the formal clinical definition of post-traumatic stress disorder, see American Psychiatric Association, *Diagnostic and Statistical Manual of Mental Disorders,* 4th ed. (Washington, D.C.: American Psychiatric Association, 1994), 424–429 (hereafter cited as *DSM-IV*).

26. *Double Indemnity,* dir. Billy Wilder, perf. Fred MacMurray, Barbara Stanwyck, Edward G. Robinson, Paramount, 1944. Screenplay by Billy Wilder and Raymond Chandler, from the novel by James M. Cain.

27. "Just as the city–mystery [of the 1830s and 1840s] registered the dreaded rise of the metropolis, *film noir* registered its decline, accomplishing a demonization and an estrangement from its landscape in advance of its actual 'abandonment'—the violent reshaping of urban life sponsored by the Federal Housing Administration, the Housing Act of 1949, and in New York City the force of nature known as Robert Moses." David Reid and Jayne L. Walker,

"Strange Pursuit: Cornell Woolrich and the Abandoned City of the Forties," in Copjec, *Shades of Noir,* 68–69.

28. Michael J. Lyons, *World War II: A Short History* (Englewood Cliffs, N.J.: Prentice-Hall, 1989), 235.
29. John Campbell, "The Bombing of Cities," in *The Experience of World War II* (New York: Oxford University Press, 1989), 174–181.
30. Nicholas Christopher, *Somewhere in the Night: Film Noir and the American City* (New York: Free Press, 1997), 35.
31. Richard Schickel describes the professionalism of Hollywood's noir screenwriters: "It is not that they aspired to and failed to attain the standards of high literature. Most of them aspired instead to 'professionalism' (a word they often used), the ability to make a decent job of work out of anything they turned their hands to—which often included 'serious' literature." Schickel, *Double Indemnity,* 19.
32. Cameron Crowe, *Conversations with Wilder* (New York: Alfred A. Knopf, 1999), 20, 183–184. Ellipses in original.
33. Richard Dyer, *White* (New York: Routledge, 1997), 28.
34. The sign "Los Angeles Railway Corp. Maintenance Dept." in the opening shot, "Pacific All-Risk Insurance, Founded MCM, Main Office, Los Angeles" lettered on the glass office doors, and on Walter Neff's dictated memorandum: "Los Angeles, July 13, 1938."
35. Alan Spiegel, "Seeing Triple: Cain, Chandler, and Wilder on *Double Indemnity,*" *Mosaic: A Journal for the Interdisciplinary Study of Literature* 16, nos. 1–2 (1983): 91.
36. Dyer, *White,* 122.
37. See photograph and caption on page 43 of Richard Schickel's monograph on *Double Indemnity:* "Stanwyck and MacMurray shooting at a Los Angeles supermarket in wartime, the shelves groaning with food and guarded by members of the L.A.P.D."
38. Cheever, "Country Husband," 325.
39. Wanda Coleman, *Los Angeles Times Magazine,* October 17, 1993, 6. Quoted in Naremore, *More Than Night,* 237.
40. John A. Williams, "Chester Himes—My Man Himes" (interview), in *Flashbacks: A Twenty-Year Diary of Article Writing* (Garden City, N.Y.: Anchor, 1973), 323.
41. bell hooks, "The Oppositional Gaze: Black Female Spectators," in *Feminist Film Theory: A Reader,* ed. Sue Thornham (New York: New York University Press, 1999), 309.
42. Chandler, "Simple Art of Murder," 533.
43. Arna Bontemps and Jack Conroy, *Anyplace but Here* (New York: Hill and Wang, 1966), 267, 9.
44. James Sallis, "In America's Black Heartland: The Achievement of Chester Himes," *Western Humanities Review* 37 (Fall 1983): 198.
45. James Wolcott, "Raymond Chandler's Smoking Gun," *New Yorker,* September 25, 1995, 101.
46. David Fine, "Nathanael West, Raymond Chandler, and the Los Angeles Novel," *California History* 68 (Winter 1989/1990): 51; Graham Hodges, introduction to *If He Hollers Let Him Go,* ix.
47. Himes's use of the southern terms *cracker* and *peckerwood* to describe white bigots reflects the recent influx of white and black southerners into Los Angeles.
48. Williams, "Chester Himes," 314.
49. Chester Himes, *The Autobiography of Chester Himes,* vol. 1: *The Quality of Hurt* (Garden City, N.Y.: Doubleday, 1972), 73.

50. Sides, "Battle on the Home Front," 252.

51. Elizabeth Cowie, "*Film Noir* and Women," in Copjec, *Shades of Noir*, 136.

CHAPTER 2. POST-TRAUMATIC FICTION

1. *The Man in the Gray Flannel Suit,* dir. Nunnally Johnson. Twentieth Century Fox, 1956.

2. Herman, *Trauma and Recovery,* 67.

3. Ibid., 32.

4. George Lipsitz, *Rainbow at Midnight: Labor and Culture in the 1940s* (Urbana: University of Illinois Press, 1994), 47.

5. Barbara Ehrenreich, *The Hearts of Men: American Dreams and the Flight from Commitment* (New York: Anchor Doubleday, 1983), 17.

6. Herman, *Trauma and Recovery,* 66.

7. Thomas Frank, "The Rebel Consumer," in Frank and Weiland, *Commodify Your Dissent,* 33. See also Thomas Frank, *The Conquest of Cool: Business Culture, Counterculture, and the Rise of Hip Consumerism* (Chicago: University of Chicago Press, 1997).

8. Robert A. Hipkiss, " 'The Country Husband': A Model Cheever Achievement," *Studies in Short Fiction* 27 (Fall 1990): 577.

9. Ehrenreich, *Hearts of Men,* 36.

10. William H. Whyte, *The Organization Man* (New York: Simon and Schuster, 1956), 310.

11. Paley, "Two Ears, Three Lucks," xi.

12. Grace Paley, "An Interest in Life," in *Collected Stories,* 61.

13. Tillie Olsen, "I Stand Here Ironing," in *The Best American Short Stories, 1957,* ed. Martha Foley (Boston: Houghton Mifflin, 1957), 271.

14. Wini Breines, *Young, White, and Miserable: Growing Up Female in the Fifties* (Boston: Beacon Press, 1992), xiii.

15. Betty Friedan, *The Feminine Mystique* (New York: Norton, 1963), 15, 22.

16. Michael Lambek, "The Past Imperfect: Remembering as Moral Practice," in *Tense Past: Cultural Essays in Trauma and Memory,* ed. Paul Antze and Michael Lambek (New York: Routledge, 1996), 246.

17. Tal, *Worlds of Hurt,* 8–19.

18. *DSM-IV,* 424–425, 428.

19. Cathy Caruth, *Unclaimed Experience: Trauma, Narrative, and History* (Baltimore: Johns Hopkins University Press, 1996).

20. Cathy Caruth, "Recapturing the Past: Introduction," in *Trauma: Explorations in Memory,* ed. Cathy Caruth (Baltimore: Johns Hopkins University Press, 1995), 152–153.

21. Lawrence J. Kirmayer, "Landscapes of Memory: Trauma, Narrative, and Dissociation," Antze and Lambek, *Tense Past,* 189–190.

22. Herman, *Trauma and Recovery,* 9.

23. Kirby Farrell, *Post-traumatic Culture: Injury and Interpretation in the Nineties* (Baltimore: Johns Hopkins University Press, 1998), 14.

24. Cheever, "Country Husband," 335. Subsequent page references appear in the text.

25. Jackson, *Crabgrass Frontier,* 241.

26. *DSM-IV,* 424.

27. Lawrence L. Langer, *Holocaust Testimonies: The Ruins of Memory* (New Haven: Yale University Press, 1991), 5–6.

28. Breines, *Young, White and Miserable,* 28.

29. Lawrence Jay Dessner, "Gender and Structure in John Cheever's 'The Country Husband,' " *Studies in Short Fiction* 31, no. 1 (Winter 1994): 63.

30. Ibid., 65.

31. John Cheever himself served in the U.S. Army during World War II but never saw combat duty, although he wished to. He was transferred from E Company of the Twenty-second Infantry to the Signal Corps. He spent most of the war in New York and Hollywood writing propaganda. Soon after Cheever's transfer to the Signal Corps, "E Company was blasted to pieces on the beach at Normandy." It is perhaps no accident that Cheever places Francis's war flashback in Normandy. See Susan Cheever, *Home before Dark: A Biographical Memoir of John Cheever by His Daughter* (New York: Washington Square Press, 1984), 56–57.

32. David Riesman, introduction to *Crestwood Heights* (Toronto: University of Toronto Press, 1956), xiii. Quoted in Breines, *Young, White and Miserable,* 43.

33. See Stan Yogi, "Legacies Revealed: Uncovering Buried Plots in the Stories of Hisaye Yamamoto," *Studies in American Fiction* 17(Autumn 1989): 169–181; Cheung, *Articulate Silences;* Sau-Ling Cynthia Wong, *Reading Asian-American Literature: From Necessity to Extravagance* (Princeton: Princeton University Press, 1993); and Elaine H. Kim, *Asian American Literature: An Introduction to the Writings and Their Social Context* (Philadelphia: Temple University Press, 1982).

34. Fine, "Nathanael West, Raymond Chandler, and the Los Angeles Novel," 196.

35. Hisaye Yamamoto, "Wilshire Bus," in *Seventeen Syllables and Other Stories* (Latham, N.Y.: Kitchen Table: Women of Color Press, 1988), 37. Subsequent page references appear in the text. A subsequent edition of *Seventeen Syllables* has been published by Rutgers University Press.

36. Yogi, "Legacies Revealed," 179.

37. *DSM-IV,* 428.

38. Reminiscences of Bob Kono, former camp internee, lecture, University of Oregon, February 4, 1999.

39. Dorothy Ritsuko McDonald and Katharine Newman, "Relocation and Dislocation: The Writings of Hisaye Yamamoto and Wakako Yamauchi," *MELUS* 7 (Fall 1980): 23.

40. Indeed, young Nisei, even the highly educated, rarely obtained employment outside the Japanese American world. Historian Ronald Takaki writes: "The Nisei were trapped in an ethnic labor market. Only a very tiny percentage of them worked for white employers." Takaki, *Different Mirror,* 275.

41. Carey McWilliams, *North from Mexico* (Philadelphia: Lippincott, 1949), 227.

42. See Mazon, *Zoot Suit Riots,* and Carey McWilliams, *Southern California: An Island on the Land* (1946; reprint, Salt Lake City: Peregrine Smith, 1973), 319–321.

43. Carey McWilliams might argue that it goes back to the mid-nineteenth century, when the Chinese replaced Native Americans at the despised low end of the labor market. See McWilliams, *Southern California,* 47.

44. Arna Bontemps and Jack Conroy, *They Seek a City* (Garden City, N.Y.: Doubleday, 1945), 205.

45. John Modell, *Economics and Politics of Racial Accommodation: The Japanese of Los Angeles, 1900–1942* (Urbana: University of Illinois Press, 1977), 10.

46. Hisaye Yamamoto, "Yoneko's Earthquake," in *Seventeen Syllables,* 52.

47. Charles L. Crow, "A *MELUS* Interview: Hisaye Yamamoto," *MELUS* 14 (Spring 1987): 78.

48. John Okada, *No-No Boy,* 202.

49. Bess Myerson, quoted in Susan Dworkin, *Miss America 1945: Bess Myerson's Own Story* (New York: Newmarket Press, 1987), 7.

50. Takaki, *Different Mirror,* 399.

51. Cheung, introduction to *Seventeen Syllables*, xiv.

52. Takaki, *Different Mirror*, 276.

53. As Elaine Kim writes, "Family members drifted apart in the camp environment. . . . Finally, *nisei* children stopped meeting with their parents even at the mess halls, gathering instead with persons of their own age group. . . . The War Relocation Authority established governing bodies within the camps that reversed the traditional Japanese community structure and pattern of leadership." *Asian American Literature,*134–135.

54. Monica Sone, *Nisei Daughter* (Seattle: University of Washington Press, 1953), 237–238.

55. On the FHA loans, see Gwendolyn Wright, *Building the Dream: A Social History of Housing in America* (New York: Pantheon Books, 1981), chap. 13: "The New Suburban Expansion and the American Dream."

56. Robert Fishman, *Bourgeois Utopias: The Rise and Fall of Suburbia* (New York: Basic Books, 1987), 170–171.

57. Sucheng Chan, *Asian Californians* (San Francisco: MTL/Boyd & Fraser/Golden State Series, 1991), 105–106.

58. Robert M. Fogelson, *The Fragmented Metropolis: Los Angeles, 1850–1930* (Cambridge: Harvard University Press, 1967), 188.

59. Wong, *Reading Asian American Literature,* 136.

60. Ibid., 123.

61. Hisaye Yamamoto, "Life Among the Oil Fields: A Memoir," in *Seventeen Syllables,* 89.

62. Wong, *Reading Asian American Literature,* 141.

63. Modell, *Economics and Politics;* Elisabeth Kornhauser, reminiscences of life in prewar Los Angeles, conversation with the author, May 10, 1994; Ronald Takaki, *Strangers from a Different Shore* (Boston: Little, Brown, 1989), 203–208.

64. Mitsuye Yamada, "Desert Run," in *Desert Run: Poems and Stories* (Latham, N.Y.: Kitchen Table: Women of Color Press, 1988), 5. A subsequent edition of *Desert Run* has been published by Rutgers University Press.

65. Mazon, *Zoot Suit Riots,* 16–17.

66. Jeanne Wakatsuki Houston and James D. Houston, *Farewell to Manzanar* (Boston: Houghton Mifflin, 1973), 114.

67. Hisaye Yamamoto, "The Brown House," in *Seventeen Syllables,* 45.

68. Yogi, "Legacies Revealed," 80.

69. Dori Laub, M.D., "Truth and Testimony: The Process and the Struggle," in Caruth, *Trauma,* 73.

70. Hisaye Yamamoto, "After Johnny Died," *Los Angeles Tribune,* November 26, 1945, 1 ff.

71. Don Parson, " 'This Modern Marvel': Bunker Hill, Chavez Ravine, and the Politics of Modernism in Los Angeles," *Southern California Quarterly* 75 (Fall/Winter 1993): 335.

72. See Elizabeth A. Wheeler, "Bulldozing the Subject," in *Essays in Postmodern Culture,* ed. Eyal Amiran and John Unsworth (New York: Oxford University Press, 1993), 199–228.

73. Parson, " 'This Modern Marvel,' " 343.

74. Andrew Lind, *Hawaii's Japanese: An Experiment in Democracy* (Princeton: Princeton University Press, 1946), 162. Quoted in Takaki, *Different Mirror,* 385.

75. Gunnar Myrdal with Richard A. Sterner and Arnold Rose, *An American Dilemma: The Negro Problem and Modern Democracy* (1944; reprint, New York: Harper & Row, 1962), lxxi, 100.

76. Cheung, *Articulate Silences,* 64–65.

77. Yamamoto, " . . . I Still Carry It Around," *RIKKA* 3, no. 4 (1976): 11.
78. Cheung, *Articulate Silences,* 72.

CHAPTER 3. AMERICAN NOVELS BEFORE AND AFTER BROWN

1. Jackson, *Crabgrass Frontier,* 209.
2. Lipsitz, *Rainbow at Midnight,* 20.
3. Robin D. G. Kelley, "Congested Terrain: Resistance on Public Transportation," in *Race Rebels: Culture, Politics, and the Black Working Class* (New York: Free Press, 1994), 55–56.
4. See Wright, *Building the Dream;* Hirsch, *Making the Second Ghetto;* and Jackson, *Crabgrass Frontier.*
5. Jackson, *Crabgrass Frontier,* 241.
6. Barbara Christian, "Nuance and the Novella: A Study of Gwendolyn Brooks's *Maud Martha,*" in *A Life Distilled: Gwendolyn Brooks, Her Poetry and Fiction,* ed. Maria K. Mootry and Gary Smith (Urbana: University of Illinois Press, 1987), 239.
7. See Gwendolyn Brooks, *Report from Part One* (Detroit: Broadside Press, 1972), 175–177 and passim.
8. Frank Chin et al., *Aiiieeeee!: An Anthology of Asian American Writers* (Washington, D.C.: Howard University Press, 1974).
9. Hirsch, "Epilogue: Chicago and the Nation," in *Making the Second Ghetto,* 259–275.
10. Richard C. Berner, "Seattle, 1921–1940," in *Seattle in the Twentieth Century,* vol. 2 (Philadelphia: Charles Press, 1992), 210.
11. Carlo Rotella, *October Cities: The Redevelopment of Urban Literature* (Berkeley and Los Angeles: University of California Press, 1998), 124.
12. Percy, *Moviegoer,* 82.
13. Quoted in David Halberstam, *The Fifties* (New York: Villard Books, 1993), 141.
14. Dyer, *White,* 18.

CHAPTER 4. HANGING CURTAINS IN CHICAGO

1. St. Clair Drake and Horace R. Cayton, *Black Metropolis: A Study of Negro Life in a Northern City* (1945; reprint, Chicago: University of Chicago Press, 1993), 114.
2. Ibid., xxxv; Alan B. Anderson and George W. Pickering, *Confronting the Color Line: The Broken Promise of the Civil Rights Movement in Chicago* (Athens: University of Georgia Press, 1986), 53.
3. Hirsch, *Making the Second Ghetto,* 17.
4. Anderson and Pickering, *Confronting the Color Line,* 67; Drake and Cayton, *Black Metropolis,* 12.
5. Anderson and Pickering, *Confronting the Color Line,* 59.
6. The conflicts began in May 1944 and became sporadic sometime in 1952 (Hirsch, *Making the Second Ghetto,* 52, 63); Brooks submitted a synopsis and ten chapters of *Maud Martha* to her publisher in January 1945 and then worked on the novel on and off until the full manuscript's acceptance at Harper's in October 1952 (D. H. Melhem, *Gwendolyn Brooks: Poetry and the Heroic Voice* [Lexington: University Press of Kentucky, 1987], 80, 83).
7. Patricia H. Lattin and Vernon E. Lattin, "Dual Vision in Gwendolyn Brooks's *Maud Martha,*" in *On Gwendolyn Brooks: Reliant Contemplation,* ed. Stephen Caldwell Wright (Ann Arbor: University of Michigan Press), 140.
8. Gwendolyn Brooks, *Maud Martha* (New York: Harper & Brothers, 1953), 101. Subsequent page references appear in the text.
9. Hirsch, *Making the Second Ghetto,* xi.

10. Ibid., 215–216.
11. Ibid., 133; C. K. Doreski, *Writing America Black: Race Rhetoric in the Public Sphere* (New York: Cambridge University Press, 1998), 121.
12. Hirsch, *Making the Second Ghetto,* 119, 207.
13. Christian, "Nuance and the Novella," 241.
14. Drake and Cayton, *Black Metropolis,* 747, 749.
15. Anderson and Pickering, *Confronting the Color Line,* 63.
16. Quoted in Hirsch, *Making the Second Ghetto,* 61.
17. See Maria K. Mootry, " 'Tell It Slant': Disguise and Discovery as Revisionist Poetic Discourse in *The Bean Eaters,*" in Mootry and Smith, *Life Distilled,* 179–180; Hortense Spillers, " 'An Order of Constancy': Notes on Brooks and the Feminine," *Centennial Review* 29 (Spring 1985): 223–248; and Christian, "Nuance and the Novella."
18. Claudia Tate, "Anger So Flat: Gwendolyn Brooks's *Annie Allen,*" in Mootry and Smith, *Life Distilled,*143, 149.
19. Drake and Cayton, *Black Metropolis,* 112, 101, 102.
20. Drake and Cayton, *Black Metropolis,* 660.
21. Hirsch, *Making the Second Ghetto,* 25–26.
22. Carla Cappetti, *Writing Chicago: Modernism, Ethnography, and the Novel* (New York: Columbia University Press, 1993), 122.

CHAPTER 5. QUESTIONING SEATTLE

1. Yasuko I. Takezawa, *Breaking the Silence: Redress and Japanese American Ethnicity* (Ithaca, N.Y.: Cornell University Press, 1995), 61, 74.
2. Okada, *No-No Boy,* 52. Subsequent page references appear in the text.
3. Takezawa, *Breaking the Silence,* 126.
4. Ibid., 84.
5. Stan Yogi, "'You Had to Be One or the Other': Oppositions and Reconciliation in John Okada's *No-No Boy,*" *MELUS* 21 (Summer 1996): 61–63.
6. War Relocation Authority Application for Leave Clearance, 1943. See Michi Weglyn, *Years of Infamy: The Untold Story of America's Concentration Camps,* (New York: William Morrow, 1976), 136.
7. Jere Takahashi, *Nisei/Sansei* (Philadelphia: Temple University Press, 1997), 123.
8. Takezawa, *Breaking the Silence,* 120–121.
9. "Diagnostic Criteria for 309.81 Posttraumatic Stress Disorder," Criterion C (7), *DSM-IV,* 428.
10. S. Frank Miyamoto, *Social Solidarity among the Japanese in Seattle* (1939; reprint, Seattle: University of Washington Press, 1981), 9.
11. Celene Idema, conversation with the author, July 25, 1999.
12. Quintard Taylor, *The Forging of a Black Community: Seattle's Central District from 1870 through the Civil Rights Era* (Seattle: University of Washington Press, 1994), 160–161.
13. Takezawa, *Breaking the Silence,* 114.
14. Ibid., 111.
15. "The House I Live In (That's America to Me)," music and words: Earl Robinson and Lewis Allan, 1942. Frank Sinatra recording, August 22, 1945, arranger: Axel Stordahl; conductor/band: A. Stordahl/studio orchestra, *The Frank Sinatra Story in Music,* vol. 2 (Columbia Records, 1959).
16. Takahashi, *Nisei/Sansei,* 121.
17. Disneyland opened July 17, 1955. Karal Ann Marling, ed., *Designing Disney's Theme Parks: The Architecture of Reassurance* (Canadian Centre for Architecture [Montreal], 1997), 220.
18. On barriers to suburban residence, see Takezawa, *Breaking the Silence,* 115,

117; Takahashi, *Nisei/Sansei,* 161. For year of novel's composition, see auto-biographical note by John Okada quoted in Frank Chin's afterword to *No-No Boy,* 260.

19. Jinqi Ling, "Race, Power, and Cultural Politics in John Okada's *No-No Boy,*" *American Literature* 67 (June 1995): 363, 375.

20. Gayle K. Fujita Sato, "Momotaro's Exile: John Okada's *No-No Boy,*" in *Reading the Literatures of Asian America,* ed. Shirley Geok-lin Lim and Amy Ling (Philadelphia: Temple University Press, 1992), 257.

CHAPTER 6. NEUTRALIZING NEW ORLEANS

1. Joel Williamson, *The Crucible of Race: Black-White Relations in the American South since Emancipation* (New York: Oxford University Press, 1984), 253.

2. Patrick H. Samway, S.J., *Walker Percy: A Life* (New York: Farrar, Straus, and Giroux, 1997), 187.

3. Max Webb, "Binx Bolling's New Orleans: Moviegoing, Southern Writing, and Father Abraham," in *The Art of Walker Percy: Stratagems for Being,* ed. Panthea Reid Broughton (Baton Rouge: Louisiana State University Press, 1979), 6.

4. Kim Lacy Rogers, *Righteous Lives: Narratives of the New Orleans Civil Rights Movement* (New York: New York University Press, 1993), 46.

5. Percy, *Moviegoer,* 17–18. Subsequent page references appear in the text.

6. Rogers, *Righteous Lives,* 37, 45.

7. Samway, *Walker Percy,* 208, 212.

8. Rogers, *Righteous Lives,* 55. See also Philip A. Grant Jr., "Archbishop Joseph F. Rummel and the 1962 New Orleans Desegregation Crisis," *Records of the American Catholic Historical Society of Philadelphia* 91, nos. 1–4 (1980): 59–66.

9. Samway, *Walker Percy,* 186; Jay Tolson, *Pilgrim in the Ruins: A Life of Walker Percy* (New York: Simon & Schuster, 1992), 269.

10. Walker Percy, "The Southern Moderate," in *Signposts in a Strange Land,* ed. and with an introduction by Patrick Samway (New York: Farrar, Straus, and Giroux,1991), 90.

11. Tolson, *Pilgrim in the Ruins,* 274.

12. Kelley, *Race Rebels,* 57.

13. A rare exception, Michael Pearson, writes: "Appropriately, in many ways, the critical focus has been on 'isms' in his fiction—existentialism, stoicism, Catholicism—for Percy is a novelist of ideas. However, it is interesting to note that at least one 'ism' is missing from critical discussion. What does Walker Percy have to say about racism?" ("The Double Bondage of Racism in Walker Percy's Fiction," *Mississippi Quarterly* 41 [Fall 1988]: 480–481). Pearson goes on to link the antiracist statements from Percy's essays with the more general humanism of the novels.

14. Samway, *Walker Percy,* 207.

15. Robert Coles, *Walker Percy: An American Search* (Boston: Atlantic Little Brown, 1978), 142.

16. See Bertram Wyatt-Brown, *The House of Percy: Honor, Melancholy, and Imagination in a Southern Family* (Oxford: Oxford University Press,1994).

17. Tolson, *Pilgrim in the Ruins,* 283–284.

18. Interview with Barbara King, in Lewis A. Lawson and Victor A. Kramer, eds., *Conversations with Walker Percy* (Jackson: University of Mississippi Press, 1985), 91.

19. Andrew Ross, "Hip, and the Long Front of Color," in *No Respect: Intellectuals and Popular Culture* (New York: Routledge, 1988), 84.

20. Walker Percy, "Stoicism in the South," in *Signposts in a Strange Land,* 84.

21. Samway, *Walker Percy*, 203, 205.
22. Percy, "New Orleans Mon Amour," in *Signposts in a Strange Land*, 21.
23. See George Lipsitz, "Mardi Gras Indians: Carnival and Counter Narrative in Black New Orleans," *Cultural Critique* 10 (Fall 1988): 108–109.
24. See Rogers, *Righteous Lives*, 76.
25. Ibid., 71–72. See also Donald E. DeVore and Joseph Logsdon, *Crescent City Schools: Public Education in New Orleans, 1841–1991* (New Orleans: Orleans Parish School Board, 1991), 245–255.
26. John Edward Hardy, *The Fiction of Walker Percy* (Urbana: University of Illinois Press, 1987), 41.
27. Percy, "Southern Moderate," 100–101.
28. Kelley, *Race Rebels*, 75.
29. Fishman, *Bourgeois Utopias*, 4.
30. Harry R. Greenberg, *The Movies in Your Mind* (New York: Saturday Review Press, 1975), 4. Quoted in Lewis A. Lawson, "The Dream Screen in the Moviegoer," in *Walker Percy's Feminine Characters*, ed. Lawson and Elzbieta H. Oleksky (Troy, N.Y.: Whitston Publishing Co., 1995), 8.
31. Percy was not himself a veteran of World War II or the Korean War.

CHAPTER 7. "A RITUAL FOR BEING BORN TWICE"

1. Elinor Langer, "Notes for Next Time," quoted in Breines, *Young, White, and Miserable*, 135.
2. Jo Sinclair, *The Changelings* (1955; reprint, New York: Feminist Press, 1983), 12. Subsequent page references appear in the text.
3. Jack Kerouac, *On the Road* (New York: Signet/NAL, 1957), 51.
4. Sylvia Plath, *The Bell Jar* (1963; reprint, New York: Bantam Books, 1971), 199.
5. Paule Marshall, *Brown Girl, Brownstones* (1959; reprint, New York: Feminist Press, 1981), 228. Subsequent page references appear in the text.
6. Schaub, *American Fiction in the Cold War*, 75.
7. Jack R. Sublette, *J. D. Salinger: An Annotated Bibliography, 1938–1981* (New York: Garland Publishing, 1984), 30–31; Sanford Pinsker, *The Catcher in the Rye: Innocence under Pressure* (New York: Twayne Publishers, 1993), xiv–xv; Warren French, *J. D. Salinger, Revisited* (Boston: Twayne Publishers, 1988), 34–35.
8. *Statistical Abstract of the United States*, 118th ed. (Washington, D.C.: U.S. Department of Commerce, 1998).
9. Ralph Ellison, "On Initiation Rites and Power," *Going to the Territory* (New York: Vintage Books, 1987), 44.
10. Ralph Ellison, *Invisible Man* (New York: Vintage Books, 1952), 269. Subsequent page references appear in the text.
11. Erving Goffman, *Asylums: Essays on the Social Situation of Mental Patients and Other Inmates* (1961; reprint, Chicago: Aldine, 1962), 319, 320.
12. Joel Schwartz, *The New York Approach: Robert Moses, Urban Liberals, and the Redevelopment of the Inner City* (Columbus: Ohio State University Press, 1993), xviii, xvi.
13. Robert A. Caro, *The Power Broker: Robert Moses and the Fall of New York* (New York: Random House, 1974), 20.
14. James Baldwin, "Fifth Avenue, Uptown: A Letter from Harlem," in *Nobody Knows My Name: More Notes of a Native Son* (New York: Dell Publishing, 1961), 55, 61.
15. Caro, *Power Broker*, 983.
16. Charles S. Wright, *The Messenger* (1963; reprint, New York: Fawcett Crest paperback, 1963), 10. Subsequent page references appear in the text.
17. Many thanks to Lawrence Hogue for introducing me to *The Messenger*.

18. Plath, *Bell Jar,* 1. Subsequent page references appear in the text.
19. Todd W. Bressi, ed., *Planning and Zoning New York City: Yesterday, Today, and Tomorrow* (New Brunswick, N.J.: Rutgers Center for Urban Policy Research, 1993), 51–53.
20. Barbara Kruger, "An 'Unsightly' Site," in *Remote Control: Power, Cultures, and the World of Appearances* (Cambridge: MIT Press, 1993), 6, 18.
21. Jackson Lears, "A Matter of Taste: Corporate Cultural Hegemony in a Mass-Consumption Society," in *Recasting America: Culture and Politics in the Age of Cold War,* ed. Lary May (Chicago: University of Chicago Press, 1989), 45.
22. Louis Chu, *Eat a Bowl of Tea* (Secaucus, N.J.: Lyle Stuart, 1961), 245–246.
23. An exception is Gavin Jones's article " 'The Sea Ain' Got No Back Door': The Problems of Black Consciousness in Paule Marshall's *Brown Girl, Brownstones,*" *African American Review* 32, no. 4 (1998): 597–606.
24. Philip Roth, *Goodbye, Columbus* (1959; reprint, New York: Bantam paperback, 1963), 48–49.
25. Ronald Sukenick, *Down and In: Life in the Underground* (New York: Beech Tree Books/William Morrow, 1987), 13.
26. Robert Stern, Thomas Mellins, and David Fishman, *New York 1960: Architecture and Urbanism between the Second World War and the Bicentennial* (New York: Monacelli Press, 1995), 917.
27. Ibid., 9.

CHAPTER 8. CAMPING OUT IN CULT NOVELS

1. Gore Vidal, *The City and the Pillar* (New York: Grosset & Dunlap, 1948), 140.
2. Walt Whitman, "Crossing Brooklyn Ferry," in *Leaves of Grass.* 1892 ed. (New York: Bantam Books, 1983), 129.
3. This analysis provides a literary counterpart to historian Wini Breines's excellent work on fifties women. See, for instance, Breines, "The 'Other' Fifties: Beats, Bad Girls, and Rock and Roll," in her *Young, White, and Miserable,* 127–166.
4. Schaub, *American Fiction in the Cold War,* 154.
5. See Barbara Ehrenreich, "The Beat Rebellion: Beyond Work and Marriage," in *The Hearts of Men: American Dreams and the Flight from Commitment* (New York: Anchor Doubleday, 1983), 52–67.
6. William Burroughs, *Naked Lunch* (New York: Grove Press, 1959), 28.
7. Interview with Ann Bannon in Maida Tilchen, "Ann Bannon: The Mystery Solved," *Gay Community News,* January 8, 1983, 10. Quoted in Suzanna Danuta Walters, "As Her Hand Crept Slowly up Her Thigh: Ann Bannon and the Politics of Pulp," *Social Text* 23 (Fall/Winter 1989): 86.
8. Steven Seidman, *Difference Troubles: Queering Social Theory and Sexual Politics* (New York: Cambridge University Press, 1997), 193.
9. David van Leer, *The Queening of America: Gay Culture in Straight Society* (New York: Routlege, 1995), 59.
10. Leslie Feinberg, *Stone Butch Blues: A Novel* (Ithaca, N.Y.: Firebrand Books, 1993), 56.
11. Tal, *Worlds of Hurt,* 18.
12. Ginsberg used the term to describe the regulars at the San Remo bar in Greenwich Village. Steven Watson, *The Birth of the Beat Generation: Visionaries, Rebels, and Hipsters, 1944–1960* (New York Pantheon Books, 1995), 121.
13. Sukenick, *Down and In,* 15.
14. For pre-Stonewall gay history and the postwar era as a time of both repression and growth, see Corber, *In the Name of National Security* and *Homosexuality in Cold War America: Resistance and the Crisis of Masculinity*

(Durham, N.C.: Duke University Press, 1997); Joseph A. Boone, "Queer Sites in Modernism: Harlem/The Left Bank/Greenwich Village," in *The Geography of Identity*, ed. Patricia Yaeger (Ann Arbor: University of Michigan Press, 1996), 243–272; Lillian Faderman, *Odd Girls and Twilight Lovers: A History of Lesbian Life in Twentieth-Century America* (New York: Columbia University Press, 1991); John D'Emilio, *Sexual Politics, Sexual Communities: The Making of a Homosexual Minority in the United States 1940–1970* (Chicago: University of Chicago Press, 1983); and David Comstock, *Violence against Gay Men and Lesbians* (New York: Columbia University Press, 1992).

15. Faderman, *Odd Girls and Twilight Lovers*, 171.
16. Ibid., 157.
17. Dee Garrison, " 'Our Skirts Gave Them Courage': The Civil Defense Protest Movement in New York City, 1955–1961," in Meyerowitz, *Not June Cleaver*, 201–226. Subsequent page references appear in the text.
18. Andrew Ross, "Uses of Camp," in *Camp Grounds: Style and Homosexuality*, ed. David Bergman (Amherst: University of Massachusetts Press, 1993), 74; Susan Sontag, "Notes on 'Camp,' " in her *Against Interpretation and Other Essays* (New York: Farrar, Straus, and Giroux, 1966), 275–292.
19. See Barbara Ehrenreich, "Early Rebels: The Gray Flannel Dissidents," in *Hearts of Men*, 29–41.
20. Scott Long, "The Loneliness of Camp," in Bergman, *Camp Grounds*, 79.
21. David Bergman, introduction to *Camp Grounds*, 13.
22. "Snapshots of the Interstate Metropolis," *Reporter* 13 (September 8, 1955), 18–23. Quoted in Stern, Mellins, and Fishman, *New York 1960*, 21.
23. Stern, Mellins, and Fishman, *New York 1960*, 432, 62.
24. Ibid., 61–62; Schwartz, *New York Approach*, xx.
25. Serge Guilbaut, *How New York Stole the Idea of Modern Art: Abstract Expressionism, Freedom, and the Cold War*, trans. Arthur Goldhammer (Chicago: University of Chicago Press, 1983), 1.
26. Shaun O'Connell, *Remarkable, Unspeakable New York: A Literary History* (Boston: Beacon Press, 1995), 233.
27. Lorde, *Zami*, 177, 179.
28. Kaiser, *Gay Metropolis*, 98. Watson, *Birth of the Beat Generation*, 119–121.
29. Kaiser, *Gay Metropolis*, 98.
30. Ibid., 107.
31. Allan Berube, "Marching to a Different Drummer," *Advocate*, October 15, 1981; quoted in George Chauncey, *Gay New York: Gender, Urban Culture, and the Making of the Gay Male World, 1890–1940* (New York: Basic Books, 1994), 10.
32. Faderman, *Odd Girls and Twilight Lovers*,125.
33. Kaiser, *Gay Metropolis*, 27–28.
34. Chauncey, *Gay New York*,10.
35. Kaiser, *Gay Metropolis*, 38, 51.
36. Faderman, *Odd Girls and Twilight Lovers*, 126.
37. Michael Warner, introduction to *Fear of a Queer Planet: Queer Politics and Social Theory* (Minneapolis: University of Minnesota Press, 1993), xvi–xvii.
38. Kenneth C. Davis, *Two-Bit Culture: The Paperbacking of America* (New York: Houghton Mifflin, 1984), 73, 12, 146, 72, 74.
39. J. D. Salinger, *The Catcher in the Rye* (New York: Signet paperback, 1951), 5.
40. Schaub, *American Fiction in the Cold War*, 73.
41. Davis, *Two-Bit Culture*, 2, 3, 202, 292.
42. Ehrenreich, *Hearts of Men*, 65.
43. Percy, *Moviegoer*, 19–20.

44. Wright, *Messenger*, 31–32.
45. Davis, *Two-Bit Culture*, 203.
46. Ibid., 149.
47. Burroughs cover reproduced in Davis, *Two-Bit Culture*, 175; Bannon cover in Jaye Zimet, *Strange Sisters: The Art of Lesbian Pulp Fiction, 1949–1969* (New York: Viking Studio, 1999), 47.
48. Ann Bannon, foreword to Zimet, *Strange Sisters*, 13.
49. Roth, *Goodbye, Columbus*, 52.
50. Wright, *Messenger*,16.
51. Truman Capote, *Breakfast at Tiffany's* (New York: Signet, 1958), 51.
52. Burroughs, *Naked Lunch*, 12, 3–4.

CHAPTER 9. THE DISCOURSE OF SADOMASOCHISTIC VIOLENCE

1. Catharine Stimpson, "The Beat Generation and the Trials of Homosexual Liberation," *Salmagundi* 58–59 (Fall 1982–Winter 1983): 380.
2. Corber, *In the Name of National Security*.
3. Vidal, *City and the Pillar*, 138. Subsequent page references appear in the text.
4. In *Homosexuality in Cold War America*, Robert Corber uses *The City and the Pillar* as part of his evidence that the gay rights movement began long before Stonewall (18–19, 135–159).
5. Davis, *Two-Bit Culture*, 263.
6. Hubert Selby Jr., *Last Exit to Brooklyn* (New York: Grove Press, 1964), 11. Subsequent page references appear in the text.

CHAPTER 10. SIDESTEPPING ASSAULT

1. Ann Bannon, *The Beebo Brinker Chronicles: Odd Girl Out, I Am a Woman, Women in the Shadows, and Beebo Brinker,* omnibus volume. (Tallahassee: Naiad Press, 1995), 503, 497, 433. Subsequent page references appear in the text.
2. On dueling voices and perspectives in Bannon's work, see Walters, "As Her Hand Crept Slowly," 87; Michele Aina Barale, "When Jack Blinks: Si(gh)ting Gay Desire in Ann Bannon's *Beebo Brinker*," *Feminist Studies* 18 (Fall 1992): 542.
3. Faderman, *Odd Girls and Twilight Lovers*, 146–147.
4. See Walters, "As Her Hand Crept Slowly," 87: "Bannon's work, it seems to me, escapes the narrative of damnation not only through the complexity of its content and characterization, but through its use of the "low" genre of the pulp/romantic paperback."
5. Long, "Loneliness of Camp," 87.
6. Tilden interview, quoted in Walters, "As Her Hand Crept Slowly," 86.
7. Barale, "When Jack Blinks," 537, 539.
8. Tilden interview quoted in Walters, "As Her Hand Crept Slowly," 86.
9. Kaiser, *Gay Metropolis*, 86, 101.
10. See Faderman, *Odd Girls and Twilight Lovers,*179: "In the years after the war, when butch/femme roles became so intrinsic to the young and working-class lesbian subculture, a good deal of hostility developed between those who did and those who did not conform to roles. Butches and femmes laughed at middle-class 'kiki' women for their 'wishy-washy' self-presentation." Bannon's novels show no such hostility between groups.
11. Chauncey, *Gay New York*, 347.
12. Long, "Loneliness of Camp," 79.
13. Edmund Begler, quoted in Faderman, *Odd Girls and Twilight Lovers*, 132.
14. Many thanks to James Erb for pointing out that *Breakfast at Tiffany's* passes for straight.

15. George Plimpton, *Truman Capote* (New York: Anchor Books, 1997), 163–165.
16. Capote, *Breakfast at Tiffany's*, 35–36. Subsequent page references appear in the text.
17. Van Leer, *Queening of America*, 52
18. Many thanks to Tison Pugh for spotting the joke and sharing it.
19. Chauncey, *Gay New York*, 347.

CHAPTER 11. HIPSTER MEETS HOUSEWIFE

1. Diane Di Prima, *Memoirs of a Beatnik* (1969; reprint, San Francisco: Last Gasp of San Francisco Press, 1988), 51. Quoted in Breines, *Young, White, and Miserable*, 139.
2. Stimpson, "Beat Generation," 374.
3. Kerouac, *On the Road*, 5. Subsequent page references appear in the text.
4. Dennis McNally, *Desolate Angel: Jack Kerouac, the Beat Generation, and America* (New York: Random House, 1979), 6, 61.
5. Dyer, *White*, 34.
6. Ehrenreich, *Hearts of Men*, 60.
7. Gore Vidal interview in Kaiser, *Gay Metropolis*, 98; "[Kerouac] told Ginsberg that he was prepared to accept every facet of his sexuality and to let all his inhibitions 'dissolve' in the heat of his homoeroticism." Ellis Amburn, *Subterranean Kerouac: The Hidden Life of Jack Kerouac* (New York: St. Martin's Griffin, 1998), 93. See also 91–95.
8. Quoted in Watson, *Birth of the Beat Generation*, 142.
9. Ibid., 82–88; McNally, *Desolate Angel*, 93; Kaiser, *Gay Metropolis*, 99.
10. Jack Kerouac, *The Subterraneans* (New York: Grove Press, 1958), 31.
11. Joyce Pettis, *Toward Wholeness in Paule Marshall's Fiction* (Charlottesville: University Press of Virginia, 1995), 45.

CONCLUSION

1. Tom Brokaw, *The Greatest Generation* (New York: Random House, 1998), xx–xxi.

Index

African Americans: as audience, 36–37; and Avati, 209; in Chicago, 103; and civil rights movement, 107; in *Double Indemnity,* 34–36; and gaze, 36–37; and Himes, 36, 37–38, 41, 78; and Kerouac, 256–257; in Los Angeles, 21–22, 76–77, 78; male, 36–37; and Marshall, 245, 255; middle-class, 46; and Myrdal, 91; and noir, 20, 27; and Percy, 139, 143, 144, 146–147, 152, 155, 157–158; and Roth, 187, 188, 189–191; and segregation, 13, 98–99; and Sinclair, 164, 165, 166; stereotypes of, 34; and work, 21, 36. *See also* race; segregation; *specific writers*

aftershock: and Okada, 122, 123; and postwar novel, 167; and Yamamoto, 72. *See also* memory; post-traumatic stress disorder; shock

alienation: and Cheever, 58, 59, 62; and hipster, 52; and Marshall, 254; and Okada, 121, 122; and Percy, 135, 141, 144; and postwar fiction, 2, 261; and postwar generation, 163–164; and privilege, 262; and Salinger, 169; and subculture, 193;

and violent man, 1; and Yamamoto, 59, 71. *See also* detachment; existentialism; isolation; loneliness

Alien Land Laws, 85

Allan, Lewis, 128

aloneness, 1, 2–5, 19–47, 24, 71, 87, 121, 122, 263, 266. *See also* alienation; detachment; loneliness

America, 90–91, 127–128, 249–250

American Beauty (film), 52

amnesia, 261; and Okada, 12, 102, 121, 122, 128, 262; and Percy, 102; and Roth, 181; and violence, 12; and whites, 266. *See also* forgetting; memory

anger, 104, 112, 146. *See also* emotion

anonymity, 33, 121

anti-Semitism, 186

Armed Services Editions, 205–206

Asian Americans, 4, 13. *See also* *specific groups and writers*

Asians, 77

assimilation, 121

asylum, 170. *See also* safety

audience: African American, 36–37; and *Double Indemnity,* 28, 32;

audience (*continued*)
Japanese American, 49; and noir,
23, 26, 27, 35; and Yamamoto, 49,
74, 76. *See also* reader
Avati, James, 209

Baldwin, James, 171
Bannon, Ann, 6, 195, 196, 224–235;
Beebo Brinker, 230–231; and
Capote, 237; and confinement, 16,
228; and homosexuality, 16, 225,
261–262; and housewife, 8, 195,
224, 226, 227, 228, 231; *I Am a
Woman,* 227; and New York City,
224; *Odd Girl Out,* 209; on self,
228; and subculture, 226, 229,
263; and violence, 229, 230,
231–235, 266; *Women in the
Shadows,* 228, 232
Barale, Michele, 226
Barbadian Americans, 179, 182, 186,
252
Barbados, 185
bars, 203–204, 205, 223, 230, 231,
235, 243, 247, 248.
Beats: and exposure, 244; and
housewife, 195; and Kerouac, 245,
246, 247, 248, 249; and lone,
alienated man, 263; and Marshall,
252, 253, 255, 258, 259; and Open
City, 261
beauty, 108–110, 111. *See also* fashion
beauty parlor, 109–110, 115, 116
Bedford-Stuyvesant (Brooklyn, N.Y.),
183
Bellow, Saul, *The Adventures of
Augie March,* 176
bisexuality, 244. *See also* gays;
homosexuality; lesbians; sex/sexu-
ality
body: and Kerouac, 246; and
Marshall, 185, 252, 253, 254, 257;
and noir, 30; and Okada, 124; and
Percy, 150; and Yamamoto, 73
bohemia, 197, 203, 204, 244, 245,
252–253, 256, 259. *See also* cult
novel; subculture
Bontemps, Arna, 38, 76–77

Boyarin, Daniel, 7
Breines, Wini, 3, 54–55, 63
Brooks, Gwendolyn: and Chicago,
100, 110, 113, 262; and Himes,
104, 114; and housewife,
101–102, 104, 107, 266; influences on, 99–100, 116–117; *In the
Mecca,* 117; and Marshall, 183;
Maud Martha, 7–8, 13, 97–98,
103–105, 106–108, 109–119, 121,
262, 276n6; and Okada, 121, 130,
131; and Percy, 134, 149, 152,
153; and place, 100, 101, 106; and
race, 13, 102, 107; and racism, 7,
108, 109, 110, 111, 115–116; and
segregation, 7, 104, 116; and
Sinclair, 165; and urban renewal,
7, 101–102, 114, 183, 262; and
white privilege, 99; and whites,
13, 99; and Wright, 104; and writing, 276n6; and Yamamoto, 110,
111
Brown v. Board of Education, 98, 99,
105, 137
Burroughs, William S., 6, 220;
Junkie, 209; *Naked Lunch,* 2, 176,
195, 196, 211, 213–215
buses, 74, 75, 89, 98, 122, 135, 136,
138, 139
business, 144. *See also* corporations
butch lesbians, 196, 197, 230,
232–233. *See also* lesbians

Cain, James M., 25; *Double
Indemnity,* 25, 41
Caldwell, Orville, 21
California, 84–85. *See also* Los
Angeles
camp: and Bannon, 224, 226, 231,
233; and Capote, 224, 235, 237,
239, 241, 242; and City Hall Park,
198, 200–201; and housewife, 7;
and Okada, 123; and Open City,
196; and sadomasochism, 213; and
Selby, 219, 222; and subculture,
262–263; and Wright, 218
camping out, 171–177; and Capote,
241, 242, 243; defined, 176, 196;
and Kerouac, 246; and Marshall,

community (*continued*)
127, 275n53; and lesbians, 203,
204–205, 225; and noir, 24; and
Okada, 121, 122, 125, 126, 127; of
paperback readers, 206; and post-
traumatic stress disorder, 57; and
Selby, 223; and Wright, 174; and
Yamamoto, 50, 58, 59, 71, 76, 79,
86
commuting, 51, 61, 70, 72
concentration camps. *See* internment
concrete island, 8–15, 155, 157, 163
conformity, 3, 6, 7, 64, 65, 66
Conroy, Jack, 76–77
conscience, 73. *See also* morality
consumers, 52, 80, 107–108, 163,
263
containment: and Brooks, 104, 106,
108, 112; and Cheever, 59; and
Chicago, 106; and City Hall Park,
199; and Cold War, 1, 8; and
Commission on Human Rights,
106; and cult novel, 15, 261; and
Ellison, 170; and emotion, 50, 56;
and flashback, 11; and Himes, 38;
imagery of, 1; and Los Angeles, 2,
38–39; and masculinity, 3; and
material history, 8–15; movement
beyond, 1, 15, 163, 167, 261, 265,
267; and noir, 22, 30; and numbness, 11, 49; and Percy, 140, 141,
143; and post-traumatic stress disorder, 56; and race, 3, 22; and segregation, 97; and style, 49; and
subculture, 1; and violence,
10–11; and whiteness, 3; and
World War II, 105–106
contemplation, 110, 111, 121
Corber, Robert, 214
corporations, 53, 171, 172, 174, 175,
193. *See also* business
costume, 200, 201, 202, 240, 241.
See also fashion
counterculture, 197. *See also* subculture
Cowie, Elizabeth, 46
critique, 7, 208. *See also* satire

Cronkite, Walter, 92, 93
crucifixion, 220–221
cult novel, 6, 193–211; and containment, 15, 261; and gays, 15; and
lesbians, 15; and narrator, 15; and
New York City, 207; and Open
City, 15–16; and reader, 15, 213,
264; and shock, 11; and subculture, 163, 193–194; and tourism,
207, 213; and violence, 2, 11, 264;
and Wright, 217

dance, 253, 255, 256
Davis, Kenneth, 206–207
Davis, Mike, 24
Day, Dorothy, 79, 200
death: and Cheever, 59, 60, 61; and
city, 26; and Himes, 46; and noir
hero, 25–26; and Okada, 124; and
Plath, 173; and postwar novel,
169; and Roth, 188, 191
decoration, 65–66, 106, 107, 108,
119
description: and Bannon, 230; and
Brooks, 108; detachable, 39–42,
72; and Himes, 39–41, 42–43; and
Kerouac, 247; and Percy, 149; and
Yamamoto, 72, 84. *See also* image;
style
desegregation: and camp, 196; and
New Orleans, 148–149; and Percy,
134, 135, 137, 139, 148, 149, 153;
and subculture, 193. *See also* integration; segregation
Dessner, Lawrence Jay, 66, 68
detachment: and camping out, 176;
and Himes, 27, 37–38, 39, 43,
46–47; and hipster, 52; and
Kerouac, 245, 246, 248, 250; and
Marshall, 185, 253; and noir, 20,
23, 26; and Okada, 101, 121; and
Percy, 101, 135, 141; and self, 176;
and veteran, 52, 168; and violence,
263; and Wright, 176; and Yamamoto, 71, 84, 91, 92. *See also*
alienation; aloneness; neutrality
detective, 2, 37, 132, 158, 226, 263.
See also film noir; noir

Catholic Workers, 79; and Cheever, 74, 79, 84, 88; "A Day in Little Tokyo," 87; and housewife, 7, 48–49, 53, 71, 75, 82, 86, 91, 266; "The Legend of Miss Sasagawara," 92; and Percy, 136, 140, 149, 157; on self, 12, 79, 84, 92; "Seventeen Syllables," 87; and Sinclair, 165;

"Wilshire Bus," 12, 48–49, 50, 51, 53, 55, 58, 70–76, 77–79, 80, 81–82, 84, 85–88, 89, 91–93
Yogi, Stan, 87–88
youth, 167–168, 171, 245. *See also* child/children

Zoot Suit Riots, 22, 76, 90

About the Author

Elizabeth A. Wheeler is an assistant professor of English at the University of Oregon. Her articles have appeared in the *Journal of Film and Video, Southern California Quarterly,* and *Essays in Postmodern Culture.* She codirects the University of Oregon Literacy Initiative and has run neighborhood youth centers in New York City and Oakland, California.